HAWAI'I

OFF THE BEATEN PATH®

OFF THE BEATEN PATH® SERIES

ELEVENTH EDITION

HAWAI'I

OFF THE BEATEN PATH®

SEAN PAGER

REVISED AND UPDATED BY

CATHERINE CALDWELL

Essex, Connecticut

All the information in this guidebook is subject to change. We recommend that you call ahead to obtain current information before traveling.

Globe Pequot

An imprint of The Rowman & Littlefield Publishing Group, Inc.
4501 Forbes Blvd., Ste. 200
Lanham, MD 20706
www.rowman.com

Distributed by NATIONAL BOOK NETWORK

British Library Cataloguing in Publication Information available

ISSN 1535-8313
ISBN 978-1-4930-7820-2 (paper : alk. paper)
ISBN 978-1-4930-7821-9 (electronic)

∞™ The paper used in this publication meets the minimum requirements of American National Standard for Information Sciences—Permanence of Paper for Printed Library Materials, ANSI/NISO Z39.48-1992

Contents

About the Author

Sean Pager first came to Hawai'i at the age of six months. It didn't make much of an impression at the time, but he enjoyed growing up in the islands and appreciated them even more when he continued to travel and live elsewhere. Sean did his first paid travel writing for the *Let's Go* series as a summer job while in college and liked it enough to stick with it after graduation. *Hawai'i: Off the Beaten Path* is his first book-length publication. In his free time, Sean likes to go off the beaten path in the islands by hiking the hills or sailboarding the coast. He currently lives with his wife, Sheryl, and daughter, Sophie.

About the Reviser

Reviser **Catherine Caldwell** is a writer and editor who lived in Honolulu and dearly misses Hawai'i. While now based abroad in France, she is still a regular contributor and editorial assistant to *HILuxury*, Hawai'i's luxury magazine. When she is not writing, Catherine spends her time traveling, playing with her snow bengal cat, and taking vinyasa yoga classes, as she is a former trained yogini, thanks to CorePower Honolulu.

HAWAI'I

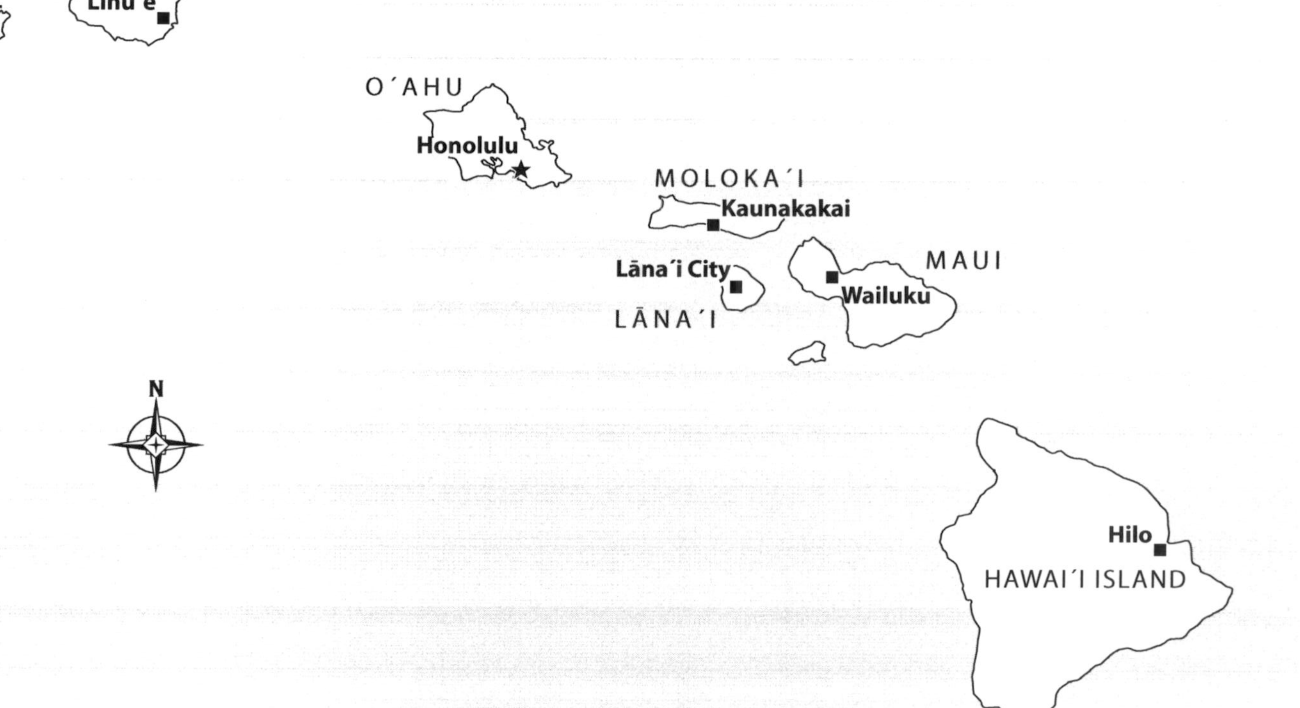
KAUA'I
Līhu'e
O'AHU
Honolulu
MOLOKA'I
Kaunakakai
Lāna'i City
LĀNA'I
MAUI
Wailuku
N
Hilo
HAWAI'I ISLAND

Introduction

Welcome to Hawai'i! These words are heard by over nine million tourists each year who storm the islands to roast themselves on Waikīkī Beach and sip mai tais topped with paper parasols. Despite this annual onslaught, there remains a Hawai'i that few tourists see and many hardly suspect exists. This book will take you there.

Bypass the tourist centers, and you can lose yourself in the midst of untouched natural beauty. You'll travel the back roads that tour buses cannot follow, or take to the hills on foot. Discover beaches empty of human footprints and remote valleys guarding sparkling waterfalls. Experience a Hawai'i enriched by its diverse immigrant cultures and native Polynesian roots. You'll learn the legends of prehistoric temples, wander through royal palaces and missionary homes, shop in local craft shops, and sample multiethnic cuisines. All this awaits you in the Hawai'i that lies off the beaten path.

A Setting of Superlatives

You could live here all your life and still discover new ways to appreciate Hawai'i's charms. These islands boast the world's best surfing waves, the highest sea cliffs, the rainiest mountain peak, the largest and most active volcanoes, and the clearest night skies. They belong to the longest and most isolated archipelago in the world. More than 90 percent of the approximately 1,400 plant taxa (species, subspecies, and varieties) native to Hawai'i are found nowhere else on the planet.

For all their beauty and wonder, the islands are newcomers as landforms go. They represent the peaks of enormous undersea volcanoes fueled by primeval fires welling up from deep within the earth. Because the ocean floor is shifting northwest over the underlying source of magma, the zone of active volcanism resembles a geological assembly line, with each island forming and then moving over to make way for its successors. The oldest islands, worn away by erosion and sinking under their own weight into the earth's mantle, have all but disappeared, while the youngest and largest island grows almost daily as eruptions continue to build new land, much to the delight of tourists lucky enough to witness this volcanic genesis.

Long before geology became a science, the ancient Hawaiians understood the natural forces governing their island home. Their legends told of the epic battle between Pele, the fire goddess, and her older sister Nāmaka, goddess of the sea. Pele came to Hawai'i to escape her older sister's wrath after she had stolen Nāmaka's suitor. The sea goddess followed her and flooded the first shallow fire pits that Pele had dug. Pele moved from island to island, going southeast down the Hawaiian chain and building newer and taller mountains from the volcanic fires she summoned. Yet each time, the power of the ocean wore down Pele's island fortresses and drove her onward. Although her current home on the Big Island continues to grow, Pele knows that it too will have to be abandoned in time. Already, new undersea volcanoes farther southeast are rising to form the islands of the future. Other legends told of Pele's brother, Kamohoali'i, taking the form of a shark to lead Pele and her sisters to the islands.

Of the 132 volcanic peaks that rise above the highest tide, only the youngest 8 were large enough to be settled permanently by the early Hawaiians. Visitors today can explore 6 of these islands: Kaua'i, O'ahu, Moloka'i, Lāna'i, Maui, and Hawai'i ("the Big Island"). Each maintains its own distinct identity. Even within the individual islands, you will marvel at the diversity of habitats. The most obvious contrasts are between windward (northeast) and leeward (southwest) coasts. Crossing a mountain barrier can bring you from rain forest into desert within the distance of a few miles. Weather patterns are also extremely localized. It rarely rains in one place for long, and it's almost always sunny somewhere.

Hawai'i's human history is as unique as its natural setting. Polynesian voyagers in double-hulled canoes followed the stars from other Pacific islands across thousands of miles of open ocean to settle these lands more than 1,500 years ago. They developed a sophisticated culture governed by various *kapu* (taboos). Elaborate *heiau* (temples) enshrined beautifully crafted *ki'i akua,* or *ki'i* (idols), which accepted divine offerings from citizens, *ali'i* (chiefs), and *kāhuna* (respected experts) to achieve their means, such as to request support and assistance or for intervention.

The arrival of the English explorer Captain James Cook in 1778 brought the archipelago into contact with the modern world. Western weapons, as well as a massive army, knowledge of Hawaiian and foreign consuls, and support from a personal *akua* (divine spirt), enabled a Hawai'i chieftain named Kamehameha to, over the span of 20 years, forge a unified kingdom. After his death, his son abandoned the old gods and ordered all the ki'i destroyed in island-wide bonfires. Today only the stone foundations of the heiau remain as vestiges of a once-flourishing civilization.

Congregationalist missionaries soon arrived to convert the people of Hawai'i to Christianity beginning in 1820. Half a century later, the rise of sugar plantations in Hawai'i began to import laborers from around the world. Out of this immigrant pool grew a multiethnic society blending East and West. First a kingdom, then a republic, later a territory, and finally the 50th state in the Union; Hawai'i is the only US territory that was formerly a sovereign kingdom. Hawai'i also remains one of the few places in the world where no ethnic group can claim a majority.

On the Practical Side

Heading off the beaten path in Hawai'i can pose some special challenges. Most of the islands have a single main highway that hugs the coast. The Hawai'i Visitors and Convention Bureau (HVCB) has erected roadside marker signs styled in the shape of a Hawaiian warrior to designate the main points of interest. Green mile markers help you keep track of distances, but there are few street signs to guide you along secondary routes. Many places of interest can be reached only by unpaved roads.

As an off-the-beaten-path traveler in Hawai'i, you assume certain obligations. These are small islands, with fragile environments. Many of the sites described here rely on their inaccessibility as their only protection against abuse. Keep in mind that Hawai'i's heiau and wilderness remain sacred sites to some, as you'll see by the offerings left (often a simple ti leaf wrapped around a rock).

Most people come here to bask in Hawai'i's natural beauty, and happily, the best parts are usually free. Natural attractions fall into two main categories: *mauka* (meaning "mountain"—you pronounce it maow-kuh) and *makai* (meaning "ocean"—you pronounce it mah-kye). You'll hear these two words used frequently in the islands as directions, as you can almost always use one or the other as a convenient landmark. Going *mauka* (inland) often involves hiking, and Hawai'i has some of the world's best trails. Depending on the season, you might find guavas, passion fruit, mangos, mountain apples, and other tropical fruits that grow wild in the hills. You needn't worry about poisonous or predatory animals here, but other dangers exist. Volcanic soil and rock can often be treacherously crumbly and undergrowth impossibly thick. Illicit backwoods *pakalolo* (marijuana) patches can put unwary trespassers at risk. Stick to posted trails, and you'll be fine. Bring mosquito repellent for wet valley hikes and flashlights to explore the occasional cave.

Going *makai* (seaward) eventually means hitting the beach. A simple rule: If a sign says beach park, you can usually expect facilities (but not necessarily a sandy beach). If it says just beach, the reverse is usually the case. Keep in mind that all of Hawai'i's shoreline up to the highest high-water mark is public property. Public shoreline access, where possible, is required by law. Hawai'i has an amazing variety of beaches, but again, the visitor should proceed cautiously. Depending on the season and location, surf and currents can make swimming unsafe. In particular, the northern and western shores of all islands are exposed to dangerous surf in winter. The well-fed reef sharks almost never attack humans in Hawaiian waters, but the occasional jellyfish or Portuguese man-of-war can sting painfully. Razor-sharp coral reefs will cut unprotected feet, and crevices may conceal spiny sea urchins and moray eels. Conditions change rapidly, so never turn your back on the ocean. Also, be aware that all marine mammals and

Speak Like a Hawaiian

Hawaiian words are used for most place names in Hawai'i and are sprinkled throughout the everyday speech of islanders. With a little practice, you too can speak like a *kama'aina*. The Hawaiian language has only twelve letters: seven consonants—*h, k, l, m, n, p, w*—and five vowels—*a, e, i, o, u*. Pronounce the consonants as you would in English, except for *w,* which is pronounced as a soft *v* after *e, i,* or *a*. (Yes, it's technically pronounced "Havai'i.") Vowel sounds are more like Spanish: *a* as in *father, e* as in *acorn, i* as in *macaroni, o* as in *solo, u* as in *union.* Always pronounce each letter separately. Special cases are *ao* or *au,* which are usually pronounced "ow"; *ae* and *ai,* which sound like "eye"; and *ei,* which becomes "ay." A ' symbol before or between vowels indicates a glottal stop or slight pause in the sounds (think of the phrase, "uh-oh"). Give each syllable an even stress. When you see an eye-popper such as *humuhumunukunukuapuaa* (the state fish), don't panic. Just take it one group at a time: humu-humu-nuku-nuku-a-pu-a-a. It's easy!

Here is a selected list of Hawaiian terms used in this guide.

ali'i *(ah-lee-eee):* Hawaiian chief or royalty

aloha *(ah-loh-ha):* greetings, love

hala *(hah-lah):* pandanus, screwpine, or tourist pineapple; a Polynesian introduction, this tree has stilt-like aerial roots, pineapple-like fruit, and long fibrous leaves used for weaving (*see* lauhala).

hale *(hah-leh):* house

haole *(how-leh):* foreigner

heiau *(hay-ow):* ancient Hawaiian temple

hula *(hoo-lah):* Hawaiian dance

kāhili *(kah-hee-lee):* a feathered standard held on a pole as the symbol of royalty

kahuna *(kah-hoo-nah):* "one who knows the secrets"; Hawaiian priest, healer, or other skilled professional

kalua *(kah-loo-ah):* steam-cooked in leaves in an underground oven

kama'aina *(kah-mah-eye-nah):* longtime island resident

kane *(kah-neh):* man; also the name of one of the principal Hawaiian gods

kapu *(kah-poo):* taboo, forbidden

ki'i *(key-ee):* an idol, statue, or image

kokua *(koh-koo-ah):* help, cooperation

konane *(koh-nah-neh):* Hawaiian game similar to checkers

kukui *(kookoo-ee):* candlenut tree; a Polynesian introduction with light green leaves whose oil-rich nuts were strung together and burned as candles

lānai *(la-nye):* large open-air veranda

lauhala *(laow-hah-lah):* "leaf of hala"; woven to make mats, sails, and so on

lau lau *(laow-laow):* Hawaiian specialty featuring pork, fish, and taro leaves wrapped and steamed in a ti leaf bundle

lei *(lay):* garland or necklace, most often made of flowers

loco moco *(loh-coh moh-coh):* a local dish based on rice, a fried egg, a hamburger patty, and plenty of gravy

luakini *(loo-ah-kee-nee):* sacrifice; describes large state temples where human sacrifices were offered

lu'au *(loo-ow):* traditional Hawaiian feast; also decribes a specific dish cooked in coconut milk

mahalo *(mah-hah-loh):* thank you

makai *(mah-kye):* toward the sea, coastal

mana *(mah-nah):* spiritual power, prestige

mauka *(maow-kah):* toward the mountains, inland

Menehune *(men-eh-hoo-nay):* legendary race of "little people"

'ono *(oh-noh):* delicious

pali *(pah-lee):* cliff

paniolo *(pah-nee-olo):* cowboy

poi *(poy):* mashed vegetable paste, usually made from taro tubers

tapa *(tah-pah):* Polynesian bark cloth; called *kapa* in old Hawai'i

taro *(tah-roh):* traditional food staple, source of poi

wahine *(wah-hee-nay):* woman

Much of the foreign-sounding speech you'll hear in the islands isn't Hawaiian but pidgin, a unique vernacular that grew out of the mongrelized vocabularies of multiethnic plantation workers. It continues to thrive today as a "locals only" slang. A glossary to pidgin is impractical, as word usages are nonstandard; you just have to get a feel for it. Just remember to say "howzit"—it's the way locals say hello.

sea turtles are protected by federal law, and visitors can be fined for disturbing their natural activity.

You shouldn't overlook Hawai'i's cultural offerings, either. In many ways, the Aloha State still feels like its own country, and you may as well enjoy its differences. Wear a flower lei. Listen to a Hawaiian music station like KAPA Hawaiian FM (kaparadio.com), or the popular University of Hawai'i at Mānoa college station, KTUH FM (90.1 FM in Honolulu or streaming online at KTUH.org). Look for cultural festivities listed in the local newspaper or check out the events calendar at gohawaii.com. Sample some diverse foods, and order out a local-style "plate lunch" to eat at a picnic. In addition to the islands' Polynesian heritage, Asian influences are especially strong. You'll find many Buddhist temples. Most of these temples welcome visitors, but they ask that you remove your shoes before entering. As for shopping, try the gift shops of the attractions listed throughout the guide. Many stock unusual items at very reasonable prices.

One of Hawai'i's unadvertised charms is its rainbow of people, who make up an American melting pot of diverse origins. Almost everyone speaks English, but you might not feel sure of this when they're laying on the pidgin, a unique local dialect (and, as of 2015, an official language of the state) that incorporates foreign words, slang, and a singsong inflection. If you stay mellow and say "howzit" (hello), you'll still get a lot of *aloha.*

For offbeat accommodations, try one of the many bed-and-breakfast outfits (B&Bs). Besides the ones listed in this guide, you can book with several statewide agencies. Those with Internet access can find additional accommodation listings plus other useful visitor information at the following websites: gohawaii.com; hawaii.com; and bestplaceshawaii.com. ***Lanikai Beach Rentals*** (808-261-7895 or 808-476-7195; lanikaibeachrentals.com) is based on O'ahu. ***Hawai'i's Best B&Bs*** (bestbnb.com) concentrates on upscale listings. If you want more rugged lodgings, camping is safe and practical on most islands. To get the scoop on state campgrounds, contact the Department of Land and Natural Resources Division of ***Hawai'i State Parks*** (808-587-0300; dlnr.hawaii.gov/dsp) at Kalanimoku Building, 1151 Punchbowl St., Rm. 310, Honolulu 96813. For ***county campgrounds,*** get in touch with the particular island's department of parks and recreation. Contact Kaua'i's DPR (808-241-4463; kauai.gov) at 4444 Rice St., Ste. 150, Līhu'e 96766; O'ahu's DPR (808-768-3003; honolulu.gov) at 1000 Ulu'ohia St., Ste. 309, Kapolei 96707; Maui County's DPR (808-270-7389; co.maui.hi.us) at 700 Hali'a Nakoa St., Unit 2, Wailuku 96793; and Hawai'i's DPR (808-961-8311; co.hawaii.hi.us) at 101 Pauahi St., Ste. 6, Hilo 96720. For additional camping options, see chapters on individual islands. Hostel accommodations are also available on most islands; see chapter listings.

The only regularly scheduled interisland transport is by air. Needless to say, the biggest airline in the state is ***Hawaiian Airlines*** (800-367-5320; hawaiianair.com), although Alaska Airlines and Southwest Airlines have recently become interisland competitors offering cheap flights. Getting around on the islands themselves will require a rental car, except on O'ahu, where the nationally award-winning bus system might be adequate. All the major national firms, as well as local independents, are represented on the larger islands. It is a competitive market, so call around. It also pays to ask your interisland airline for special fly-drive rates.

There are any number of commercial alternatives to driving that will take you off the beaten path—from submarine tours to mountain biking to kayaking. Space does not permit a full listing here, but most advertise in the free, weekly tourist publications available for all major islands except Lāna'i. Specially recommended are the highly informative ***101 Things to Do*** booklets for Kaua'i, O'ahu, Maui, and Hawai'i Island; you'll find them for free at brochure racks throughout those islands. Hikers can take advantage of weekend Sierra Club outings on the four major islands. Write the Hawai'i chapter office at PO Box 2577, Honolulu 96803; call (808) 538-6616 for a statewide schedule; or visit sierraclubhawaii.org.

As for using the guide itself, you should note that it is written as a narrative, designed to be used on the scene. Attractions are listed geographically in the order you will encounter them, except within individual towns, where accommodations and restaurants are grouped together. Items of special interest appear in boldface italic type. Accommodation prices are based on a double room. Unless noted otherwise, the label "B&B" implies that continental breakfast is included.

Restaurant prices are given by category based on the cost of an average entree: inexpensive—less than $15; moderate—$16 to $24; expensive—$25 to $32; and investment-caliber—more than $33.

Kaua'i

Kaua'i stands apart from the other islands of Hawai'i. The farthest north of the main islands, Kaua'i is the oldest geologically. Six million years have given erosive forces the time to sculpt its mountain slopes with a delicate scalpel. An eternity of waves has wreathed the island in a white lei of sand. Kaua'i is also the wettest Hawaiian island. Its central peak, Mount Wai'ale'ale ("overflowing waters"), held the world's record for annual rainfall. The overflowing waters from such constant precipitation feed Kaua'i's seven full-fledged rivers, where other islands have mere streams. The unrivaled lushness of this "Garden Island" has lured Hollywood here to film countless motion pictures, including *Jungle Cruise*, *Raiders of the Lost Ark*, *Jurassic Park* (and *World*), *Avatar*, and *Pirates of the Caribbean: On Stranger Tides*.

Kaua'i has always stood apart in human terms as well. The Kaua'i Channel is wider, deeper, and rougher than those between other islands. Scientists think Kaua'i and its nearest neighbor, Ni'ihau, remained fairly isolated in ancient Hawai'i. These were the only islands Kamehameha did not conquer. Two invasion fleets failed, one beaten back by storms, the next devastated by sickness. In the end, Kaua'i's King Kaumuali'i

KAUA'I

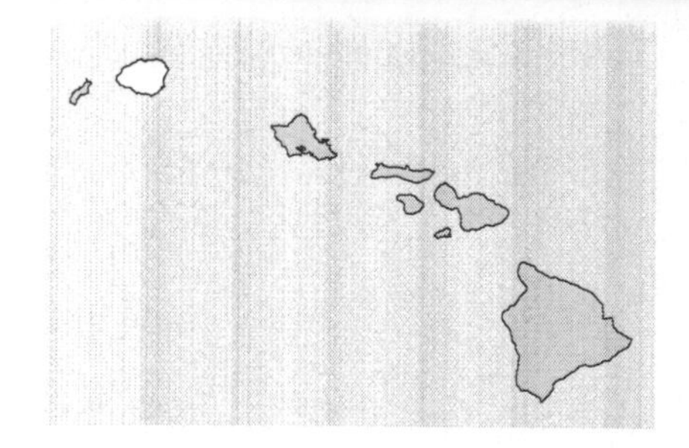

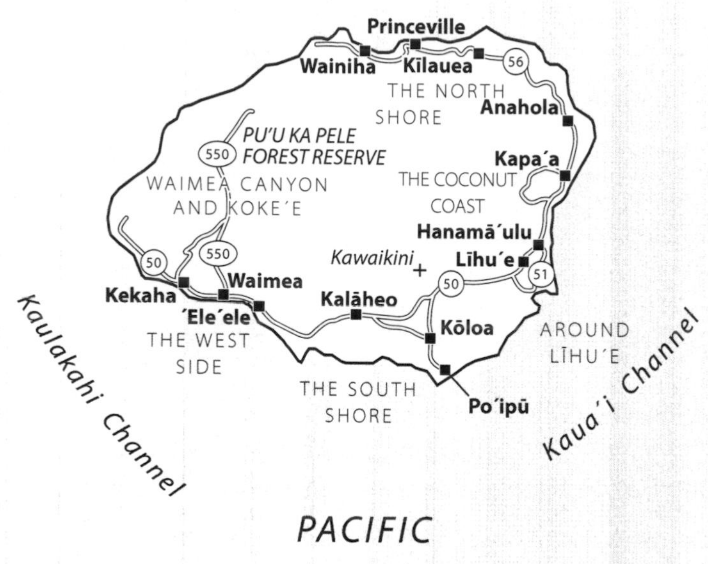
Princeville
Wainiha
Kīlauea
56
THE NORTH SHORE
Anahola
PU'U KA PELE FOREST RESERVE
550
Kapa'a
WAIMEA CANYON AND KOKE'E
THE COCONUT COAST
Hanamā'ulu
50
550
Kawaikini
Līhu'e
51
Kekaha
Waimea
50
Kalāheo
'Ele'ele
Kōloa
THE WEST SIDE
AROUND LĪHU'E
THE SOUTH SHORE
Po'ipū
Kaulakahi Channel
Kaua'i Channel

PACIFIC
OCEAN

N

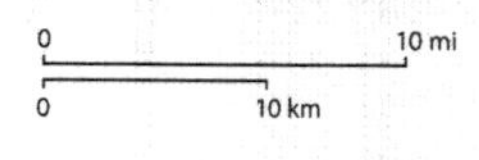
0
10 mi
0
10 km

voluntarily acknowledged Kamehameha's sovereignty and became Kamehameha's vassal, opting for peaceful resolution instead of bloodshed.

islandfacts

Nickname: Garden Isle

Dimensions: 33 x 25 miles

Highest elevation: Mt. Kawaikini (5,243 feet)

Population: 73,454 (2021)

Principal city: Līhu'e

Flower: Mokihana Berry

Color: Purple

Two main highways, Kaumuali'i (HI-50/Route 50) and Kūhiō (HI-56/ Route 56), reach like arms around the island, with a third main roadway branching off Route 50, also known as the Kaumuali'i Highway, to climb the inland heights of Kōke'e State Park. Starting from Līhu'e, the central town, you can drive slightly more than 40 miles in each direction before running into the impassable barrier of the Nā Pali Coast. Throughout your stay on Kaua'i, look for the Sunshine Farmers' Markets that rotate through the island towns throughout the week. They combine local color with real bargains. Check online at kauai .gov for the current schedule.

A great way to go off the beaten path on Kaua'i is by paddling a kayak. Even novices can safely navigate the island's rivers to reach secluded waterfalls. Experienced ocean paddlers can explore sections of otherwise inaccessible coastline. Several local firms rent kayaks and supply racks to transport them. ***Outfitters Kaua'i*** (808-742-9667; 888-742-9887; outfitterskauai.com) in Līhu'e also leads hiking, zip-line, biking, and kayaking tours. They have a permit for tours in Waimea Canyon and Kōke'e and can supply detailed route maps for suggested activities. ***Kayak Kaua'i*** (808-826-9844 in Hanalei; 888-596-3853; kayakkauai.com) offers similar services on the North Shore and Coconut Coast.

In addition, look in the local paper for listings of the Kaua'i Sierra Club's outings. While planning your stay, contact the Kaua'i Visitors Bureau to learn more about Garden Isle activities (808-245-3971; gohawaii.com/kauai).

Around Līhu'e

Located on the southeastern corner of Kaua'i, Līhu'e serves as the county seat, the main air and sea port, and the midpoint from which highway mileage is numbered. Surrounded by sugarcane and hemmed in on all sides by mountains, Līhu'e town is relatively new as a settlement. The ancient Hawaiians usually bypassed this section of the coast, following instead an inland route behind the mountains. Sugar, centrality, and proximity to O'ahu conspired to put Līhu'e on the map. Recent tourist developments favoring other coasts have had the opposite effect.

At the junction of the two main highways, turn into Līhu'e on Rice Street, named for an early manager of the Līhu'e Sugar Plantation. Almost immediately on your left, the ***Kaua'i Museum*** (808-245-6931; kauaimuseum.org) stands behind an imposing classical facade. The well-organized exhibits within cover the story of Kaua'i from many angles. You can see photos of Ni'ihau (as close as most people will ever get), study a model Hawaiian village, rattle a gourd, read excerpts from Captain Cook's log on "discovery" day, and even take a video tour, shot by helicopter, of the island's remote interior. The museum is open Mon through Fri from 9 a.m. to 4 p.m. and Sat 9 a.m. to 2 p.m. $15 admission fee. Guided tours are offered Mon, Wed, and Fri at 10 a.m.

On the next block, the 1913 former ***County Building*** reposes in a stately, royal palm–lined park. The ***Kaua'i Historical Society*** (808-245-3373; kauaihistoricalsociety.org) has its office inside, with books on island history and self-guiding "history maps" for sale. Normally open weekdays 8 a.m. to 4 p.m., you can get state camping permits (808-274-3444) from the State Building behind the old county building for $18 per night ($20 for Nā Pali Coast). Permits for the county's excellent campgrounds (808-241-4463; kauai.gov) are issued for $3 per adult at the cylindrical county building at the top end of Rice Street. Permits can be issued for up to seven days and can be requested up to one year in advance. Haleko Road runs west off Rice Street just inland of the museum, directly behind the now-silent Līhu'e sugar mill. On the way down, notice the ***Haleko Shops*** on the right, near the corner. Severely damaged in the 1992 hurricane, these four concrete remnants and ornate marble horse trough came from a plantation housing camp for German workers.

hawai'itrivia

There are more miles of beach per coastline here than on any other island.

By law, no building here can be taller than a palm tree.

Kaua'i hosts the largest coffee plantation in Hawai'i.

Kaua'i's Mount Wai'ale'ale is one of the wettest spots on Earth.

Wailua River is the only navigable river in Hawai'i.

Kaua'i's tropical beauty has been filmed in more than 70 Hollywood movies and television shows.

As a side trip, you can find the ***Lutheran Church of All Nations,*** which these devout immigrants built atop "German Hill" on the other side of the mill. (An HVCB marker points up Ho'omana Road from Route 50.) This 1885

Geography of Kaua'i

The oldest and northernmost of the Hawaiian Islands, Kaua'i ranks fourth by size and population. Built from a single massive volcano, the island has been eroded into a series of mountain ridges, valleys, and canyons. Its two central peaks usually remain shrouded in clouds. Of the two, Kawaikini is the highest at 5,243 feet, but Wai'ale'ale, 100 feet lower, once held the record for the world's highest annual rainfall. The island has 113 miles of shoreline (much of it sandy beaches), 16 of which, along the spectacular Nā Pali Coast, are inaccessible by road.

Lutheran church has an attractive baroque altar inside. But look more closely. The floor is actually bowed like the deck of a ship, with the pulpit, the elevated forecastle, and the balcony the quarterdeck. The church design symbolizes not only the ship that carried these immigrants to their new home but also the ship of faith that sustained them on their voyage.

Continuing on Haleko Road past the mill takes you on a winding path through lush jungle. Take the next left onto Nāwiliwili Drive, which skirts the cane fields on its way to the harbor. You'll pass a sign on your left marking ***Grove Farm Homestead & Sugar Plantation Museum*** (808-245-3202). Book well in advance for a tour of this historic 80-acre estate. Often led by descendants of Kaua'i's plantation families who offer insider "gossip" about the past, the 2-hour tours of Grove Farm are offered Mon, Wed, and Thurs at 10 a.m. and 1 p.m. for a $20 donation. Reservations are recommended.

The homestead's founder, George Wilcox, was a son of missionaries. He raised tuition for his engineering degree by collecting bird guano to sell as fertilizer. After purchasing the dry land for next to nothing, Wilcox brought irrigation water from the mountains to create a profitable sugar plantation in 1864. A visit to Grove Farm provides a timeless glimpse of the plantation lifestyle he helped pioneer. Designed as a self-contained community, the beautifully maintained grounds still yield harvests of fruits and vegetables. Those who are game can taste raw coffee beans and macadamia nuts.

The Wilcoxes were true pack rats who collected much and threw away nothing. All the furnishings and personal possessions remain as if the inhabitants were due to return momentarily.

You'll also visit the spartan dwelling of the Moriwake family. Mrs. Moriwake, a picture bride from Japan, lived here with her family through 52 years of service as the Wilcoxes' laundress. A print of Mount Fuji on the wall provides a touch of the old country. The main house, built and furnished from beautiful native woods, is where George Wilcox lived with his brother Sam and Sam's family. Among the antique furniture, you'll find an embroidered settee that Helen Lehman, a longtime houseguest, took 10 years to complete.

To escape the family bustle, George later built himself a bachelor pad, designed with two bedrooms (winter and summer) draped with mosquito nets. The unadorned rooms are almost bare of furnishings. Although a millionaire, the frugal mission son kept his fragments of soap in an old sardine can.

Nāwiliwili Road continues down to its namesake harbor, Kaua'i's main shipping port ever since its completion in 1930. In your mind, try to screen out the heavy dock machinery and industrial warehouses and focus on the lovely setting of the bay, with the Ha'upu (or Hoary Head) Mountains closing in on its western edge. In the opposite direction, Nāwiliwili Beach Park abuts Kalapaki Beach, the site of the Marriott. But you can enjoy the same views at considerably less cost by staying at the ***The Kauai Inn*** (808-245-9000; 2430 Hulemalu Rd.; kauaiinn.com). The rooms are comfortable, and the inn boasts an outdoor pool and views of the green Hula'eia Mountains. From $230. If you just want a place to lay your head, try the ***Tip Top Motel*** (808-245-2333; 3173 Akahi St.) in Līhu'e. It's known locally for its bakery/café of the same name. Doubles start at $153.

Return to Nāwiliwili Road and turn west onto Niumalu Road, 2 blocks above the harbor. Niumalu climbs behind a bulk-sugar warehouse and sidles along the cane fields. Pause at the unmarked turnout ahead for another view of the bay. The road then descends through the rustic Hawaiian village of Niumalu.

At Niumalu Park, turn right onto Hulemanu Road, which curves uphill again. About 0.5 mile farther, stop at the overlook to view ***Alakoko Fishpond,*** tucked below along a bend in Hulē'ia Stream, backdropped by the rugged beauty of the Ha'upu Mountains. Alakoko is also known as Menehune Fishpond because of its legendary builders. A supposedly reclusive, dwarf-like people, the Menehune were said to be expert masons who performed miraculous construction feats overnight for payment in food. Menehune legends are part of the folklore throughout Hawai'i, and theories vary as to their origin. The bird chatter you hear comes from ***Hulē'ia National Wildlife Refuge,*** just upstream. ***Outfitters Kaua'i*** (808-742-9667; outfitterskauai.com) offers a variety of kayak tours ranging from river to ocean, plus ziplining. Visit their brick-and-mortar location at 230 Kipu Rd. or their curbside shack on Niumalu Road.

Hulemanu Road continues past the overlook, shadowing the Ha'upu Mountains as it cuts through green waves of endless cane. Turn right on Puhi Road to rejoin the highway. On your way back to town, you might visit ***Kilohana***

(808-245-5608; kilohanakauai.com), another restored plantation estate on the inland side of the highway. Gaylord Wilcox, the head of Grove Farm, brought renowned architect Mark Potter from O'ahu in 1935 to build his dream house. The name *Kilohana* means "not to be surpassed," and Potter made a strong bid to design and furnish a home worthy of this name. Stop at the main house to get a map of the 35-acre estate and restored farm area. To learn more about Hawai'i agriculture, past and future, hop a ride on the ***Kaua'i Plantation Railway*** (808-245-5608), which will take you through an additional 60 acres in a progression from taro (the staple of ancient Hawaiians) to tropical fruit trees and other niche crops that are replacing sugar. A string of reproduction vintage cars is pulled by a 1939 Whitcomb diesel engine on the 40-minute train ride. Admission is $21.50. While at Kilohana, taste their local rum on-estate. The Kōloa Rum Company is a single-batch, craft distiller, and bottler of premium Hawaiian rums right on the plantation. Tastings are available Mon through Sat 10 a.m. to 4 p.m. The shop closes at 5 p.m.

The inside of Kilohana is part museum and part boutiques specializing in Kaua'i-made wares. Kilohana's courtyard provides a romantic setting for alfresco dining at ***The Plantation House by Gaylords*** (808-245-9593; kilohanakauai.com). Continental entrees come with vegetables and fruits from Kilohana's own gardens. Mon through Sat lunch is served from 11 a.m. to 3 p.m. Dinner is offered Mon through Sat 5 to 8 p.m. Reservations suggested. Investment-caliber. Kilohana opens daily at 11 a.m.

Farther west on Route 50, shortly after Kaua'i Community College in the town of Puhi, is a small take-out restaurant, ***Mark's Place*** (808-245-2522), specializing in the local plate lunch with an upscale twist. Chef Mark Oyama teaches culinary arts at the college, and this is where he practices what he preaches. It is open Mon through Fri 11 a.m. to 4 p.m. Inexpensive.

Back in town, dining options consist mostly of mom-and-pop restaurants serving ethnic cuisine in unadorned settings. Two blocks seaward of the County Building, off Rice, a number of eateries cluster around Kress Street. Disguised as a camp house kitchen with its trademark corrugated orange Formica counter, ***Hamura Saimin*** (808-245-3271; 2956 Kress St.) ladles out Kaua'i's best bowl of saimin (like Japanese ramen or Chinese mein in a hot fish-and-kelp dashi broth). Select your own add-ins to slurp with your noodles and find a stool to sit on, but heed the sign on the wall that says please don't put gum under the counter. Hamura's is open Mon through Thurs 10 a.m. to 10:30 p.m., Fri and Sat 10 a.m. to midnight, and Sun 10 a.m. to 9:30 p.m. Inexpensive. In the same building, ***Halo Halo Shave Ice*** cranks out a fruity Filipino version of this Hawaiian frozen treat daily until 4 p.m.

Brief History of Kaua‘i

Captain James Cook's arrival on the west coast of Kaua‘i in 1778 touched off a new era that would transform the Hawaiian Islands. A steady stream of Western ships followed in his footsteps, many of them anchoring at the protected Waimea harbor that Cook had described in his journals, making Kaua‘i an early center of trade.

The separate political status retained by the island in the early days of the Hawaiian Kingdom made it the focus of international intrigue, most notably by a German adventurer acting in the service of the Russian czar.

As the site of Hawai‘i's first commercial sugar plantation, Kaua‘i was also at the forefront of another watershed, the birth of an industry that dominated the islands' socioeconomic landscape for more than a century. Strangely, sugar's successor, tourism, has come later to Kaua‘i than to some of its neighbors, although the Garden Isle has long been the darling of Hollywood filmmakers. Kaua‘i suffered widespread devastation at the hands of two hurricanes, Iwa in 1982 and Iniki in 1992, which further slowed development on the island.

Nearby is ***Kiibo Restaurant*** (808-245-2650; 2991 Ume St.), a traditional sushi house where Japanese art lines the walls and menu favorites include donburi bowls, ramen, and teriyaki dishes. Open Mon to Sat from 5 to 8 p.m. Another hotspot is the family-run ***Greenery Café*** (808-246-4567; thegreenerycafe.com), situated in a cozy cottage with a menu that uses locally grown greens. Open Mon and Wed 10:30 a.m. to 5 p.m., Tue 10:30 a.m. to 4 p.m., Thu 8 a.m. to 5 p.m., and Fri 8 a.m. to 4 p.m. Inexpensive to moderate.

More Līhu‘e eateries lie along Route 56, also known as the Kūhiō Highway, north of Rice Street. For those who like seafood, ***Fish Express*** (808-245-9918; 3343 Kūhiō Hwy.), across the street from the hospital, offers unbeatable values. Its tiny lunch counter serves gourmet fish specials: Choose from among the daily fresh-catch and organic selections prepared in intriguing ways, such as macadamia-nut-encrusted fish with *liliko‘i* (passion fruit) sauce or salmon lumpia over Kīlauea greens. At a price less than $15, you can't eat this well anywhere else on the island. (Fish haters can sample Hawaiian plates instead.) The lunch counter operates every day from 10 a.m. to 4 p.m. A more limited hot menu is served at other times. (The Oriental fried chicken and ginger shrimp are popular choices.) The deli counter also offers an impressive selection of poke, the local version of seafood salad made from (mostly raw) fish, seaweed, crab, or octopus. Fresh fish fillets are also available to grill for your own beachside barbecue.

For beachfront dining and live Hawaiian music, locals favor ***Duke's Canoe Club*** (808-246-9599; dukeskauai.com), adjacent to the Marriott on Kalapaki Beach. Roaming aunties bearing guitars make the rounds in the upstairs restaurant, but the Barefoot Bar is where the music lingers, and if you are upstairs, you won't even know anything is going on below. The latter is open for lunch and dinner 11 a.m. to 10 p.m. Inexpensive.

If you want a taste of Italian luxury, visit ***Volcano Pizza Kauai*** (808-742-2226; volcanopizza.com) for wood-fired Neopolitan pizzas or NY-style pies to-go at an outdoor window. Open Mon to Sat 4 to 9 p.m. Closed Sun. Inexpensive to moderate.

There are things to see on the way to Hanamā'ulu. One hill closer to Līhu'e, Route 56 passes through Kapaia, where you can stop to admire the handcrafted fabric creations at ***Kapaia Stitchery*** (808-245-2281), housed in a red plantation store. You will find everything from traditional kimonos to quilt-making kits—or choose your own fabric and have something custom-made. Open Mon through Sat 9 a.m. to 3 p.m.

For a scenic jaunt inland, take Mā'alo Road uphill from the stitchery through 3 miles of sugarcane with steadily improving mountain views. At the end of the road, your reward is a bird's-eye view of mighty ***Wailua Falls,*** featured on the TV show *Fantasy Island.* Those feeling adventurous (and sure of foot) can leave their fellow tourists gawking at the lookout and head 100 yards back up the road. At the far edge of the second guardrail, a steep and very slippery trail leads down to the pool at the base of the falls. Wave to the people above as you back float.

If a waterfall dip sounds too cliché, how about rafting an inner tube down a mountain flume? ***Kaua'i Backcountry Adventures*** (808-245-2506; 855-846-0092; kauaibackcountry.com) offers mountain tube rides down a two-mile stretch of a former sugar irrigation ditch not far from here. The 40-minute ride passes a few small rapids but is fairly tame; it goes through five tunnels totaling about a half mile in all; headlamps are provided. On the ride up to the ditch, you'll get to see some of the scenic backcountry the ditch traverses and learn the history of the plantation that the ditch once served. Part of a larger irrigation system that consisted of 51 miles of ditch in all, the flumes were built in the 1870s, largely by Chinese immigrants, many of whom had come from California after the Gold Rush fizzled. Because the ground was too brittle for dynamite, the tunnels were all dug by hand, with workers receiving 50 cents per day for this dangerous, backbreaking labor. After the tube ride, you get a picnic lunch by a mountain pool. The full experience lasts about 3 hours. Call for reservations; cost is $149. The same company also operates a zip-line adventure as an aerial alternative for $149.

The South Shore

Departing west from the Līhu'e area, the Kaumuali'i Highway (Route 50) crosses through the Knudsen Gap between Kāhili Ridge and the Ha'upu Range to enter the ***Kōloa District,*** birthplace of the Hawaiian sugar industry. The word *kōloa* is usually translated as "tall cane." The region, blessed with ample irrigation and yearlong sunshine, has yielded bumper crops since antiquity.

Turn left onto Maluhia Road (Route 520), 5 miles west of Līhu'e, and head through the ***Tree Tunnel,*** a fragrant double row of overhanging eucalyptus trees planted in 1911. Continue through more tropical foliage, then sugarcane, as you descend upon Kōloa Town, now known to tourists as **Old Kōloa Town** (oldkoloa.com). Maluhia Road ends at a T junction with Kōloa Road. On the right-hand side as you enter town, a tiny anonymous park commemorates Hawai'i's sugar heritage. Erected in 1985 for the 150th anniversary of commercial sugar production in Hawai'i, a small concrete monument symbolizes an opened millstone. Inside, a set of bronze bas-relief carvings portrays the different ethnic groups that figured in sugar's past. Careful readers of the accompanying plaque will notice historical revisionism at work: Someone has taken the *haole* plantation manager, formerly represented on horseback, out of the scene entirely.

The plaque gives a brief overview of the sugar industry's evolution. The story begins with William Hooper, who arrived from Boston in 1833 at age 24 with little expertise in agriculture and no knowledge of Hawai'i. Yet somehow he secured enough native cooperation to begin the first large-scale sugar plantation in the islands. The plaque neglects to mention that Hooper and his two partners became embroiled in an international investment scandal and went bankrupt. Despite such rocky beginnings, sugar went on to become Hawai'i's dominant industry and the mainstay of its economy for almost a century. At one point, 60 percent of the island's electricity was generated by burning sugar by-products. In spite of this, labor costs and foreign subsidies have put sugar on the decline since World War II. Up until recently, Kaua'i's Gay & Robinson was one of two remaining sugar plantations in the state (the other was on Maui), but both have closed. Although the burning of leftover bagasse from harvested cane no longer contributes directly to the island grid, hydroelectric generators installed by the sugar industry continue to supply most of Kaua'i's electricity.

Near the monument, a small garden displays different varieties of sugarcane, and behind (partially engulfed by a banyan tree) stand the remains of the third mill built in Kōloa.

Across Kōloa Road from the park, the Yamamoto Store is the focus of more town history. On the sidewalk in front of the store stand cartoon-style sculptures by Maui artist Reems Mitchell, depicting a pair of Kōloa old-timers,

Toshi Freitas, the mechanic, and "Chinaman" Lickety Split. Wander into the courtyard behind the store to explore the ***Kōloa History Center,*** a collection of exhibits and artifacts portraying aspects of plantation life, from the different immigrant groups housed in camps to the itinerant "drummers" and "shibai" artists who passed through the town hotel. You can also pick up a free brochure for the self-guided ***Kōloa Heritage Trail*** to other south-shore spots of historical interest.

Kōloa Fish Market (808-742-6199; 3390 Po'ipū Rd.), just down the road, serves a tasty Hawaiian plate lunch, with rotating multiethnic specialties, plus sushi and an assortment of poke waiting for the choosing behind its small deli counter. Open Mon through Sat 10 a.m. to 3 p.m. Closed Thurs and Sun. Inexpensive.

For a tour of Kōloa's churches and temples, continue east on Kōloa Road to the Big Save market at the corner. Craftspeople from Japan built the two Buddhist temples here in 1910 to cater to immigrant cane workers. The ***Hongwanji Mission*** has its temple behind the green YBA (Young Buddhists Association) Hall. Its carved roof and decorative metal inlays form a delicate black-on-white pattern. Around the corner, on Waikomo Road, ***Jodo Mission*** competes with two temples. The smaller original has an elaborate altar inside.

Turning from sutras to rosary beads, follow the signs to ***St. Raphael's Church*** from Kōloa onto Weliweli Road (between Maluhia and Waikomo), then turn right onto Hapa Road to reach Kaua'i's oldest Catholic church. The original Calvinist missionaries strove to exclude Catholicism, convincing their Hawaiian converts that papistry was "just another form of idolatry." Gunboat diplomacy by French warships brought an end to such discrimination.

Several church buildings lie scattered in this peaceful lot, bordered by cane fields. The current church dates from 1866, but the graves of Portuguese immigrants in the cemetery are older. In the corner, behind the rectory, stands a beautiful ruinlike shrine built from black lava rocks arranged in steps and levels seemingly at random, highlighted by white marble statuary. The remains of the original 1841 church, rediscovered a century later in an adjacent field, have been shaped into a grotto accented by a giant cross.

Returning onto Weliweli Road, turn left onto Waikomo Road and notice the rickety plantation homes as yet untouched by the tourist traffic a few blocks over. Waikomo Road runs into Po'ipū Road and ***Kōloa Church,*** which dates from 1837. The tall steeple of this New England–style edifice built by missionaries served as a landmark for whaling ships approaching port.

Turn left onto Po'ipū Road and bear left at the Y junction ahead to pass through Po'ipū Beach (poipubeach.org), an area thickly populated with plush hotels. A visual oddity among these is the ***Po'ipū Crater Resort***

(844-860-6181; suite-paradise.com) off Pe'e Road, the tiny villas of which sprout like acne on the steep walls inside a crater formed by Kaua'i's last volcanic gasp. You might also visit ***Kiahuna Plantation Resort*** (808-742-6411), which engulfed the former Moir Garden. Former plantation manager Hector Moir and his wife, Sandy, planted this attractive assortment of cacti and succulents suited to Po'ipū's arid climate back in 1938.

The family-run ***Little Fish Coffee*** (808-742-2113; 2294 Po'ipū Rd.; littlefishcoffee.com) is good, serving fair-trade coffees and coffee drinks, a variety of acai bowls, and hearty bagel sandwiches. Open daily, 7:30 a.m. to 1 p.m. Inexpensive.

Po'ipū's most notable eatery, however, is ***The Beach House Restaurant*** (808-742-1424; 5022 Lāwa'i Rd.; the-beach-house.com) on the way to Spouting Horn. The stunning oceanfront location provides the perfect setting for inventive Pacific Rim cuisine such as the restaurant's signature wasabi-buttered fresh island fish. Open daily 3:30 to 9 p.m. Happy hour served 2:30 to 4 p.m. daily. Investment-caliber. Reservations are recommended.

There is little point tarrying in crowded Po'ipū, though, when the coast is clearer farther on in ***Mahaulepu.*** Follow the main cane road extension from Po'ipū for almost 2 miles until you come to a stop sign at another major cane road. Turn right (following the utility poles) and continue another mile past the quarry. Check in at the guard station to sign a liability release. From here, various turnoffs lead to distinct beaches along the Mahaulepu coast. *Mahaulepu* means "falling together," referring to the remnants of Kamehameha's abortive 1796 invasion force that staggered ashore here to face a brutal ambush.

Start your exploring at the nearest beach access straight ahead and park at the stone barrier. Walk back toward Po'ipū until you reach the stream at the end of the beach, and follow the faint trail that runs through cane grass along the far bank. The trail continues a quarter mile inland and disappears into the mouth of a cave. You have to duck at the entrance, but the rest of the way is okay. Keep a hand above your head just in case, as you grope your way toward the light at the other side. Dense vines hang from the large opening here like a sixties bead curtain. And behind the curtain? A Chinese banyan in a natural courtyard of stone. As for the rest of Mahaulepu, you can play Robinson Crusoe, hunting for hidden footprints on a series of deserted beaches alternating with rocky outcrops. The farthest beach, ***Haula,*** cannot be reached by road; you have to hike a half mile east along low sea cliffs at the foot of the Ha'upu Mountain Range.

Retrace your steps to the Y junction at the entrance to Po'ipū Beach, where the right fork, Lāwa'i Road, leads to attractions of its own. Tucked inside the Y is Kōloa Landing, a narrow coastal inlet at the mouth of Waikono Stream. Nothing remains of this once-crowded port from whaling's heyday, but accommodation bargains cluster nearby. Book well in advance for any of these. ***Garden Isle Cottages Oceanfront*** (808-639-9233; 2658 Pu'uholo Rd.) overlook the water. Nestled in lush gardens, the self-contained units are decorated with original artwork. Or enjoy chic accommodations right on the water at nearby ***Whalers Cove Resort*** (808-742-7571; 2640 Pu'uholo Rd.; whalerscoveresort.com), complete with an outdoor pool and ocean views. Prices above $350.

Kōloa Landing Resort (808-500-7742; koloalanding.com) nearby also have sumptuous gardens and similar amenities, as well as large studios and villas. Rates range from $115 and up. Please keep in mind that there is a cleaning fee and a daily resort fee.

The main scenic attraction along Lāwa'i Road is the ***Spouting Horn.*** Hidden behind the tour buses in the parking lot, this surf-driven geyser does its best "thar she blows" imitation through a submerged lava tube. Rumor has it that the spout went much higher before plantation owners dynamited the opening to prevent salt sprays from damaging their crops. On the way to the Spouting Horn, you'll pass another neglected park of historical interest. ***Kūhiō Park*** marks the birth site of Kaua'i's favorite son, Prince Jonah Kūhiō Kalaniana'ole, heir to the Hawaiian monarchy and one of Hawai'i's first delegates to Congress. The park also includes the remains of an ancient fishpond and a small *heiau.*

At the end of Lāwa'i Road, a 1920s plantation home serves as the visitor center for the ***National Tropical Botanical Garden*** (808-332-7324; ntbg .org). Reserve in advance for one of the two tours per day for an experience that even nongreen thumbs will appreciate. Lawa'i Valley is a sunken oasis of tropical vegetation surrounded by former sugar land. The gardens are roughly segregated into botanical classes and beautifully landscaped around natural streambeds and hillsides. Robert Allerton and his adopted son (some say lover), John, used their Chicago mercantile fortune to create a tropical Eden here on an estate originally owned by Queen Emma. Emma herself was known as the first Hawaiian monarch to cultivate a garden for aesthetic rather than functional purposes; she began gardening at Lawa'i in 1870. The Allertons greatly expanded her efforts throughout five decades in the 20th century and were instrumental in establishing the National Tropical Botanical Gardens under congressional charter in 1964. The garden management now oversees the 286-acre property, which is divided into the separate Allerton and McBryde Gardens.

The visitor center is open daily from 8:30 a.m. to 5 p.m. Guided walking tours of the ***Allerton Garden*** are offered seven times daily. The two-and-a-half-hour tours require advance reservations (808-742-2623) and take you where many TV shows and movies were filmed, like *Jurassic Park*; the cost is $60 for adults. The Allerton Garden is a masterwork of landscape design. The formal geometry of the reflective pools and fountains blends harmoniously with the wildly tropical vegetation and colorful flowers, accented by art pieces from around the world. The adjacent ***McBryde Garden*** serves as the botanical gardens' research collection and contains some 270 different types of palms as well as a broad representation of Hawaiian flora, including endangered and endemic species. Self-guided tours of McBryde are available for all ages without reservations; the cost is $30 for adults. All tours involve a 2-mile ride on a tram and at least a mile and a half of walking on a gravel path up and down stairs. Along the way, you gain hands-on exposure to some of the world's most remarkable tropical flora, including four different colors of hibiscus (white, red, yellow, orange) and the rarely seen brighamia, which looks like a cabbage on a bowling pin. The latter grows only on the edge of the remote sea cliffs of Kaua'i and Moloka'i. Driven to near extinction when the sphingid moth that used to pollinate its yellow-white, trumpet-shaped flowers became extinct itself, the brighamia survives only through the efforts of botanists, who must hand-pollinate each plant, often rappelling down steep rock faces to reach them.

Return along Lāwa'i Road until it dead-ends at Kōloa Road and turn left onto Route 530, which cuts west through rolling hills carpeted with sugarcane to rejoin the Kaumuali'i Highway at Lawa'i. These upland fields once grew pineapples, but by 1970 all had switched to sugar, a less labor-intensive crop. The old pineapple cannery has been converted to retail space near the junction with Route 50.

If you're hungry, pizza lovers will want to continue west to ***Brick Oven Pizza*** (808-332-8561), on the mountain side of Route 50 in Kalāheo. The freshly risen crusts brushed with garlic come laden with tummy-pleasing toppings. Open 11 a.m. to 9 p.m. daily, except Tues. Inexpensive to moderate. For a more elaborate dinner, ***Kalaheo Café & Coffee Company*** (808-332-5858; 2-2560 Kaumuali'i Hwy.; kalaheo.com) offers much more than coffee—prime rib, island fresh fish, meat loaf, omelets—in a charming, rustic setting. Open for breakfast, lunch, and dinner Wed to Sat. Breakfast available all day on Sun. Moderate to expensive.

Turn left from the end of Route 530 to continue west on Route 50 to the town of Kalāheo. Turn left onto Papalina Drive near the center of town to enjoy the scenic vistas over the Lawa'i Valley and Po'ipū Coast on your way to ***Kukuiolono Park***. This cool hilltop sanctuary includes a nine-hole public golf course and a small pseudo-Japanese garden. Follow the road up to the clubhouse for a panoramic view stretching all the way to Ni'ihau. You can loop back to the highway on Pu'u Road.

The fields west of Kalāheo have been planted with coffee bushes as a replacement for sugar. Coffee's commercial history began in Hawai'i on this island, and although the baton has since passed to the Big Island's Kona Coast as the industry center, the 3,400 acres here now constitute Hawai'i's largest coffee plantation. You can learn more about island coffee (and sample the final product) by stopping at the ***Kaua'i Coffee Visitor Center*** (808-335-0813; 800-545-8605; kauaicoffee.com), just ahead on the left. Housed in two former sugar camp homes, the center has displays on the plantation's sugar past as well as its coffee future. Open weekdays 9 a.m. to 5 p.m., and weekends from 10 a.m. to 4 p.m. Free.

The West Side

About 2 miles west of Kalāheo on Kaumuali'i Highway, be sure to stop at the ***Hanapēpē Valley Overlook*** for a technicolor vision of red canyon walls rising vertically above a tree-carpeted valley floor. Continue on Route 50, which curves around the mouth of the canyon to descend into Hanapēpē town. A roadside sign welcomes you to KAUA'I'S BIGGEST LITTLE TOWN, part of an attempt to lure westbound tourists. Fortunately, they have not yet been too successful. To see for yourself, veer right beneath the bougainvillea-draped cliffs and park on Hanapēpē Road.

Hanapēpē has its share of history to relate. The valley you admired from above witnessed the bloody suppression of Kaua'i loyalists who revolted against the Kamehameha dynasty in 1824. A hundred years later, 16 Filipino workers and four police officers were killed here during a plantation strike. But Hanapēpē's main attraction springs from its vintage plantation shops, still infused with the rhythm of small-town life. Much of *The Thorn Birds* was filmed here.

Begin your walking tour at ***Taro Ko Farm*** (also known as Taro Ko Chips Factory) (808-335-5586), a tiny one-room factory that Mr. and Mrs. S. Nagamine, the former owners, started as a retirement project. The taro comes from nearby valley fields. Open daily from 8 a.m. to 5 p.m. Next, you can explore a series of ***art galleries*** notable not so much for the originality of their work—you can judge that for yourself—as for the accessibility of the tenant-artists, many of whom paint in studios on the premises and are happy to discuss their work. Most stay open Mon through Sat. ***Kaua'i Fine Arts*** (808-335-3778; brunias.com) sells a different kind of artwork, though; it specializes in antique maps and prints.

You shouldn't overlook Hanapēpē's more traditional vendors, either. Sample the spicy confections at the ***Crackseed Center*** or pop inside the ***Talk Story Bookstore*** (808-335-6469; talkstorybookstore.com), which prides itself on being "the westernmost bookstore of the United States," offering new and used books, comics, vinyl, plus vintage collectables. Look for historic plaques in Hanapēpē that tell the history of the area; for example, Talk Story was once Yoshiura's General Store, known as the Mikado until World War II.

Before you leave, have a swing on the rope bridge over Hanapēpē River next to the old church. Continue on the road across the 1911 bridge farther downstream. From here, you can turn up Awāwa Road into the valley for a scenic digression along the west canyon wall past sugarcane and taro fields. Distinctive for its large forked leaves, the taro plant served as the early Hawaiians' staple crop. They mashed its starchy roots to make *poi* and cooked the stem and leaves as vegetables. The Hawaiians believed that the taro plant grew from the grave of humankind's elder brother, who had died in infancy. Taro was their link to the land and their "staff of life." Out on the highway, galleries await, including some with "surfboard art." Friday evenings from 5 to 9 p.m., the town galleries host a free open house called Hanapēpē Art Night, with live music, hula, storytelling, and Hawaiian craft demonstrations.

Naturally, no self-respecting art town could long survive without a decent coffeehouse. In addition to hot java, enjoy tasty artisan breads, croissants, and panini made with organic ingredients at ***Midnight Bear Breads*** (808-335-2893; 3038 Hanapēpē Rd.; midnightbearbreads.com). Open Wed and Sat 9 a.m. to 3 p.m., Thurs 8 a.m. to 2 p.m., and Fri 8 a.m. to 8 p.m. Inexpensive to moderate.

Near the edge of town, turn left from the highway onto Lele Road, then right onto Lolokai Road to ***Salt Pond Beach Park.*** Besides offering a beautiful protected beach, the park abuts ancient salt ponds used to harvest sea salt. Rights of use pass through descent. Captain Cook got his salt here, and if you ask someone in the Hui Hana Pa'akai, which still operates these evaporative basins, you may be able to as well. State health department regulations prevent the "impure" salt from being sold commercially, but the impurities add flavor.

West of Hanapēpē, a number of small, working sugar towns are strung along the highway. Looking out onto the horizon, the remote and mysterious islands of Ni'ihau and uninhabited Lehua hover across Kaulakahi Channel. Owned by a missionary-descended ranching family, Ni'ihau is the only private island in the state. The pure-blooded Hawaiians who live here still speak their native tongue and eke out a rustic existence tending the island ranch and gathering honey. Although residents remain free to come and go, uninvited visitors are strictly forbidden. Ni'ihau was another Hawaiian island "invaded" during the Pearl Harbor attack. A downed Japanese fighter pilot terrorized inhabitants until a Hawaiian man, disregarding three bullet wounds, killed the pilot and was awarded the Medal of Merit and the Purple Heart for his actions.

Past the 18-mile marker in Kaumakani, the ***Ni'ihau Helicopter*** office (877-441-3500; niihau.us) offers exclusive tours of the "Forbidden Isle," including a 3-hour beach landing with swimming and snorkeling if weather permits. The half-day tours cost $630; reserve in advance.

From here another 2 miles takes you to Waimea, once the largest settlement on this coast and a historical center of interest. Waimea Bay served as Kaua'i's first major port, beginning with two celebrated British vessels that anchored offshore in 1778. A small marker in ***Lucy Wright Park*** marks the spot where Captain Cook first stepped ashore at 3:30 p.m. in January of that year, bringing Hawai'i into contact with the Western world. This metal plaque and another modest statue in the center of town (cast from the original in Whitby, England, Cook's birthplace) constitute the sole acknowledgment of the historic visit by one of the world's greatest explorers and Hawai'i's first tourist. Cook's journals became best sellers back in Europe. His description of Waimea Bay as a safe anchorage on Kaua'i made it the port of call for a steady stream of Western vessels crossing the Pacific. Waimea became the island's de facto capital as Kaua'i's ruling chiefs gathered here year-round to take advantage of the trading opportunities. Waimea Bay also witnessed the abduction of Kaua'i's King Kaumuali'i, when Kamehameha II invited him on what became a one-way sailing cruise to O'ahu in 1821. Ka'ahumanu, the queen regent, then forced both Kaumuali'i and his oldest son to marry her. These unorthodox tactics ensured Kaua'i's allegiance to the unified Hawaiian Kingdom.

At the entrance to town, turn left into ***Russian Fort Elizabeth State Park*** (fortelizabeth.org) to absorb some more history. One of three forts on Kaua'i built by Georg Anton Schaeffer, a German adventurer acting in the service of the Russian czar, Fort Elizabeth dates from 1815. Schaeffer persuaded King Kaumuali'i to permit these outposts in defense of Russian trading interests. Other foreign powers objected, and the Kamehameha monarchy protested this bid by Kaumuali'i to bolster Kaua'i's autonomy. Schaeffer had overstepped himself, and in 1817, having fallen out of favor, he departed the islands for good. Hawaiian troops completed the construction and occupied the fort until 1864, when it was dismantled.

The fort's outer walls are still readily apparent, and a path leads through the main gate to the interior. Climb the steps to the battlements to gain a view of the coast. Inside the fort, various signs along the path label random piles of rubble or empty spaces, according to the architectural feature of the fort believed to have stood there. Look for dark green clumps of "sleeping grass" scattered around the parking lot and entrance sign. In reality a relative of the giant koa tree, the "grass" has tiny branches sprouting miniature purple-tinged leaves paired in two symmetric rows. Touching the leaves causes each pair to fold tightly closed as if curled up to sleep.

Cross the bridge across flood-prone Waimea River into town. *Waimea* means "reddish waters." Although Hawaiian legend ascribes the river's color to blood from an unjustly slain maiden, the ruddy water bleeds from a far greater wound—Waimea Canyon. Stop by the public library (808-338-6848) on the highway to pick up a copy of a self-guided walking tour of Waimea's historic buildings.

Highlights include the privately owned ***Gulick-Rowell House,*** begun in stone in 1829 by the Reverend Peter Gulick and completed with wooden porches and balconies 17 years later by the Reverend George Rowell. This building is notable for its adaptation of New England designs to Hawaiian building materials and climate. Rowell, "the builder missionary," also completed the current ***Waimea United Church of Christ*** in 1859 from sandstone cut nearby. The two buildings stand on Huakai Road 1 block on either side of Waimea Canyon Drive (Route 550).

Back on the highway, notice the open-wall frame of the old Waimea Mill. The damage predates Hurricane Iniki to the earlier Hurricane Iwa in 1982. You'll find a third building by Rowell opposite the Big Save. After a personal dispute with the established mission, Rowell built ***Waimea Hawaiian Church*** for his breakaway congregation around 1865.

Not included in the walking tour but worth a gander is the ***Menehune Ditch,*** part of an ancient irrigation system diverting the Waimea River to surrounding taro fields. Follow the HVCB warrior onto Menehune Road from the highway and drive about 1.3 miles, stopping where the cactus-draped cliffs crowd in on the river. What little remains of the ditch, sandwiched between the road and cliffs, may not impress you, but the significance of this still-functioning watercourse lies in its use of dressed lava stone, which some argue indicates more sophisticated masonry than the Hawaiians were known to have—hence the credit to the Menehunes.

On the way back, you will see taro fields on your right, which the ditch irrigates. A little farther on, follow the sign to ***Waimea Shingon Mission*** at the end of Pule Road, where a sci-fi vision confronts you. Rows of silver, conical-topped cylinders line the temple perimeter, illuminated by red shower-nozzle lights. In the corner, a multiplatform monument supported by these silver cylinders glistens like a wedding cake. Inscribed with Asian characters, each of these bizarre concrete blocks also houses a miniature statuette. These figurines are traditional in Shingon temples. Each represents 1 of the 88 sins described in Buddhist sutras, and making the tour past all 88 supposedly inoculates you against temptation. But what is unique about this shrine is the unusual shape and appearance of the containers in which the statuettes are housed. They were designed to mimic the appearance of missile shells. Gold-star mothers of Japanese-American soldiers who fought in World War II commissioned these monuments to honor their fallen sons. Ancient Hawaiian burial caves dot the cliffs above.

A unique way to experience plantation living is to stay at the ***Waimea Plantation Cottages*** (808-338-1625; 9400 Kaumuali'i Hwy.; coasthotels.com). Scattered among clusters of coconut trees in a huge garden lot bordering a silty black-sand beach on the west end of town, the cottages are renovated homes brought in from sugar camps all along the coast and furnished with understated charm. The resort was started by descendants of Hans Peter Faye, a Norwegian immigrant who rose to become one of the early sugar barons in the area. Rates average $400 for a one-bedroom cottage.

To explore Waimea's heritage as a sugar town, consider taking the historical walking tour with trail maps provided by the ***West Kaua'i Heritage Center*** (808-338-1332; wsmmuseum.org). The cultural and resource center explores the missionary stories as well as ancient and modern Waimea. The center is open every Tue to Fri 9 a.m. to 3 p.m. Closed holidays.

If Waimea's sugar heritage lies increasingly in its past, the displays at the center chronicle the promise of a high-tech future. This facility, located on the highway at the corner of Waimea Canyon Drive, is part of a campaign to attract technology companies to West Kaua'i. The exhibits describe the activities of some of these companies, which rent space at the center. But it has a much broader focus, covering technology used in the region from the days of the ancient Hawaiians to the present day's solar-powered aircraft tested at the nearby Pacific Missile Range. The center also holds classes in lei making for $10 for adults and $5 for children; reservations required. The center has a wealth of visitor information on the island, as well as a museum and gift shop.

Back in town, shoppers will enjoy browsing through the tchotchkes at ***Paradise Shells & Souvenirs*** (9728 Kaumuali'i Hwy.), where you'll find everything from novelty local T-shirts to keychains and assorted trinkets. The hot climate on this side of the island makes it a great place to try shaved ice (a local version of snow cones), and Waimea has some of the best on the island at ***Jojo's,*** a colorful roadside shack. Choose from a variety of unique flavorings, such as *li hing mui,* a tangy Chinese salty-sour candy made from preserved plums, or try *halo halo,* a kind of Filipino tropical smoothie. For local treats, stop by ***Ishihara Market*** (808-338-1751), which serves take-out plate lunches and sells sushi and poke from the deli counter throughout the day. Open Tue to Sat 6 a.m. to 7:30 p.m., and Sun 6 a.m. to 7 p.m. A more contemporary hotspot is ***Porky's Kaua'i*** (808-631-3071; 9899 Waimea Rd.; porkyskauai.com), a hip food cart serving hot dogs, sausages, and grilled cheese sandwiches loaded with toppings and your choice of their signature "Porky's" sweet or sweet and spicy BBQ sauce.

For dinner, the town favorite is ***Wrangler's Steakhouse*** (808-338-1218), decorated in predictable Western style but with a much broader menu than the name suggests. Save room for the peach cobbler, which is baked to order—yum!

Open Tue through Sat from 5 to 9 p.m. Moderate. The casual alternative is ***Chicken in a Barrel BBQ & Bar*** (808-320-8397; 9400 Kaumuali'i Hwy.), offering chicken, baby back ribs, and hoagies with a mission: The proceeds also benefit an outdoor camp for Hawai'i youth. Open daily 8:30 a.m. to 9 p.m. Inexpensive.

If instead of taking Waimea Canyon Road up to its namesake you continue west, Route 50 leads next to Kekaha, the largest settlement on the west coast. Kekaha's giant mill once set the tone for this blue-collar community. Although the mill no longer operates, it remains part of the landscape. Just past the mill on Kekaha Road, the former post office building now houses famed former woodworker Ray Nitta's ***Westside Wood Designs Studios*** (808-337-1875). Unlike most artisans of his caliber who fashion objets d'art that never get used, Ray's former shop is full of beautiful-yet-functional items, from canoe paddles to Zen Buddhist drums. He worked mostly in native woods on commission; variable hours.

From Kekaha north stretches an almost endless beach, but the park here has the only facilities before Polihale. Kekaha is also the turnoff for Kōke'e Road, an alternate route to Waimea Canyon. Sticking to the coast, Route 50 continues as far as Mana and the Pacific Missile Firing Range at Barking Sands. In dry weather, a portion of the beach here sometimes emits "barking" sounds when you walk on it. Locals, however, say that "the dog stay old already" and has grown silent.

Just as the state highway ends and swings inland to connect with some closed military roads, a single-word sign, POLIHALE, designates the cane road access to ***Polihale State Park*** (808-587-0400; dlnr.hawaii.gov). The price you pay for admission here is 5 miles along a bumpy dirt road. Your reward is a beautiful desolate beach extending across windswept sand dunes as far as the eye can see. Check ahead for road conditions and closures.

About 3.5 miles in, the road approaches a large monkeypod tree fronting a scrub-covered hill with another sign indicating Polihale straight ahead. If you turn left at the tree instead, the road leads seaward toward some enormous sand dunes. Park safely so as not to get your wheels stuck and climb over the dunes to ***Queen's Pond,*** a reef-protected lagoon. This is the only part of Polihale Beach safe for swimming (in moderate surf). After a dip here, continue on to the state park at the end of the road.

As you drive the final miles past the camping area, the mountain ridges edge closer to the shoreline until they loom directly overhead. Beyond Polihale begins the Nā Pali Coast, 16 miles of jagged cliffs plunging directly into the ocean. Hanging valleys, hidden sea caves, and ancient ruins lie shrouded in mystery—incomparable and all but impenetrable.

The park itself offers a pleasant setting with beach pavilions and picnic tables surrounded by native beach vegetation. The shrubbery bush covering the dunes here is beach naupaka. Because of its tolerance to salt spray, this is often the closest-growing plant to the ocean. Besides its stubby leaves and small white pods, naupaka is distinguished by its "half flowers" that appear to be missing petals on one side. A related variety, mountain naupaka, shares this trait and is found only atop the highest peaks. According to Hawaiian legend, the two represent parted lovers whose half-formed flowers reflect a single broken heart. Ni'ihau and Lehua float serenely above the horizon, and if you scoop sand near the shoreline, you may find some of the tiny shells from which the famous Ni'ihau necklaces are made.

Polihale means "house bosom." At the very edge of the beach, where it tapers off beneath the encroaching cliffline, an ancient *heiau* marks the site from which, according to Hawaiian belief, the souls of fallen warriors would depart the earth to the drumbeat of kāhuna. A sacred spring still bubbles beneath the sands nearby. Standing amid this desolate setting, the meager trappings of civilization that the park provides seem foreign to and dwarfed by the power of the natural splendor. Sunset at Polihale feels like the end of the world.

Waimea Canyon and Kōke'e

The drive-by scenery in these adjacent state parks is unmatched in Hawai'i. ***Waimea Canyon*** (808-274-3444; hawaiistateparks.org) serves up eyefuls of choice canyon vistas along the 12-mile cleft in the island's west flank, while higher up Kōke'e luxuriates in a cool, nontropical setting with breathtaking overlooks onto the Nā Pali Coast. To get to these views, take Waimea Canyon Road, which offers the most scenic views on the way up from the highway merging into Kōke'e Road near the entrance to the park. Stop at the first turnout once you climb above Waimea town for a view of the western coastline. A display board explains the changing land use of this region. As you continue on your way up, note the many dead or toppled trees left in Hurricane Iniki's wake.

Besides checking your gas gauge, it's a good idea to check the weather before embarking on the long haul up the canyon roads. Call the ***Kōke'e Museum*** at (808) 335-9975, or peer up the valley from Waimea and gauge the cloud cover. Most of the scenery lies at elevations between 3,000 and 4,000 feet. If the whole area appears fogged in, you may prefer to hang out on the beach or tour Waimea town and hope things clear up on top. As a rule, more clouds tend to gather as the day goes on. If the weather looks dicey, head straight to the Nā Pali overlooks at the end, as they tend to cloud over first. If it does rain while you are up there, don't lose hope. Retreat to the ***Kōke'e Lodge*** (808-335-6061; kokeelodge.com) for a cup of hot caffeine and let the trade winds do their work. You may witness some stunning rainbows to reward your patience.

Three designated canyon overlooks along the upper Kōke'e Road fill their railings with gawking crowds. The ***Waimea Canyon Lookout,*** first at 11 miles in and 3,120 feet elevation, offers the most dramatic frontal view into the main canyon and its three tributaries. Mark Twain, who toured the Hawaiian Islands in his youth and got in first with the most quotable quotes, billed this "the Grand Canyon of the Pacific." While nowhere near as large as Arizona's famous hole, Waimea Canyon boasts a lusher climate that adds a vibrant green to the palette of reds, oranges, and browns used to paint its mainland counterpart. Clouds float in and out of the 3,000-foot-deep gorge, redefining the landscape by shape and shadow and sometimes dissolving reality into mist. Helicopters make a less-welcome intrusion.

The next stop, at ***Pu'u Ka Pele,*** provides picnic tables and a side view of the canyon, while the third turnoff, at ***Pu'u Hinahina,*** features yet another angle as well as a separate view toward the coast and out to Ni'ihau. The brightly colored wildfowl you see strutting and pecking in the parking lots are moa, descendants of the original Polynesian chickens brought to Hawai'i. They are protected by park statute and fed by tourists, and their clucking and crowing are heard everywhere. In between these official lookouts, frequent bends in the highway provide space to safely pull over and find your own preferred vantage point.

An even better option is to take a hike. Anyone ambulatory can and should enjoy the ***Iliau Nature Trail,*** a 0.3-mile loop through sporadically labeled native vegetation leading to an impressive canyon overlook and a glimpse of Wai'alae Waterfall on the far rim. Look for the signposted Kukui trailhead just before the 9-mile point. The stars of the show here are the rare iliau, relatives of the silversword plants found on Haleakalā and the Big Island that are unique to Kaua'i. These branchless plants topped with spiky leaves wait until the end of their life before erupting in hundreds of yellow blossoms. Branching off from the loop, the longer ***Kukui Trail*** drops 2,000 feet to connect with the extensive trail system and wilderness camps on the canyon floor.

A mile past the third posted canyon lookout, the NASA tracking facilities mark the boundary between Waimea and Kōke'e Parks. The first right (Halemanu Road) leads to yet another canyon viewpoint (looking back down the canyon) as well as to trails to the Waipo'o Falls and beyond. Unpaved Halemanu Road is often unsuitable for conventional vehicles, but it's less than a mile hike to the lookout just off Halemanu to the right on the ***Cliff Trail.*** Branch left from the trail to the waterfalls for a dip in a refreshing pool surrounded by ginger.

From here on, the main highway moves away from the canyon rim and continues climbing to ***Kanaloahuluhulu Meadow,*** the center of Kōke'e activity. The god Kanaloa supposedly fashioned this clearing to prevent malevolent forest sprites from preying on passersby. You can get a meal returning to the ***Kōke'e***

Lodge from 10 a.m. to 4:30 p.m. Mon to Fri, and 9:30 a.m. to 4:30 p.m. Sat and Sun., including a delicious Portuguese bean soup and corn bread. The small gift shop inside the lodge features local artisans' handiwork. The lodge also rents comfortably equipped housekeeping cabins sleeping three to seven, ranging from $109 to $169. Early bookings are essential, especially for weekends and holidays (300 Kōke'e Rd., Waimea 96796). ***Camp Sloggett,*** run by the YWCA

Garden Isle Celluloid

Kaua'i's jagged green mountains and dazzling white beaches would stir any cinematographer's soul. So it's no surprise that the island has become Hollywood's venue of choice whenever a script calls for a tropical setting. Throughout the years, Kaua'i has doubled for Vietnam's rice paddies *(Uncommon Valor, Flight of the Intruder),* Costa Rican rain forest *(Jurassic Park),* African jungle *(Outbreak),* and even the Australian outback *(The Thorn Birds).* It served as Peter Pan's Never-Never Land *(Hook), South Pacific*'s Bali Hai, television's *Fantasy Island,* and the original *Gilligan's Island.* The island has also put in more than a few appearances as itself. Elvis Presley got married at the Coco Palms in 1961's *Blue Hawai'i* and returned to croon his way through two other movies set here. More recently, Nicolas Cage and Sarah Jessica Parker's *Honeymoon in Vegas* devolved into a Garden Isle romp. In all, Kaua'i has been filmed in more than 60 full-length motion pictures, beginning with 1933's *White Heat.* Steven Spielberg alone has made four of them, including *Raiders of the Lost Ark.*

Almost any old timer on the island can tell you stories about how John Wayne came drinking at the local saloon while filming *Donovan's Reef.* Or how Frank Sinatra nearly drowned at the beach in Wailua while making *None but the Brave.* With as many as three different movies under production at the same time in recent years and with so many celebrities owning vacation homes on Kaua'i's North Shore, island residents have become almost blasé about their Hollywood connection.

For visitors to Kaua'i, however, the chance to brush against movie history has proven a great selling point. The official *Kaua'i Visitors Bureau Map Guide* includes markers of 39 different film locations for visitors to inspect. You can pick one up at the bureau's office at 4334 Rice St. in Līhu'e or at many other locations around the island. Local bookstores and gift shops stock copies of *The Kaua'i Movie Book,* the definitive guide to moviemaking on the Garden Isle; it is full of photos and anecdotes about the shoots, as well as a map of their locations.

For those wanting help in reaching some of the more out-of-the-way sites (many of which are on private property), Hawai'i Movie Tours (robertshawaii.com/kauai/tours/hawaii-movie-tours) provides a fully narrated tour service. You also learn a wealth of insider gossip about the goings-on behind the scenes and even sing show tunes from *South Pacific.* The tours run approximately eight hours Mon, Wed, and Fri from 7 a.m. to 3:30 p.m. The cost is $164 for adults (ages 12 and older) and $138 for children ages 4 to 11. Reserve in advance at (808) 539-9400, as space is limited.

(808-245-5959 for YWCA main office; campingkauai.com), rents its lodge and bunkhouse for roughly $250 to $300. Linens are not provided; reserve well in advance. Tent camping is available on the property provided you make reservations with the YWCA (808-245-5959). Tent sites are also available throughout the park with a state permit.

Next to the lodge, the ***Kōke'e Museum*** (808-335-9975; kokee.org), run by the Hui o Laka in honor of Laka, the goddess of the forest, offers hiking information and maps (including a giant 3-D topological map of West Kaua'i with all the trails marked). The two-room museum also crams in a wealth of natural-history lore. Well-organized exhibits touch on Hawaiiana, geology, and botany and display stuffed wildlife (including a ferocious boar's head). Be sure to strike the bell stone to hear a working example of these geologic curiosities used by the Hawaiians. Open daily 9 a.m. to 4 p.m.

Outdoors enthusiasts will delight in Kōke'e's many activities. Hunters (with a state permit) track pigs year-round. Frugivores descend upon Kōke'e during late June and July for the Methley plum season. The first Saturday of August kicks off trout season. Anglers can tackle rainbow trout (stocked annually) for the next 16 days, then on weekends through Sept. Licenses are available at Kōke'e Lodge.

The Camp 10 Road, the second right after the lodge, leads through 2 miles of sylvan splendor to picnic areas around the Sugi Grove. The latter half of the road usually requires four-wheel drive. Cedar, fir, eucalyptus, and even redwood trees line the forest paths here. At dusk, look for Hawaiian bats, the islands' only endemic mammal, fluttering from the treetops. From Sugi Grove, you can hike to some upper canyon vantage points. But for scenic destinations, most Kōke'e trails head for ridgetop views above the Nā Pali Coast or make soggy forays through the Alakai Swamp.

You can get a taste of both without departing pavement by continuing on Kōke'e Road to the ***Kalalau*** and ***Pu'u o Kila Lookouts.*** Both overlook the lushly carpeted amphitheater of Kalalau Valley 4,000 feet below. Waterfalls spill silently down the razor-slashed walls. Kalalau Beach, the end point of the Nā Pali Coastal trail (see The North Shore), lies just beyond the left rim of the valley. Uninhabited since the 1920s, the hidden depths of the Kalalau radiate a remote and mysterious power. Here, in a real-life story immortalized by Jack London's pen, Ko'olau the Leper hid with his family to escape exile to Moloka'i. After World War II, Bernard Wheatley, the "Hermit of Kalalau," lived alone in the valley for more than 10 years before disappearing.

From Pu'u o Kila, at the end of Kōke'e Road, you can also scan the vast acreage of the ***Alakai Swamp,*** which stretches across the sunken volcanic basin of Kaua'i's original caldera. The remnant of an aborted road project designed to reach Hanalei extends from the lookout along the narrow ridge dividing Kalalau and the Alakai. Free yourself from human static (if not the inescapable buzz of helicopter sorties) by walking a short distance along ***Pihea Track*** and contemplating the changing angles into Kalalau Valley. Follow your nose to the spicy anise aroma of berries from the *mokihana* trees along this trail. Woven with the equally fragrant leaves of the maile vine, which grows here also, the combination forms Hawai'i's most sacred lei. (If you find mokihana trees, look but don't touch; the tree's berry is extremely acidic and can burn bare skin.)

After a half mile, the "road" narrows; a trail continues to Pihea Overlook, then drops into the murky depths of the Alakai Swamp. The largest wetland area in Hawai'i, the Alakai extends to the summit of Wai'ale'ale, absorbing the prodigious rainfall this peak attracts. The swamp provides refuge for countless endangered native birds, shielded from predators in the mire and, at 4,000 feet, out of range of mosquito-borne diseases. Keep your eyes peeled for the brilliant red 'i'iwi or, if you're lucky, the lime-green nukupu'u. Both have curved beaks; the latter exists only in the eastern Alakai. The almost totally endemic vegetation creates a unique moss-covered environment for hardy souls to explore, but be prepared for rain and mud. Fortunately, a boardwalk bridges the worst patches of muck along the way.

If mud-soaked socks do not appeal, three somewhat drier trails branch off Kōke'e Road between the lodge and the air guard station, descending parallel ridges to reach spectacular vantage points overlooking the Nā Pali Coast. Here you can sit, deafened by silence, watching white tropical birds circle in search of nesting sites as mountain goats clamber along impossibly steep ledges. The two overlooks at the end of the ***Awa'awapuhi and Nualolo Trails*** connect via a third trail. The combined 10-mile loop makes for one of the most stunning—and strenuous—day hikes in Hawai'i. Order maps from the Division of Forestry and Wildlife, 3060 Eiwa St., Rm. 306, Līhu'e 96766; (808) 274-3433. The hike is not for those afraid of heights.

The Coconut Coast

Heading northeast from Līhu'e beyond Hanamā'ulu, the Kūhiō Highway (Route 56) descends from the edge of the Kalepa Ridge and hugs the coast for the next 10 miles or so. The profusion of coconut trees dotting the golf course on your right makes it immediately obvious how the eastern shore acquired its nickname. Before you fast-forward on to the North Shore, take some time to explore the Wailua River Valley. One of the two most sacred areas in all Hawai'i, this lush waterway was the residence of Kaua'i's ali'i nui rulers.

Start your tour on the coast at ***Lydgate Park.*** To get there, turn right onto Leho Road just past the Wailua Golf Course, then right again. The park borders a long, white-sand beach shaded by ironwood trees. Two lava-rock wading pools offer protection against the trade wind–borne swells that buffet the shore. At the far end of the beach road, just below the Aston Kaua'i Resort, scattered clusters of lava rocks mark the remains of ***Hikinaakalä Heiau,*** an ancient sanctuary at the mouth of the Wailua River. The heiau is one of seven strung along the river valley, culminating in an altar on the summit of Mount Wai'ale'ale. Keep in mind that when you look at these heiau, you're seeing only the stone foundations and walls. Kamehameha II abandoned the old religion in 1819. On his orders, all the wooden idols and altars in temples throughout the kingdom were burned to the ground. The few that survived are housed in museums. The heiau here was part of Hauola Place of Refuge. By reaching this peaceful spot, fugitives of old could gain sanctuary from their persecutors. Notice the small noni trees that grow amid the stones here. The pear-size noni fruits bulge like cancerous growths, starting off green and ripening to an unappetizing gray, translucent hue. The fruit has strong medicinal value and is used by some to control hypertension.

The next heiau of the Wailua seven lies hidden among the cane fields above the highway, but you can see numbers three and four by crossing the Wailua River and turning left from Kūhiō Highway onto Kuamo'o Road (Route 580), an ancient roadway once forbidden to commoners. Royalty would beach their canoes and be carried, still seated, along the sacred path to their homes by the lagoon. On your right is the ***Coco Palms Resort,*** the granddaddy of island resorts, built around ancient fishponds where Queen Kapule, the island's last reigning monarch, once lived. An enormous stand of coconut trees encircles the grounds, remnants of an unsuccessful 19th-century copra plantation. The hotel itself has a grand history as a pioneer of Hawaiian resort kitsch, from clamshell washbasins to palm-frond chandeliers; it was featured in several Hollywood movies, including Elvis Presley's *Blue Hawai'i.* Severely damaged by Hurricane Iniki in 1992, it has been closed ever since, but it is slated for redevelopment as a combined resort/condo project. Stay tuned.

Now on to the heiau. Only a short distance up the road, in ***Wailua River State Park*** (808-274-3444; dlnr.hawaii.gov), an HVCB warrior points to ***Holoholo Ku Heiau,*** an ancient temple of sacrifice. Some controversy exists as to the authenticity of the ruins. Queen Kapule is believed to have converted the structure into a pigpen. Notice the dense interlocking thickets of hau trees planted as a natural barrier around this sacred spot.

A few yards farther, you can visit another set of stones used for birth, not death. ***Pōhaku Hoohānau,*** a large stone set against the hillside, marks the site where royal mothers came to give birth in a rustic shelter. Infants born here absorbed the *mana* (spiritual power) of this sacred spot. The umbilical cords were stashed in the adjacent *pōhaku piko* following delivery. A special bell stone on the ridge above would be struck on the occasion of a royal birth, sounding the happy news across the valley.

Farther on, Kuamo'o Road begins to climb the ridge between the Wailua River and Ōpaeka'a Stream. Be sure to stop at the scenic lookout on top to savor the sweeping view of Wailua Valley as you watch riverboats chug slowly upstream. The Wailua River is easily the most navigable river in the state—a Yankee vessel hid here from a Confederate warship during the Civil War. The boats you see today are ferrying tourists to the ***Fern Grotto,*** a natural rock cavity draped with maidenhair ferns. If you can, consider renting a kayak and paddling up on your own (see Introduction). If you do, you can also reach "secret" Ho'olalae Falls by hiking a short distance from the river (ask for directions when you rent your kayak). Interpretive signs at the lookout also identify the adjacent ***Poliahu Heiau.*** The dedication of this temple to Poliahu, the goddess of snow (who lives on the Big Island), is left unexplained.

Your next stop just ahead looks out above ***Ōpaeka'a Falls,*** named for the tiny shrimp that frolic in the pools below. Once a year, while laying eggs, these shrimp dye the water and waterfall red. Walk across to the highway to treat yourself to yet another great view of the main valley.

Farther up Kuamo'o Road, the Wailua Valley gradually opens into Wailua Homesteads, a vast expanse of green pastures and scattered houses ringed by mountains. The cool, fresh air here brings a welcome respite from the coastal heat. To see a very different set of temples, turn left from Kuamo'o Road onto Kaholalele Road, one-quarter of a mile past the 4-mile marker, and go 1 block to the end of the road to reach ***Kaua'i's Hindu Monastery*** (808-822-3012; 107 Kaholalele Rd.; himalayanacademy.com). This active cloistered community conducts a daily *puja* (purification ritual) at 9 a.m. in the Kadavul Temple, which visitors are welcome to join. Dedicated to Shiva, the temple houses a 700-pound crystal *shivalingam* at its center, while the surrounding iconography portrays other avatars of Shiva and his family, including Ganesha, Shiva's elephant-headed son; and Nandi, the bull on which Shiva rides. Taking photographs inside the temple is not permitted. Nearby, the massive white granite Iraivan temple is slowly taking form, built in traditional south Indian style from carved blocks imported from India. Visitors are welcome to visit the complex during daylight hours, and organized tours may be available. Modest dress is requested (no shorts or T-shirts).

For those wishing to spend the night amid this bucolic beauty, there is no shortage of bed-and-breakfasts to choose from. Among the most darling is the ***Fern Grotto Inn*** (808-821-9836; 4561 Kuamoo Rd; kauaicottages.com), which offers various vacation rentals and adorable, old-style plantation cottages. And while breakfast may not be offered here, to spice things up for lovebirds, the karma sutra zen chair is available for honeymooners in certain cottages on reserve. Call for rates. ***The Secret Garden Room*** (808-822-3817; 6430 Ahele Dr.) offers a cozy room as well as a garden, koi pond, and manmade waterfall right outside. Rates begin at $180. Airbnb has become a major fixture for rentals throughout the islands in recent years; peruse the app to discover rooms that are sometimes up for rent and sometimes being occupied by the actual folks who live there.

Kuamo'o Road continues to climb deeper into the island interior. At about 5 miles in, a sign warns that the road ahead is "unimproved," but it really is not that bad. You pass hillsides carpeted with maidenhair ferns, fragrant patches of yellow ginger, and other tropical flora. At about 6.5 miles from its start, the road crosses Keahua Stream, where you can park and stretch your legs in ***Keahua Arboretum.*** Although most of the plant labels have been lost, nature paths wind along the stream through open meadows and clusters of exotic trees. The Makaleha Mountains, Wailua's rear wall, loom fairly close by, and behind them, the twin peaks of Wai'ale'ale and Kawaikiu slash upward to skewer the clouds.

For those wishing to take in more of the scenery on foot, an excellent network of hiking trails begins near Keahua. The ***Kuilau Ridge Trail,*** one of the most scenic on Kaua'i, has its signposted trailhead on the right of the highway just before you cross Keahua Stream. The 2.1-mile (1.5 hour) jaunt through diverse vegetation and fruit winds along a steep ridge to reach a shelter-picnic site. Continue on a half mile farther to get the best views. More hard-core is the ***Powerline Trail,*** which starts at the end of the road and leads you on an all-day slog across the mountains to Princeville. On clear days the views are spectacular, but expect thigh-deep mud in patches.

On your way down from Keahua, take the turnoff left onto Route 581 (Kamalu Road), which winds through lush forest and rolling pastures behind Nounou Mountain. About 1.2 miles along, a sign on the right, opposite 1055 Kamulu Rd., indicates the trailhead for the ascent up Nounou, better known as the Sleeping Giant. Hawaiian legend claims the mountain is really the overgrown body of the giant Nounou, whose recumbent form is best viewed from the coast. The trail travels 1.5 miles to Nounou's chin (about an hour's hike) and offers panoramic views from the top.

Route 581 continues for another couple of miles of mountain vistas before it swings toward the coast to rejoin the coastal highway near the center of Kapa'a, where an HCVB warrior designates the optimum viewing angle to make out the Sleeping Giant's shape, but you can see him from anywhere along the Coconut Coast. (Hint: Nounou's head rests on a pillow above Wailua, and his body stretches north.)

The Twice-Buried Lantern

In a quiet corner of Kapa'a Ball Park, next to the highway, stands an enormous Japanese stone lantern with a curious past. The saga of this monument in many ways mirrors the evolving identity of the local Japanese community that built it in 1915, using leftover funds raised during the 1905 Russo-Japanese War. In addition to honoring Japanese soldiers who fought in that war, an inscription on the lantern's face commemorates the ascension of a new emperor to the Japanese throne. With its bombing of Pearl Harbor in 1941, Japan became public enemy number one. To protect it against vandals, the 25-foot-tall, 16-ton lantern was buried soon afterward, a precaution symbolic of efforts by local Japanese to hide ties to their motherland. After World War II ended, the lantern remained forgotten underground until it was exposed accidentally in 1972. County officials turned to the local Japanese community for guidance, but no one stepped forward to take charge of this unwelcome relic from a bygone era, and the lantern was reburied soon afterward. However, by 1985, a new generation of Japanese Americans, led by then-mayor Tony Kunimura, sparked interest in the monument as a reminder of their heritage.

The lantern was unearthed for the second time and placed in a supportive brace, pending renovation. Donations for this purpose are sought by the Kaua'i Historical Society. Call (808) 245-3373 for information.

If you're more interested in exploring the diversity of Kaua'i shopping, stop by the ***Noka Fair*** (808-652-4040; nokafairkauai.com); look for the colored awnings of vendors along the highway. Open daily 9 a.m. to 5 p.m.

When hunger beckons, you will find the Coconut Coast loaded with restaurants of all stripes strung along the highway. To eat as locals do, visit ***Pono Market*** (808-822-4581), at the southern edge of Kapa'a, for a take-out plate lunch and poke; the *lau lau* (a sort of steamed Hawaiian tamale) and *manju* (a Japanese filled pastry) have a special following. Open Mon through Sat 6 a.m. to 4 p.m. To eat healthy, try, well, ***Russell's By Eat Healthy*** (808-822-7990; 4-369 Kūhiō Hwy.; eathealthykauai.com), a chill, BYOB café offering a mix of vegan and gluten-free breakfast, lunch, and dinner options. Open Tues to Sat 8 a.m. to 2:15 p.m. Last seating at 2 p.m. Moderate to expensive.

Those with a yen for Japanese should visit ***Restaurant Kintaro*** (808-822-3341), where you can order either *teppanyaki* dishes prepared at your table or sushi and other delicacies from the kitchen. Open Mon through Sat 5:30 to 9:30 p.m. Expensive. Or build-your-own thin crust pizza at ***Bobby V's Italian Restaurant Pizzeria*** (808-821-8080; 4-484 Kūhiō Hwy.; bobbyvpizzeria.com) and enjoy your tasty creation sitting in the garden outside. Open daily 11 a.m. to 9 p.m. Inexpensive to moderate. Another good option is ***Kenji Burger*** (808-320-3558; 4-788 Kūhiō Hwy.; kenjiburger.com), where you can enjoy casual bento boxes, the eponymous burgers, poke, and shakes in a hip, new-school spot. Open Sun, Mon, Wed, and Thurs 11 a.m. to 8:30 p.m., and Fri to Sat 11 a.m. to 9 p.m. Inexpensive to moderate.

Finally, tucked inside the Kaua'i Coast Resort behind the Coconut Marketplace is the ***Hukilau Lāna'i Restaurant*** (808-822-0600; hukilaukauai.com). This establishment is also owned by The Plantation House by Gaylords. Early birds who arrive before 5:45 p.m. can enjoy a special tasting menu that features five courses and five wines for $65 per person ($45 for food only). Open Wed through Sat from 5:30 to 8:30 p.m. Expensive to investment-caliber.

Those craving another waterfall-fed pond to frolic in can take Kawaihau Road off Kūhiō Highway (near the north edge of town). On the way, you will pass ***St. Catherine of Alexandria Parish,*** which looks like an aircraft hangar but harbors beautiful murals by prominent local artists portraying Christian scenes in a Hawaiian and Asian idiom. Continue on for another 2 miles, then turn right onto Kapahi Road, which angles back to end at a dirt road. Follow this dirt road to a narrow trail and keep on the left fork as you zero in on the sound of the falls. Kapa'a Stream funnels over ***Ho'opōuli Falls*** into a narrow steep-walled pool formed by an exposed lava tube.

The North Shore

Those striking "Bali Hai" peaks you've admired all the way from Līhu'e rise from the edge of the Anahola Mountains at the northern limit of the Coconut Coast. North of Kapa'a, Kealia Beach marks the beginning of undeveloped coastline; however, Kūhiō Highway turns inland as it climbs over the Anahola Mountains, leaving the beaches ahead hidden from tourist traffic. WARNING: With all North Shore beaches, extreme caution must be exercised while swimming. Dangerous currents form along the coast, and monstrous surf appears during winter.

After crossing the Anahola Mountains, you enter a vast clearing, but surprise, no sugarcane: The climate on the North Shore is too wet. Sugar has given way to niche farms such as the small papaya plantation about a half mile past the 16-mile marker. Turn right here onto Ko'olau Road to do some exploring. To reach secluded ***Moloa'a Bay,*** take the next right and follow bumpy Moloa'a Road to its end. Park and walk past the cluster of beach homes along the public right-of-way to the beach. Sheltered inside the steep walls of the bay, this beautiful curving strand is bisected by Moloa'a Stream. Windblown debris accumulates at the far end of the beach. You may get lucky and discover a Japanese fishing float, a hollow ball of glass that has floated thousands of miles across the Pacific.

To cool your thirst after your seaside frolics, you might stop at ***Moloa'a Sunrise Fruit Stand*** (808-822-1441; moloaasunrisefruitstand.com), back at the turnoff from the highway, for a tropical fruit smoothie. Open Mon through Fri 9 a.m. to 4 p.m.

Ko'olau Road winds uphill past Moloa'a to cross rolling pastureland. For diehards who thought Moloa'a wasn't deserted enough, turn back on the angled cane road on your right just more than a mile farther on Ko'olau Road, then take an immediate left. Follow this second dirt road to the end and hike the remaining half mile down to ***Ka'aka'aniu*** or ***Larsen's Beach.*** All this effort guarantees seclusion on a lovely stretch of shoreline that is a traditional harvesting site for *limu,* an edible seaweed. Ko'olau Road continues past an 1853 cemetery and affords ocean and mountain vistas before it rejoins Kūhiō Highway.

At the 23-mile marker you reach the first real settlement on the North Shore, at Kīlauea. A plantation town that refused to die, Kīlauea now thrives on the tourist traffic lured by ***Kīlauea Lighthouse.*** Turn right off the highway onto Kolo Road to enter town. You take the first left to reach the lighthouse, but before doing so, have a look at tiny ***Christ Memorial Episcopal Church,*** a charming lava-rock edifice set amid a peaceful garden and cemetery. Inside the church are some colorful stained-glass windows imported from England and a hand-carved altar fashioned by a parishioner, Mrs. William Hyde Rice. The present church dates from 1941, but many of the plots in the cemetery hark back to the original Congregational mission church. Farther along Kolo Road, ***Saint Sylvester's Catholic Church*** claims its share of attention for its innovative octagonal design. Inside, painted ceiling panels by Jean Charlot depict the Stations of the Cross.

At the end of the road, ***Kīlauea Point National Wildlife Refuge*** (808-828-1413; fws.gov) surrounds the old lighthouse standing on Kaua'i's northernmost tip. Stop first at the visitor center to take in some information-packed displays on Pacific wildlife. You can then walk out to the end of the point and enjoy sweeping views along the coast in both directions while looking for the critters you've just read up on. Dolphins, green sea turtles, monk seals, and even humpback whales can all be spotted on occasion, as well as dozens of seabirds whirling overhead.

The old lighthouse is no longer used and is closed to visitors, but a separate set of displays tells the story of its rare "clamshell" lens. Designed by French physicist Augustin Fresnel in 1913, using thousands of fragile interlocking pieces, the 4-ton lens beamed its light 20 miles out to sea. Volunteers lead informative and very scenic hikes along the cliffside terrain and native vegetation of adjacent Crater Hill. The refuge is open Wed to Sat 10 a.m. to 4 p.m. Admission is $10. On the way to the lighthouse, you'll pass the Kong Lung Center, a historic trading post turned tourist complex.

Across the road from the Kong Lung Center, ***Kīlauea Fish Market*** (808-828-6244) offers the North Shore's best dining value. Gourmet plate lunch, including fresh fish specials, is served Mon through Sat 11 a.m. to 8 p.m. Inexpensive to moderate.

These gardens are but a prelude to the horticultural wonders of ***Na 'Aina Kai*** ("Lands by the Sea") (808-828-0525; naainakai.org), a 12-acre tropical extravaganza, complete with a landscaped waterfall, a Japanese teahouse, a koi pond, and bronze statuary. The gardens consist of six major sections, from the bog house to the obligatory poinciana maze, as well as an "international desert," jungle rain forest, and beachside wetland. The landscaped plots are surrounded by 45 acres of exotic fruits and 110 acres of tropical hardwood forest—planted as a revenue source for the garden's future. There's also a whimsical childrens' garden for tots to explore. The gardens are open for guided tours once or twice Tues to Fri, depending on the tour. Reservations recommended. The tours involve walking and/or riding in an open cart, and each emphasizes different aspects of the gardens. They range from 90 minutes to a 5-hour walking tour and cost $45 to $85. Call for a complete schedule.

If you glanced along the western shoreline from Kīlauea Point, you probably saw a wide patch of sandy beach. Getting there is another story. ***Kauapea Beach*** once bore the nickname Secret Beach because of its hidden access. The secret is out now, and there is no reason why you should not enjoy its charms. Take Kalihiwai Road, the first right past Kīlauea, and then turn right again onto a dirt road. From the end of this road, you have a short (5-minute) hike down a very steep hill. Popular with alternative lifestyle types, Kauapea Beach at the bottom is much bigger than you might expect, but it is partitioned by lava-rock outcrops into cozy subsections. Although calmer in the summer, the beach is not recommended for swimming any time of year due to dangerous currents.

Kalihiwai Road continues on through lush foliage and then curls around the mouth of beautiful ***Kalihiwai Bay*** to descend to yet another pristine North Shore beach. Children swing on a rope over the lagoon formed at the mouth of Kalihiwai Stream. Tidal waves in 1946 and 1957 twice flattened the entire valley. As a result, a broken circuit has left a second Kalihiwai Road joining the highway farther along.

On your way there, park at the scenic overlook near the 24-mile marker and walk onto the highway bridge to savor the tropical vision of Kalihiwai Valley. The waterfall you see upstream can be reached by kayak or jeep trail. The trailhead begins at the next turnout a mile farther at the falling rocks sign. Bear left at the meadow. Past the bridge, turn onto the western branch of Kalihiwai Road, choosing the left fork (Anini Road) unless you want to admire Kalihiwai Bay from the other side. Anini Road passes some elegant beach homes (which may explain its good state of repair) on its way to ***Anini Beach Park,*** a huge, grassy expanse with the usual facilities. WARNING: One of the largest fringing reefs in Hawai'i protects the coastline here, but dangerous currents still form in the winter, especially through Anini Channel, a gap in the reef where sailboarders romp on windy days.

Back on the highway, you next pass 1 Hotel Hanalei Bay, formerly known as the Princeville Resort. Built onto bluffs overlooking magnificent Hanalei Bay, the ultraluxury ***1 Hotel Hanalei Bay*** (883-623-0111; 1hotels.com/hanalei-bay) has perhaps the most scenic location of any in Hawai'i. The only luxury resort on the island without resort or parking fees, this 1 Hotel is the first of its kind on the island, merging sustainability and wellness into a 2.0 lifestyle hotel with cutting-edge fitness, spa, and wellness offerings.

Princeville Ranch (808-855-0064; princevilleranch.com) offers private horseback lessons for children and adults on private ranch land. Their sister company, Kaua'i Backcountry Adventures, invites you to hike and/or paddle your way to remote waterfalls or soar across jungle canyons on a zip line. Popular tours for tubing and ziplining cost around $149 and include lunch. Reserve in advance.

You can also explore Princeville's remote interior on your own by hiking the ***Powerline Trail,*** a rough, unpaved road that crosses the island to emerge at Keahua Arboretum in Wailua. The one-way trip takes several hours and can get very wet and muddy as you climb toward the rain-soaked summit. But if the weather's good, heading even a few miles in can yield spectacular views of mountain ridges and waterfalls. To reach the trailhead, turn inland at the Princeville Ranch onto Pooku Road, then drive 1.7 miles to the pavement's end; the trail follows the Hanalei River upstream.

On the other side of the highway from the Princeville entrance, be sure to stop at the ***Hānalei Valley Overlook*** on the left for one of the classic vistas in Hawai'i. The Hanalei River emerges from the mouth of a deep valley and curves gently west through fields of taro. When it rains in the mountains, tiny waterfalls appear—local lore warns not to visit Hanalei when more than eight cascades are gushing, or you risk being stranded by flash floods. Most of the land before you belongs to the Hanalei National Wildlife Refuge (808-828-1413; fws.gov/hanalei). The Hanalei Valley has been farmed by different people throughout the years through a cycle of crops. Now, as a protected wildlife refuge, the land has reverted to the taro cultivation of ancient times in a cooperative venture whereby flooded taro fields, regulated by terracing, provide a favorable habitat for endangered wildfowl. Birders can study an illustrated placard to bone up on the different species they might encounter below.

As the highway begins its descent to the valley floor, a wide strip around the first bend allows space to pull over and admire ***Hānalei Bay*** ("Crescent Bay"), the companion view to the valley overlook. Surfers stop here and check out the breakers through binoculars to decide which part of the bay to paddle out to below. Keen eyes may spot the buffalo that graze in Bill Mowry's farm in front of the bay; this meat is featured on local restaurant menus.

At the bottom of the hill, you reach the famous single-lane ***Hānalei Bridge,*** a symbolic gateway to the scenic wonders ahead. Mileage numbers are zeroed from this point, and as a practical benefit, weight restrictions prevent tour buses from crossing. The bridge is actually two in one: a 1912 Pratt truss bridge reinforced below by a late-1960s Warren pony truss. Additional one-lane bridges span the 10 miles of highway ahead, enforcing a slower pace of life. By custom, traffic on the bridge alternates, allowing cars gathered on the one side to clear while the other side waits to cross. Etiquette dictates that you wave to acknowledge other motorists' courtesy in yielding.

To explore the upper valley you saw from the overlook, turn left after the bridge onto Ohiki Road, which heads upriver through the taro fields/wildlife refuge. A turnoff just ahead to the right leads to an old cemetery. A little bit farther on, there's a parking lot where a quarter-mile nature loop leads to a recently discovered heiau. The steep powerline trail behind the cemetery serves as the beginning of the ***Hānalei Okolehao Trail,*** named for the *okolehao* liquor distilled from *ki* plants along this ridge during Prohibition. The 2.25-mile hike takes about 2 hours and offers great views of Hanalei Bay. Another 1.5 miles inland, the main road ends at the easier ***Hānalei Valley Trail,*** which heads 2 miles upstream through fruit trees and bamboo forests.

After the bridge, the Kūhiō Highway follows the Hanalei River into Hanalei Town. Stop when you spot the soothing green of ***Wai'oli Hui'ia Church*** on your left. If you come by on Sunday morning, you will hear the church's famous choir fill the rafters with Hawaiian hymns. The building to the right, ***Wai'oli Mission Hall,*** built in 1841, housed the original congregation.

The real treat, however, awaits at the end of the long driveway between these two buildings. Park in the lot behind the Mission Hall to visit ***Wai'oli Mission House*** (grovefarm.org), the 1837 residence of the Alexanders, the first Congregationalist missionaries on the North Shore. Restored in 1921 by three Wilcox sisters whose missionary grandparents succeeded the Alexander family here, the mission house is run by the same trust that oversees Grove Farm. Where Grove Farm portrays life during sugar's heyday, this Hanalei museum returns to an even earlier time for a glimpse at the lives of Bedford missionaries in "Owhyhee," as it was referred to back then. Docents lead tours of the property, revealing the stories behind its contents, while the letters and portraits on display chronicle the early inhabitants. The prefab house and most of the furniture (including a bed warmer!) were shipped around Cape Horn. A garden in back made this isolated mission self-sufficient in food supplies. Tours are offered Tues, Thurs, and Sat 10 a.m. to 1 p.m.; donations voluntary.

From the mission, take any road seaward and then turn right to backtrack along the bay to ***Black Pot Beach Park*** at the mouth of the Hanalei River. The park name honors a tradition of seaside festivities held on this spot in decades past. Local fishermen, visiting yacht crews, and anyone else who cared to join in would gather nightly to cook in a communal black pot. "Uncle" Henry Kalani Tai Hook, the unofficial mayor of Hanalei, set records with the enormous outdoor banquets he organized here. An old pier that juts offshore once served to load rice from the valley mill (note the faint rail tracks). Kids play on and around the crumbling pier, and swimming in these estuarine waters is the safest in the bay.

Most of the restaurants in Hanalei cater to tourists and price accordingly, so you might want to bring a picnic lunch. ***Postcards Cafe*** (808-826-1191; postcardscafe.com), first in line as you enter town from Princeville, serves decent, albeit pricey, fish and veggie fare with some Pacific Rim touches in an old plantation-style house decorated with vintage photos and guess what else. Expensive to investment-caliber prices. Open for dinner daily 5 to 9 p.m. What Hanalei lacks in eateries it makes up for in its bars. ***Tahiti Nui*** (808-826-6277; thenui.com), on the highway in the center of town, is practically an institution. There is live music nightly 6:30 to 9 p.m. and various special events. The venue's Family Luau is also held every Tue and Wed at 6 p.m. Brunch is available during weekends. This South Seas watering hole dates from over 40 years ago, when original owner Louise Marston arrived as a war bride from Tahiti and fell in love with Hanalei. Polynesian architecture and decor run from floor to ceiling. The glass fishing-float lanterns and carved-coconut-stump barstools are especially nice touches. Bar dining is available. Also popular after dark is the ***Hānalei Gourmet*** (808-826-2524; hanaleigourment.com), a deli bar housed in the restored 1926 Old Hanalei Schoolhouse across the street. Try the chicken salad in a papaya or avocado boat, if it's on the specials menu. The deli is open Sun to Thurs 11:30 a.m. to 8 p.m. Live music every Sun 6 to 8 p.m.; moderate.

For those wishing to stay the night, Hanalei has a few options. The ***Hānalei Inn*** (808-826-9333; hanaleiinn.net) offers country studios with individual lānais and kitchens, as well as barbecue areas. For something even more chill, enjoy a laid-back retreat at ***Hānalei Surfboard House*** (808-651-1039; hanaleisurf boardhouse.com), with its spunky decor and studios plus a lānai. You can also book a variety of rental properties, some owned by absentee celebrities, through ***Oceanfront Rentals on Kaua'i*** (808-826-6585; 800-222-5541; PO Box 223190; rentalsonkauai.com).

As Route 56 climbs around the western edge of Hanalei Bay, the road widens at two pullout spaces, from which a steep, often muddy trail descends

Hānalei Rice Mill

Deep within the Hānalei National Wildlife Refuge, unobtrusively located on the banks of the Hānalei River, sits the state's only rice mill. Included on the National Register of Historic Places, the mill was built by a Chinese farmer in the late 1880s and came into the (Japanese) Haraguchi family in 1924. Rice was harvested here until the 1960s, when the rice industry collapsed, and the land reverted to taro. Having already rebuilt the mill once after a 1930 fire, the Haraguchi family never intended to restore the historic property twice more after it closed, but hurricanes Iwa and Iniki had other plans. The building and all its original equipment had stood in disarray until the early 1980s, when the family formed a nonprofit organization and slowly began moving toward restoration. Their efforts included taking an oral history from family patriarch Kayohei Haraguchi, who died shortly before Iwa demolished the building in 1982. The mill was fully restored and operating as an education center for schoolchildren when Iniki hit in 1992 and again leveled the structure. The family's homes and farm also were devastated, delaying further reconstruction efforts until 1996. Besides rebuilding the mill, workers also labored for months to restore the ancient equipment. It's the only such building of its kind in the state.

Now rebuilt, the facility is open to the public on a limited basis but remains temporarily closed. Call (808) 651-3399 (haraguchiricemill.org). Stop by the roadside informational kiosk at the entrance to Hanalei town (next to the Bike Doktor); the Hariguchis also own the adjacent Hanalei Taro & Juice stand, which sells a wide range of island produce and special taro smoothies.

through the forest of hala trees to ***Lumahai Beach.*** This lovely strand starred in *South Pacific* as Nurses' Beach, where Mitzi Gaynor tried to "wash that man right out of my hair." Waters here are very treacherous, so best stick to the sand.

The highway next crosses Lumahai Stream to enter ***Wainiha***—Valley, River, Bay, Beach, and General Store. The latter is your last stop for provisions. WARNING: *Wainiha* quite appropriately means "unfriendly waters." Not only is the beach treacherous, but the river mouth is a nursery for baby sharks—so steer clear. Consider turning inland onto Powerhouse Road to explore wide-mouthed Wainiha Valley, where an early census listed 52 residents as menehune. You'll pass the standard North Shore offerings of lush vegetation, waterfalls, and ancient taro terraces before ending up 2 miles in at the 1906 hydroelectric power station.

Back on the highway, the YMCA's ***Camp Naue*** (808-826-6419) lies at the 8-mile marker, spread over a choice beachfront lot. Often the site of community functions, the camp rents dorm bunks for $20 to those who can furnish their own bedding in between group bookings. No reservations are accepted, but call ahead to check availability.

After rounding a final curve, the highway crosses a small stream (and quite often vice versa) where, yawning open as if to swallow unwary motorists, ***Maniniholo (Dry) Cave*** appears on the left. Park at Hā'ena Beach Park across the road to explore this cavernous chamber, named for the head fisherman of the menehune who lived here. Sinuous vines hang over the rim, and wild taro grows near the entrance. Inside, with the aid of a flashlight, you can follow a passage opening from the back left wall a good distance in before the ceiling becomes uncomfortably low. This ancient lava tube helped form the sea cave through which you entered. Hā'ena Beach Park has facilities, but a nicer stretch of sand lies back around the bend toward Hanalei. Take the beach access road a quarter mile before Maniniholo Cave to ***Tunnels,*** a popular surfing spot with outstanding snorkeling during calm summer months. Sandlubbers can simply admire the mountain and ocean views.

Kūhiō Highway presses on through lush vegetation darkened by the shadow of the mountains overhead. About a half mile past the 9-mile marker, on the mountain side of the road, you will see the entrance to ***Limahuli Gardens*** (808-826-1053; ntbg.org), the North Shore satellite of the National Tropical Botanical Garden in Lawa'i, with an environmentally friendly visitor center intended to be visually compatible with its fabulous setting. The structure began as a 10-by-32-foot office trailer, which was transformed into a building resembling a historic, plantation-style home. Call to check conditions and reserve your visit.

The center displays Hawaiian crafts and offers information about the environment and the garden, a 17-acre facility that features a large collection of rare and endangered native Hawaiian plants and many tropical species. The plantings here focus on ethnobotany. You can learn about the plants the ancient Hawaiians used in their daily life as you explore this spectacular valley setting via a three-quarter-mile loop trail. Black lava rock contours the green valley slopes in an age-old system of terraces built for taro. A coastal overlook offers stunning views. Guided tours are $60 (reserve in advance); self-guided, $30. Open Tues through Sat 8:30 a.m. to 4 p.m.

Back on the highway, ***Hā'ena State Park*** (808-274-3444; dlnr.hawaii.gov) just ahead was the site of the infamous Taylor's Camp, a 1960s hippie community in which free-living style did not include plumbing or waste disposal. State authorities eventually condemned the land. Like Limahuli Gardens, call ahead to check about flooding. Park at the visitor parking area, cross the street, and take the short but steep trail ahead to the ledge overlooking ***Waikapalae (Wet) Cave.*** To get the full spelunking effect, you should ease your way down to the edge of the water. Daylight, tinted green by the foliage overhead, filters through the mouth of the cave, and the soundless water inside acquires an eerie blue hue.

A second wet cave, ***Waikanaloa,*** opens onto the highway just ahead. Peering inside, you can see through to a second chamber. One of the legends of Pele explains how these two caves became wet. It seems the volcano goddess dug her fire pits here when she came to Kaua'i in search of a home. Her sister, the ocean, flooded her out of Waikanaloa; Pele tried higher up at Waikapalae, but the ocean followed still. Defeated, Pele took her fires to O'ahu.

As you return to your car, keep your eye on the cliff-top peaks above the highway. These silent sentinels loom ever closer, choking off the road against the sea, until all at once it ends at ***Ke'e Beach;*** beyond lies only the remote Nā Pali Coast and the start of the Kalalau Trail. Ke'e Beach, at the far end of the parking lot, provides ample reward for your perseverance in coming this far. Dominated by the spires of rock overhead and sheltered by a protective reef, this tiny cove offers excellent snorkeling in calm waters and is usually safe for a dip in moderate surf. Long stretches of hidden sandy beach extend around the right side of the lagoon. You can walk there or drive from the parking lot, but the swimming is less protected.

The left side of Ke'e Beach conceals secrets of its own. Follow the short sidewalk strip from the edge of the parking lot toward a narrow trail skirting the edge of the former Allerton estate, just above the rocky border of the lagoon. You get a magnificent glimpse of the endlessly silhouetted *pali* (cliffs) ahead that give this coast its name. Near the end of the point, the trail turns left and climbs steeply through vegetation to emerge in the clearing that was once ***Ka 'Ulu o Laka Heiau,*** dedicated to Laka, the patron of the hula. The rocky remains of this ancient temple have weathered considerably, but you can still feel the power of the setting, hovering midway between mountain and ocean, encircled by jungle, at the very edge of civilization. The ancient Hawaiians held night rituals on this site, hurling special burning branches from the cliffs nearby in a natural display of fireworks. Hula *hālau* (hula schools) still return today to leave offerings and rededicate their arts in this sacred spot. Casual visitors are requested to refrain from entering beyond the marked boundary.

Across the parking lot from Ke'e Beach begins the ***Kalalau Trail,*** Hawai'i's most celebrated wilderness experience. Along the way, you take in magnificent scenery, lush tropical vegetation, dramatic seascapes, hidden valleys cloaked in mist, and, above all, the magnetic presence of *na pali,* the endless sea cliffs whose sheer edges the trail traverses. This is no cakewalk. It's made worse by—you guessed it—flooding. Further research is needed to see if the trail has reopened after excess water levels. To travel the full 11 miles along the Nā Pali Coast to Kalalau Beach takes at least two days. There are numerous spur trails heading inland to explore. State camping permits are required. A popular day hike goes 2 miles to ***Hanakāpī'ai Beach*** (swimming not recommended) and then an

Lohi'au's House or the Tale of Three Sisters

Countless hikers head into the Nā Pali every day without noticing an archaeological site that the Kalalau Trail passes scarcely 50 feet from the trailhead. Just to the left of the trail, keen eyes will discern the vine-draped lava-rock foundation that is reputedly the site of Lohi'au's house. Legends recount that Lohi'au was a handsome chieftain associated with the hula hālau at the nearby Ka 'Ulu o Laka temple. In one legend, when the volcano goddess Pele arrived on Kaua'i, she was fleeing the wrath of her elder sister, a powerful ocean goddess. Hearing the sounds of the drums at Ka 'Ulu o Laka, Pele drew near to watch the ritual hula. With his graceful dancing, Lohi'au won Pele's favor. They vowed to live together as man and wife.

Unfortunately, Pele's older sister, Nāmaka (or Nāmaka-o-Kaha'i), had followed her to the island. When Pele attempted to dig for fire to build a home for her and her beloved, the ocean goddess rushed in with crashing waves to squelch Pele's fire. Pele's flooded fire pits remain known as the wet caves of Waikapalae and Waikanaloa. With a heavy heart, Pele had to leave Lohi'au in quest of fire elsewhere. As she moved from island to island, Pele longed for her beloved mortal. When at last she settled on the Big Island, her volcanic fires secure in the mighty lava fortress she had built, she sent her younger and favorite sister, Hi'iakaikapoliopele (meaning "Hi'iaka, in the bosom of Pele," the patron goddess of hula dancers, chant, medicine, and sorcery), to summon her paramour within 40 days—but Pele insisted that Hi'iaka not fall in love with Lohi'au.

Hi'iaka encountered many adventures and challenges along the way, such as having to duel with the *kupua* (demons) of the island forests, but finally reached Kaua'i. Lohi'au had since died a lonely death, but Hi'iaka was able to revive his spirit with chanting and prayer and bring him back to life. The two then embarked on an arduous journey down the Hawaiian island chain, battling monsters and overcoming obstacles. Pele, believing that Hi'iaka had betrayed her (it had been more than 40 days), destroyed Hi'iaka's sacred Lehua forest.

Upon her return, Hi'iaka saw Pele's destruction and embraced Lohi'au in revenge. Upon seeing them together, Pele's wrath overflowed. Torrents of fire gushed down the slopes, causing Lohi'au to die a second death engulfed in molten lava. Again, Hi'iaka revived him. Regretting her actions, Pele decided to let Lohi'au choose whom he wanted to be with. Different versions of the legend say Lohi'au decided to remain with both goddesses. Others say he returned to Kaua'i alone. But it is most widely believed that Lohi'au had come to love and admire Hi'iaka for her beauty, bravery, and kindness during their dangerous travels together, and that he chose her for his wife and took her back to Kaua'i to be together.

optional 2 miles upstream past ancient taro terraces and remnants of an 1890 coffee plantation to the 300-foot ***Hanakāpī'ai Falls*** for a chilling plunge in the pool below.

Those with less time or stamina might consider hiking only a half mile in on the trail until you catch the first full glimpse of the Nā Pali Coastline spread out before you. You'll know when you're there. Finally, to explore the Nā Pali Coast by catamaran or zodiac, call ***Captain Andy's Sailing and Rafting*** (808-335-6833; napali.com).

Places to Stay on Kaua'i

HĀNALEI

Hānalei Inn
5-5468 Kūhiō Hwy.
(808) 826-9333
hanaleiinn.net
Rustic studios with BBQ areas, individual lānais, and private kitchens. Rooms $219 to $330. Two-night minimum stay. Discount after seven days.

KAPA'A

Fern Grotto Inn
(808) 821-9836
4561 Kuamoo Rd.
kauaicottages.com
Adorable plantation cottages and vacation rentals. Call for rates.

Starry Night Lodging
'Melemele' Kapa'a Cottage
starrynightlodging.com
2-bedroom, 1-bathroom retreat in Kapa'a. $449 average a night.

KŌLOA

Whalers Cove Resort
2640 Pu'uholo Rd.
(808) 742-7571
whalerscoveresort.com
Chic accommodations with a beautiful pool right on the water. Call to check seasonal condo rates.

LĪHU'E

The Kauai Inn
2430 Hulemalu Rd.
(808) 245-9000
kauaiinn.com
From $230.

WAIMEA

Waimea Plantation Cottages
9400 Kaumuali'i Hwy.
(808) 338-1625
coasthotels.com
Charming individual cottage-type accommodations. Call to check seasonal rates.

Places to Eat on Kaua'i

KALĀHEO

Kalaheo Café & Coffee Company
(808) 332-5858
2-2560 Kaumuali'i Hwy.
kalaheo.com
Prime rib, island fresh fish, meat loaf, omelets, and excellent coffee in a charming, rustic setting.

KAPA'A

Greenery Café
3146 Akahi St.
(808) 635-2752
Delicious and light breakfast and lunch, made with locally grown ingredients.

KŌLOA

The Beach House Restaurant
5022 Lāwa'i Rd.
(808) 742-1424
the-beach-house.com
Hawaiian regional cuisine served in a romantic oceanfront setting. Expensive to investment-caliber.

FOR MORE INFORMATION ABOUT KAUA'I

kauai.com

gohawaii.com/islands/kauai

kauai-hawaii.com

LĪHU'E

The Plantation House by Gaylords
3-2087 Kaumuali'i Hwy.
(808) 245-9593
kilohanakauai.com
Continental entrees come with veggies and fruit grown on the property. Revered island-wide. Expensive to investment-caliber.

Hamura Saimin
2956 Kress St.
(808) 245-3271
Ladles out Kaua'i's best bowl of saimin. Open from 10 a.m. until late in the evening. Inexpensive.

WAIMEA

Porky's Kaua'i
9630 Kaumuali'i Hwy.
(808) 631-3071
porkyskauai.com
Hot dogs, sausages, and grilled cheese sandwiches, loaded with toppings.

O'ahu

With 81 percent of the state's population on this island, it's not surprising that O'ahu is commonly (if erroneously) translated as "the gathering place." The fact that the state capital resides here is almost redundant. However, officially, O'ahu itself does not exist anymore. The entire island belongs to the city and county of Honolulu, which also includes the uninhabited Leeward Islands that stretch a thousand miles northwest of Kaua'i, making it the largest "city" in the world. This semantic confusion only serves to underline the extent to which Honolulu dominates the islands.

Honolulu Harbor assured O'ahu commercial preeminence, and Pearl Harbor to the west made it a vital strategic asset as well. On the other side of Honolulu Harbor, Waikīkī Beach gave O'ahu a jump start into tourism far ahead of the other islands. It still bears the brunt of Hawai'i's visitors, and some say O'ahu is past its prime. This is grossly unfair. Honolulu has grown into a vibrant, culturally sophisticated city, and O'ahu, although undeniably more built up than its neighbors, still retains a scenic beauty rivaling the best in Hawai'i. What's more, unlike most of the other islands, O'ahu has only one concentrated resort center along a single beach. Much of its shoreline remains public beach

O'AHU

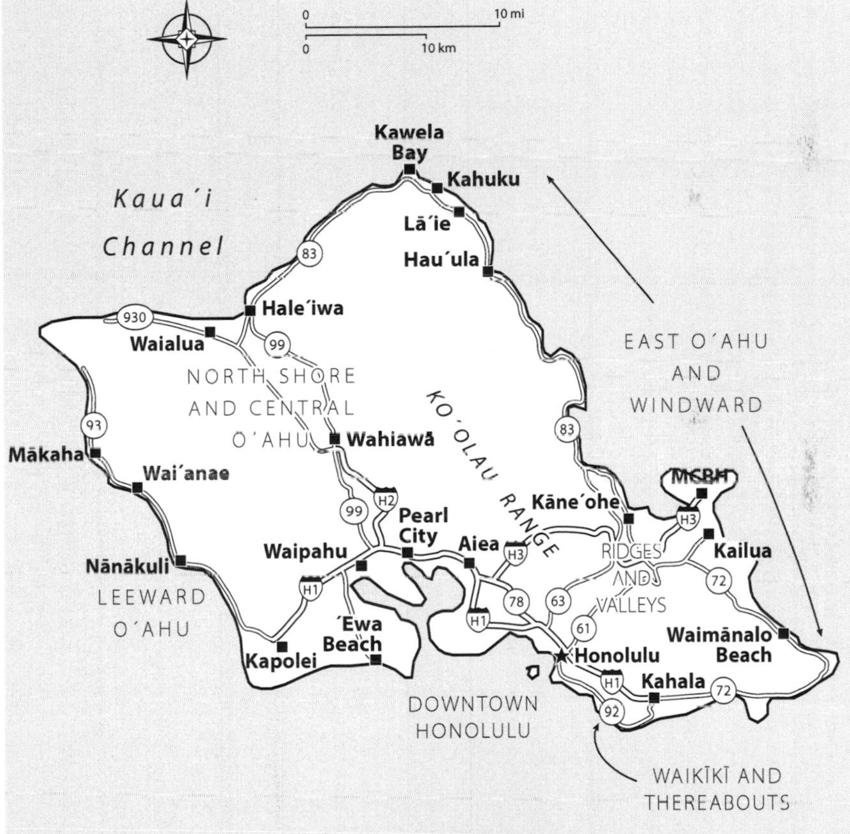

N
0
10 mi
0
10 km
Kawela Bay
Kahuku
Kaua'i Channel
Lā'ie
Hau'ula
83
Hale'iwa
930
Waialua
99
NORTH SHORE AND CENTRAL O'AHU
KO'OLAU RANGE
EAST O'AHU AND WINDWARD
93
Mākaha
Wahiawā
Wai'anae
83
MCBH
Kāne'ohe
H2
H3
99
Pearl City
Aiea
Waipahu
H3
Kailua
Nānākuli
RIDGES AND VALLEYS
LEEWARD O'AHU
H1
72
78
63
'Ewa Beach
H1
61
Waimānalo Beach
Kapolei
Honolulu
H1
Kahala
72
DOWNTOWN HONOLULU
92
WAIKĪKĪ AND THEREABOUTS
PACIFIC OCEAN

park. O'ahu boasts more miles of swimming beaches than any other island, and its surfing beaches on the North Shore are unmatched anywhere.

Measuring 44 by 30 miles in a sort of squashed parallelogram, O'ahu rests on the overlapping slopes of two extinct volcanoes. Their heavily eroded remains extend as parallel mountain ranges running northwest to southeast. Urban Honolulu spreads along the southern shore, walled in by the Ko'olau Mountains, the younger and larger volcanic range. For travel information on the island of O'ahu, contact the O'ahu Visitors Bureau (visit-oahu.com).

Downtown Honolulu

The heart of historic Honolulu resides in its downtown area by the harbor. Downtown divides naturally into three sections, reflecting distinct stages in its development. The business district remains at the center, flanked by the enclaves of government and Chinatown. The scarcity of parking makes driving a burden, however. Consider taking ***TheBus*** (808-848-5555; thebus.org) or the slightly more expensive ***Waikīkī Trolley*** (808-591-2561; waikikitrolley.com), which operates narrated tourist circuits throughout the city using old-style streetcars. Tickets may be purchased through any concierge desk.

Begin your tour where the town itself began—at the harbor waterfront. Water from Nu'uanu Stream prevented coral growth offshore, making this the only natural harbor on the islands. In 1792 William Brown, a British merchant captain, discovered this large protected harbor, which he named Fair Haven.

Brief History of O'ahu

In 1795 O'ahu bore witness to Kamehameha's final victory, a brutal conquest that made him supreme in the islands. A century later O'ahu also witnessed the overthrow of the monarchy that Kamehameha had established. But of all the landmark events of Hawaiian history, the Japanese attack on O'ahu's Pearl Harbor stands out. December 7, 1941, "a date which will live in infamy," changed the course of World War II and the postwar order that followed.

In other respects, too, O'ahu occupies center stage in Hawai'i. For years the islands remained synonymous with Waikīkī in the eyes of the world, and even today Waikīkī receives the lion's share of visitors. The military presence at Pearl Harbor and other bases around O'ahu continues to provide an important source of revenue to the state's economy. Likewise, as the state capital and the only major urban population center, Honolulu dominates educational, cultural, and professional life in Hawai'i. As the Pacific Rim continues to gain in economic and geopolitical significance, policy makers hope to capitalize on Honolulu's strategic mid-Pacific location.

Other merchants followed, first China clippers, then whalers. Local inhabitants gathered to barter provisions and sandalwood, and Westerners began to settle as well. A new village arose on the hot, dusty plains inland of the harbor, taking for its name the Hawaiian translation of "protected bay"—Honolulu.

The growing community of *mahilini* (newcomers) included all kinds of miscreants who jumped ship and caused trouble. Other menaces came from outside. French warships shelled Honolulu more than once, demanding tolerance of Catholics and lower tariffs on French champagne. A hotheaded British captain briefly took over the entire kingdom in 1843. Still, the harbor commerce brought great wealth to the island kingdom and made for a colorful chapter in Hawai'i's maritime history.

Up until 2009, the ***Hawai'i Maritime Center*** (808-847-3511, The Bishop Museum) at Honolulu Harbor's Pier 7 explored this ocean heritage, beginning with the ancient Polynesian mariners who settled these distant islands and continuing through to the jet age that made tourism king. The center's Kalākaua Boathouse was designed to change the minds of those who think that museum is a four-letter word spelled b-o-r-e. Multimedia exhibits and snazzy decor helped bring the subject matter to life. Life-size dioramas of Hawai'i's maritime past took you from the cabins of luxury liners to the waterfront tattoo parlors of World War II. You could also learn how sharks played an important role in Hawaiian culture, admire a rare 46-foot skeleton of a female humpback whale, take a video tour of the remote Leeward isles, and play with hands-on ocean ecology exhibits. Sadly, the museum closed its doors and couldn't survive.

Neither, it seems, could the *Falls of Clyde,* reputedly the last four-masted sailing clipper afloat that had been docked outside the boathouse for many years. Built in Glasgow in 1878, *Falls of Clyde's* worldwide travels included cargo duties in the Hawaiian Islands, but it ended up being used as a floating oil depot in Alaska and was slated for grounding in Seattle as a breakwater. Local citizens raised money to save it, and the vessel was restored but began sinking in early 2019, and its current fate as a seaworthy nautical vessel remains, strangely, up in the air.

islandfacts

Nickname: The Gathering Place

Dimensions: 44 x 30 miles

Highest elevation: Mount Ka'ala (4,025 feet)

Population: 1,016,508 (2020)

Principal city and state capital: Honolulu

Flower: 'Ilima

Color: Yellow

At the ***Marine Education Training Center*** on Sand Island, the *Hōkūle'a* ("star of gladness") has an even more remarkable story. This replica of the ancient double-hulled Polynesian voyaging canoes was the first to grace Hawaiian waters in more than 700 years. When Western sailors began to arrive in the Pacific, the secrets of ocean seafaring had largely been forgotten in the widely scattered islands of the "Polynesian Triangle." Western egos refused to accept that the Polynesians could have carried out such long-distance exploration centuries before the Vikings. In 1976, the *Hōkūle'a* silenced skeptics by retracing the ancient sea route from Hawai'i to Tahiti relying solely on traditional methods of navigation. Members of the Polynesian Voyaging Society, who sail the *Hōkūle'a* and its successors, can tell you how they did it on their regularly scheduled tours of the canoe.

If all this talk of ocean vessels is making you itch to get out on the water, there are always 1.5-hour sunset cocktail cruises available, which start around $79 and are run by ***Atlantis Submarines*** (800-381-0237; atlantisadventures.com). Nearby is ***Aloha Tower*** (808-544-1453), built in 1926 as Honolulu's tallest building and remodeled in 1992 as part of a harbor-front marketplace. The observation deck is open daily from 9 a.m. to 5 p.m. In former times the tower's four-sided clock face and single-word message greeted passengers arriving on Matson's weekly steamships from the mainland, Hawai'i's only link to the outside world before the jet age.

A mural in the arrival hall recalls the pageantry of a 1930s "boat day." As island residents gathered, leis in hand, a flotilla of local craft would escort the steamer into dock while the Royal Hawaiian Band played, hula dancers swayed, and boys dived for tossed coins. The return of passenger cruise ships to Honolulu Harbor has prompted a revival of this tradition. Cruise ships dock at least twice a week (more during winter). The boats usually come in to port at 7 a.m. and leave port at 7 p.m. Contact the Aloha Tower Marketplace concierge (808-544-1453) for a daily schedule of boat dockings, events, and entertainment. Tours of the tower can also be arranged by advance request; free.

Olympic gold medalist Duke Kahanamoku set his first world record swimming in the water off Pier 8 in 1911. Mainland swimming officials refused to believe the unofficially clocked time. Their suspicions were briefly vindicated when Duke finished dead last in his first mainland race. He'd never swum in water that cold and hadn't warmed up. In his next race, he broke his own world record and went on to compete in four Olympics, striking Olympic gold in 1912 and 1920.

A century earlier, Honolulu Fort occupied this spot, the focus of several tumultuous events. Today, the only reminder is a solitary cannon on Fort Street. Cross Nimitz Highway to reach ***Walker Park,*** where the cannon mingles with other historical relics from the area's past. Continue across Queen Street to the ***C. Brewer Building.*** Now home to the University of Phoenix, this 1930 beauty huddles at the foot of Fort Street Mall, enclosing its charms in a walled garden. Note the sugarcane motif in the lobby grillwork, recalling the agricultural heritage of C. Brewer, which remains the oldest US company west of the Rockies.

Continue to the end of the block and turn right onto Merchant Street, where most of Honolulu's early trading houses set up shop. Just around the corner, look for the ornate facing of the 1905 ***Stangenwald Building,*** Honolulu's first skyscraper. This New York–style brownstone edifice housed a notorious furniture store whose owner had connections with city hall. Word seeped out that madams in the area had to buy their brothel beds here to stay open.

At the next corner, stop to take in the architectural splendor of the ***Alexander & Baldwin Building.*** Originally based on Maui, A&B hired two of Honolulu's leading architects to build this lavish 1929 headquarters as a memorial to its founders. The tile work of the Bishop Street portico depicts Hawaiian fish in a Chinese motif. These and other historic buildings blend seamlessly among the many mirrored-glass high-rises nearby. Thanks to downtown's strict zoning laws regulating urban density and greenery, these modern office blocks retain a tropical charm with miniparks, sculpture gardens, and artificial waterfalls. One such park at the corner of King Street and Fort has a noteworthy statue of Robert Wilcox, Hawai'i's first congressional delegate. You can also check out the ***Honolulu Museum of Art***'s (808-532-8700; 999 Bishop St.; honolulumuseum.org) satellite gallery in the First Hawaiian Center (also the tallest building in the

hawai'itrivia

O'ahu is home to world-famous surfing beaches, the state capital, and a historic naval base.

'Iolani Palace, located in downtown Honolulu, is the only royal palace in the United States.

More than 14,000 coral blocks were taken from offshore reefs to build Kawaiaha'o Church in 1836.

Jurisdictionally speaking, Honolulu is the largest "city" in the world.

Geography of O'ahu

The third-largest island, O'ahu has a 112-mile coastline with the most swimming beaches of any Hawaiian island, as well as some of the world's most famous surfing breaks. Formed from two overlapping volcanoes, the island's population center, Honolulu, hugs the southern shore. The peaks of the younger and larger Ko'olau range rise more than 3,000 feet, with nearly vertical cliffs along their windward edges. The older Wai'anae Mountains harbor the island's summit, Mount Ka'ala, at 4,025 feet.

state; it's the one that looks like a giant playing deck with a tilted middle card). The gallery within is open Mon through Thurs 8:30 a.m. to 4 p.m., and Fri to 6 p.m. Free. Notice that many men working downtown wear reverse-print aloha shirts instead of suits, especially on "Aloha Friday." Welcome to Wall Street in the Pacific.

The Hawaiian government allowed haole businesses to stay in Hawai'i, although they kept an eye on foreign troublemakers. The early Hawaiian monarchs resented the time they were obliged to spend here, preferring the old capitals of Lahaina (Maui) and Kailua (Kona) or even the beach at Waikīkī; but finally, by 1850, Kamehameha III yielded to the inevitable and made Honolulu the capital. Government took up its positions to the east of business. Merchant Street appropriately slants into King Street, where most of Honolulu's monarchy-era buildings cluster.

On the ocean side of King, Hawai'i's founding monarch, ***King Kamehameha,*** presides in statue form. The heroic image of the king poses with outstretched arm, clad in the traditional yellow feather cloak and helmet of a Hawaiian chieftain. The money for the statue was originally appropriated to commemorate the 100th anniversary of Captain Cook's landing, but most Hawaiians found little to celebrate in that milestone. The committee in charge deemed Kamehameha a better choice to rekindle the people's pride in their own history, leaving Cook's discovery of the islands relegated to a plaque on the pedestal. The statue here is actually a duplicate. The first casting made in Italy was lost at sea, and this one was paid for with the insurance money. (The original was later recovered and is currently displayed on the Big Island, Kamehameha's birthplace.) During Aloha Week and Kamehameha Day, the statue is draped with 18-foot-long leis.

Behind the statue stands ***Ali'iolani Hale*** (House of Heavenly Kings), commissioned in 1869 as a palace for Kamehameha V. The designs were modified for government use. Its attractive Renaissance Revival chambers housed the cabinet and legislature under Kalākaua. Unfortunately, around this time, relations between business interests and the government began to sour, culminating in the 1893 overthrow of the monarchy. Some argue that the paramount interest of sugar plantation owners in protecting their access to US markets made the revolution and subsequent annexation to the Union inevitable. Ali'iolani is where the fateful events began. Haole businessmen occupied the building as the opening move in their bloodless takeover. The US ambassador ordered American troops to land from a warship, ostensibly to protect American lives; many saw the act as a sign of US backing for the coup. (In 1993 President Clinton issued a formal apology for the US involvement.) Once in power, the new regime shifted the executive and legislative organs of government across the street to 'Iolani

Palace and renamed Ali'iolani the Judiciary Building. It remains home today to the Hawai'i Supreme Court. Step inside to admire the skylit octagonal rotunda. If you arrive Mon through Fri between 8 a.m. and 4 p.m., you can visit the ***Judiciary History Center*** (808-539-4999; jhchawaii.net) here. Displays trace the evolution of Hawaiian justice from the days of the kahuna and kapu through the bumpy transition to Western law under the monarchy. Free guided tours are available by reservation.

Facing Ali'iolani Hale across the street stands ***'Iolani Palace*** (808-522-0822; iolanipalace.org), the only seat of royalty in the United States. A palace has stood here ever since Kamehameha III moved his court to Honolulu. Built in so-called American Florentine style, the present two-story palace was occupied by only two monarchs, King Kalākaua and his sister, Queen Lili'uokalani, before the 1893 revolution. Then 'Iolani served as the "executive building" under the republican, territorial, and state governments that followed, not to mention its stint as the nerve center for television's *Hawai'i Five-0*. With the completion of the new state capitol next door in 1968, the Friends of 'Iolani Palace began a $7 million restoration of the palace. They now offer guided or self-guided tours (for $32.95 and $26.95, respectively) that run about 60 to 90 minutes, which includes a self-guided visit to the basement gallery housing the crown jewels and other royal regalia, plus a short video. If you would prefer to visit only the basement, tickets can be purchased separately. Book at the Royal Barracks office (808-522-0822 or online) between 9 a.m. and 4 p.m.

The admission ticket is made up as an invitation to King Kalākaua's ball. You make the magical leap in time after donning protective shoe covers. A guide welcomes you in the name of His Majesty and ushers you through the staterooms of the palace, chatting about royal banquets and distinguished visitors—all in the present tense. Much of the palace's original contents "wandered" during the coup. The Kingdom's crown jewels were literally gambled away by a looter ignorant of their true value. The Friends are gradually recovering the original furnishings or commissioning exact replicas. One piece was even found in a local thrift shop! A regal staircase handcrafted entirely from koa wood leads upstairs to the living quarters. The indulgent guides reserve a single original pillar for visitors to stroke. Upstairs, you visit his-and-hers bedrooms in opposite corners of the palace. Kalākaua grew to resent the separate rooms and moved to a private bungalow outside the palace.

The king's office is dominated by a huge desk cluttered with papers of state written in Hawaiian. Kalākaua was quite the Renaissance man: He became the first monarch to sail around the world; he teamed up with bandmaster Henry Berger to compose the islands' anthem, "Hawai'i Pono'ī"; he mounted a campaign to revive the hula and other aspects of the old culture that the missionaries had suppressed; and he personally recorded many of the legends of his people. The king also took an active interest in the progress of science, and he corresponded with Thomas Edison regularly. Not bad.

ʻIolani Palace was one of the most technologically advanced buildings of its age. All the bathrooms had flush toilets. A dumbwaiter outside the dining room connected to the basement kitchen. Electric lights illuminated ʻIolani four years before the White House wired up. Kalākaua even installed Honolulu's first telephone so that he could call to the royal boathouse. The "Merrie Monarch" had his vices, however, and spending money was one of them. His profligacy helped provoke the overthrow of the monarchy.

hawaiʻitrivia

Electric lights illuminated ʻIolani Palace four years before the White House wired up.

The tour culminates in the grand throne room, which spreads across half the ground floor. Decorated in crimson and gold, it has crystal chandeliers hanging from the ceiling and a floral carpet print designed by Kalākaua himself. Bishop Museum returned the original thrones and crowns, which are displayed within, along with a royal kapu stick crafted from the tusk of a narwhal. At night, an entire wall of French windows opened onto the garden, admitting perfumed breezes to festive balls that ran into the wee hours of the morning. In less happy times, the wall portraits of past monarchs in this room looked on as Queen Liliʻuokalani stood trial for treason after an attempt by her supporters failed to win back her throne. The deposed queen spent nine months confined to the guest room upstairs.

While waiting for your tour to begin, explore the grounds outside. You'll find many distinctive trees, such as the banyan "forest" that grew out of two trees planted by Queen Kapiʻolani. Moving counterclockwise from the banyans, the next building is the Royal Barracks, a medieval-looking bastion that was moved brick by brick to make way for the new state capitol. Nearby stands the Royal Bandstand, site of King Kalākaua's coronation, staged nine years into his rule. (His original investiture had been unchivalrously rushed due to rioting by the losing side in the election.) Hawaiʻi's governors today conduct their own inaugural rites at this same pavilion. The Royal Hawaiian Band gives free concerts here most Fridays at noon, weather permitting, except for the month of August. Farther around the palace is the former Royal Crypt, where Gerrit Judd carried on a literal "underground government" at night during the British occupation of Honolulu.

From the crypt, you will see a small rock platform in the far corner of the palace grounds. This *ahu,* or offering stand, was built from stones hand-carried from each Hawaiian island in 1993 during ceremonies marking the centennial of the overthrow of the Hawaiian monarchy. The structure remains a focus for activists demonstrating for a return of sovereignty to the Hawaiian people. Continuing your circle from the crypt, find your way to the plaque on an upright boulder commemorating Captain Cook.

hawai'itrivia

Built in 1843, Our Lady of Peace in Honolulu is the oldest Catholic cathedral in the United States.

Turning from the secular to the religious, walk east down King Street from Ali'iolani Hale to ***Kawaiaha'o Church*** (808-469-3000; kawaiahaochurch.com), built on the site of a former spring. (The name means "the waters of Hao.") Known as Hawai'i's Westminister Abbey, this was Honolulu's largest building until 'Iolani Palace was built. Hiram Bingham, the leader of the early missionaries, drew the plans from memories of his native New England. Almost 14,000 half-ton coral blocks were cut from underwater reefs to build it. Trees from northern O'ahu were floated to Kāne'ohe and carried over the mountains. Bingham did not remain to witness the church's dedication in 1842; his wife's ill health forced a return to Massachusetts.

From the very beginning, Kawaiaha'o became an institution of the Hawaiian monarchy. The church provided the setting for royal marriages, funerals, successions, and other courtly ceremonies. Feather *kāhili* (flags) above the velvet pews at the rear of the church signify royalty; the pews are reserved for royal descendants today. Portraits of the entire royal family adorn the walls, with plaques commemorating various historical events. The public is welcome to attend Sunday services, conducted in Hawaiian and English, beginning at 8:30 a.m. Signposts designate other interesting features around the churchyard. The Gothic-looking crypt near the church entrance figures in a real-life Hawaiian ghost story. Its occupant, King Lunalilo, Hawai'i's first elected monarch, had died within a year in office. Instead of burial in the Royal Mausoleum, the king's final wish was to be "entombed among my people" in Kawaiaha'o Cemetery. His successor, King Kalākaua, had lost to Lunalilo in the original election and remained bitter. He refused to order a royal salute from the Punchbowl cannons, saying that if Lunalilo wanted to be buried with the people, he could be buried like a commoner. Instead, eyewitness accounts of the ceremony reported that just as the body was being interred, exactly 21 bursts of thunder sounded a supernatural salute to the fallen king.

Surrounded by a wrought-iron fence, the smaller cemetery behind the church belongs to the ***Mission Houses Museum*** (808-447-3910; missionhouses.org) across the road. The names on the tombstones reflect descendants of the various mission companies. Cross Mission Lane to visit the museum's restored mission buildings and learn about the missionaries' lifestyles.

The first Congregationalist missionaries arrived here in 1820, establishing their headquarters on the outskirts of Honolulu before dispersing to mission stations throughout the islands. In 1821 precut lumber arrived from Boston to erect the Frame House, the oldest Western-style structure surviving in Hawaiʻi. As many as four mission families lived in this house at one time. Cramped bedrooms with trundle beds reflect the lack of space.

The deep cellar caused suspicion among Hawaiians when it was dug. They thought the missionaries might be hiding weapons. The cellar now houses a diorama of 1820 Honolulu. Note that the ocean came within 300 feet of the Mission Houses before landfills pushed back the shoreline. In 1831 Levi Chamberlain, the mission's secular agent, built a larger building from coral blocks and scrap lumber. Most of the space was taken up by stockpiled supplies waiting to be transferred to the 17 other mission stations around the islands.

In these crowded conditions, babies were born and Hawaiian orphans taken in. The women were kept busy running the home, teaching school in the parlor, sewing dresses to clothe the congregation, and cooking for the endless succession of Hawaiian visitors that had to be entertained. They had to learn how to prepare native foods in a tropical climate without refrigeration, cooking mostly in a large wall oven. Murky water from the local wells had to be drip-strained through porous coral stone. Through all of this, Hawaiians crowded at the windows, fascinated by the chance to watch Western women at work. (In ancient Hawaiʻi, the men did the cooking.)

Heading to Market

For a taste of local color and the chance to pick up some unique souvenirs, visit the ***Aloha Stadium Swap Meet*** (808-486-6704; alohastadiumswapmeet.net). The event is held each Wed, Sat, and Sun in the parking lot of the Aloha Stadium (except when the stadium is otherwise in use), close to Pearl Harbor. Admission is $2, and the place is packed with booths selling everything from garage-sale items to diverse foods to custom-designed clothing. The market runs 8 a.m. to 3 p.m. on Wed and Sat and 6:30 a.m. to 3 p.m. Sun. Come early to catch the best finds and beat the heat.

Also popular with visitors is the ***People's Open Market,*** a farmers' market held Mon through Sat at different sites rotating around the island. Call (808) 768-9266 for market times and locations. Other open-air markets in Honolulu include Oʻahu Market in Chinatown, for tasty victuals, and the weekend art mart outside the zoo in Waikīkī.

Meanwhile, the missionary men busied themselves translating the Bible into Hawaiian, writing sermons, and conducting church business. The printing house next door churned out some 30 million pages of Hawaiian-language Bibles and other educational materials by hand. The pages were hung like laundry to dry and then bound. In 1853 almost 75 percent of the Hawaiian population was literate, an achievement exceeded at that time only by New England and Scotland—this from a people who didn't even have a written alphabet half a century earlier. The missionaries became victims of their own success when in 1863 their governing body in New England withdrew its support, forcing the missionaries to seek employment to feed their families. Many left Hawai'i, some to continue mission work in the South Pacific. Those who stayed founded the commercial dynasties that came to wield considerable power in the islands.

The Mission Houses are open Tues through Sat 10:30 a.m. to 2:30 p.m. Tours are offered daily every hour from 11 a.m. to 3 p.m. for $20. Although separate from the museum, the old mission Adobe Schoolhouse can be seen nearby on Mission Lane. Constructed between 1833 and 1835 using air-dried adobe bricks and lumber, this building replaced an earlier school and meeting house (which were made of straw). It was also rented to the local government during the 1870s for use as a public school.

Return to Kawaiaha'o Church and cross King Street to ***Honolulu Hale,*** at the corner of Punchbowl, aka city hall. Its Spanish Mission architecture became a signature of C. W. Dickey's much-copied Hawaiian Mediterranean style. Take a stroll through the lofty central atrium that often houses art displays. For functional city bureaucracy, such as county camping permits (808-768-2267; 650 S. King St.; camping.honolulu.gov), head a block farther to the Municipal Building. Except for Kualoa, O'ahu county campgrounds carry a security risk. For state camping permits (808-587-0300; 1151 Punchbowl St.; camping.ehawaii .gov), go inland to the corner of Beretania Street.

Moving away from downtown on Beretania brings you to Honolulu Police Department headquarters, which harbors its own ***Law Enforcement Museum*** (808-529-3111; 801 S. Beretania St.; honolulupd.org) within. You can learn how Honolulu's finest, including Hawai'i's original supercop, ***Chang Apana***, kept the peace from Kamehameha's day onward. Armed with his trademark whip in lieu of a firearm, Chang went undercover through back-alley Chinatown, where he once arrested 70 suspects single-handedly in a gambling bust. Over the course of his career, Apana was stabbed six times, thrown out a second-story window, attacked with sickles, run over by a horse-and-carriage—and every time, he still managed to book his suspects. Vacationing author Earl Biggers heard of Chang's exploits and fictionalized them in his Charlie Chan novels (the first of which, *The House Without a Key* in 1925, has since been immortalized as an upscale restaurant at Halekulani Hotel in Waikīkī, where Biggers wrote the story). Open Mon through Fri 9 a.m. to 3 p.m. Free guided tours of the museum and police station are available; book online. On your way out, you might visit the two nearby ***Robyn Buntin galleries*** (808-523-5913; robynbuntin.com), which have an impressive collection of contemporary and traditional Asian and Pacific Island art and antiques. Open Mon through Sat from 10 a.m. to 3 p.m.

Continue on Beretania Street to ***Thomas Square,*** a wooded park commemorating British Admiral Thomas's restoration of Hawaiian sovereignty after his countryman Captain Paulet seized power in 1843. Across Beretania Street on the inland side of the park, the ***Honolulu Museum of Art*** (808-532-8700; honolulumuseum.org) occupies a rambling Mediterranean villa located on land donated in 1927 by its founder, Mrs. Charles M. Cooke. The 32 galleries surround six garden courts and include a creditable collection of works by European masters. But the real draw is the museum's top-notch collection of Asian art, from samurai armor to T'ang horses plus a collection of Hiroshige *ukiyo-e* prints amassed by James Michener, a famed former novelist. Guided tours are offered Thurs through Sat at 10 a.m. to noon. Admission is $20. The museum has also acquired a sizable trove of Islamic art from the estate of tobacco heiress Doris Duke, much of it on view in the museum. To see the rest, take a tour of Shangri-La (see Waikīkī and Thereabouts), which you can reserve through the museum (808-532-3853; shangrilahawaii.org). Shangri La tours are available Thurs to Sat, at 9 and 11 a.m., and 1 and 3 p.m. Lunch and brunch are available Thurs through Sat from 11 a.m. to 2 p.m. in the ***HoMa Café + Coffee Bar*** for a moderate price. The museum is open Thurs through Sun 10 a.m. to 4:30 p.m. Admission is $20.

On the other side of King Street stands the concert hall of the Blaisdell Center and, farther down to the left, the grand entrance of McKinley High School. Note the Asian architecture of the ***First Chinese Church of Christ*** across the street and the ***Makiki Christian Church*** around the corner on Pensacola Avenue. The latter has five stories of dreamlike pagoda roofs modeled on Tamon Castle, the first Christian church in Japan.

Returning toward downtown on Beretania Street across Punchbowl brings you to the modern ***State Capitol Building,*** which stands behind and dwarfs its adjacent predecessor, 'Iolani Palace. The capitol's innovative design draws on elements symbolic of Hawai'i: Its two legislative chambers taper vertically like the volcanoes on which the islands rest; its pillars represent palm trees, and the reflecting pools surrounding the capitol symbolize the ocean. You can pick up a brochure covering the capitol district from the governor's office on the fifth floor.

Be sure to peek into the legislative chambers. The house has warm earth tones and a chandelier called Sun. The senate has blue shades of sky and sea and a chandelier called Moon. Both chambers feature enormous hanging tapestries by Ruthadell Anderson. Other artwork on the grounds includes *Aquarius,* a mosaic by Tadashi Sato; a statue of Queen Lili'uokalani, invariably clutching a fresh flower; and a controversial statue of Father Damien by Marisol Escobar. Damien was a Catholic priest who contracted leprosy while ministering to victims of the disease on the island of Moloka'i. Escobar portrays Damien as a frail old man, deformed but radiating inner peace.

More art awaits across Richards Street in the ***Hawai'i State Art Museum***, now called ***Capitol Modern*** (808-586-0305; capitolmodern.org), on the second floor of the Number One Capitol District Building. By law, 1 percent of all state construction money goes to fund the state's "art in public places" program (Hawai'i was the first state in the Union to offer such a program). This museum showcases local and contemporary art from across the islands, with different rooms highlighting aspects of the state's diverse heritage. Events include First Fridays. Call (808) 586-0305. Open Mon through Sat 10 a.m. to 4 p.m. Free.

Farther down Richards, opposite 'Iolani Palace, stands the 1927 ***YWCA Building,*** designed in Mediterranean style by Berkeley Arts and Crafts architect Julia Morgan. Popular with the ladies who lunch, ***Cafe Julia*** (808-533-3334), inside the courtyard, features fresh local produce on its seafood, salad, and sandwich menu. Open Mon to Fri, 11 a.m. to 2 p.m. Moderate.

On the other side of the Capitol Building, across Beretania Street, next to the war memorial, stands ***Washington Place*** (808-586-0248), which is now the governor's home. John Dominis died at sea soon after building this home for his family. The building's name arose when his widow rented rooms to the US commissioner. Her son inherited the house and lived there with his wife, Lydia Kapa'akea, until she ascended to the throne as Queen Lili'uokalani. Later the deposed and widowed queen moved back across the street from 'Iolani Palace and lived there until she died in 1917. All state governors reside with their families at Washington Place, and Hawai'i's "White House" has been converted to a state museum; public tours are available Thurs at 10 a.m. by reservation.

Walk next door from Washington Place to Episcopalian ***St. Andrew's Cathedral,*** founded by Kamehameha IV and Queen Emma, both ardent Anglophiles. Continue along Beretania Street to reach the last of Honolulu's Big Three churches. Completed in 1843, ***Our Lady of Peace*** is the oldest Catholic cathedral in the United States. It doesn't look like much from the outside, but the interior has beautiful gilded ceiling panels, statuary, and stained glass. Our

Lady stands in front of the top end of Fort Street Mall; diverse eateries of all stripes and cultures line this pedestrian arcade and surrounding alleyways along Bishop Street.

Glance down adjacent Chaplain Lane and see what movie is currently being projected up on the big wall opposite ***Proof Social Club*** (808-537-3080; proofsocialclub.com), a dive punk bar that offers tasty slices of gourmet pizza (with ingredients like Portuguese sausage, ponzu chicken, and smoked duck breast that rotate daily), as well as plenty of hard liquor and a good selection of beers. (Just don't spill on the pool table.) Open every day 4 p.m. to 2 a.m. Brunch served on third Sat from 11 a.m. to 4 p.m. Inexpensive.

The next alley over, where Pauahi Street asphalt blends with the tiled brick of Fort Street Mall, sits ***Döner Shack*** (808-744-4784), selling freshly sliced schwarma and loaded sandwiches. Bring a photo of yourself eating döner to place on the wall to score a free entree—make it a "Downtown Döner," with beef, lamb, sliced cucumbers, tomatoes, onions, yogurt sauce, and hummus. Open Mon to Fri 10 a.m. to 5 p.m. and Sat 10 a.m. to 3 p.m. Inexpensive. For fresh poke, sushi, and ice cream-size scoops of spicy ahi tuna, head around the corner to ***Ahi And Vegetable*** (808-599-3500; ahiandveg.com). Farther down, ***Rada's Piroscki*** (808-526-3950) sells the deep fried Russian pastries in three styles (beef and cheese with mushroom or cabbage, or chicken and cheese and mushroom) from a window counter for a couple of bucks per piroscki. Open Mon to Fri 6:30 a.m. to 5 p.m. and Sat 7 a.m. to 3:30 p.m.

At the end of Fort Street Mall, ***Marugame Udon*** (808-545-3000) offers white 'n' ropey Japanese udon noodles in a variety of broths for cheap, plus assorted musubi and tempura-fried chicken and veggies. There's another Marugame in Waikīkī, but over there you'll be stuck in a line out the door. This downtown branch, with plenty of seats to people watch, is the one to visit. Open Mon to Sat 10 a.m. to 7 p.m. Inexpensive.

One block past Fort Street you'll find Bethel Street, home to two historic theater venues. The ***Hawai'i Theatre*** (808-528-0506; hawaiitheatre.com), on the corner of Pauahi, has been renovated to its original 1922 splendor, lavish with murals and gilding. Tours are offered at 11 a.m. every first Tues of the month for $10. Farther down, on the corner of Merchant Street, ***Kumu Kahua Theatre*** (808-536-4441; 46 Merchant St.; kumukahua.org) performs in smaller but equally historic digs in the old Kamehameha V Post Office Building. Built in 1871, this was the first building in the Hawaiian Islands (and the oldest building in the United States) to be constructed solely of reinforced concrete; the success of this style of construction led to the same style being used to build the royal palace, Ali'iolani Hale, the following year. Kumu Kahua

Theatre produces and stages plays about life in Hawai'i, written by Hawai'i playwrights, for the people of Hawai'i. It is the only theater of its kind, creating and showcasing works related to its own geographical region and the related cultures, known to exist in the world.

While here, take a peek inside the ***Walter Murray Gibson Building*** diagonally opposite. One of the most colorful personalities in Hawaiian history, Gibson came to the islands as a Mormon pioneer on Lāna'i. Excommunicated, he entered politics as a Hawaiian populist, rising to power as Kalākaua's "minister for everything" before losing out to the opposing missionary-sugar-growers' faction. This building is the only reminder of his brief but dazzling career. Its patterned tile interior looks more like a hotel lobby than the former police station it was.

For a unique shopping trip, stop in at ***Lai Fong*** (808-537-3497; 1118 Nu'uanu Ave.). It's a kind of Chinese department store full of imported fabrics, Chinese antiques, and crafts. Original owner Fong came to Hawai'i as a picture bride and got her start as a seamstress. You can still order tailor-made clothing here. The office is open Mon to Sat 10 a.m. to 6 p.m.

One block farther, ***Ramsay Museum*** (808-537-2787; 1128 Smith St.) bears another locally prominent name. Ramsay's beautifully rendered pen-and-ink drawings are no longer for sale here except as limited-edition reproductions, although an extensive collection awaits viewing upstairs. It makes something of a statement for historic preservation to realize that many of the subjects of her drawings no longer exist. The museum is housed in the historic 1926 Tan Sing building. Ramsay's success has inspired a new crop of galleries to open downtown. ***The ARTS at Marks Garage*** (808-521-2903; 1159 Nu'uanu Ave.) is a cooperative effort run by local artist organizations, spearheaded in recent years by local nonprofit whiz and "arts whisperer" Donna Blanchard. Open Tues through Sat noon to 5 p.m. The gallery publishes a free walking tour brochure that will guide you to other downtown galleries. Most of these galleries stay open late on the first Fri of each month, as local art mavens gather for evening receptions, refreshments, and live street entertainment from 5 to 8 p.m.

This section of Hotel Street, from Nu'uanu Avenue to Smith Street, becomes a bar and club scene after 9 p.m., with revelers dropped off by Uber or Lyft and filling the streets. Lucky for them, there are plenty of spots to visit.

Honolulu's restaurants are every bit as international as its populace. The variety of restaurants here is probably unequaled in a city of its size. Cross-pollination between these diverse culinary traditions has led to some unusual hybrids. Amid the creative energies unleashed by such culinary fusion, a new school of Hawai'i regional cuisine (HRC) has emerged. Its leading proponents are scattered among the islands, but common threads link the restaurants. Following the trend of New American regional cuisine, the menus revolve around island-grown produce and fresh seafood, served crusted in, say, a coating of macadamia nuts, then seared, blackened, or wok-charred, and sauced with Pacific Rim flavorings enhanced through classic French reductions. Presentations dazzle with vertiginously layered towers erected in the center of an oversize plate and a multicolored wasabi/sesame/miso/ginger-something drizzled around the edges. Decor is deliberately understated, often with an open kitchen as the centerpiece, and the service is casual, albeit attentive.

Many of today's top HRC performers got their start in hotel restaurants on the neighbor islands. But almost all of them have opened restaurants in Honolulu of late, and the competition has gotten fierce. ***Roy's*** (808-396-7697; royyamaguchi.com), in Hawai'i Kai, features such specialties as hibachi-style grilled Atlantic salmon with a Japanese citrus *ponzu,* blackened Island ahi with a spicy soy mustard butter sauce, and roasted macadamia-nut-crusted mahimahi with a lobster cognac butter sauce. Open Sun to Thurs 4:30 to 9 p.m., and Fri and Sat until 9:30 p.m. Expensive to investment-caliber. Owner Roy Yamaguchi has recently expanded to create a new restaurant line specifically designed to pay homage to local culinary heritage: ***Eating House 1849*** (808-924-1849; royyamaguchi.com/eatinghouse1849-waikiki) in Waikīkī, offers similar high-quality seafood and signature dishes. Open daily; 10:30 a.m. to 2 p.m. weekend brunch; 4 to 5 p.m. Happy Hour; dinner until 9 p.m. Expensive to investment-caliber. Another favorite is Peter Merriman's ***Merriman's Honolulu*** (808-215-0022; 1108 Auahi St., #170; merrimanshawaii.com). Peter Merriman has restaurants throughout the Hawaiian Islands that offer delicious farm-to-table fare. The Honolulu location oozes local neighborhood vibes with warm, friendly service and small and large plates that will warm your belly. Open 11 a.m. to 9 p.m. daily. Other standouts include Russel Siu's ***3660 On the Rise*** (808-737-1177; 3660 Wai'alae Ave.) in Kaimukī, which is slightly less expensive than the rest; open Wed through Sun 5:30 to 8 p.m. ***La Mer*** (808-923-2311) offers prix-fixe French cuisine in an open-air fine dining setting at the Halekulani Hotel where you can enjoy ocean views off Waikīkī Beach. Open daily 5:30 to 8:30 p.m. Investment-caliber. The newer kid on the block is ***Senia*** (808-200-5412; restaurantsenia.com), a 50-seat restaurant in Chinatown quickly becoming known for its tasting menu served at the chef's counter, where you can chat with owners (celebrity chefs at this point) Chris Kajioka and Anthony Rush. The offerings rotate regularly but often include caviar, truffles, and beyond. Open 5:30 to 9:30, Tues to Sat. Investment-caliber.

If Hawai'i regional cuisine has traditionally been the future of Hawai'i's upscale dining culture, ***La Mariana Restaurant*** (808-848-2800), located in the sailing club of the same name, retains something of its past. To get there, take Sand Island Access Road from Nimitz Highway north of downtown and look for the sailing masts on the right after the first traffic light. Having survived at least one tidal wave and several lease foreclosures, this rustic beach shack has been around ever since Keehi Lagoon was opened as a "poor man's yacht club." The Polynesian kitsch decor harks back to the classic South Seas restaurants of the 1920s and 1930s—and with good reason: Original owner Annette Nahinu bought much of it from her more illustrious but less long-lived predecessors such as Trader Vic's and Don the Beachcomber. A circus sideshow of multicolored bulbs illuminates your choice of lamps made from shells, bamboo, puffer fish, and Japanese fishing floats. Thronelike rattan chairs encircle wooden tables; carved tikis serve as pillars; and, of course, the ubiquitous fishing nets drape both ceiling and walls. No fewer than two trees grow within the restaurant, while a row of coconut palms frames the harbor views. The local American fare and daily fresh fish on the menu are passable, but you might just come here for drinks. Open Tues to Sat 11 a.m. to 8 p.m.

In the past 12 years, an entirely new neighborhood has emerged off Ala Moana Boulevard, between Ward and Restaurant Row: ***Kaka'ako***, once a congregation of mostly empty warehouses, auto-body shops, garages, and a CompUSA. Beginning around 2011, Kamehameha Schools (the private, charitable educational trust endowed with the former estate of Princess Bernice Pauahi Bishop, the last direct descendant of King Kamehameha I) began a major construction boom. They rebranded the area around Halekauwila, Cooke, and South Streets as "Our Kaka'ako," a planned community development of nearly a dozen mixed-use, mostly high-income apartment high-rises and multistoried structures.

At its core: ***SALT at Our Kaka'ako*** (691 Auahi St.; saltatkakaako.com), a multifarious complex of pseudo-industrial structures stacked together and designated for retail and dining. Most of the buildings resemble converted shipping containers with exposed concrete and I-beams, an homage to this area's manufacturing history as the former home of Honolulu Iron Works, a metal foundry and machine shop. (The titular "salt" refers to ancient times, when this area was mostly low-lying fish and salt ponds.)

There's plenty to see, eat, and especially drink at SALT. Begin at ***Bevy Bar*** (808-594-7445; bevyhawaii.com), an industrial-chic hideout behind lava rock walls, serving thoughtfully handcrafted cocktails created by owner (and award-winning mixologist) Christian Self, with more than 25 restaurant and bar openings under his belt. Open Tues to Wed 5 to 10 p.m., Thurs 5 p.m. to midnight, and Fri and Sat 5 p.m. to 2 a.m. Moderate. For more casual drinks and to catch the game, head upstairs to ***Pitch Sports Bar*** (808-379-2550; pitchsportsbar

.com) for draft beers and local Asian-inspired shareable appetizers, including kalbi (Korean ribs), poustine fries, and truffle teriyaki chicken wings. Enjoy seating inside or outside on the green AstroTurf lawn out front. Open Mon to Thurs 11 a.m. to midnight, Fri and Sat 11 a.m. to 2 a.m. and Sun 8 a.m. to midnight. Inexpensive to moderate. If even this is too much ceremony, grab your own beers yourself from coolers lining the walls at ***Village Bottle Shop & Tasting Room*** (808-369-0688; villagebeerhawaii.com) to take home or enjoy on-site at long benches inside. Open Sun to Wed 11 a.m. to 9 p.m., and Thurs to Sat noon to 11 p.m. Inexpensive to investment-caliber—depending on the brew you grab.

For drinks of a nonalcoholic nature, try ***Insomnia Espresso Coffee*** (808-545-4160), one of the last original holdouts before Kaka'ako's transformation. Selling a variety of coffee drinks plus breakfast and—why not?—Vietnamese fare since 2004. Open Mon to Fri 8 a.m. to 2 p.m., and Sat 9 a.m. to 2 p.m. Inexpensive.

For restaurants, the crowds gather at ***Moku Kitchen*** (808-591-6658; mokukitchen.com). You can't miss this place—it's the biggest restaurant in the complex, with the mascot of a rooster staring out over the parking lot. This is a nod to Hawai'i's upcountry farming and ranching heritage. Serving American/local fusion, cocktails, and live music nightly. Open Mon to Wed 11 a.m. to 10 p.m., and Fri and Sat 11 a.m. to 10 p.m. Moderate to expensive. Moku shares the boulevard-facing parking lot with ***Highway Inn*** (808-954-4955; myhighwayinn.com), a family-run Hawaiian restaurant whose original location in Waipahu has been a beloved local institution since 1947. Come with a big appetite for equally big trays of lau lau, *kalua* pig, lomi salmon, taro, chicken, plus poke, salads, and sandwiches. Open Mon to Sat 10 a.m. to 8 p.m., and Sun from 10 a.m. to 2:30 p.m. Moderate.

SALT's second most famous eatery is possibly ***Hank's Haute Dogs*** (808-532-4265; hankshautedogs.com), where restauranteur Hank Adaniya, former owner of the award-winning Chicago Trio restaurants (and whose parents previously opened a hot dog stand in Kapi'olani Park in the 1940s), returned to Hawai'i to create this "slow fast food" eatery on Cooke Street, serving sausages ranging from traditional Chicago-style hot dogs to lobster, boar, and kobe sausages. Open Mon to Thurs 11 a.m. to 4 p.m., and Fri to Sun 11 a.m. to 6 p.m. Inexpensive. Need more sausage? Head back upstairs to ***The Butcher & Bird*** (808-762-8095; butcherandbirdhi.com), which is both a full-service butcher and deli shop offering locally sourced, handcrafted sausage. For cooking at home—or enjoying right on the balcony seating area outside. Open Tues to Sun 11 a.m. to 6 p.m. Inexpensive to moderate. ***Pioneer Saloon at SALT*** (808-600-5612; 675 Auahi St.) offers the best of local Hawaiian plate lunches in a funky, laid-back setting. Whether it's chicken katsu or garlic ahi plate, nothing tastes more fresh or local. Don't miss the miso butterfish! Moderate.

There's plenty of good shopping here, too—from the old-school vinyl afficiandos at ***Hungry Ear Records*** (808-262-2175; hungryear.com), selling new and used LPs, including rare Hawaiian albums daily, 10 a.m. to 6 p.m., to the film photography experts at ***Treehouse*** (808-597-8733; treehouse-shop .com), loaded with camera equipment, art books, photo kits, as well as drop-off film processing. Open Mon to Sat 10 a.m. to 6 p.m., and Sun from 11 a.m. to 5 p.m.

SALT may be where the action is centered in the neighborhood, but there are great attractions also in the area. One spot worth visiting is ***Holey Grail*** (1001 Queen St. #101; holeygraildonuts.com), which is known for their original taro donut. Open 7 a.m. to 7 p.m. daily, extended hours until 9 p.m. on Fri and Sat.

Enjoy locally brewed craft beer from ***Honolulu Beerworks*** (808-589-2337; honolulubeerworks.com), a microbrewery in a warehouse producing beverages like the Pia Mahi'ai Honey Citrus Saison, made with Big Island honey, and the Cocoweizen, featuring hand-toasted coconut and flavors of pineapple, banana, and clove. Open Mon to Thurs noon to 10 p.m., and Fri to Sat noon to midnight. Inexpensive.

Craft beer fans have much to celebrate—they can head three blocks up to Queen Street and enjoy more local beer at ***Aloha Beer Company*** (808-544-1605; alohabeer.com) sitting on casual benches on the first floor, or in the more sophisticated Hi-Brau Room speakeasy on the second floor. Or to ***Waikīkī Brewing Company*** (808-591-0387; waikikibrewing.com) down the street, to enjoy their signature Aloha Spirit Blonde Ale, featuring slightly bitter and balancing perle and tettnang hops, or Ala Moana Amber, made with five different types of malt. Open Mon to Thurs 2 to 10 p.m., Fri 11 a.m. to 11 p.m., Sat 9:30 a.m. to 11 p.m., and Sun 8 a.m. to 10 p.m. Inexpensive to moderate. Brewery fans will also appreciate ***Hana Koa Brewing Co.*** (808-591-2337; 962 Kawaiaho'o St.; hanakoabrewing.com) in the neighborhood. Open Tues to Thurs noon to 10 p.m., Fri and Sat 11 a.m. to 11 p.m., and Sun 10 a.m. to 9 p.m.

While you're in the Kaka'ako area, you may see a medley of colorful murals painted on the sides of buildings and wooden construction site walls. They're the latest creations by artists brought in from the international street art collective ***POW! WOW! Hawai'i*** (powwowhawaii.com), which hosts a weeklong event every February of live art, educational programming, and a concert series. The event began in Honolulu but has since spread to other cities around the globe.

Another neighborhood with a rich history that's having something of a renaissance is the often-overlooked community of McCully/Mōʻiliʻili, nestled between Mānoa Valley to the north and Waikīkī to the south.

Look no further than the James M. Chrones Building at the intersection of King and McCully for a few hip destinations. There's ***Truest Hawaiʻi*** (808-946-4202), a shoe haven for sneakerheads open Mon to Sat noon to 6 p.m.; and ***Mono Hawaiʻi*** (808-955-1595), selling stationery, backpacks, photography equipment, and travel gear. Open Mon to Sat 11 a.m. to 4 p.m. ***Lightsleepers MC*** (facebook.com/lightsleepers) is a clothing store and lifestyle brand. Check the Facebook page for updates and locations. And at the corner, "stay handsome, not hammajang" at ***Mojo Barbershop & Social Club*** (808-800-3960), offering shaves, lineups, and cuts for men. Open Mon to Sat 9 a.m. to 7 p.m.

If shopping and haircuts make you thirsty, head across the street to ***Pint + Jigger*** (808-744-9593; pintandjigger.com), boasting dozens of craft beers and smokey cocktails, plus a hearty pub and brunch menu with items like Scotch egg and a "Hulk"-size BLT with fried green tomatoes. The Doobie Brothers would've felt right at home in ***Anna O'Brien's*** (808-946-5190) a few blocks away. It's an Irish dive bar with a decent stage for stand-up comedy or small bands upstairs; Anna's is a holdout from 1970s Hawaiʻi, the kind of place that attracts visitors like Bill Murray, Hannibal Buress (who jumped in for an improv sesh with the local comics of Comedy U), and Reel Big Fish (who could've performed any venue when they once came to Hawaiʻi but chose here). Open Mon to Sat 11 a.m. to 2 a.m. and Sun 7 a.m. to 2 a.m. Inexpensive.

Farther down King Street, near Stadium Park, ***Maple Garden*** (808-941-6641; 909 Isenberg St.) specializes in northern Chinese dishes for inexpensive prices and offers the best all-you-can-eat Chinese buffet in Honolulu, complete with deep-fried prawns, spicy kung pao chicken, honey spareribs, tea-smoked duck, cold ginger chicken, and more for less than $20. Open daily 11 a.m. to 2 p.m. and 5:30 to 10:30 p.m. Moderate.

This area has also become home to a variety of Japanese izakayas, serving delicious grilled and fried appetizers alongside a mix of beers, highball cocktails, sake, and soju to crowds nightly. They all range from inexpensive to expensive. Beginning on McCully Street and moving east, there's ***Izakaya Torae Torae*** (808-949-5959) specializing in sushi and sashimi with a cheap late-night happy hour (try the "everything" seafood shooter for just $5). Open daily 6 to 11:30 p.m. With the best name on the list, there's ***Fujiyama Texas*** (808-955-0738; fujiyamatexas-hi.com) around the corner, specializing in deep-fried kushi katsu meats and veggies served on skewers. Open daily for breakfast and dinner. ***Tori Ton*** (808-260-1478) is opposite ***Old Stadium Park***, where the Honolulu Stadium once stood, entertaining audiences with football games, stock car racing, and performances by Irving Berlin and Elvis Presley. This izakaya offers a mix of dishes, including Japanese oden veggies and yakitori skewers, plus assorted beers and flavored highballs. Open every day except Monday. ***Izakaya Naru*** (808-951-0510; asia-kitchen.co.jp/naru_honolulu) serves Okinawan-inspired dishes, like bittermelon-spam-egg-and-tofu stir-fry, housemade peanut tofu, and stewed pork belly. Open Mon to Sat 5:30 p.m. to 2 a.m. and Sun 5:30 p.m. to 1 a.m.

If you're craving American fare with local flavor, check out ***Betty's Burgers*** (808-762-0099; 1025 University Ave.; bettysburgershi.com), which brings Hawaiian flare to the silver spoon, fast-food diner scene. Come here for smash burgers, fries, and uber-thick shakes. Vegetarians also welcome. Open daily from 11 a.m. to 9 p.m.

To get your just desserts, head to ***Frostcity*** (808-947-3328; 105 S Beretania St.; frostcityhi.com). This Taiwanese snow-ice shop serves delicious Hawaiian-style shave ice alongside sweet Taiwan-inspired taro balls. Open Tues through Sun 12:30 to 10 p.m., and until 11 p.m. on Fri and Sat. Or find your way to ***La Gelateria*** (808-591-1133; 819 Cedar St., off King Street between Pi'ikoi Street and Ke'eaumoku Street) to sample Maurice Grasso's inventively indulgent flavor infusions, from rose-petal sorbet to liliko'i champagne. Open weekdays noon to 4 p.m. A great place for brunch and the famed milk 'n' cereal pancakes or the loco moco is ***Scratch Kitchen*** (808-589-1669; 1170 Auahi St., Ste. 175; scratch-hawaii.com). Scratch also serves hearty dinner favorites like bacon mac and cheese and lilikoi bbq short ribs. ***Side Street Inn*** (808-591-0253; 1225 Hopaka St.), near the northwest corner of Ala Moana Shopping Center, one block in from Kapi'olani Boulevard, is where you'll find some of Honolulu's top chefs gathering after hours in this bare-bones diner, lured by gourmet comfort food, including a famous pork chop. Open Tues to Fri 4 to 8:30 p.m., and Sat and Sun noon to 8:30 p.m. Moderate. (There's a bigger location on Kapahulu Ave. if the Hopaka St. location fills up. Same menu, slightly more upscale.)

But for now, we're still exploring downtown Honolulu. Beginning at the corner of Nu'uanu Avenue and N Hotel Street, ***Fête*** (808-369-1390; fetehawaii.com) is equal parts Honolulu and Brooklyn, offering New American cuisine like twice-fried locally grown Ludovico chicken and foie gras gyoza. Open Mon to Thurs 11 a.m. to 9 p.m., and Fri and Sat 11 a.m. to 10 p.m. Moderate to expensive. Next door is ***Brick Fire Tavern*** (808-379-2430; brickfiretavern.com), whose head chefs trained with master Neopolitan pizza maker Enzo Coccia in Naples to create Italy-quality margherita pizza right in Chinatown. Open Mon to Sat 11 a.m. to 2 p.m. and 5 to 10 p.m., and Sun 5 to 10 p.m. Moderate to expensive. Meanwhile, the chefs at ***Yakitori Hachibei*** (808-369-0088) are creating high quality Japanese barbecued yakitori on skewers to dip in various seasonings and sauces. Open Tues to Sat 5 to 10 p.m. Expensive. They're all located in the historic Encore Saloon building, the name of which is now shared by the restaurant ***Encore Saloon*** (808-367-1656; encoresaloon.com), where they sell Mexican food and drinks, plus an amazing $2 Taco Tuesday special. During renovations in 2015, baggies of drugs tucked away from decades ago fell out of the walls. Local historians reported that in 1980, workers discovered hidden passageways believed to have been used to shanghai sailors who would later awaken at sea.

Across the street is the oldest bar in Honolulu, ***Smith's Union Bar*** (808-538-9145; 19 N. Hotel St.), which has been serving beers and liquor to patrons dating back to WWII. (The decor hasn't changed from since then, either.) Open daily 8 a.m. to 2 a.m. Inexpensive. Next door is ***Maria Bonita*** (808-536-6185), where chef Diego Gallardo makes authentic cuisine inspired by his hardworking mother, Maria, who raised Diego along with his five brothers and two sisters. Open Mon to Sat 11 a.m. to 3 p.m. Inexpensive. ***Bar 35*** (808-537-3535; 35 N. Hotel St.; bar35hawaii.com), down the street, is home to a 100-plus selection of brews from around the world and craft pizzas. Open Thurs and Fri 4 p.m. to 2 a.m., and Sat 6 p.m. to 2 a.m. Inexpensive to moderate. Up the narrow staircase next to the entrance to Bar 35 is ***The Tchin Tchin! Bar*** (808-528-1888; thetchintchinbar.com), a hip rooftop bar pouring craft cocktails, whiskies, and wine—plus small plates to share. Enjoy in the industrial inside or the garden deck outside. Open Tues to to Thurs 5 to 10 p.m., and Fri and Sat 5 p.m. to midnight. Moderate. Next door is, well, ***NextDoor*** (808-200-4470; 43 N. Hotel St.; nextdoorhi.com), a nightclub with loft ceiling. Open Wed to Fri 5 p.m. to 2 a.m., and Sat 9 p.m. to 2 a.m. Inexpensive.

For more drinks, head back across the street to ***The Manifest*** (32 N. Hotel St.; manifesthawaii.com), with a mega selection of spirits (and a mean cocktail selection to boot), plus artisanal small plates. Open Mon to Thurs 10 a.m. to midnight, and Fri and Sat 10 to 2 a.m. Inexpensive to moderate. For drinks, food, and live music, there's ***The Other Side Diner*** (808-533-2328; 42 N. Hotel St.; theothersidehi.com), a punk, '50s-esque diner that offers breakfast, burgers, wings, and wraps—which can also all be made vegetarian or vegan. Local musician and original owner Serena Hancock wanted a restaurant that would stay open late enough to feed her after shows, a matter complicated by her being vegan. She couldn't find a place—so she decided to open one herself in 2011. Open Tues to Thurs 4 to 10 p.m., Fri 4 p.m. to 2 a.m., Sat 11 a.m. to 2 a.m., and Sun 11 a.m. to 10 p.m. Inexpensive.

At the corner of Hotel and Smith Streets are two hearty eateries: ***Livestock Tavern*** (808-537-2577; livestocktavern.com), specializing in stick-to-your-ribs Amerian stews, roasts, and big plates on a menu that rotates seasonally. Open every day 5 to 10 p.m., and Sat and Sun for brunch from 10 a.m. to 2 p.m. Moderate to expensive. And ***Lucky Belly*** (808-531-1888; luckybelly.com), offering big bowls of ramen in rich pork broths with a wide selection of sake and Japanese beer. Open Mon to Thurs 5 to 10 p.m., and Fri and Sat 5 to 11 p.m. Moderate to expensive. (Pro tip: Swing by Thurs through Sat after 10 p.m. when the restaurant opens a window facing Smith Street and sells bowls and bentos for around $10.)

For those who like a beer with their art, ***Hank's Cafe*** (808-888-3988; 1038 Nu'uanu Ave.) beckons. Owner Hank Taufaasau hangs his own paintings, as well as those of others, on the walls of this cozy tavern. Most people come here for the live music nightly. Open daily 7 a.m. to 2 a.m. To see a different kind of artistry, pause to smell the flowers at the lei stands on Beretania Street between Smith and Maunakea Streets, with others on Maunakea itself. The stringers work right in the store, and the variety of colors and textures is staggering. Some have strong fragrances such as *pīkake* (jasmine). Others, such as woven *haku lei* (worn on the head), retain their beauty after drying. Choose one to enjoy all day. Prices range from single digits into the hundreds at various shops.

By now you've reached the border of ***Chinatown.*** This part of downtown developed later than the other two. Sugar plantations began to import Chinese laborers in 1852, but as soon as their contracts expired, the Chinese fled the fields to open shops and small businesses in town. Chinatown soon became a hotbed of gambling, opium dens, and brothels. The Chinatown underground literally ran underground. As developers remodel the buildings here, they keep finding tunnels.

This crowded enclave of wooden shops and homes burned to the ground twice. The second blaze in 1900 started when the Board of Health torched homes contaminated with the bubonic plague, and the fire spread. The Chinese suspected a haole conspiracy to drive them out. During World War II the rebuilt district became a GI vice center. Chinatown today thrives as a magnet for immigrants from everywhere throughout Asia. Its mysteries unfold like layers of a fortune cookie.

The ***Hawai'i Heritage Center*** (808-521-2749) offers morning walking tours of Chinatown center on Wed and Fri at 9:30 a.m. Call for prices.

It can be just as much fun to poke around on your own. Walk down Maunakea to the corner of Hotel Street. This is the center of Chinatown, where the lion dancers prance during the Chinese New Year. Hotel Street is also Honolulu's principal red-light strip, flush with peep shows and porn shops on adjacent blocks. With its ornate pagoda roof, ***Wo Fat,*** once home to Hawai'i's oldest restaurant, keeps a benevolent watch over the comings and goings at the corner from its second-story perch. A pan-Asian galaxy of eating possibilities lurk within the food court of ***Maunakea Marketplace*** on the opposite corner. A statue of Confucius presides over the courtyard. Farther up Maunakea Street on the corner of Pauahi, a Chinese hole-in-the-wall, ***Lam's Kitchen*** (808-536-6222; 1152 Maunakea St. A), makes their own white 'n' flat look funn noodles and pairs them with tasty wontons in clear, deceptively complex broth. Just be prepared to wait for a table among the Chinatown regulars; they love this place, too. Open daily 8 a.m. to 4 p.m. Inexpensive.

Duc's Bistro (808-531-6325), an elegant French-Vietnamese restaurant, is a few doors down. Duc's is open Mon to Fri noon to 8 p.m., and Sat and Sun for dinner only 5 to 8 p.m. Live music Wed through Sat evenings. Expensive. If it's *pho* you're looking for, follow the faithful to ***Phở Tô Châu Restaurant*** (808-533-4549), 2 blocks down King Street at the corner of River Street. The lunchtime lines out the door testify to the superiority of the steaming Vietnamese noodle broth ladled out in this bare-bones diner. Open daily 9:30 a.m. to 2:30 p.m.

For those still looking to explore, ***Legend Seafood Restaurant*** (808-532-1868), in the intricate ***Chinatown Cultural Plaza*** farther up River Street, has its following. Open daily for lunch and dinner. (Legend also has a vegetarian twin next door—a gesture of filial piety for the owner's Buddhist mom.) For great dim sum, hit ***Mei Sum*** (808-531-3268; 1170 Nu'uanu Ave.) where you can devour these Hong Kong–style delicacies by the cartload. Open Sat and Sun 8 a.m. to 8 p.m., and Mon through Fri 9 a.m. to 8 p.m. Closed Wed. Across Nu'uanu Street, ***Hasr Wine Company*** (808-535-WINE; hasrwineco.com) reflects Honolulu's dual East-West personalities, combining fine California wines from one-of-a-kind case lots with an extensive sake collection. Wine tastings are offered regularly. More delicious Chinese food can be found at ***Ginger and Garlic*** (808-537-3883) on Smith Street. This inexpensive to moderately priced restaurant specializes in hearty, family-style Chinese fare. Open every day from 10 a.m. to 9 p.m..

A potpourri of vintage Chinatown shops lines the rest of Maunakea Street. The buildings here mostly date from the two decades following the 1900 fire. You'll find acupuncture clinics, martial arts studios, Asian groceries and importers, watch repair shops, and tattoo parlors. Much of the action is out in the streets themselves. People of all ages rush about on various missions. You'll hear bantering in a dozen Asian dialects.

You can balance your yin and yang at ***Chinese Herbs & Acupuncture*** (808-947-7103; 1911 S. King St. A). Specializing in Chinese herbs and acupuncture, seek your inner zen 9 a.m. to 5:30 p.m. Mon through Sat.

Lower Maunakea has a string of antiques shops that offer a dragon's lair of hoarded treasure, including Ni'ihau shells, samurai swords, Tibetan bronze, vintage aloha shirts, and much more. If you build up an appetite for more dim sum during your shopping, ***Golden Palace*** (808-521-8268; 111 N. King St.) offers a great selection.

Continuing your exploration on King Street, heading away from the capitol, you'll pass the open-air ***O'ahu Market,*** where vendors display food products such as pig snouts, quail eggs, and lotus roots. You can sample all sorts of tropical fruits you may not have seen before. Open every day 6 a.m. to 5 p.m.

A block farther on King Street brings you to Nu'uanu Stream, flanked by River Street. Farther up River Street, across Beretania Street, a statue of Chinese nationalist leader Sun Yat-sen greets you. Sun got his education here in Honolulu and helped launch his revolution with funds raised from Hawai'i's Chinese community. The Filipino community has placed a statue of its own hero, Jose Rizal, across the bridge. Listen to the click-clack of mahjong played by old men at the pavilion tables.

The Asian Mall and upstairs Sun Yat-sen Hall display vintage photos, including some "class portraits" of Sun and his émigré cohorts plotting their revolution. The ***Lum Sai Ho Tong*** has its headquarters at the corner of River and Kukui Streets. The many tongs in Chinatown served as cultural societies for immigrant clans. If the gate to the stairway is unlocked, you can visit the elaborate Taoist shrine on the second floor. Across the river, the ***Izumo Taisha Shrine*** houses the *kami,* Okuninushi-No-Mikoto, a universal god of love and happiness. The shrine property was seized during World War II and only returned by court order in 1962. Shinto services usually are held on the tenth day of each month, and members also visit at significant milestones in their lives, such as reaching the ages of 3, 5, 7, 61, and 88.

Continue up River Street across Vineyard Boulevard to visit a temple for yet another Eastern religion, Buddhism. The ***Kuan Yin Temple*** (808-533-6361) has Western-style walls joined to a traditional Chinese ceramic tile roof. Inside, enormous statues stand behind the altars, the largest of which represents the bodhisattva, Kuan Yin, goddess of mercy. Wei Tor (faith) and Kuan Tai (truth) guard her flanks. You can burn a stick of incense to add to the fumes already present. Some worshipers even burn money. Temple priests and priestesses rattle joss sticks to tell fortunes. Open to visitors daily from 8:30 a.m. to 2 p.m.

If you need a waterfall in your garden to meditate properly, the little-known ***Lili'uokalani Gardens*** lies close at hand. Take Nu'uanu Avenue across the freeway and turn left onto School Street. The second right, a small side street, leads to the banks of Nu'uanu Stream. Queen Lili'uokalani used to picnic here, and so can you. Most of the plants here are native species. The garden is open daily from sunrise to sunset.

Ridges and Valleys

Above the city, the ridges of the Koʻolau Mountain Range reach like fingers toward the sea, with a series of valleys spaced in between. As Honolulu grew, the city pushed inland from the harbor, first into Nuʻuanu ("cool height") Valley. Hawaiians preferred the mild climate and lush beauty, and the many churches and consulates here seem to echo this view today. As you enter the valley, Asian temples predominate along upper Nuʻuanu Avenue. Most of these also function as cultural centers. Ironically, some of the only civilian casualties of the Pearl Harbor attack happened when a stray artillery shell exploded in one such Japanese-language school.

First up as you cross the freeway on Nuʻuanu Avenue is the ***Chinese Buddhist Society*** building on your left. The large meeting hall has a lovely altar in back. A couple of doors farther along is the ***Soto Mission.*** The stylized geometry of this Japanese Zen Buddhist temple reflects the Soto sect's homage to Buddhism's Indian origins.

The ***Myohoji Temple*** comes next on the right, 2 blocks farther at 2003 Nuʻuanu Ave. It's set back from the street along the banks of Nuʻuanu Stream, sheltered beneath high-rise condos. As you continue on Nuʻuanu Avenue up a short hill, take a peek left down Judd Street at the traffic light to see what seems to be another Asian temple. In fact, you're looking at ***St. Luke's Episcopal Church.*** Just ahead, turn right onto Craigside Drive to visit ***Honolulu Memorial Park.*** Sloping down the gulley of Nuʻuanu Stream, this Japanese cemetery enjoys a picturesque setting highlighted by detailed replicas of two famous buildings in Japan. The Sanju Pagoda is an enlarged model of the one in Nara's Minami Hokke-ji Temple. A winding garden path leads to a replica of the Kyoto Kinkaku-ji ("golden pavilion"). Note the phoenix on the roof, a symbol of immortality. Both buildings serve as columbariums for cremated remains.

Just uphill on the left side, the Ten Ri Kyo faith (an offshoot of Buddhism) maintains a small shrine within a charming Japanese garden. On the right-hand side, turn through wrought-iron gates into the grounds of the ***Royal Mausoleum*** (808-587-2590; hawaiistateparks.org). Completed in 1865 as the burial ground for Hawaiʻi's royalty, the mausoleum chapel takes the shape of a Greek cross. Remains from earlier royal graves were transferred here, except for those of Kamehameha I, whose burial place remains a secret as that was the old Hawaiian custom. The chapel did not hold all the caskets, and they were moved into underground crypts. Three trusted advisers also occupy places of honor here. John Young helped train Kamehameha I's army; Robert Wylie served as Kamehameha III's foreign minister; and Charles Bishop founded Bishop Estate, which remains the state's largest landowner. William Maioho, the former curator, was a descendant of the chiefly line that has guarded the Kamehameha family bones since antiquity. The mausoleum is open Mon through Fri and Memorial Day 8:30 a.m. to 4:30 p.m. Guided tours are available with advance reservations.

Turn left onto Kawananako Place to see the final temple of the strip, ***Hsu Yun Temple.*** This one is Chinese Buddhist and has bolder colors than its Japanese neighbors. Inside, its double-sided altar glistens with gold-trimmed grillwork, and incense perfumes the air. You can follow the life of the Buddha through illustrated serial posters around the room. Two other buildings behind the temple house cremation urns stacked in crowded rows of bleachers. Full-time monks live next door, praying for earthly peace.

From the end of Nu'uanu Avenue, take the overpass to get onto the Pali Highway heading toward Kailua. About a mile along, turn right after the first traffic light to ***Queen Emma's Summer Palace*** (808-595-3167; daughters ofhawaii.org). Emma's uncle, John Young II, erected the house, which arrived prefab from Boston in 1847, and called it Hānaiakamalama ("adopted child of moonlight"). Emma inherited the property and spent a lot of time here with her husband, King Kamehameha IV. Feather *kāhili,* emblematic of royalty, stand in every room. Woven *lauhala* (pandanus) mats cover the floors, except for Western carpets in the Edinburgh Room, an extension built in anticipation of a visit from the Duke of Edinburgh. The building lacks the regal appearance of 'Iolani Palace, but a visit here provides a much more personal experience. Docents guide you around the palace, where almost every furnishing has a story.

A rare feather cape that Kamehameha I won in battle displays the yellow feathers of the now-extinct *'o'o 'a'a* bird. A tiger-claw necklace from an Indian maharaja and a lithograph of Napoleon III number among the many gifts from monarchs around the world. Notice the tiny red jacket that belonged to Prince Albert. Like many little boys, the royal heir wanted to be a fireman when he grew up, so Honolulu firefighters made him a miniature uniform.

Despite these tokens of happy times, a sense of tragedy pervades the house. Prince Albert, the only son of Kamehameha IV and Queen Emma, took sick and died at the age of four in 1862. A silver christening cup and holy water sent by Britain's Queen Victoria, who had agreed to be the child's godmother, arrived only hours after his death. Albert's father, the king, blamed himself for his son's death and shut himself in the Summer Palace for almost 15 months of mourning before dying of what the community called a broken heart.

Faced with a double bereavement and a house full of painful memories, Emma took to traveling and social work. She auctioned off much of the home's furniture to help fund the Queen's Hospital, which she and her husband had founded. Later the house itself was scheduled to be torn down and the grounds converted into a ballpark, but the Daughters of Hawai'i intervened. They restored the palace, recovered much of the original contents, and now operate it as a museum. The palace welcomes visitors Tues, Thurs, Fri, and Sat 10 a.m. to 3:30 p.m.; $10 admission fee.

A trio of Asian temples flanks the Summer Palace. The most interesting of the three, the Shinto shrine of ***Daijingu,*** sits behind the palace on Pū'iwa Road. Stone lions guard the entrance, and offerings of 100-pound rice bags and 3-gallon jugs of soy sauce rest before the altar.

About a half mile from the Summer Palace, turn right onto Nu'uanu Pali Drive for a scenic detour. The road winds through 2 miles of lush rain forest and bamboo thickets. Halfway along, following a sharp bend in the road, look for a turnoff into a small forest clearing. (You'll recognize it by the litter.) The ***Judd Memorial Trail*** begins here, an easy 1.3-mile loop that leads to a grove of Norfolk pines named for an early forest ranger. Locals come here to mud-slide down the hill slopes on plastic bags, large pieces of cardboard, or ti leaves (the old Hawaiian way); you can wash off in Jackass Ginger, a naturally formed pool reached by taking the right fork of the trail immediately across Nu'uanu Stream. Nu'uanu Pali Drive continues past a grassy embankment, where kids fish for crayfish in the stream pools, before rejoining the Pali Highway.

As you continue through rain forest on the highway, glance up at the steep walls of the valley above you. Waterfall paths scar the green cliff faces; if it has been raining, the walls sparkle with rivulets. A mile farther, take the turnoff to the ***Pali Lookout*** for a magnificent view of O'ahu's windward coast. From this cliff-top perch you see at once the dramatic contrast between the two sides of the Ko'olau Range. The gentle ridges and valleys that slope upward from the "town" side terminate here in an unbroken wall of *pali* (cliffs). Rising vertically as high as 3,000 feet, these Ko'olau cliffs tower above the bowl-shaped coastal plains below. Their wind-eroded faces are cloaked in greenery, moistened by a misty crown of rain clouds that the trade winds deposit on their peaks. At just less than 1,200 feet, the Nu'uanu Pali represents a low point in the chain; jagged spires on either side of the pass rise 1,000 feet above. Winds funneling through the pass often reach gale force, so hold onto your hat and tether small children securely (just kidding).

The view below encompasses the sweep of Kāne'ohe Bay, the largest in the state. Below the lookout, the Pali Highway emerges from tunnels to descend to Kailua, the next bay off to the right. Part of the original Pali Highway follows an ancient Hawaiian pathway from the lookout itself. You can walk along this abandoned road to enjoy the view in solitude.

Kamehameha's conquest of the islands reached its terrifying conclusion in 1795 at this very spot. His army had routed a combined opposition of O'ahu and Maui chieftains and driven them up Nu'uanu Valley. Many of the defeated warriors leaped over the cliffs to avoid capture. More than 800 skulls have been found at the bottom.

The windward coast is described in a later section; for now, let's stay in town. To the right (east) of Nu'uanu Valley, the green volcanic form of Punchbowl Crater rising above downtown Honolulu makes a striking landmark, whose English name makes obvious visual sense. Hardened ash ejected during violent steam explosions formed this tuff cone in less than a day. *Pū-o-waina,* its original Hawaiian name, translates to "hill of sacrifice," an ironically appropriate epithet for the ***National Memorial Cemetery of the Pacific*** (808-532-3720) inside. Ernie Pyle, the famous World War II correspondent who covered one battle too many, and Ellison Onizuka, a Hawaiian-born astronaut who died in the *Challenger* crash, lie entombed here along with countless others. You enter from the mountainside on Puowaina Drive. Open daily from 8 a.m. to 6 p.m.

Art lovers may want to stop on the way to the cemetery at the ***Cedar Street Gallery*** (808-589-1580; 866-498-7700; 817 Cedar St.; cedarstreetgalleries .com). It features artwork by an impressive roster of more than 100 island artists in a midtown location off King Street. Open Sat noon to 4 p.m., and Mon through Fri until 5 p.m.

The various ridges above Honolulu have dense housing tracts whose twinkling lights at night reflect the star-filled sky. Most have scenic drives, the oldest and nicest of which is the Tantalus/Roundtop loop, inland and east of Punchbowl. Take Punahou Street off King past the cactus-covered walls of missionary-founded Punahou School. Turn left onto Nehoa Street at the light and then right 2 blocks up Makiki Street, which takes you to the start of the loop. Bear left onto Makiki Heights Drive. Just ahead at the hairpin bend, outdoors enthusiasts can stop in at the ***Hawai'i Nature Center*** (808-955-0100; hawaiinaturecenter.org) to get island trail maps as well as advice on the network of trails that crisscross the ridges. Two of the trails begin right behind the center.

Makiki Heights Drive runs into Tantalus Drive, which takes you to the top of the loop. The road passes more elegant homes (one of which was the residence-in-exile for Ferdinand and Imelda Marcos) spaced between amazing rain-forest growths of bamboo, ferns, and philodendron creepers. Roll down your window to inhale the smell of ginger and pīkake flowers. With every bend in the road, you get treated to another breathtaking view of Honolulu. Tantalus Drive climbs to 2,000 feet and then loops back as Roundtop Drive on the other side of the ridge, providing new viewing angles to contemplate. Halfway down, take the turnoff to ***Pu'u Ualaka'a State Park*** and walk out onto the lookout platform at the lower parking lot. Be sure to bring your wide-angle camera lens because all of Honolulu spreads out below your feet.

Next up comes Mānoa ("vast") Valley, an enormous clearing famous for its "Mānoa mist," whereby the sun shines through a veil of mistlike rain and forms intense rainbows. This time take Punahou Street to its end and bear left onto Mānoa Road.

Follow this tree-lined drive just less than a mile into the valley, and on your left you'll see the entrance to the ***Wai'oli Kitchen & Bake Shop*** (808-744-1619; 2950 Mānoa Rd.; waiolikitchen.com). The restaurant here dates from the 1920s; photos from the tearoom's past hang alongside portraits of Hawaiian royalty. Grab a table in the open-air lānai and enjoy light cafe fare while admiring the lushly tropical garden. Inexpensive to moderate. Another attraction on the property is a replica of ***Robert Louis Stevenson's grass shack,*** brought here from Waikīkī, in which the author penned some of his famous works.

Continue on Mānoa to ***Lyon Arboretum*** (808-988-0456; manoa.hawaii .edu/lyonarboretum) at the back of Mānoa Valley. Harold Lyon was a sugar botanist in the 1920s. He belonged to an elite team of roving naturalists who traveled the world, paddling upriver through Malaysian jungle and scaling South American peaks in a never-ending search for specimens of interest or value to the Hawaiian sugar industry. He introduced several thousand new plant species to the islands, many of which you can see today growing in a seminatural state on the 194-acre grounds of the arboretum.

A Hawaiian garden displays the trees and plants used in ancient times. They are grouped according to usage: Foods include mountain apples and breadfruit; clothing came from *wauke* (a mulberry) bark; musical instruments could be a gourd or bamboo rattle; building materials ranged from vines to trees; medicines came from almost anything. You can see how limited the original flora of the islands was, but the Hawaiians found ingenious uses for almost everything. Open Mon through Fri 9 a.m. to 3 p.m. $10 donation suggested. The arboretum also offers regular tours as well as other interpretive activities and classes. Call for a schedule.

Just ahead, the road ends at the trailhead to ***Mānoa Falls.*** Although often muddy, this popular trail offers a delightful stroll through rain-forest jungle, some of which was planted by the arboretum. Look for mountain apples and guava along the way and expect mosquitoes. The veil-like ribbon of the 100-foot waterfall spills into a shallow pool less than a mile up the canyon. It takes about 45 minutes going up. Just before you reach the falls, the Aihualama Trail branches off to the left to connect with the Tantalus trail system. The first part of the trail offers a good view across Mānoa Valley.

Inside the Mānoa Marketplace is a mix of retail and restaurants, plus a large selection of bakeries, including French-inspired ***Fendu Boulangerie*** (808-988-4310; instagram.com/fendu.boulangerie) carrying fresh 'n' flaky croissants, sandwiches, plus gourmet pizzas and sandwiches. Open daily 7:30 a.m. to 3 p.m. Inexpensive. There's also ***BRUG Bakery*** (808-589-2200; brugbakery.com), baking assorted breads and pastries. Open Mon to Sun 8 a.m. to 6 p.m. Inexpensive. If you grow tired of French, why not Italian? ***Paesano Ristorante Italiano*** (808-988-5923), with its white tablecloths and traditional Italian cuisine, has been a Mānoa mainstay for years. Open Mon to Fri 11 a.m. to 2 p.m., and daily 5 to 9 p.m. Moderate to expensive. Make it dinner and a show at nearby ***Mānoa Valley Theatre*** (808-988-6131; manoavalleytheatre.com), "Hawai'i's Off-Broadway," hosting a mix of six or more plays and musicals a season throughout the year.

On your way out of the valley, take the left fork onto O'ahu Avenue, which turns into University Avenue and bends sharply left as it approaches the University of Hawai'i's Mānoa campus; a trio of art galleries here is worth noting. The Art Department displays rotating exhibits in its two art galleries (808-956-6888; hawaii.edu/artgallery): the ***Art Gallery***, open Mon to Fri 10 a.m. to 4 p.m., and Sun noon to 4 p.m.; and the ***Commons Gallery***, open Wed through Sun noon to 4 p.m. during fall and spring semester hours. Nearby Kraus Hall harbors the ***John Young Museum*** (808-956-3634; hawaii.edu/johnyoungmuseum), a collection of Asian-Pacific works, mostly donated by noted island painter John Young. Open weekdays from noon to 4 p.m. Built in 1931, Kraus Hall holds historical interest as the former site of the Pineapple Institute, which did much to establish this iconic crop in the islands. Finally, the ***East-West Center*** (808-944-7111; eastwestcenter.org) has its own rotating Pacific Rim exhibits at the corner of Dole Street and East-West Road. Open Mon through Fri 7:45 a.m. to 4:30 p.m. All three are free. The main East-West Center building farther up the drive (on the right just after the guard post) has a pleasant Japanese garden and koi pond in back; a colorful Korean building waits just up the road. ***Kennedy Theatre*** (808-956-7655 or 808-944-2697; manoa.hawaii.edu/liveonstage/kennedy-theatre), the Brutalist concrete cube across the street, stages some culturally adventurous performances worth checking out.

Just off University Avenue heading away from campus, O'ahu's most intimate luxury accommodation, the ***Mānoa Valley Inn*** (808-926-0888; manoavalleyinn.com), awaits on Vancouver Drive. This three-story mansion bristles with gables and buttressed eaves. Built in 1919 by businessman John Guild and now on the National Register of Historic Places, the home was refurbished by Crazy Shirts founder Rick Ralston with nostalgic touches, from patterned wallpaper to brass fixtures. Many of the antique furnishings come from Ralston's personal collection. All the necessary ingredients for gentle living are supplied in this self-styled country inn: croquet and billiards, a veranda facing a shady yard, wine, daily newspapers, and fresh-cut flowers. Rooms range from $220 to $249, continental breakfast included. A block seaward of the inn on Seaview Avenue, you can obtain far more modest lodging at Hosteling International's ***Mānoa Hostel*** (808-946-0591; hostelsaloha.com). Rates start at $34 per night for dorm rooms; private rooms are also available.

Wai'alae Avenue, the continuation of King Street, leads past other ridges and valleys of interest. Pālolo Valley hides a startling sight in its rear canyon, the ***Mu-Ryang-Sa Buddhist Temple.*** Take Tenth Avenue deep into the valley and bear right onto Wāi'oma'o Road. You'll see the vibrant orange-and-green colors of the temple's pagoda rooftops before you get there. Hawai'i's first Korean Buddhist temple is a massive complex. Fierce larger-than-life statues of "Buddha's guards" secure the entrance to the three temple buildings. The oldest one, on the right, displays the most authentic architecture. Inside, bleacher rows of golden miniature Buddhas surround a central altarpiece. The entire building swims with colors and textures that boggle the mind. Flower children might appreciate the equally colorful ***Kawamoto Orchid Nursery*** (808-732-5808; 2630 Wāi'oma'o Rd.; kawamotoorchids.com), just around the bend. Open Mon through Sat from 8 a.m. to 3 p.m.

The next ridge is Maunalani Heights. Take Wilhemina Rise to Maunalani Circle to reach the trailhead for ***Lanipō.*** This is the best of the many ridge hikes leading up to a Ko'olau pali overlook. You pass through a variety of vegetation, including seasonal strawberry guavas, and are afforded great views into the surrounding valleys; the thin ribbon of civilization along the coast recedes with every mile into virgin forest. Three miles along you reach a staggering panorama of the windward coast, 2,500 feet below. The hike is strenuous and takes at least 3 hours going up. Make sure it's clear up top before setting out; otherwise, your only view will be of your hands groping through the mist.

Waikīkī and Thereabouts

Waikīkī is like a concrete castle guarded by a less-than-shimmering moat—specifically, the polluted Ala Wai Canal, where a guy in 2006 once contracted flesh-eating bacteria and died days after he drunkenly tumbled in. The area (Waikīkī, not the canal) is a giant tourist mill, cut off from reality and quarantined lest it contaminate the rest of Honolulu. Yet Waikīkī has its own perverse charm in spite of its monumental tackiness and congestion. Long before the first tourists arrived, Hawai'i's royalty luxuriated on the golden crescent of Waikīkī Beach and surfed its endlessly rolling breakers, with the regal profile of Diamond Head

Crater rising in the distance. As the birthplace of Hawaiian tourism, Waikīkī has an added nostalgia lacking in other island resorts. While today's clamorous crowds may detract from the beach's beauty and the high-rise hotels block each other's views, Waikīkī remains a world-class resort destination that has undergone a continuing multimillion-dollar makeover over the last decade. You may not like it, but you owe yourself a look.

In days gone by, most of Waikīkī inland of the beach was a productive wetland with 51 acres of fishponds surrounded by taro and rice paddies. The word *Waikīkī* means "spouting waters." Beachgoers increasingly complained about the swarming mosquitoes bred in "the swamp," and in 1922 the Ala Wai Canal drained the land, allowing Hawai'i's first destination resort to be born. Emerging from the primordial slime, greedy developers soon raised a bumper crop of architectural hideousness. The main one-way thoroughfares are Kalākaua Avenue, heading toward Diamond Head past the beach hotels, and Ala Wai Boulevard, running toward Ala Moana along the canal, where outrigger canoe teams practice.

When local people go to the beach in town, they usually head for Ala Moana Beach Park, just west of Waikīkī. ***Aina Moana*** (better known as Magic Island), an artificial peninsula at the Waikīkī end of the park, offers great views and protected swimming. Come here at sundown to watch Friday evening sailboat races at the adjacent Ala Wai Yacht Club. On the other side of the beach park lies Kewalo Basin, home port for many of the island's commercial fishermen. You can check out their catch (and bid on it) at the morning fish auction that takes place Mon through Sat at 1131 N. Nimitz Hwy. on the downtown side of the basin docks. The ocean's colorful bounty—from half-pound snappers to 500-pound swordfish—is laid out on ice-packed pallets for dealers to inspect, and it's then auctioned off fish by fish from 6 a.m. onward. Wear closed shoes.

Crossing the bridge over the Ala Wai Canal and harbor, Ala Moana Boulevard enters Waikīkī itself. Make a right on Kālia Road after the road curves past the Hilton Hawaiian Village and stop at ***Fort DeRussey Beach Park,*** one of the two public areas bordering Waikīkī Beach. Southern Californians at heart can find pickup games of two-person beach volleyball here. Actor Tom Selleck used to play almost every Sunday while filming the TV series *Magnum P.I.* The ***US Army Museum of Hawai'i*** (808-955-9552; hiarmymuseumsoc.org) next to the park bristles with weaponry of varying ages and has some realistic Vietnam-style dioramas for Rambo types wanting to experience ersatz jungle combat. Open Tues through Sat, 10 a.m. to 5 p.m. Free; donations appreciated.

Saratoga Road leads from the museum back inland to Kalākaua Avenue. Nestled nearby, Lewers Street has been given a massive facelift in recent years and is worth a stroll. ***Taormina Sicilian Cuisine*** (808-926-5050; taorminarestaurant .com) offers Southern Sicilian dishes and a formidable wine selection. Open daily 11 a.m. to 2 p.m. and 5 to 9 p.m. Expensive. At the end of the block, ***Halekulani Hotel*** (808-923-2311) is a destination unto itself with several upscale attractions, including the iconic outdoor restaurant ***House Without a Key*** and ***Lewers Lounge***, a wood-trim jazz lounge you have to cross the courtyard to reach. But it's worth the trip to catch jazz, clarinet, flute, and saxophone man Rocky Holmes doing his thing. House Without a Key is open daily 7 to 10:30 a.m. and 11:30 a.m. to 8:30 p.m.; and Lewers is open Tues through Sat 7 p.m. to midnight or 12:30 a.m. Both are investment-caliber.

On Wed and Fri between 10 a.m. and noon, you can visit the ***Urasenke Foundation*** (808-923-3059; 245 Saratoga Rd.; urasenke.org) to watch a ritual performance of the *cha-no-yu,* the ancient Japanese tea ceremony. $3 donation. Reservations required. Around the bend from Urasenke on Kalākaua sprawls the massive ***Royal Hawaiian Shopping Center*** (808-922-2299; royalhawaiian center.com), which offers free lessons in hula on Tues 11 a.m. to noon for adults and on Thurs at 11 a.m. for children. Open daily from 10 a.m. to 9 p.m. There are also hula and music shows Tues, Wed, and Fri at 5:30 p.m. Free. If you shop here and love art and may be looking for a souvenir, check out the ***Lu Koa Collection*** (808-636-3218; 2201 Kalakaua Ave.), which houses handcrafted Hawaiian jewelry and art.

Threaded between the A and B buildings of the shopping center, Royal Hawaiian Avenue ushers the faithful to the vintage hotel of the same name. It's worth making the pilgrimage to the ***Royal Hawaiian Hotel*** (808-923-7311; 888-236-2427; 2259 Kalākaua Ave.; royal-hawaiian.com) to bask in the lingering romance of old Waikīkī. Built in 1927 as the glamour destination Matson needed to attract passengers on its luxury liners, the "Pink Palace" welcomed an endless stream of Hollywood stars. Its Valentino-era Moorish architecture and quiet, grassy courtyard remain an island of grace amid an ocean of vulgarity. Rooms in the historic wing feature four-poster beds, floral wallpaper, and Queen Anne furnishings. The hotel offers guests free experiences such as lei making, hula lessons, and storytelling sessions. Rates start at $469. Farther down Kalākaua, the ***Moana Surfrider, a Westin Resort and Spa*** (808-922-3111; moana-surfrider.com), also known as "The First Lady of Waikīkī," claims its own share of nostalgia. Step through the elaborate colonial porte cochere that fronts the lobby to travel back in time. Built in 1901, the Moana was Waikīkī's first hotel. Live music plays throughout the day in the beachfront banyan tree court, where Robert Louis Stevenson once composed and the Prince of Wales caroused. The historical room above the lobby chronicles this glamorous past with photos, video, and memorabilia, and the hotel offers free historical tours lasting more than an hour on Mon and Wed at 1 p.m. Guest rooms have been refurbished with period touches, such as Hawaiian quilts on the beds and old-fashioned fixtures for the plumbing. Rates start at $399.

While you're here, you might as well visit the new ***International Market Place*** (808-931-6105; shopinternationalmarketplace.com), which feels more like a greener Ala Moana Shopping Center than the old-school (slightly dingy) outdoor shopping bazaar, originally built in 1956, that proceeded it. The new developers left the signature Indian banyan tree, though, and added a statue of Don Ho. It's not the same but such is the modern, ever-changing face of Waikīkī. Open daily 11 a.m. to 9 p.m.

Across the street from the Moana Surfrider, the ***Sheraton Princess Kai'ulani Hotel*** (808-922-5811 or 888-236-2427; princess-kaiulani.com) takes its name after Princess Kai'ulani, who grew up on these grounds. Historical exhibits on display include a poem Robert Louis Stevenson wrote to the princess in an autograph book. Sent to London for her education, Kai'ulani was recalled to Washington and charged by her aunt, the deposed Queen Lili'uokalani, to intercede with President Cleveland for the queen's restoration. Her mission proved unsuccessful, and the princess tragically perished at the age of 23, a death that Western medicine attributed to pneumonia, but Hawaiians knew was from a broken heart. Cultural activities on the grounds include hula lessons, pineapple carving, Hawaiian quilting, and flower lei making. Free. Rooms from $217.

Beyond the Moana the shoreline reverts to public beach park, attractively landscaped with garden statuary and lots of waterfall thingies burbling out of nowhere. There are several features of interest (not counting the ones in swimsuits on the beach). Right next to the police substation, four large boulders lounge incognito in the sand. A plaque explains how these ***kahuna stones*** came to contain the healing powers of four powerful kāhuna visiting from Tahiti in the 13th century. Not far from the stones stands a bronzed statue of Duke Kahanamoku, Olympic medalist, a Waikīkī beach boy, and international surfing hero. Raised in a family of eight boys, Duke was taught to swim the old-fashioned way: tossed off a canoe to sink or swim. He learned well enough to garner six medals (three gold) in four Olympics from 1912 to 1932. (He could have competed in six had it not been for World War I's cancellation of the 1916 games and his own illness in 1928.) Named for the Duke of Edinburgh, who had visited the islands the day he was born, Hawai'i's Duke rode his Olympic fame to a series of Hollywood roles and traveled the world to hobnob with royalty as the island's unofficial ambassador. He brought his surfboard with him on his travels and did much to spread the sport internationally by demonstrating his prowess. Elected sheriff of Honolulu, Kahanamoku continued his ambassadorial role, taking visiting celebrities, including the Prince of Wales, to surf at Waikīkī. Local surfers bemoan the fact that the statue has its back to the ocean, something the experienced waterman would never have done while living. A torch-lighting ceremony and free hula performance are staged on the beach here nightly at sunset. Modern-day beach boys ply their trade from a concession stand nearby. For around $35 you can help paddle an outrigger canoe out to sea and ride the waves in. For around $125 you can get an hour's surfing lesson with individual instruction. The waves here offer long, gentle rides, making Waikīkī one of the best places on the island to learn to surf. If you rent a board on your own, you'll want to get one with a leash so that the board stays with you.

Continue down the street to watch old-timers face off on the checkered tables of the Kūhiō chess pavilions. Across the street, look for the blue V-shaped roof of St. Augustine Church.

The main hotel strip ends at Kapahulu Avenue opposite the entrance to the Honolulu Zoo. Look for a schedule of nearby bandstand events and read some park history at the corner visitor kiosk. Those interested in learning more Waikīkī history can find self-guiding tour information at waikikihistorictrail .org. Next to the kiosk sits a controversial burial mound, Na Iwi Kupuna Waikīkī, which translates roughly as "the bones of our ancestors in Waikīkī," and it houses just that (said bones having been unearthed during work on a water main).

Behind the burial mound is the entrance to the ***Honolulu Zoo*** (808-926-3191; honoluluzoo.org). You can shop for sidewalk art along the fence outside the zoo on Monsarrat Avenue on weekends, purchasing directly from the artists. The zoo itself is fairly standard, but visitors (especially prospective snorkelers) definitely should visit the 120-year old ***Waikīkī Aquarium*** (808-923-9741; waikikiaquarium.org) farther along Kalākaua Avenue. It isn't a big facility, but the exhibits illustrate the colorful diversity of marine life surrounding these islands. You can see some of the world's first chambered nautiluses hatched in captivity, see Hawaiian monk seals at play, and handle marine life in the Edge of the Reef exhibit. Ask about reef walks and other aquarium excursions and events. Open daily 9 a.m. to 4:30 p.m. Admission $12.

Next to the aquarium, note the elaborate facade of the oceanside ***War Memorial Natatorium.*** An enclosed, saltwater bathing pool built in honor of World War I vets, the natatorium has been the subject of a decade-long debate: What do you do with an aging war monument no one wants to use anymore? The city restored the facade, but the pool could not be reopened due to sanitation concerns about inadequate water circulation. In November of 2009, it was announced that the pool and bleachers would be demolished and replaced with sandy beach. It was also announced that the entrance arch would be relocated. Now, there are talks of restoring and reopening the pool to the public. Follow the conversation on the Natarium's Facebook page: facebook.com/natatorium.

Kapi'olani Park sprawls along the opposite side of the street. A staging ground for community activities on weekends, it is also a top-rated kite-flying venue. Farther down Kalākaua stands the ***Kaimana Beach Hotel*** (808-923-1555 or 808-921-7092; 2863 Kalākaua Ave.; kaimana.com). This small "boutique" hotel enjoys a less frenetic, off-Waikīkī location on Sans-Souci Beach, another Robert Louis Stevenson hangout. Rooms start at $212. The hotel's ***Hau Tree*** restaurant sits right on the beach. For a bed-and-breakfast alternative, try a gracious estate on the slopes of Diamond Head, overlooking Waikīkī. The rooms and apartment rent for $150 to $160 and are full of original artwork and heritage koa furnishings, including a 100-plus-year-old bed that belonged to Princess Ruth. Two-day minimum stay. Call ***Diamond Head B&B*** (808-923-3360; diamondheadbnb.com).

hawai'itrivia

O'ahu boasts more miles of swimming beaches than any other island.

Kalākaua Avenue ends near the foot of ***Diamond Head Crater.*** The largest of the tuff cones on the island, Diamond Head received its English name when British sailors caught the glint of what they thought were diamonds reflecting from its slopes. King Kamehameha I promptly slapped a kapu on the entire mountain, only to discover the "gems" were calcite crystals. You can enter the crater interior via a military tunnel through the inland walls. To do so, turn left onto Paki Avenue, then right at the traffic lights onto Monsarrat. A paved road less than a mile long leads through the tunnel. The military installations inside share space with ***Diamond Head State Monument*** (808-587-0300; dlnr.hawaii.gov/dsp/parks/oahu/diamond-head-state-monument/), which the public can visit from 6 a.m. to 4 p.m. From the parking lot a well-graded trail ascends the 760-foot summit, emerging through the inside of a World War II bunker. The panoramic view from the top extends across half the island. The hike up takes about a half hour. Bring water and a flashlight. Admission is $5 paid by credit card only, and all non-residents must pay a $10 parking fee. Children three and under, free.

If you'd rather sun by the shore than hike in the hills, turn right from the end of Kalākaua onto Diamond Head Road, which skirts the seaward edge of the crater around the southern tip of the island. The road climbs high onto the slopes past Diamond Head Lighthouse. Just ahead, a paved pathway leads down the steep cliffside to ***Diamond Head Beach,*** a secluded gem. A fringing reef extends close to shore, making swimming difficult at this spot. Surfers and sailboarders who come here launch through a reef channel a few hundred yards to the left. If you keep walking that way toward Black Point, you'll find some nicer swimming holes and maybe a stretch of sand to call your own.

You can also watch the action from up top at the two lookout points farther along. During summer, the surf off Diamond Head reaches as high as 8 feet, providing exciting conditions for expert wave riders. The first lookout also offers a view east of distant Koko Head and Koko Crater and has a plaque commemorating Amelia Earhart's solo flight across the Pacific.

Some of Honolulu's finest homes are here, with none finer than ***Shangri-La*** (808-532-3853; 4055 Papu Circle; shangrilahawaii.org), the Islamic pleasure palace that on Diamond Head did Doris Duke decree. In 1935 Duke, a newlywed tobacco heiress, embarked on a round-the-world honeymoon that sparked a lifelong passion—not with her husband (that marriage ended in divorce), but rather with Islamic art. Hawai'i was the last stop on Duke's voyage, and, equally captivated by the relaxed island lifestyle, she would return here to build a unique hideaway that combined her two loves. Duke's virtually limitless resources enabled her to amass an amazing trove of art, antiques, tapestries, textiles, metalwork, lusterware, ceramic tiles, and mosaics from Morocco to Molucca and everywhere in between, in what gradually became a monument to pan-Islamic architecture and decor. She often disassembled entire rooms from historic buildings and had them transported to Hawai'i. If she couldn't buy an object, she would commission an exact replica of it or order a custom-made design. The result is a dazzling mélange of architectural styles that blends textures and forms with a daring aesthetic that beguiles without overwhelming. The 5-acre property enjoys a dramatic oceanfront perch, providing an almost surreal contrast to the sophisticated splendor within. Two-and-a-half-hour tours of Shangri-La are offered Thurs through Sat at 9 a.m., 11 a.m., 1 p.m., and 3 p.m. by reservation; they begin at the Honolulu Museum of Art and cost $25. Reservations needed. Call (808) 532-8700 or go online at honolulumuseum.org to make a reservation.

If instead of continuing on Kalākaua past the zoo, you turn left up Kapahulu Avenue, you'll come to some interesting antiques stores. Step inside ***Bailey's Antiques & Aloha Shirts*** (808-734-7628; 517 Kapahulu Ave.; alohashirts.com) and you enter a three-ring bazaar. The eclectic inventory creates a carnival atmosphere rich in color and texture. Most of the items fit the category of Hawaiiana kitsch and collectibles, such as the dancing hula-girl lamps popular in the 1950s. Bailey's specializes in classic aloha shirts, including original 1940s "silkies," whose wild floral patterns became a symbol of the islands. Some of the shirts have celebrity connections and fetch upward of $1,000. You can also find contemporary reproductions for about $50 and used shirts starting at $9.99. Original owner David Bailey scoured thrift shops in California to find these forgotten treasures and has been known to buy the shirt off a stranger's back. Open daily 11 a.m. to 5 p.m.

Other antiques shops space themselves along Kapahulu Avenue, with the biggest cluster at the far end near the freeway. The five antiques shops in back of the ***Kilohana Square*** shopping complex, at 1016 Kapahulu Ave., mostly specialize in decorative art and furniture from Asia. On the way down, you might also stop in at Aunty Mary Lou's ***Na Lima Mili Huli No'eau*** (808-499-7048; 762 Kapahulu Ave.), a craft shop devoted to the traditional Hawaiian art of feather working. (The name means "skilled hands touch the feathers.") Students take lessons here and then sell their completed projects by consignment. Open Mon through Fri 10 a.m. to 5 p.m., and 11 a.m. to 5 p.m. on Sat.

Kapahulu also has a variety of good restaurants. Beginning at Waikīkī, across from the Ala Wai Golf Course, is ***Tonkatsu Tamafuji*** (808-922-1212), serving Japanese comfort food, especially breaded pork tonkatsu. Open Mon and Wed to Fri 4 to 9:30 p.m., and Sat and Sun 11 a.m. to 2 p.m. and 5 to 9:30 p.m. Moderate. ***Rainbow Drive-In*** (808-737-0177; 3308 Kana'ina Ave.; rainbowdrivein.com) is the local's favorite, an iconic Hawaiian plate lunch destination serving BBQ chicken and beef, mahimahi, and chili counter-side. Open daily 7 a.m. to 9 p.m. Inexpensive.

Sunrise Restaurant (808-737-4118; pigsfromthesea.com) offers Okinawan cuisine in a no-frills environment. Inexpensive to moderate. For more local fare, ***Uncle Bo's Pūpū Bar & Grill*** (808-735-8310) is a contemporary hangout (the original is in Hale'iwa) specializing in large portions of seafood, like steamer clams and oysters Rockefeller. Open daily 5 to 10 p.m. Moderate to expensive. ***Tenkaippin Hawai'i*** (808-732-1211; facebook.com/tenkaippin hawaii) is a cozy ramen shop with wraparound bar seating. Open Mon to Thurs 11 a.m. to 1:30 p.m. and 5 to 8:30 p.m., and Fri and Sat 11 a.m. to 1:30 p.m. and 5:30 to 9 p.m. Inexpensive. ***Yakitori Glad*** (808-734-0077) is a Japanese izakaya where all items—from chicken skewers to a mug of beer—cost just $3.90. Open Mon to Sun 5 to 10 p.m. Inexpensive. Across the street is ***Haili's Hawaiian Foods*** (808-735-8019; hailishawaiianfood.com), a long-running local fixture specializing in hearty Hawaiian plates. Open every day except Mon 10 a.m. to 2 p.m. Expensive.

The Kapahulu area used to be heavily settled by Honolulu's Portuguese community. Near the inland end of Kapahulu Avenue, ***Leonard's Bakery*** (808-737-5591; leonardshawaii.com) keeps tradition alive with fresh-baked

Portuguese *pao doce* (sweetbread) and hot *malasadas* (doughy, holeless doughnuts). Open daily 5:30 a.m. to 7 p.m.

A quick right turn up Wai'alae Avenue at the freeway end of Kapahulu Avenue brings you to ***Kaimukī***, a trendy enclave where locals gather to sip lattes and dine at an eclectic array of restaurants, a trio of which is owned by restauranteur Ed Kenney, son of legendary hula practitioner Beverly Noa. He's created a popular farm-to-table eatery at the intersection of 9th Avenue. ***Mud Hen Water*** (808-737-6000; mudhenwater.com) offers Hawaiian fusion dishes, like fresh fish in pastele and Portuguese sausage and mussels, that evolve depending on what local produce and seafood is available. Open Tues to Sat 8 to 11 a.m. for breakfast, and 11 a.m. to 2 p.m. for lunch. Dinner is served Tues through Thurs 5 to 9 p.m., and Fri and Sat until 9:30 p.m. Brunch on Sun from 9:30 a.m. until 2 p.m. Moderate.

For dessert, head down the street to ***Otto Cake*** (808-834-6886; ottocake.com), baking more than 286 different rotating flavors of the best cheesecake in Hawai'i, ranging from liliko'i to almond cookie. Each one, mixed by hand by Otto, a local punk and ska musician and baker extraordinaire. Open Mon to Sat 11 a.m. to 7 p.m., and Sun 11 a.m. to 3 p.m. Inexpensive.

Just Up the Freeway

Hawai'i does have "interstate" highways, despite the irony of being completely isolated in the middle of the Pacific Ocean. The main route through town is the H-1 Freeway. Take any on-ramp and head west to see some more of Honolulu. If you really want to experience the soul of Hawai'i, visit the ***Bishop Museum*** (808-847-3511; 1525 Bernice St.; bishopmuseum.org), a repository of Hawaiian culture, artifacts, and history, spanning from archaeology to zoology. Princess Bernice Pauahi, the last heir of the Kamehameha Dynasty, left her immense landholdings to educate Hawaiian students. Her private possessions, however, were left to benefit the people of Hawai'i, as the beginnings of the museum established by her American banker husband, Charles Reed Bishop. Today, a century later, the museum's exhibits have swelled to include 76,000 Hawaiian artifacts alone, not to mention an estimated 14 million insect specimens (making Bishop Museum home to the third largest insect collection in the US). Bishop Museum has become the world's leading research institution on Pacific cultures. To reach it, take the Houghtailing Street turnoff from the H-1 Freeway and take the second left.

Budget plenty of time for your visit, as there's lots to see. The bulk of the exhibits fill the massive Hawaiian Hall inside the castle-like main building. The three levels focus on different aspects of Hawaiian culture and society. The first floor is the realm of Kai Ākea, representing Hawaiian gods, mythologies, beliefs, spirituality, and precontact Hawai'i. The second floor, Wao Kanaka, represents traditional day-to-day life, how people live and work, and the importance of land and nature. The third floor, Wao Lani, focuses on Hawaiian ali'i, and important moments in Hawaiian history, from the turbulent changes of the 19th century to today's multiethnic society. From the ceiling hangs the 50-foot skeleton of a sperm whale. In the entrance room, look for Kūka'ilimoku, the personal war god of Kamehameha I. The great conqueror carried this flaming orange-feathered apparition into battle, and its wide staring eyes were witness to the years of carnage. You might also see Kamehameha's full-length yellow feather cloak, the result of more than 100,000 mamo birds that were gathered to provide the necessarily plumage. Each bird yielded only a few yellow feathers plucked from among the black.

Next door is Pacific Hall, a two-story gallery where visitors can explore Moananuiakea and the various cultures of Oceania. The first floor is filled with cultural artifacts, such as woven mats, model canoes, contemporary artwork, and videos of Pacific scholars. The second floor details the origins and migrations of Pacific peoples through linguistics, oral storytelling traditions, and archaeology.

Other key attractions include the Abigail Kinoiki Kekaulike Kāhili Room, displaying portraits of the Hawaiian Monarchy as well as some of their effects (such as the feather standards associated with them); the Nā Ulu Kaiwi'ula Native Hawaiian Garden, where you can stroll past dozens of plant species from the endemic to the nonnative; and the 16,500-square-foot Richard T. Mamiya Science Adventure Center facility, which showcases Hawai'i's natural sciences and has received international recognition in recent years for cutting-edge research in the fields of oceanography, volcanology, and biodiversity.

Open daily, the planetarium introduces you to the world of stars, with various shows. For more information on programming—including demonstrations of feather work, quilting, lei making, hula, and "living stories" tours, visit bishopmuseum.org. The Bishop Museum is open daily from 9 a.m. to 5 p.m.; $28.95 general admission.

Past the museum, the freeway splits temporarily, with H-1 bending seaward to the airport. Continue straight on what's now Route 78 for another mile. Take the Pu'uloa Road/Tripler Hospital turnoff and make a quick right into ***Moanalua Gardens*** (moanaluagardens.com), which are temporarily closed to the public, with the exception of private events. Prince Lot, who later became Kamehameha V, kept a summer home here, where he encouraged a partial revival of the hula art forms. The annual Prince Lot Festival, held at 'Iolani

Palace, commemorates his efforts with a weekend of Hawaiian dance during July. The prince's elaborate cottage still stands beside koi and taro ponds.

You can soak up additional historic scenery by hiking the nearby ***Kamananui Valley Trail,*** which passes petroglyphs and other historic sites deep into the valley. Kamehameha I (Lot's grandfather) capped his conquest of O'ahu by sacrificing rival chief Kalanikupule on an altar here. Stop by the ***Moanalua Gardens Foundation*** (808-839-5334; moanaluagardens foundation.org; 1414 Dillingham Blvd, St. 211) to purchase "A Walk into the Past," an interpretive trail guide keyed to numbered posts along the way. Open Wed 9 a.m. to 2 p.m.

The best signs to follow to the ***Pearl Harbor*** and *Arizona* Memorial are along H-1. If you're already on Route 78, follow signs to the Aiea exit, about 4 miles farther, and turn left over the bridge. This section of Kamehameha Highway runs past the stadium along the East Loch of Pearl Harbor. The cauliflower-like lakes of this enormous inland lagoon were cut by river valleys during a time of lower sea levels. Oyster beds thrived in the shallow flats, hence the name Pearl.

The American military acquired base rights to Pearl Harbor during King Kalākaua's reign in exchange for tariff-free access to US markets for Hawaiian sugar, but the military didn't get around to dredging the harbor opening until 1902. Hawaiians were perturbed when the US Navy chose to dig its dry dock on the very island where the shark goddess, Ka'ahupahau, supposedly lived. Their dire warnings came true when, four years into construction, a structural collapse wiped out all the work that had been done to that point. A giant shark skeleton was found amid the rubble.

The Japanese attack on December 7, 1941, brought Pearl Harbor before the eyes of the world and catapulted the United States into World War II. Contrary to popular belief, the attack did not come entirely without warning. A Japanese mini-sub had been found and sunk near the mouth of the harbor hours earlier. Experimental radar stations even tracked the incoming attack squadrons (until their commander told them to turn off their screens). More intriguing yet, American intelligence forces had recently cracked the Japanese code and by monitoring cable transmissions were alerted to the likelihood that Japan was planning a military strike. Some have suggested that top American officials secretly planned to absorb the damage so as to commit the United States to entering the war against Hitler. These "conspiracy theorists" claim that the fortuitous absence of the carrier fleet at the time of the attack was more than a stroke of luck.

You can grapple with your own interpretation as you come face-to-face with the monuments left from that day's violence. Take the turnoff from

Kamehameha Highway to the **Arizona *Memorial*** (808-422-3399; nps.gov/perl) at the World War II Valor in the Pacific National Monument. The 184-foot, white concave hull of the monument sits like a shroud across the sunken hull of the battleship *Arizona,* whose number-three gun turret pierces the surface at low tide. More than a thousand sailors and marines perished in this single battleship's destruction—almost half the total deaths in the attack. Most of the victims remain entombed in the ship, which sank within minutes of the explosion in the forward-deck powder magazine. More than 60 years later the *Arizona* continues to bleed, oozing gallons of oil every week.

Free boat trips to the memorial depart from the National Park Service visitor center on a first-come, first-served basis. However, many open-air museum exhibits are available to browse. One display tells the story of Hawai'i's Americans of Japanese descent. At a time when mainland cities were incarcerating their Japanese populations, Hawai'i's Japanese Americans refused to allow their patriotism to be doubted. Their patient resolve won them the chance to prove themselves in combat in Italy, where they became one of the most decorated battalions in US military history. Equally compelling is the story of Admiral Yamamoto, a Harvard-educated military genius who masterminded the Pearl Harbor strike despite a personal opposition to the war. The museum is open daily 7 a.m. to 5 p.m.; programs run 8 a.m. to 3:30 p.m. Free. Reservations recommended.

There are also multiple other historic sites to visit. Amble over to nearby ***USS* Bowfin *Submarine Museum and Park*** (808-423-1341; bowfin.org). You can take in the exhibits of the Pacific Submarine Museum and then enter an actual World War II submarine, the USS *Bowfin,* moored nearby. Dubbed the "Pearl Harbor Avenger," the *Bowfin* was launched exactly a year after the Japanese attack and went on to claim 44 kills (23 confirmed) in Japanese craft sunk. Open daily 7 a.m. to 5 p.m. Admission is $21.99, which includes an audio tour in English and Japanese of both the submarine and the museum. The last tour starts at 4:30 p.m. On Wed and weekends, check out the massive "swap meet" flea market at nearby Aloha Stadium from 8 a.m. to 3 p.m.

At the USS *Bowfin* Submarine Museum and Park, you can also purchase tickets for Pearl Harbor's newest visitor attraction, the ***Battleship* Missouri *Memorial*** (808-455-1600, x251; ussmissouri.org). One of the most formidable battleships ever built, the USS *Missouri* saw duty in three wars, from World War II to the Persian Gulf. It earned its spot in the history books, however, not for its role in the fighting, but rather as the place where World War II ended with Japan signing instruments of surrender on its aft deck. Anchored only 1,000 yards from another World War II battleship, the sunken USS *Arizona,* the two form perfect bookends to America's involvement in the war, from defeat to victory.

Hit the highlights, including the main bridge, armory, wardroom, the panoramic views from the "flying bridge," the retrofitted Tomahawk missile launchers, and, of course, the "surrender deck." Exhibits recount the details of daily life on board ship, and war stories abound, including a heart-stopping moment when a Japanese kamikaze pilot slammed his fighter plane into the starboard side of the ship. Part of the experience is merely appreciating the size of this floating behemoth. Launched in 1944, the USS *Missouri* was the last battleship the US Navy ever built and one of the largest. Its entire 887-foot-long hull is encased in steel armor plating more than a foot thick. Its massive 16-inch guns, each weighing 116 tons and measuring 65 feet in length, are capable of launching a shell as heavy as a Volkswagen Beetle more than 20 miles—with pinpoint accuracy. Just designing the USS *Missouri* took 175 tons of blueprint paper. Built in three years, the ship required more than three million man-days to complete (and, more recently, 25,000 volunteer hours to renovate). The Battleship *Missouri* Memorial is open daily 8 a.m. to 4 p.m. Tickets must be purchased by 3 p.m. and cost $34.99 for general admission ($17.49 for kids aged 4 to 12), which comes with a 35-minute guided tour of the main historical areas of the ship, including the Surrender Deck. History buffs will want to snag tickets for the Chief Engineer's Tour instead (an additional $30 for adults and kids), which lets you explore the engineering spaces, including the engine rooms, gun turrets, and fire rooms. Book early though: This tour is limited to only 10 guests per time slot and only 6 time slots available each day.

Going straight from the same Aiea freeway exit puts you on Moanalua Road (moving parallel to and inland of Kamehameha Highway, past the stadium). Turn right at the mall just ahead and take Aiea Heights Drive up the hill to ***Keaiwa Heiau State Recreation Area*** (808-483-2511; dlnr.hawaii.gov/dsp/parks/oahu/keaiwa-heiau-state-recreation-area). You get some good views of Pearl Harbor and Central O'ahu on the way up. The heiau sits at the park entrance, one of the few healing temples of ancient Hawai'i that remain. Here the *kāhuna lapa'au* (medicine men) mixed herbs and prayers to cure a variety of ailments. Many of the medicinal plants they used still grow around the heiau grounds. The rest of the park consists of groves of ironwoods and eucalyptus and cool fresh air. At the top of the road, the ***Aiea Loop Trail*** offers an easy 4.5-mile hike through a variety of forest cover and occasional views. You can see the wreckage of a C-47 cargo plane about 3 miles along on your right. The round-trip trek takes about 3 hours. Free.

A Night on the Town (and Daytime, Too)

Waikīkī is the entertainment capital of Hawai'i. It has plenty of nightclubs for owls on the prowl, and almost all the big hotels book prominent local talent to perform at dinner shows. For free outdoor entertainment, pick an evening with clear skies and stroll along Waikīkī Beach. At night the beach is empty and you hear the gentle lap of waves against the shore. As you walk, you can hear the sounds of the many hotel shows staged on oceanfront lānais and linger to watch part of the acts.

If you feel like stopping in for a drink, a good candidate is ***Duke's Waikīkī*** (808-922-2268; dukeswaikīkī.com) in the Outrigger Waikīkī. Top-notch local entertainers perform contemporary island music Sun 7 a.m. to midnight. In between, the "aunties" serenade individual tables. Moderate to expensive.

For food (and drinks) with a view, head to ***SKY Waikīkī*** (808-979-7590; skywaikiki.com) to enjoy colorful cocktails and light bites 19 stories above the city. But arrive dressed to impress; at night, SKY turns into a dedicated nightclub. Open every day from 4 to 10 p.m.; hours extended until midnight on Fri. Moderate to expensive. Another rooftop destination is ***Buho Cocina y Cantina*** (808-922-2846; opentable.com/buho-cocina-y-cantina), serving up Mexican cuisine like burritos, tacos, and fresh ceviche with local ingredients in an open-air lounge. Open Sun, Mon, and Tues 4 p.m. to midnight, and Sat, Tues, and Thurs to Fri from 4 p.m. to 1:30 a.m. Moderate.

For equally classy dining and digs, ***Mahina & Sun's*** (808-924-5810; mahinaandsuns.com), overlooking the Instagram-famous "Wish You Were Here!" pool in the courtyard of the '60s-themed ***Surfjack Hotel & Swim Club,*** offers breakfast, lunch, dinner, and drinks. Order the "Presidential Martini," with Grey Goose and Noilly Prat vermouth served shaken, not stirred—it's the one that Hawai'i's own Barack Obama had when he visited back in December 2016. Open daily 6:30 a.m. to 10 p.m. Moderate to expensive. Equally fancy is ***Hideout*** (808-628-3060; hideoutwaikiki.com) at The Laylow hotel, with its lobster frittatas for breakfast and flatbread pizzas for lunch, dinner, or anytime. Sit by the fire pits as a bonus flourish. Ask the bar to make you an elegant tropical cocktail, or perk up with a trendy Stumptown coffee. Open daily 6 a.m. to midnight. Moderate to expensive.

Those feeling less fancy can head to ***Duke's Lane Market & Eatery*** (808-923-5692; dukeslanehawaii.com) just a couple of blocks over; a still-classy food court and bar to enjoy a mix of dishes—from creamy gelato to spitfire rotisserie. Open daily 7 a.m. to 11 p.m. Inexpensive to moderate.

For late night fun, visit ***Wang Chung's Karaoke Bar*** (808-201-6369; wangchungs.com) off Koa Avenue, a cozy, colorful bar where you will find surprisingly good fried chicken bites, pork hash sliders, and tacos. Pick your song carefully; it'll come up on every screen in this LGBTQ+ friendly hangout. Open daily 7 a.m. to 2 a.m. Inexpensive.

Night action outside Waikīkī has a few areas of interest: Collegiate crowds gather at a cluster of bars near the intersection of King Street and University Avenue. Hawai'i Pacific University has mostly taken over ***Aloha Tower Marketplace,*** converting the once-tallest building in Honolulu and its surrounding complex into a dorm and extended campus for its students. People who work at nearby ***Restaurant Row*** near the ocean end of Punchbowl Street will have lunch or get drinks at the restaurants and bars downstairs of their office buildings.

Honolulu has a few standing monthly events that never fail to attract a crowd. The biggest is the ***First Friday*** of every month in Chinatown, where art lovers and 20-somethings (not necessarily two mutually exclusive crowds but the vibe at 6 p.m. is much different from the vibe at 11 p.m.) mingle and explore the neighborhood. Every Fri and Sat, the Honolulu Museum hosts ***HoMA Nights*** until 9 p.m., which enables guests to enjoy live art and music and stroll through the latest exhibitions with drinks in their hands. (The security guards love it.) Other street events include nightly pop-up marketplaces and food festivals by ***Art + Flea*** (artandflea.com), ***Honolulu Night Market*** (honolulunightmarket.com), and ***Eat the Street Hawai'i*** (eatthestreethawaii .com). These events had live art demonstrations, street food vendors, fashion shows, and local businesses selling wares—and were a regular fixture that packed the warehouses and streets of Kaka'ako with thousands of people from 2011 to 2016 but have trickled down once the artsy neighborhood settled into its final form and converted the collaborative spaces and construction sites into permanent, million-dollar condos.

Whatever the event, if your night on the town stirs an appetite, ***M.A.C. 24-7*** (808-921-5564; mac247waikiki.com) in the Hilton Waikīkī Beach Hotel serves good-value grub (especially breakfast). Attempt the giant pancake challenge if you dare. Open 24 hours every day. Inexpensive to moderate.

Almost every weekend in the summer, Japanese temples schedule bon dances to honor ancestral spirits, and the public is always welcome. Local hula hālau also hold fund-raisers at sites around the island—a great way to catch authentic Hawaiian culture. A number of groups schedule ***biking trips*** on weekends.

To see the island on foot, consider hikes with the ***Sierra Club*** (808-538-6616; sierraclubhawaii.org) or ***Hawaiian Trail and Mountain Club*** (check online at htmc1910.org).

Michael Walther's ***O'ahu Nature Tours*** (808-924-2473; oahunaturetours.com) offers a daily schedule of interpretive outings to island ecosystems; tours range in price. To give you an idea, the Ultimate Circle Island Tour costs around $125.

Wild Side Tours (808-306-7273; sailhawaii.com) offers marine ecotours along O'ahu's remote, relatively pristine Leeward Coast. Founded by a husband-and-wife team of marine biologists with intimate knowledge of the local terrain, the trips take place on a 42-foot catamaran and may involve dolphin or humpback whale watching, reef snorkeling, and visits to a turtle "cleaning station," with the focus of activity varying according to participant interest and marine conditions. The "Best of the West" option includes snorkel gear, lunch, snacks, and in-water guides for $205 per person. ***Twogood Kayaks*** (808-321-9900; adventuretourshi.com/twogood-kayaks) offers a guided nature tour in Kailua Bay. An all-day package features an excursion to an offshore island with hiking and exploration of secluded coves for $169, including lunch. A self-guided version of this tour is available for $59.

More conventional walking treks covering historic downtown, island temples, petroglyphs, waterfalls, and rain forests can be arranged through the ***Hawai'i Geographic Society*** (808-782-3562). Learn more about their offerings by messaging them on their Facebook page: facebook.com/HawaiiGeogSociety.

Those of a crafty bent might consider taking a Hawaiian class. Besides the Royal Hawaiian Shopping Center and Bishop Museum (see Waikīkī and Thereabouts), other places offering instruction in Hawaiian crafts and hula include the ***Waikīkī Community Center*** (808-923-1802; waikīkīcommunitycenter.org) and the ***Lyon Arboretum*** (808-988-0456; manoa.hawaii.edu/lyonarboretum). The ***Japanese Cultural Center*** (808-945-7633; jcch.com) has its own offerings from time to time.

For many visitors, the number one activity is shopping. Most tourists find their way to ***Ala Moana Shopping Center*** (808-955-9517; alamoanacenter.com), the world's biggest open-air shopping center. Locals increasingly shop at the many outlets that populate Central O'ahu. But Honolulu has plenty of quirky, offbeat shopping venues as well. The gift shops at the major museums here provide fertile ground to hunt for that one-of-a-kind special find. The newly branded community of Ward Village, off Ala Moana Boulevard between Ward Avenue and Ala Moana Center, has a nice array of boutiques inside the ***South Shore Market*** (808-591-8411), patronized by visitors and locals alike Mon to Thurs 10 a.m. to 8 p.m., Fri and Sat until 9 p.m., and Sun until 6 p.m. ***Nā Mea Hawai'i*** (808-596-8885; nameahawaii.com), at Ward Centre, has a fine selection of island crafts and books; it's owned by a consortium of local artisans working in media ranging from wood carving to Hawaiian quilts. Open

Mon through Thurs 10 a.m. to 6 p.m., Fri and Sat until 7 p.m., and Sun until 5 p.m. Also good is the ***Nohea Gallery*** (808-762-7407; noheagallery.com), also with space at Kahala Mall. Antiques hunters should visit ***Antique Alley*** (808-941-8551), a cluster of shops near Ala Moana Center at 1030 Queen Street. Open 12:30 to 5:30 p.m. everyday except Sun and Wed.

Curious about crack seed? This local treat of preserved fruits that have been split with the seed and salted or sweetened may have originated in China (brought over by plantation workers) but has found a huge local audience in Hawaiʻi. Some of the best, including rock salt plum, li hing mui, Japanese arare crackers, preserved orange peels, and licorice peaches, are available at ***Lin's Hawaiian Snacks*** (808-597-8899; linsmarkethawaii.com) at the corner of Queen and Kamakeʻe Street. Enjoy these or Taiwanese "bubble" milk tea, complete with chewy tapioca balls, perfect for hot days in Hawaiʻi. Open Mon to Sat 10 a.m. to 7 p.m., and Sun 10 a.m. to 7 p.m. Inexpensive.

East Oʻahu and Windward

All right, enough big-city stuff. You came here to see natural beauty, and Oʻahu's got plenty outside Honolulu. To do the main "circle island" tour, driving up the windward coast and back through the center in a single day, is impractical though. If you're based in Honolulu, take advantage of the scenic trans-Koʻolau highways—the Pali, Likelike, and H-3—to break the trip into smaller loops.

Start the southern circuit on Kalanianaʻole Highway at the east end of H-1, "heading Koko Head" (which is how locals say "go east" when you're east of Diamond Head). Four miles along the highway, you reach Hawaiʻi Kai, a large suburb built around a converted fishpond. ***Mariner's Ridge*** is one of the few built-up hillsides here, but it's private property. Check alltrails.com/trail/hawaii/oahu/mariners-ridge-trail for updates and alternatives. If you take Kaluanui Street off Hawaiʻi Kai Drive all the way to the top, there's an excellent 1.5-hour hike to a Koʻolau pali overlook. It's similar to Lanipō but not as long or hard, and the view is almost as good.

After Koko Marina, the divided highway ends. Continue up the hill between Koko Head and Koko Crater, two large tuff cones formed during Oʻahu's most recent eruption. (Not to worry, it happened about 100,000 years ago.) At the top of the hill, turn right into ***Hanauma Bay Beach Park*** (808-768-6861; hanaumabaystatepark.com). Peering over the rim into this unique indentation on Koko Head's east flank from the parking lot, you won't need a geology degree to recognize that the bay was once a volcanic crater, part of a chain of craters along the east coast. Hanauma's seaward wall has yielded to the assault of the ocean. You'll find a unique, sheltered bay with large coral deposits and a white-sand beach.

As a state underwater park off-limits to fishing, Hanauma has blossomed into a natural aquarium with fish of every shape, stripe, and color. You'll see giant rainbow parrotfish, banded convict tangs, yellow-and-black Moorish idols, and maybe even reed-thin trumpet fish. The different schools glitter like so many points of light. If the water inshore is murky, try the outer reef (but not in big surf). Newcomers have to watch a short video before they walk or ride a trolley down the steep path to the beach. A concession rents snorkeling equipment, and if you want to make yourself really popular with the fish, buy some food packets. There is a $25 entry fee ($3 parking). Open 6:45 a.m. to 4 p.m. (no entry after 2 p.m.). Due to overcrowding, the park is closed on Mon and Tues and exercises capacity controls on parking.

Before you leave Hanauma, there are a few more options for the adventurous to explore. Look for the ***Toilet Bowl***, a unique rock formation in a hidden inlet just outside the mouth of the bay. Incoming waves are channeled into an exposed lava tube; as they ebb and flow, they "flush" a small pool at the end in a vigorous imitation of your household porcelain pot. The rocks around the edge are slippery, so be careful getting in. Once inside, it's safe as long as you stay in the center of the pool, and it's loads of fun. To get here, you used to be able to walk from the beach along the left side of the bay and around the outer rim. Access has been closed of late due to fear of falling rocks. Instead, you will need to find your way down from the parking lot following the top of the crater rim through an arid scrubland toward the mouth of the bay and then descending into the narrow canyon that opens into the back of the inlet. (There is no marked trail.) For those who prefer the high road, an alternative to visiting the Toilet Bowl is to ascend the spine of the crater by taking the blocked-off road that splits off near the park entrance from the highway. Your reward is a sweeping view of the island's southeastern coastline.

Past Hanauma Bay the highway swoops around another sunken crater (used as a firing range), then clings to the striated slopes of ***Koko Crater***, which overlooks the deep blue of the Kaiwi Channel. This is the sort of drive you see featured in sports-car commercials. You wind in and out of the volcano's ridges and grooves, while beneath the highway the ocean crashes against the coast in a fury of foam and spray. Across the channel, Moloka'i darkens the horizon. If conditions are clear, you can make out Maui and Lāna'i as well.

Less than a mile along the road, look for a small stone monument on your right, a hundred yards *before* the ***Hālona Blowhole*** parking lot where the tour buses disgorge their loads. Pull over here instead and walk up the steps to this

The Case of the Missing (Half) Island

One of the most striking features of O'ahu is its Nu'uanu pali, a wall of sheer cliffs that extends along half the island from Waimanalo to Waikāne. Rising more than 3,000 feet at their highest point, the pali dominate the landscape of the southern windward coast. Their characteristic fluted indentations add an element of delicate beauty to the drama of their near-vertical slope.

This sheer cliff face stands in marked contrast to the gently sloping ridges of the Ko'olau Range's leeward slopes, which reach like so many fingers toward the coastal settlements of Honolulu, with deep valleys etched in between. Trails leading up these ridges to an overlook offer some of the island's most dramatic vistas. But what accounts for this very different topography on either side of the same mountain mass? Originally, the Ko'olau—along with most of the island—formed as a single volcano with roughly symmetrical edges. The summit of this ancestral volcano, which once reached perhaps 5,000 feet in elevation, was centered above the windward coast, roughly where Kailua and Kāne'ohe are today. Somehow, a huge chunk of this island mass disappeared along its southern windward edge, leaving only the leeward slopes, whose abrupt end at the *pali* bears witness to a now-vanished mountain.

That much of the geologic evidence is clear. The chain of islands dotting the windward coast offshore mark the outer edges of where the Ko'olau volcano once stood. Geologists tried to account for this disappearing mountain by citing the normal forces of erosion—the constant trade winds that weather the windward side and the ocean waves that tear against the coast.

fishing shrine built by the Honolulu Japanese Casting Club. Carved into the upright rock, Ojisan, a guardian spirit, keeps a watchful eye on anglers casting from the wave-swept lava shelf below. The view from the monument extends along the coast in both directions. Below to your left, the tiny picturesque cove you see earned a cameo in the "kiss in the sand" scene in *From Here to Eternity.* Beware of currents beyond the rim if you swim here. Just around the cove, the Hālona Blowhole sprays a fine mist through a hole in the lava shelf, driven by incoming waves that fill a sea cave underneath.

Past the blowhole, the highway straightens as it descends to the flat coastline of ***Sandy Beach.*** The bodysurfing here is famous, but for experts only. Because of the steep slope of the beach, waves crash with spine-snapping force directly onto the shore, and the undertow from the backwash is fierce. Red flags mean stick to the sand. In the summer, when trade-wind swells build up, the surfing circuit migrates here for bodyboarding contests. Youngsters favor "Sandy's" year-round as the hangout of choice for sand, sun, and scoping. The windswept field next to the beach is popular for stunt kites.

The problem was that O'ahu is simply not old enough (geologically speaking) for these slow-moving forces to have carved away that much rock in such a short time. It was a mystery.

More than a decade ago, however, an unmanned navy submarine made a remarkable discovery. Operating in very deep waters many miles off the coast of O'ahu, the sub was searching for the "black box" flight recorder from a downed airplane. The sub's sonar revealed a strange accumulation of debris—giant boulders, rubble, and so on—piled along the ocean floor. Subsequent investigation revealed that this debris had the same geologic composition as the Ko'olaus. The stuff down there had come from up above.

Scientists calculated that for so many tons of rock to have traveled so far and so deep offshore, it had to have been moving very, very fast. This discovery led to a new explanation for the formation of the pali. Geologists now believe that somehow half of the island all at once took a cataclysmic plunge into the sea.

It turns out the Nu'uanu pali are not the only example of such massive island-wide landslides. The sea cliffs along the north shore of Kaua'i and Moloka'i also appear to have formed in a similarly abrupt fashion. The lava flows that built these islands hardened into unstable layers like a pile of bricks without mortar. The impact of so much rock crashing into the ocean all at once gave rise to some amazing splash waves. Scientists have traced a massive prehistoric tsunami that flooded the island of Kaho'olawe up to the 500-foot level to one such monster landslide along the Big Island's Kona Coast.

This process is continuing still. A new peninsula formed off Moloka'i's North Shore from a recent collapse. For young islands, Hawai'i's geologic history has been anything but dull.

Just ahead you might turn up Kealahou Street and take another left to visit the ***botanical gardens*** inside steep-walled Koko Crater (808-768-7135; honolulu.gov/parks/hbg/honolulu-botanical-gardens/182-site-dpr-cat/572-koko-crater-botanical-garden). Known as Kohelepelepe ("the fringed vagina") to the ancient Hawaiians, the crater's resemblance to that portion of the female anatomy is explained by legend. It seems that the swinish pig-god Kamapua'a had been in amorous pursuit of Pele. To distract him, Kapo, Pele's sister, threw her magically detachable vagina to O'ahu; its imprint remains on this spot. Notice that, as with Diamond Head, the higher southwestern walls reflect the direction of the trade winds when the crater formed. The garden inside mostly features xerophytic plants appropriate to the dry climate. Open daily sunrise to sunset. Allow 1.5 hours to explore the botanical gardens. Free.

After Kealahou Street, Kalaniana'ole Highway turns inland and climbs through a funnel-shaped valley between the edge of the Ko'olau Mountains and Makapu'u Point. On your right, halfway up, look for a turnoff to a paved road with a locked gate. You can park here and hike 1.4 miles to the road's end at the scenic ***Makapu'u Lighthouse*** at the eastern tip of the island. It's a great place to watch whales in winter.

You get a lesser version of the same view from the lookout farther ahead on the highway. Take a deep breath as you approach the top. More than half the windward coast unfolds before you, bordered by the bluest of ocean. From this side-on perspective, it's easy to trace the boundaries of the original 5,000-foot volcano that formed this half of the island. Instead of ending at the vertical wall of the windward cliffs, picture the Ko'olau ridges continuing to rise to a summit peak hovering somewhere above the present coastline and then descending roughly symmetrically on the other side. The line of islands dotting the coast offshore formed as rift eruptions along the outer flank of this now-vanished mountain.

Anchored in the blue waters closest to the lookout, Rabbit and Turtle Islands are the southernmost members of this chain of offshore islands. The larger of the two, Rabbit Island got its name from a rabbit farm that once flourished on its scrub-covered slopes. Appropriately, the island's shape resembles the profile of a giant rabbit's head swimming offshore. Walk a little way onto Makapu'u Head for a better view along the coast. Notice the many rounded boulders here, garlanded by tiny orange blossoms of 'ilima shrub. These are river stones. The hanging valley you just drove up was gouged by an ancient river that drained the slopes of the mountain that was.

The highway descends from the lookout to picturesque ***Makapu'u Beach.*** The waves here outdo even Sandy's and funnel into the cliff-ringed bay year-round. Surfers of all kinds come here, but inexperienced swimmers should stay out of the water. Look up to the sky to see the black *iwalani* ("bird of heaven") frigates that circle effortlessly above, watching for fish. These winged pirates often steal the catch from other birds. Trade winds running into the 1,000-foot wall of the Ko'olau cliffs create a constant updraft that hang gliders also can enjoy. Launching from the cliff top, these daring flyers have set endurance records at this spot.

Across the road from the beach park, ***Sea Life Park*** (800-259-2500; sea lifeparkhawaii.com) operates a popular Sea World–type attraction. Open daily 10 a.m. to 4 p.m. $44.99 general admission. The first show is at 10:15 a.m. Snorkeling can be good to the left of the pier just ahead.

A couple of miles farther on Kalaniana'ole Highway, you reach ***Waimanalo Beach,*** a magnificent strand that stretches more than 3 miles around the gentle curve of Waimanalo Bay. The city and state beach parks here are lined with ironwood trees, and both are popular with weekend picnickers. Waimanalo Beach does get waves, but an offshore reef provides some protection. Its shallow waters offer an ideal learning ground for bodysurfing and boogie boarding.

As you move north, the Ko'olau cliffs grow taller and more lush as they recede from the shoreline. The interior plains area of Waimanalo is mostly farms run by Hawaiian homesteaders. Signs advertising accommodations here are for horses. Turn up any country road, and you'll see pig farms, equestrian stables, and fruit and vegetable gardens galore.

If you call ahead, you can arrange to visit the ***Hawai'i Bonsai Culture Center,*** also known as Dragon Garden Nurseries (808-259-6886), open by appointment only. Home to almost 300 "elite bonsai" housed in exquisite ceramic pots with another 400 candidates in the making and 5,000 "pre-bonsai" under cultivation. The art of bonsai began more than 2,000 years ago in China, when Chinese physicians tired of constantly traveling to collect the healing herbs they needed from the mountain forests. What began as a practical method to cultivate a living pharmacy-in-miniature soon evolved into a sculptural art form. A wide variety of trees can be used, including elm, juniper, ficus, myrtle, and bougainvillea. Wires and other artifacts are used to curve the tree into the desired shape. It takes about five years to make a true bonsai, but the process can continue for decades, if not centuries. Founder Walter's former career was as an antiques dealer, and the furnishings in his warehouse office reflect this; they include a wooden one-panel carving that came from the back of a settee used by the emperor of China and his two wives in their summer palace. The back ended up with General MacArthur in Japan. (The other half of the settee became a coffee table used by William Randolph Hearst in Hearst Castle.)

Farther on, ***Honolulu Polo Club*** (honolulupolo.org) takes to the field on the inland side of the road every Sun at 3 p.m. from June to Oct. Gates open at 1 p.m. Admission is $10. As the highway continues, it skirts the green peaks of ***Mount Olomana*** ("forked mountain"). Rising 1,643 feet from flat surroundings, this daggerlike spire often splits the clouds.

On the other side of Olomana, Kalaniana'ole Highway runs into Kailua Road opposite Castle Hospital. A right turn takes you past ***Kawainui Marsh,*** a waterfowl sanctuary, into Kailua town. Kailua Road bends right at the town's main intersection, with Kuulei Road continuing straight ahead and Oneawa Street to the left.

Nature lovers should turn left onto Oneawa and continue about a mile before turning left onto Kaha Street (two streets before the canal). Park in the park at the end and follow the path that leads around to the right, across the canal, and onto the elevated ***Dike Trail*** that borders Kaiwainui Marsh. Tame mallard and Muscovy ducks beg for handouts as you leave the park. Once you reach the dike, you have an ideal perch from which to observe the rich birdlife that the marsh sustains. In the distance, a breathtaking panorama of green hills and ridges rises above the marshland, silhouetted in ascending tiers that climax with the towering wall of the Koʻolau pali. You can walk on the dike the full mile to Kailua Road, emerging just before the entrance to town.

Finally, back at the main intersection, bearing right on Kailua Road brings you to the ***Kailua Chamber of Commerce's visitor center*** (808-261-7997; kailuachamber.com), just ahead on the left in a remote section of the Kailua Shopping Center. There you can get information on other windward coast attractions. The center is staffed by volunteers Mon through Fri 10 a.m. to 4 p.m., and Sat til 2 p.m.

Those who just want to hit the beach should continue straight on Kuʻulei Road until you dead-end into Kalāheo Road, which runs along the coast. Turn right to get to ***Kailua Beach Park.*** Curving around from Mokapu Peninsula, Kailua Bay shelters its turquoise waters behind an outlying reef, where turtles are common. Flat (Popoia) Island floats offshore, but it's a long swim out. Sun worshipers delight in the fine white sand of Kailua Beach, and the onshore winds and calm seas make ideal learning conditions for windsurfing. But when the wind kicks up, the same onshore breezes turn the beach into a desert sandblast and whip the bay into a frothy mass of whitened chop. That's when Robby Naish, Kailua resident and 24-time world-champion windsurfer, rigs up. You can rent equipment or arrange lessons at ***Naish Hawaiʻi*** (naishsails.com), his shop on Hāmākua Drive (the first cross street as you enter town on Kailua Road), or at ***Kailua Beach Adventures*** (808-262-2555; kailuabeachadventures.com), near the intersection of Kailua Road and Kalāheo Avenue; both also do kite surfing and kayaks. When the wind is down, the windward coast is ideal for kayaking, as both Kailua and Kāneʻohe Bays have numerous islands and sandbars to paddle to. The view from the water looking back at the Koʻolau Mountains is unsurpassed. You can also rent equipment for kayaking from ***Twogood Kayaks*** (808-262-5656; 134B Hāmākua Dr.; twogoodkayaks.com).

If you continue east from Kailua Beach around the tip of Puʻu Halo Ridge, you enter Lanikai, a secluded residential area ringed by mountains and blessed with azure waters that beckon toward a distant pair of island peaks, the Moku Luas. Park and walk up any beach access path. If you come here at night during summer, you might see glow-in-the-dark plankton wash ashore, miniature phosphorescent specks that sparkle in the sand like fairy dust.

You can scale Kaiwi Ridge behind Lanikai for breathtaking coastal vistas. Turn up Kaelepulu Drive and pass the turnoff to the country club. The trail begins just before the entrance to the Bluestone Estates, starting from a driveway off to the left and running outside the wire fence of the estates. After the first 100 feet, you get on top of the ridge, and the views get better and better. You'll pass some military bunkers higher up. The ultimate panorama arrives with the second bunker about a half mile along.

On the other side of the Kailua–Ku'ulei Road divider, ***Casablanca*** (808-262-8196; 19 Hoolai St.), the second left as you enter town, belies its name with a cheerful blue exterior. Inside you'll find authentic Moroccan cuisine served Tues through Sat 6 to 8:30 p.m. Reservations are highly recommended. Expensive to investment-caliber.

Two more eateries await at the Kāne'ohe edge of Kailua Bay, if the bunker tours have given you an appetite. ***Nico's Kailua*** (808-263-3787; 970 N. Kalāheo Ave.; nicoskailua.com) is an upscale yet casual ranch house with nightly live music and a menu of savory seafood options, such as peppercorn swordfish and furikake pan-seared ahi, all of it hand-selected from the public auction in Honolulu each morning. Open Tues to Sat 11 a.m. to 9 p.m., and Sun from 3 to 9 p.m. Moderate to expensive. For low-key Korean home cooking, ***Willow Tree*** (808-254-1139) is a nice alternative, offering dishes like bi-bim-bap stir-fry, tofu stews, cold marinated chop chae glass noodles, and meat and fish jun fried in egg batter. Open Mon to Sat 11 a.m. to 8 p.m. Inexpensive to moderate.

To spend the night in Kailua, you can't beat the value offered by ***Kailua Beachside Cottages*** (808-261-1653; patskailua.com). Several units abut Kailua Beach Park (three have ocean views). The rentals range in price from $235 and upwards for an oceanfront unit right on the water. Three-night minimum stay. Over on Pilipu Place, ***'Ohana Beach House*** (airbnb.com) can sleep 10 in a deluxe 5-bedroom, 3-bath retreat that's less than 100 yards to the crystal clear waters of Kailua Beach. Plus a fully stacked kitchen and an outdoor shower! ***Paradise Bay Resort*** (808-239-5711; 47-039 Lihikai Dr.) offers a beautiful view of the Ko'olau Mountains and Kāne'ohe Bay. Rates from $152. ***Lanikai Beach Rentals*** (808-476-7145; lanikaibeachrentals.com) has the local bed-and-breakfast market pretty much cornered with almost a hundred listings in the area.

Backtrack on Kailua Road past Castle Hospital. Kailua Road turns into the Pali Highway as a mass of green mountains surround you. Mount Olomana juts out on the left, with the Oneawa Hills to the right. Straight ahead, the corrugated cliff line of the Ko'olau pali marches forward with Pu'u Konahuanui, the highest peak at 3,150 feet. To the right, the deeply notched V of Nu'uanu Pass stands out.

Those undeterred by Olomana's jagged profile can attempt the ascent from this side. The climb takes about 1.5 hours. The view is fabulous. To reach the start of the ***Olomana Trail*** from the highway, take the first left after the hospital (Auloa Road), then turn left again immediately and bear right after the bridge.

For an equally scenic, but less taxing trek to Maunawili Falls, continue a block farther on Auloa, bear left at the fork onto Maunawili Road, and continue until it ends at Kelewina Street. The trail meanders through 1.5 miles of lush tropical jungle that alternates between mango, kukui, banana, ginger, heliconia, (abandoned) coffee trees, and even some nice ridge views. You'll cross Maunawili Stream four times before ending at the swimming hole beneath the falls a short distance up the left fork of the stream. It takes less than an hour each way.

To call it a day, return to the Pali Highway and continue straight to climb over the mountain pass into town. Otherwise, to continue circling the island, turn right onto Kamehameha Highway, a mile farther up (at the opposite end of Auloa Road). This road cuts behind the Oneawa Hills to reach Kailua's next-door neighbor, Kāne'ohe.

Two miles off Kamehameha Highway, turn left at Luluku Road for a restful visit to ***Ho'omaluhia*** ("peaceful place") ***Botanical Garden*** (808-233-7323; honolulu.gov/parks/hbg). The road climbs into the lush Ko'olau foothills through banana farms at the edge of the park. Encompassing 400 acres of former farmland, the county's newest botanical park remains more of a forest reserve than a landscaped garden. The towering curtain of pali overhead creates a magnificent natural setting, while the 32-acre artificially created lake provides the flood protection buffer that led to the park's creation.

Stop at the visitor center a mile from the park entrance to pick up information on the park's offerings and take in some exhibits on Hawaiian ethnobotany. From here you can drive the 2 miles of winding road past endlessly varied vegetation, with views of Kāne'ohe Bay and the hypnotic presence of the pali above. For those willing to walk, a number of trails meander through the gardens. Various sections have been planted with specimens from Africa, India, tropical America, Polynesia, and Hawai'i. Ask the staff at the visitor center for free self-guiding pamphlets. The garden schedules a variety of walking tours, usually on weekends, as well as evening moon walks. Camping is allowed by advance permit Fri through Mon. Open daily 9 a.m. to 4 p.m.

After relaxing in Ho'omaluhia, those continuing onward have to make a difficult choice. Two different routes will take you north. If you like ocean views, stick with Kamehameha Highway. You'll wind through residential gardens, past stunning ocean vistas. You can stop at ***He'eia State Park*** (808-235-6509; heeiastatepark.org) at the beginning of the coastal stretch to learn some of the history of the area. The park itself juts onto Kealohi Point in the middle of Kāne'ohe Bay, the largest in the state. Coconut Island, the biggest of many offshore islands in view, appeared on television as *Gilligan's Island.* To the right of the point, you can see He'eia Fishpond, one of dozens of former aquaculture ponds the Hawaiians of old cultivated along Kāne'ohe Bay.

If you prefer the majesty of mountains, turn left at the main intersection at the end of the mall. From here, Likelike Highway and H-3 tunnel back to Honolulu. The latter, a highly controversial trans-Koʻolauan route, is something of an eyesore, rising on stilts above the misty depths of Ha'ikū Valley. To stay on the windward side, take the next right onto Kahekili Highway to continue north in the shadow of the Nuʻuanu pali. A left turn onto Ha'ikū Road, at the fourth traffic light, leads you to Ha'ikū Gardens, where ***Hale'iwa Joe's Seafood Grill*** (808-247-6671; haleiwajoes.com) serves pleasant, open-air dinners for moderate prices. Open nightly 4 to 9 p.m. Not far from here are the ***Ha'ikū Stairs,*** a heart-stopping, near-vertical ascent up the face of the *pali* to a 2,800-foot summit. The stairs were originally built by the US Coast Guard to maintain a ridgetop radio antenna. Unfortunately, legal problems have kept the city from opening them to the public. Call (808) 523-5866 to see if the situation has changed. (It hasn't.)

Farther along Kahekili Highway, you'll pass the ***Valley of the Temples,*** an interdenominational mortuary park and the late Ferdinand Marcos's temporary resting place. The Byodo-In Temple at the back is particularly picturesque. Token admission charge.

The two highways reunite at Kahaluʻu Fishpond. To visit the secluded ***Gallery & Gardens*** (808-239-8146), at a nearby mountain retreat, take the second left onto Wailehua Road, then bear right onto Lamaʻula Road and head up the hill. More than 15 years of botanical plantings enhance the already beautiful natural setting, with tropical flowers to smell and seasonal fruits to taste. Try the "magic fruit" (sepotia berry), which turns sour tastes to sweet. A garden map and labeled markers help tell you what's what. Birdsongs from the aviary and wind chimes provide soothing melodies. The architecturally intriguing, Japanese-style gallery blends well with the beautiful artwork it contains. Open Sat by appointment only.

Around the next ridge are the Waiāhole and Waikāne Valleys, havens for rural Hawaiians, with backyard taro and sweet potato patches. The demise of Oʻahu's sugar industry has freed up irrigation water for these traditional crops, which used to be diverted to the leeward side of the island. The highway leaves the valleys to slope along hills where cattle graze. As you begin to curve around the northern edge of Kāneʻohe Bay beneath the imposing Kanehoalani Ridge, look through the forest on the right-hand side to catch glimpses of ***Moli'i Fishpond,*** the only pond on the island in continuous operation since ancient times. Its harvest includes mullet, moi, and tilapia.

The fishpond belongs to ***Kualoa Ranch*** (808-237-7321; kualoa.com), which also owns the land inland of the highway. The ranch's history dates from the early Hawaiian monarchy, and it has remained under the original family ownership. The crumbled remains of a stone smokestack visible from the highway mark the site of a former mill built during owner Gerrit Judd's short-lived attempt at running a sugar plantation prior to ranching. The ranch has since diversified into several ventures, of which aquaculture is only one. It runs a range of tourism activities aimed at the adventure traveler, from ATV rides to a tour of Hollywood filming locations (in films such as *Kong: Skull Island*, *Mighty Joe Young*, and *50 First Dates*), as well as horseback riding, naturally.

At the far rim of the bay, pause for a scenic break at ***Kualoa Beach Park.*** Wiliwili trees, flaming red in late winter, line the entry road. A narrow sandy beach with adequate swimming borders the long grassy park. The views back around the bay and inland along the Koʻolau wall are breathtaking. Note the turtle profile of Kāneʻohe Peninsula—the other side of the bay—now well in the distance. Gates are locked at night here for secure camping.

Kualoa has a long history as one of the most sacred spots on the island. Oʻahu chieftains brought their children here to learn the necessary arts with which to rule. Passing canoes had to lower their sails out of respect. Offshore, Chinaman's Hat bears a close resemblance to the headgear of Chinese immigrants. Hawaiians call the island Mokoliʻi, meaning "little lizard," because their legend says the island is really the tail of a dragon that the goddess Hiʻiaka slew during her trip back from Kauaʻi. People do wade out to the island at low tide, but you need footwear to walk on the sharp coral, and you may have to swim some of the way. It's about 500 yards out.

Continue along the highway past the smokestack of an 1864 sugar mill. As you round the tip of Kanehoalani Ridge, brace yourself, because in the miles ahead your eyes will struggle with divided loyalties. On the ocean side, a series of picturesque bays beckons. In sunlight, these shallow lagoons shimmer like turquoise, sapphire, and emerald. On the mountain side, you peer into virgin green valleys bordered by steep cliffs. You'll want a third eye to negotiate the bends in the road! A string of hamlets spaces out the scenery. You can stop at any of the beach parks along the way for a dip. During the week, your only company may be a few fishermen casting bamboo poles or throw-nets from the reef.

About 3 miles along, the road curves around the deep indentation of Kahana Bay. Pass some overgrown fishponds and turn left into ***Ahupuaʻa ʻO Kahana State Park*** (808-237-7766; dlnr.hawaii.gov/dsp/parks/oahu/ahupuaa-o-kahana-state-park). Extending inland the length of the valley, this is the only publicly owned *ahupuaʻa* in the state. Ahupuaʻa were the old wedge-shaped land sections that ran from the top of the mountains down to the sea, making each community self-contained in the raw materials needed for everyday life. Wetland taro and a working fishpond help do so today. Kahana Valley still contains about 31 families, whom the state has incorporated into a "living history" program to teach schoolchildren about the valley's heritage and demonstrate traditional crafts. You can turn up the road to the park orientation office and chat with the staff, if anyone is in. If not, obtain a trail map for a valley hike from a rack outside, or take a swim in the stream mouth or ocean. The many tall trees with red-tinged leaves around here are known as false *kamani,* or tropical almonds. Free.

Past Kahana Bay, next to the 21-mile marker, you'll see the ruins of Lanakila Church next to its replacement. If you turn up Hau'ula Homestead Road and continue a few hundred yards straight ahead on the unpaved M'aakua Road, you'll reach the heads of two alternative trails. You can choose from a scenic 2.5-mile loop up the ridges on either side of the valley on the Hau'ula and Papali Trails.

Past the 20-mile point, ***Pounders Beach*** has a lovely setting and bodysurfing waves that live up to its name. Next comes the overwhelmingly Mormon town of Lā'ie. You'll see the thatched roofs of the ***Polynesian Cultural Center*** (808-293-3333 or 800-367-7060; polynesia.com) run by the church on your left. Authentically re-created villages from the major Polynesian islands are "populated" by Polynesian students attending the nearby Hawai'i campus of Brigham Young University. Various traditional crafts are demonstrated, from coconut husking to lauhala weaving. It's fairly educational but definitely geared to tourists. The full-day package with the luau dinner is priced at $269.95. Open Mon through Sat 12:30 to 9 p.m. If you visit the center, consider returning at 7:30 p.m. for the Polynesian revue, which has a cast of more than 100 performers. The Ali'i Luau package, which includes admission to the center, *luau* dinner, and show, is $189.95.

Past the cultural center, opposite Lā'ie Shopping Center, turn right onto Anemoku Street and then right again onto Naupaka Street to the tip of ***Lā'ie Point.*** A magnificent view awaits at the end of this narrow peninsula. You can see the green mass of the Ko'olau Mountains stretching as far back as Kāne'ohe. Waves crash against the many islets offshore, one of which has a natural *puka* (hole) gouged through its middle. Anglers cast their lines into the teal-colored sea. As you continue north on the highway, gaze back along the stately drive that leads to the ***Mormon Temple,*** the self-styled "Taj Mahal of the Pacific."

Malaekahana State Recreation Area, a mile farther, enjoys a truly idyllic location. Deep deposits of white sand are piled along this mile-wide bay. The steep hills backing the beach offer shade from beautifully diverse forest. If you wade a few hundred yards through the shallow waters, you'll reach ***Goat Island,*** a seabird sanctuary. You can explore the island perimeter with views along the coast, but don't disturb the nesting sites in the center.

The Kahuku section of the beach, accessed by a separate entrance, has rustic "cabins" available for rent, maintained by Malaekahana Beach Campground & Kama'aina Kids. Most are plantation suites, with a bath, that sleep four people. They rent for $117.65, and campsites cost $9.41 per person. Plantation hale, with no electricity, rent for $58.82. Gates lock at 7 p.m. Call (808) 674-7715 for information.

Beyond Malaekahana you enter Kahuku, a former plantation town largely settled by Samoans. The ***Kahuku Sugar Mill,*** which closed in 1971, still stands in the center of town. You can ogle its innards in a free self-guided tour. The flywheels, crushers, clarifiers, and myriad connecting pipes are all color coded in bright paint. When operational, the mill could churn through 50 tons of fresh cane an hour, burning the leftover bagasse for power. Gift shops and restaurants crowd the machinery in the factory center, taking the edge off the heavy industrial atmosphere.

Just ahead, the Tanaka Plantation Store complex is home to ***The Only Show in Town*** (808-293-1295)—for antiques, that is. The tiny store is crammed with antique bottles, vintage campaign buttons, classic aloha shirts, and much more. Open daily 12:30 to 5:30 p.m. The highway continues around the northern tip of the island, but it runs inland and you hardly notice the bend. Windmills on the ridge above the highway make up an experimental energy project.

North Shore and Central O'ahu

Surfing was born in the Hawaiian Islands, and the North Shore of O'ahu remains the supreme venue for the sport. Winter surf hits the north and west shores of all the islands, but Nature and her handmaiden, Geology, have conspired to make O'ahu stand apart. All along this coast, incoming ocean swells, having traveled thousands of miles from storms off Alaska, reach the beaches and rise to form the most perfect tubes and the biggest breakers in the world—and the ultimate surfing challenge.

Winter surf typically lasts from November to April, during which time the professional surfing circuit descends in force. If your visit should overlap with a major competition, the spectacle is worth taking in. The hype and hoopla of big-time surfing—with its corporate sponsors, rock music, and bikini beach contests—electrify these normally sedate beaches. Competitors are judged on the size of the waves they catch, the length of their ride, and the "radicalness" of their maneuvers.

Most of the contests are held at Sunset Beach, which stretches for more than 2 miles of wide, steeply sloping sand. The different surfing breaks all along have such names as Gas Chambers, Velzyland, and Banzai Pipeline. WARNING: At any place along the North Shore, when it's pumping, the waves can snap surfboards and spines. The backwash and undercurrent of these breakers can hold you underwater for up to 5 minutes. Needless to say, you shouldn't even walk near the shoreline. Even when the surf is down, currents pose a danger all winter.

The ***Banzai Pipeline*** has a special notoriety as the home of the "world's most dangerous wave." As big swells rise from the deep into the sudden shallow of a coral shelf, their acceleration causes the top part of the wave to curl over into a tunnel of breaking fury that combs over waters only inches deep and filled with razor-sharp coral. On days when the surf swells above 15 feet, you will find but a handful of diehards willing to brave the "tube ride" off Banzai reef. To watch them cut and slash their way in, stop at 'Ehukai Beach Park, the second beach park along Kamehameha Highway, opposite the elementary school. The Pipeline breaks just to the left of the park.

By the way, you should know that Hawaiian wave heights are measured from behind. Because the water in front of a rising wave drops an equal amount, the waves will appear twice as high from the beach. It's quite a show.

In total contrast, during the summer, Sunset Beach, like all of the North Shore, transforms into a glassy lake. The expanses of white sand broaden as the beach reclaims sand carved away by the winter surf. At the end of the day, the placid waters reflect the unforgettable sunsets that are the beach's namesake.

Beyond Sunset Beach the coastline turns rocky. Few people surf here, but ***Pūpūkea Beach Park*** has its own attraction. The waters offshore are a marine conservation zone. During calm summer months, ***Shark's Cove***, at the north end of the park, offers especially breathtaking underwater terrain, flush with fish, seaweed, coral, and lava cave formations. Don't worry: "Shark's" is a misnomer.

To the left of the cove is the site of a former rock quarry. An ancient coral reef has been excavated, leaving a horseshoe-shaped outer wall enclosing a shallow lagoon. During winter, huge waves flood the walls; as the water level inside rises, a swift current draining out to the cove can sweep the unwary off their feet. The sound and spray can be mesmerizing, but stay out of the water at these times.

Turn left up Pūpūkea Road at the Foodland supermarket, just past the quarry. Climb a half mile uphill and take the turnoff on the right for ***Pu'u o Mahuka Heiau.*** Several speed bumps later, you reach O'ahu's largest ancient temple. The low, terraced walls slope in sections down a grassy field overlooking the angled coastline. In 1793 three British sailors from one of Captain George Vancouver's ships ended up as sacrifices here. Walk to the far side of the heiau to peer down into lush Waimea Valley and Waimea Bay. On the other side of the valley, cane fields cover the ridge plateaus.

Across the highway from "three tables" reef at the southern edge of Pūpūkea Beach Park is ***Backpackers Vacation Inn & Hostel*** (808-638-7838; backpackershawaii.com). It was started by the late Mark Foo, a local boy turned surfing legend. When Mark left to paddle his surfboard around the world, his sister Sharlynn took over operations and has expanded them considerably. In addition to a hostel bunk, you can rent private rooms, cottages, and apartments in the area—some are actually beachfront. For a unique experience, ask to stay in "plantation village," a lane of tiny clapboard homes formerly used by immigrant cane workers. The colorfully painted cottages offer a range of lodging options, from dorm beds for $35 to private bedrooms in a shared cabin with kitchens for $90. Oceanfront studio apartments rent from $180. Enjoy airy lodging at ***Ke Iki Beach Bungalows*** (866-638-8229; keikibeach.com), and choose between beachfront views or garden views (many with a minimum 30-day stay). Most units come with kitchens, BBQ areas, and gardens.

South of Pūpūkea, ***Saints Peter & Paul Mission*** has a tall tower and an unusual origin. The church building was erected as a rock-crushing plant during the construction of the highway and only later was converted to a mill of a more spiritual nature. After passing the mission, the highway curves around the mouth of world-famous ***Waimea Bay.*** The island's highest ridable surf breaks on the bay's outer bowl, with monster combers that sometimes tower more than 30 feet and can flood the highway. Expert bodysurfers tackle an equally daunting shore break. In the summer, calm returns as crystalline waters mirror the beauty of Waimea's picture-postcard setting. Then you can join locals in diving off "the rock" on the left side of the bay.

Past Waimea Bay, Kamehameha Highway continues through dairy pastures past hidden surfing beaches. About 2 miles along, just after the highway's second junction with the Pohakuloa beach loop, you'll reach an unobstructed view of the shoreline at ***Laniakea Beach,*** a tiny surfing cove that is also one of the best places in the islands to see *honu* (green sea turtles). Weighing up to 400 pounds, these gentle giants feed on seaweed offshore, and usually one or two of them can be found basking on the sand, to the delight of visitors. (Look—but don't touch.) Honu can live up to 70 years, reaching sexual maturity only in their mid-20s or later. Their green color comes from the fat tissue stored inside their bodies. These turtles migrate throughout the Hawaiian Islands, nesting primarily at the remote French Frigate Shoals, 560 miles northwest of O'ahu. Nesting females deposit 100 or more ping-pong-ball–sized eggs in a sand pit that they dig and then cover with their flippers. The temperature of the eggs during incubation determines the gender of the hatchlings, with lower temperatures producing males. You can distinguish mature males from females by their much longer, wider tails.

A few miles farther down the highway, Hale'iwa sits at the crook in the angle formed by the coastline. The highway now bypasses the town, but it's worth a stop. Hale'iwa took its name from an early mission outpost here. It grew into a popular seaside resort when the Hale'iwa Hotel opened at the end of the railroad line in 1899. Things quieted down after the war, but hippies and surfers brought the town back to life in the 1960s, and artists have made up the most recent wave of invaders. Many of the original plantation shops remain along the highway, nestled in between modern plazas full of boutiques. The town's commercial district stretches almost a mile.

If you didn't get to see surfing on the beaches, you might stop before the bridge at the historic ***Surf N Sea*** (808-637-3483 or 800-899-SURF; surfnsea.com), the biggest of the many surf shops in town. Continuous surfing videos inside offer a vicarious substitute. This, coupled with an impressive collection of vintage surfboards (including legendary waterman Duke Kahanamoku's 1968 fiberglass board), nostalgic photos of pro surfers, and surf artifacts, means Surf N Sea has to double as the area's surf repository after the heartbreaking closure of the North Shore Surf Museum in the North Shore Marketplace. All the top brands of boards and designer beachwear are also here, blazing with neon color. You can buy or rent all types of water-sport equipment, as well as intriguing accessories such as Mr. Zog's Sex Wax (for your surfboard). Open daily from 9 a.m. to 7 p.m.

The attractive ***Lili'uokalani Church,*** on the Kamehameha Highway, was founded in 1832 and rebuilt in 1961. Queen Lili'uokalani attended services here during her frequent vacations in Hale'iwa. In 1892 she presented the church with an elaborate seven-dial clock that Queen Victoria had given her. Instead of numerals, the hour hand points to the 12 letters in Lili'uokalani's name. You can still see it ticking today.

Nearby, ***Matsumoto's*** perpetuates another longtime Hale'iwa tradition. This 40-plus-year-old plantation store cranks out the most famous shave ice on the island, packed into paper cones. Choose from a range of tropical fruit–flavored cane syrups to sweeten your ice or ask for a "rainbow" of any three. Local connoisseurs eat theirs with sweet azuki beans or ice cream on the bottom.

For a more substantive repast, visit ***Cafe Hale'iwa*** (808-637-5516) near the south edge of town, owned by Duncan Campbell, a noted surfboard designer. The surfing posters on the wall reflect the clientele who come by for an early-morning feed before hitting the waves. The food's great, but the catch is that they close at 2 p.m. Open Mon, Fri, Sat, and Sun from 8 a.m. Farther down, ***Kua 'Aina Sandwich*** (808-637-6067) serves a hefty grilled mahimahi sandwich and some of the best burgers in the state. Open daily 11 a.m. to 8 p.m. Or, if it's a caffeine fix you crave, visit ***Coffee Gallery*** (808-824-0368), in the North Shore

Marketplace. Order from an impressive collection of coffees grown on four different Hawaiian islands, and sip your java in a très funky painted/mosaic lānai. Open daily from 8:30 a.m. to 6 p.m. If you want a sunset dinner to remember, double back to ***Hale'iwa Beach House*** (808-637-3435; haleiwabeachhouse.com) or ***Hale'iwa Joe's*** (808-637-8005; haleiwajoes.com), across from the harbor near the entrance to town. The menu at both features fresh seafood as well as other items. But the real feast is the view as the sun drops behind Ka'ena Point, bathing the water and harbor sailboats in a rosy glow. Beach House upstairs has the better view, but Joe's has a more varied, tastier menu, and nicer ambience. Beach House is open daily 11 a.m. to 8 p.m. Expensive. Joe's is open Mon to Sun 4:30 to 9 p.m., and for additional brunch hours on Sun from 10 a.m. to 2 p.m. Moderate.

Hale'iwa has no shortage of galleries in which to browse. In the center of town, ***Wyland's Gallery*** (808-637-8729; signaturegalleries.com) has the biggest name, though the artist's most famous works don't fit in his gallery. Robert Wyland paints giant murals of humpback whales to promote marine conservation (and himself). Open daily 11 a.m. to 4:30 p.m. Inside, you'll find works in various media by a range of artists revolving around a basic ocean theme. For eclectic, island-inspired women's clothing and jewelry, check out ***Silver Moon Emporium*** (808-637-7710; silvermoonhawaii.blogspot.com) in the North Shore Marketplace. Open daily from 10 a.m. to 5 p.m.

After disporting yourself in Hale'iwa, continue straight on Kaukonahua Road, past the rotary, following the sign to Mokulē'ia. About a half mile farther, on your right, you'll pass the ***Oils of Aloha*** (808-637-5620; oilsofaloha.com), set up in a former movie house. The company is most notable for producing a unique line of cosmetics made from kukui nuts. The kukui, a relative of the castor bean, is Hawai'i's state tree, whose versatile nuts had many uses in ancient times. The word *kukui* literally means "light"; the oil-rich nuts are known in English as candlenuts and were used as just that. The meat from the kukui nut also served as a potent laxative, and the shells were polished for jewelry. Kukui oil has useful skin care properties, and the company concentrates on this angle. A kukui tree grows right outside the company building, which unfortunately is not open to visitors.

Continue on Kaukonahua Road until it runs into Farrington Highway. Turn right, and then, a half mile along, exit right from the rotary onto Goodale Avenue to enter Waialua. Waialua is Hale'iwa's less glamorous twin across the bay. While Hale'iwa basked in the limelight as a resort/recreation center, Waialua schlepped along as a working sugar town. Now that sugar has ended, its fortunes are uncertain, although a portion of former sugar land has been replanted with coffee.

Because Waialua lies off the highway, few people come here. You'll see some vintage clapboard homes and the red-dirt–stained remains of the former mill.

Return to Farrington Highway and continue west through the cane fields. ***Mokulē'ia Beach Park*** arrives a few miles farther along, but the wide sandy beach stretches for miles on either side, and unmarked turnoffs from the highway allow you to find secluded spots. Swimming can be hazardous, especially during winter surf. If you're here on a Sunday afternoon from late Apr to June or Oct to early Dec, stop by the polo grounds to watch a chukker or two. Matches start at 2 p.m. If you think beaches and polo are too down-to-earth, continue on to Dillingham Airfield, where ***Honolulu Soaring*** (808-637-0207; honolulu soaring.com) takes off daily 10 a.m. to 5:30 p.m. Rides ranging from 10 to 60 minutes are available; prices range from $85 to $275 per person. Call for more details and for reservations.

Mokulē'ia has a couple of accommodation options for those who want to spend more time on the North Shore. Spartan quarters can be had at ***Camp Mokulē'ia*** (808-637-6241), which offers lodging on a beachfront lot for $150 per couple and tent camping for $15 per person.

The road ends at the start of ***Ka'ena Point State Park*** (808-587-0300; dlnr.hawaii.gov/dsp/parks/oahu/kaena-point-state-park), a unique coastal habitat of endangered wildlife and plants. Ka'ena Point lies 2 miles farther, but the walk from the Wai'anae side is more scenic. Backtrack on Farrington Highway and continue on as the highway begins to climb onto the Leilehua Plateau between O'ahu's two mountain ranges. At a certain elevation you emerge from some trees, and, voilà, something's changed. Instead of tall cane grass walling you in, you find that your gaze stretches unobstructed across miles of spiky pineapple rows. James Dole introduced Hawai'i's first commercial pineapples in nearby Wahiawā. Unlike sugarcane, the plants are not native, but thanks to Dole, they soon became an international symbol of the islands. You can still see heavily garbed workers stooped over the fields, planting and harvesting by hand.

Four miles along the highway, take the right fork 2 more miles to Del Monte's ***Pineapple Variety Garden*** and ***Dole Plantation*** (808-621-8408; doleplantation.com), which has its own touristy visitor center, angling 1 mile back on Kamehameha Highway (Route 99). It includes the "world's largest maze," planted from hibiscus and other tropical flower bushes and forming the pattern of guess what fruit? There's also a "pineapple train" ride and a plantation garden tour. Open daily 9:30 a.m. to 5 p.m. $9.25 admission charge for the maze, $13.75 for the train ride, and $8 for the garden tour. While you're here, check out the free pineapple-cutting demonstrations held every half hour from 10 a.m. to 4 p.m.

Continue on a half mile past the garden in the same direction and turn right at the traffic light onto an unpaved plantation road. A few hundred yards into the pineapple fields, you'll reach a tight ring of eucalyptus and palm trees encircling a cluster of largish boulders. Hawaiians called this curious oasis ***Kūkaniloko,*** and women of royal descent came here to give birth so that their children would be born with the necessary *mana* to rule as kings and queens. If you look to the Wai'anae Mountains in the distance, you can trace a profile of the *wahine hāpai* (pregnant woman) to the right of the V-shaped Kolekole Pass. Kamehameha I wanted to send his sacred wife, Keōpūolani, to O'ahu to bear his first child at these birth stones, but she took sick and couldn't leave the Big Island. Some say Liholiho's early death at age 26 sprang from this inauspicious birth.

Continue on the same road, and you'll cross Lake Wilson, an artificial reservoir used for sugar irrigation, on your way into Wahiawā town. Wahiawā grew up as a plantation town, but its lifeblood today rests in the mammoth Schofield Army Barracks nearby, as the countless fast-food and chain restaurants attest. For a quiet picnic spot, turn left up California Avenue, the second cross street, and go about a half mile to the ***Wahiawā Botanical Garden*** (808-621-7321; honolulu.gov/parks/hbg). Sugar planters began the 27-acre garden as an experimental forest growth in the 1920s. The mature trees now rise majestically from the slopes of a sunken ravine, leavened with ferns, palms, and other tropical plants. Open daily 9 a.m. to 4 p.m. Free.

South of town you can loop back around the lake to Schofield Barracks. Across the highway from the base, stop at ***The Pub at Kemo'o Farm*** (808-621-1835; 1718 Wilikina Dr.; facebook.com/kemoopub) for a touch of local nostalgia. The farm got its start in 1916. It evolved from a farmers' market to an ice-cream parlor before capitalizing on the first liquor license issued after Prohibition.

Today three different bars on the premises carry on the tradition with 30 kinds of beer on tap and 45 more bottled. Live music is featured with your choice of rock 'n' roll, island style/reggae, and country music. Mon through Thurs 3 p.m. to midnight, and Fri through Sun 11 a.m. to 2 p.m.

To crown your central O'ahu visit in spectacular fashion, enter the barracks and ask the guard to direct you to ***Kolekole Pass.*** (But you need to have base access.) Lyman or Trimble Road will put you on the main road up. You can see the deep notch in the mountains as you drive up. About 5 miles from the entry gate, you reach a parking area at the top. On your right, a tall white cross stands on a nearby hill facing back toward central O'ahu. A short hike in the opposite direction brings you to a spectacular overlook onto the Lualualei Valley on the Wai'anae Coast. It's less panoramic than the Nu'uanu Pali, but at 1,720 feet, the

Magic and Mythology

The ancient Hawaiians believed in systems of order, one requiring balance between gods, themselves, and the environment. They believed that everything in nature had connections with a spiritual component that people needed to respect. Canoe builders would say a prayer before cutting down giant koa trees. Fishermen would leave offerings at fishing shrines to thank the ocean gods for the ocean's bounty. So it was with *pōhaku,* the Hawaiian word for stone or rock.

Even today in this modern age, stories abound of farmers who clear giant boulders from their fields only to return the next morning and find the stones back in their original positions. Hawaiians explain this by saying that the pōhaku "did not want to be moved." Certain pōhaku were inhabited by powerful spirits whose influence men and women could elicit through ritual offerings. For example, barren women would seek out fertility stones known to exist on each island. Moloka'i's phallic rock is the most famous example. Travelers crossing dangerous terrain would leave offerings at guardian stones, such as the giant boulder at Kolekole Pass. The sacred birth stones at Wahiawā's Kūkaniloko provide yet another well-known example.

Wahiawā is home to another set of somewhat more obscure pōhaku, the so-called Wahiawā Healing Stones, which have their own curious history. Although the stones have an ancient lineage, the origins of their healing powers remain shrouded in mystery. The stones came to the public's attention in the 1920s after some well-publicized miracles and for a time attracted mass pilgrimages, which continued until the outbreak of World War II.

Although largely forgotten since then, the stones continue to attract visitors from diverse religious backgrounds. Housed in a makeshift cinder-block shrine of sorts, the stones had a statue of the Virgin Mary placed beside them for many years.

More recently, the stones have been adopted by a group of local Hindus, who perceive one of the stones to be a Shiva *lingam* and another to bear the likeness of the elephant god Ganesh. The Hindu community has built a newer marble structure around the stones and visit on the morning of the third Sunday of each month to conduct *pooja,* a ritual ceremony.

cliff-top perch is just as exhilarating, and you may well have it all to yourself. Watch your footing, though; no handrails here!

On the way to the overlook, you pass ***Kolekole Stone,*** a massive boulder along the trail. An eroded basin on the top of the stone, drained by curious troughlike ridges, has given rise to some latter-day legends about gruesome human sacrifices. Actually, Hawaiian executioners dispatched their victims without bloodshed; a mangled corpse was not a fitting offering to place before the gods. An older, perhaps more comforting tradition holds that the stone is inhabited by a guardian spirit that keeps watch over travelers crossing this lonely mountain pass. Kolekole Road continues over and down to the other side of the pass, but only military types can drive it.

Departing from the outskirts of Wahiawā and Schofield, the H-2 Freeway whisks you back to Honolulu. As you leave the central plateau, you see mountains on both sides, pineapple fields, steep gulches, and then suddenly the blue lakes of Pearl Harbor stretched out below.

Leeward O'ahu

Having done Honolulu and the "circle island" drives, it's time to "head 'Ewa," which is the local version of "go west" toward the 'Ewa District. Honolulu itself is moving this way. Having spread all the way east to Hawai'i Kai, Honolulu has shifted course to ooze into the "second city" of Leeward O'ahu. Few tourists make it out here. Few rain clouds blow this way, either. That's what *leeward* means: sheltered from the wind. All this land was originally scrubland, too arid even to support cattle. But underground, where the folds of the island's two volcanoes had overlapped, millions of gallons of freshwater waited to be tapped. In 1877 a canny Scotsman named James Campbell bought 40,000 acres of the "worthless" land and successfully dug a series of artesian springs that made him an instant millionaire. The sugarcane that once covered these lands is being replaced by diversified crops, although the biggest new crop is housing projects.

To the west of the modern Pearl City metropolis, the town of Waipahu grew up as a separate plantation community. To explore, take the Waipahu exit from H-1 and get onto Farrington Highway. About 1.5 miles along, turn up Waipahu Depot Road toward the sugar mill.

At the mill, turn left onto Waipahu Road, and just ahead on your left is ***Hawai'i's Plantation Village*** (808-677-0110; hawaiiplantationvillage.org), surrounded by taro fields. You enter the park through a "time tunnel" to get to an authentically re-created 19th-century plantation camp inside. You can then wander through life-size dwellings representative of the many different ethnic groups that worked Hawaii's plantations.

The garden organizers have acquired many unique items, such as an antique *tofu-ya,* used to grind bean curd in Kahuku, and the Inari Shinto Shrine, rescued from destruction in Mō'ili'ili. Some of the displays offer hands-on learning; others provide fascinating vignettes. Learn the folklore that guided immigrant women facing childbirth in a foreign land. Master a few phrases of pidgin, the linguistic potpourri by which the different immigrant groups communicated. Inspect Filipino fish traps and Chinese herbal medicines. These are the ethnic threads that contribute to Hawai'i's rich social tapestry today. Open Mon through Sat 9 a.m. to 2 p.m. for guided tours only. Tickets must be purchased online ahead of time; $17 admission.

Continue on Waipahu Street to Kunia Road (Route 750). A right turn here will get you back on H-1. If it's a Sunday, you may want to turn left for a historic train ride. Take Fort Weaver Road 2.5 miles, then turn right onto Renton and drive until it ends at the 'Ewa station of the ***Hawaiian Railway Society*** (808-681-5461; hawaiianrailway.com). An old navy diesel locomotive hauls passenger cars on a 90-minute round-trip every Sat and Sun at noon and 3 p.m. Along the way you'll hear the story of O'ahu's railway and plantation history. Adult admission is $18. Reserve ahead of time to travel in style on the "parlor car," offered the second Sun of the month, for $35.

As you drive along the southern slopes of the Wai'anae Mountains, you gaze over a vast sunken plain that starts with 'Ewa cane fields and housing subdivisions and extends across Pearl Harbor all the way to Diamond Head. All this land rests on an enormous coral shelf formed at a time of higher sea levels. H-1 peters out as it rounds the bend of the mountains. Continue northwest on Farrington Highway to sidle up the shoreline of the Wai'anae (or leeward) Coast.

Sheltered behind O'ahu's tallest mountains, this dry coastal stretch provides refuge to Hawaiians clinging to a traditional rural lifestyle. Many are homestead farmers who received land grants through the Hawaiian Homelands Act. Almost everyone keeps a few pigs or chickens in their backyard, and subsistence fishing remains an important source of food. Extended families still gather for weekends on the beach.

Most tourists are put off by the region's lingering bad reputation. On the whole, you'll find the people here possessing the aloha spirit as anywhere else on O'ahu. Unfortunately, some residents (justifiably) feel that this openhearted, giving nature has left them dispossessed of their land, and now they want to keep what's left to themselves. The Wai'anae Coast has scenery rivaling the most beautiful in Hawai'i, with miles of coral beach backed by rugged mountains that open into rural valleys. It would be a shame to miss. If you exercise common sense with valuables, maintain a low-key profile, and stay away from groups of drinking locals, you should have no problems here. WARNING: As with the North Shore, beaches along this coast are exposed to winter surf; swimming is often unsafe.

Farrington Highway meets the coast at the Kahe Point Power Plant. Ignore this monstrosity and instead gaze ahead to the majestic sweep of the Wai'anae Coast spread before you. The rocky headland of Maili Point dominates the arcing shoreline, with taller mountains silhouetted beyond. The beach park on your left bears the unofficial name Tracks because of the railroad tracks from former sugar trains that parallel the highway. Continue north past other beach parks through the town of Nānākuli, where you can peer into the remote depths of Nānākuli Valley. Near the north edge of town, you pass the ***Samoan Assembly of God,*** only one of the many picturesque churches along the way.

Beyond Nānākuli, Farrington Highway skirts the Pu'u o Hulu Kai, the headland at Maili Point, to reach the town of Maili. Here you get a frontal view into the staggering expanse of ***Lualualei Valley,*** the ancestral fire pit of the Wai'anae Range. Two tall, red antennae near the mouth of the valley and a whole farm of smaller structures behind it make up the Navcom Radio Transmitting Facility, for which the navy has sequestered most of the valley floor. Pu'u Maili'ili, another headland, walls in Maili's northern limits. Consider turning onto Maili'ili Road at the edge of town to circle inland around the hill past some homestead plots. You'll see dairy farms, vegetable plots, and more stunning valley scenery. Two miles in, turn left onto Puhawai Road and left again onto Hālona. This will take you past some curious Quonset hut homes and back onto Lualualei Homestead Road to rejoin the coast.

Cross Farrington Road and continue straight onto Kaneilio Point at the southern tip of ***Pokai Bay Beach Park.*** Walk out on the peninsula through a coconut grove to ***Kū'ilioloa Heiau*** at the end. Built on three neatly terraced platforms, the heiau enjoys sweeping views along the coast. Pokai Beach, the beautiful sandy strip curving north behind the breakwater, offers the only safe winter swimming on the Wai'anae Coast. It serves as a popular canoe-launching site. The harbor here is also home port to the *e'ala,* a double-hulled Polynesian voyaging canoe, used to educate local Hawaiians about their seafaring heritage. Inland, the rear wall of Wai'anae Valley rises to Mount Ka'ala, the 4,020-foot pinnacle of O'ahu.

As far as restaurant selection goes, the Wai'anae Coast features drive-ins galore, a handful of Chinese chop sueys, and not much else. This would be a good place to acquire a taste for a plate lunch, which dominates the menus here. Try the ***L&L Drive In*** (808-696-7989), near the entrance to the beach park, for a wide selection of barbecue, fried, and sautéed entrees served with the standard two scoops of rice and macaroni salad. Open daily 7:30 a.m. to 9:30 p.m. To enjoy something completely different, try ***Organic Farm & Café*** (808-696-2655; kahumana.org), serving organic cuisine pulled from five different campuses and farm communities spanning 50 acres in nearby Lualuakei Valley. The farmers comprise a healthy collective that's also an inclusive community made up of youth, people with disabilities, and homeless families.

Continue north to Makaha, the next town and valley on Farrington Highway. The name *Makaha* means "fierce," referring to a clan of highway robbers who long terrorized passersby. The fiercest predator today is resort development.

Loop back along the north side of the Makaha Valley on Ki'i Drive to ***Makaha Beach Park*** on the coast, where pro surfing began. Spectators flock to this wide crescent of steeply sloping sand every year for the Buffalo Big Board Surfing Classic in March. Competitors ride vintage "tankers"—long boards up to 12 feet in length and weighing more than 80 pounds—as did the surfers of old.

Two miles farther, look for ***Kaneana Cave*** on the right side of the highway. The cave opening faces north, so you have to look behind you as you drive. Carved by wave action during a time of raised sea levels, the narrow, high ceiling of the cave slants 450 feet into the mountain flank. The cave's legendary denizen was a shark-man named Nanaue, who used his dual nature to prey on unsuspecting victims in the area.

Just ahead the mountains recede, opening into the amphitheatric bowl of ***Mākua Valley.*** This seemingly pristine valley harbors a deadly secret. The military has long used the area as an artillery range, and unexploded shells litter the valley floor. Across the highway, Mākua Beach continues the pearly white lining of the Wai'anae Coast. Farther up the road, the beach at ***Yokohama Bay*** marks the end of the highway. You can sift for tiny puka shells in the sand.

From here a rugged jeep trail continues 2 miles to Ka'ena Point. The Wai'anae Coast curves majestically into view, stretching back as far as Kepuhi Point. On the way, you pass more caves. Look also for *'ilima,* a native ground cover that thrives along the roadside. The tiny, pale-orange blossoms of the plant are O'ahu's official flower. Threaded by the hundreds, they form an unusual crepe-paper lei. Pregnant women used to chew the buds to stimulate their muscles during childbirth. Waves breaking near the point sometimes reach 40 feet during winter, a height unequaled anywhere else on Hawaiian shores. During calmer summer months, the tide pools can be fun to explore.

Ka'ena Point itself is a narrow, sand-dune peninsula protruding from the tapered ridge of the Wai'anae mountain range. This westernmost promontory was another legendary "jumping off" place for the souls of O'ahu's fallen warriors. A Coast Guard observation tower stands at the far end of the point. If you climb the swaying ladder to the top, you can get an exquisite view of this desolate, windswept peninsula. Incoming waves, angling from both sides of the point, sweep across a string of rocks offshore. On a clear evening, this is also a great spot to watch for the elusive "green flash" that occurs when the sun sets over a cloudless ocean horizon. Shield your gaze until the instant when the last puddle of molten sun oozes out of view. Instead of orange sun, a brilliant spot of green light will shine for the briefest moment.

Places to Stay on O'ahu

HALE'IWA

Backpackers Vacation Inn & Hostel
59-788 Kamehameha Hwy.
(808) 638-7838
backpackershawaii.com
Options range from dorm beds from $35 to oceanfront studios from $180.

HONOLULU

Mānoa Valley Inn
2001 Vancouver Dr.
(808) 947-6019
manoavalleyinn.com
This three-story mansion exudes a wonderful historic air. Rates start at $220.

Moana Surfrider, a Westin Resort and Spa
2365 Kalākaua Ave.
(808) 922-3111
moana-surfrider.com
Expensive and ultra-luxurious but definitely a place you'll remember. Built in 1901, it has been restored to perfection, and the Old World charm remains intact. Rooms from $399.

Royal Hawaiian Hotel
2259 Kalākaua Ave.
(808) 923-7311 or (866) 716-8110
royal-hawaiian.com
Although not exactly "off the beaten path," this pink palace is a landmark in Waikīkī, and its historical grandeur offers a unique type of luxury. Rooms from $469.

Surfjack Hotel & Swim Club
412 Lewers St.
(808) 923-8882
surfjack.com
A 1960s-era throwback boutique hotel in Waikīkī offering 112 bungalows and suites. Rates start at $221.

KAILUA

Kailua Beachside Cottages
204 S. Kalāheo Ave.
(808) 261-1653
patskailua.com
Offers quiet retreats on the scenic windward side. Rates start at $235.

Lanikai Beach Rentals
1277 Mokulua Dr.
(808) 261-7895 or (808) 476-7195
lanikaibeachrentals.com
A booking agency that offers a variety of budget accommodations, including some beachfront.

Places to Eat on O'ahu

HALE'IWA

Hale'iwa Joe's Seafood Grill
66-011 Kamehameha Hwy.
(808) 637-8005
haleiwajoes.com
Bring sunset serenity to your North Shore sojourn. Moderate to expensive.

HONOLULU

Fête
2 N. Hotel St.
(808) 369-1390
fetehawaii.com
New American cuisine in a red-brick corner upscale eatery. Moderate to expensive.

Hau Tree
2863 Kalākaua Ave.
(808) 921-7066
Located in the lobby of the Kaimana Beach Hotel, this open-air restaurant features a beachfront location with unsurpassed views. It's situated at the far east end of Waikīkī. Moderate.

Highway Inn
680 Ala Moana Blvd. #105
(808) 954-4955
myhighwayinn.com
Authentic Hawaiian favorites, like *lau lau* and *kalua* pig, served on big plates. Inexpensive to moderate.

Maple Garden
909 Isenberg St.
(808) 941-6641
Specializes in northern Chinese dishes and Szechuan cuisine. Moderate.

Merriman's Honolulu
1108 Auahi St. #108
merrimanshawaii.com
Lively and stylish eatery specializing in farm-to-table fare. Moderate to expensive.

Roy's
6600 Kalaniana'ole Hwy.
(808) 396-7697
roysrestaurant.com
Inventive East-West cooking in a raucous Hawai'i Kai eatery. Expensive to investment-caliber.

Senia
75 N. Hotel St.
(808) 200-5412
restaurantsenia.com
Award-winning local fusion cuisine, primarily served in rotating tasting menus, served at the "chef's counter." Investment-caliber.

Uncle Bo's Pūpū Bar & Grill
559 Kapahulu Ave.
(808) 735-8310
unclebosrestaurant.com
Pūpū platters, dumplings, and fresh seafood in a youthful, hip atmosphere. Moderate to expensive.

Moloka'i

Located midway between the bustle of Honolulu and Lahaina, the island of Moloka'i clings to a seclusion that has long been its birthright. With a legacy of ancient sorcery and the stigma of its leper colony, Moloka'i's image as the "Lonely Island" was until recently reinforced by a declining population. Moloka'i likes to bill itself as the most Hawaiian of the visitable islands; almost half of its inhabitants share Native Hawaiian ancestry. It contains only one resort and a handful of smaller hotels. There are no traffic lights or shopping malls on the island. Instead, Moloka'i offers a laid-back atmosphere, a lingering glimpse of old Hawai'i, and a low-key tourist industry conducted with a genuine warmth that has given Moloka'i its new nickname, "the Friendly Isle."

Moloka'i stretches 38 miles from end to end but no more than 10 miles in width. Three main highways partition its interior, making exploration fairly simple. The road east, Route 45, is named for Kamehameha V. Running to the west, Route 46 goes by the name of Maunaloa Highway. Branching north from the Maunaloa Highway, Route 47 provides the only access to the island's North Shore. Moloka'i hides much of its scenery within a remote interior, inaccessible by road and often

MOLOKA'I

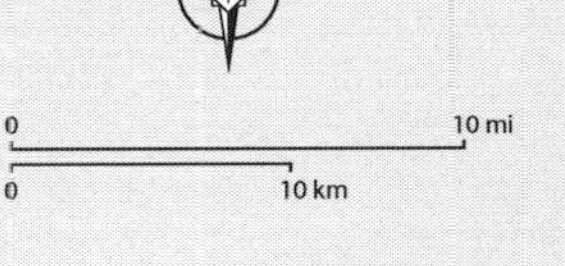
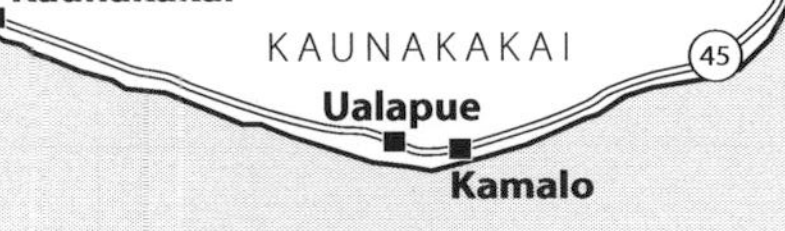
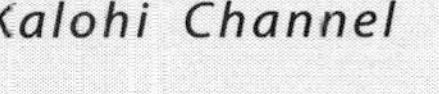
PACIFIC OCEAN
CENTRAL MOLOKA'I
AND KALAUPAPA
Ka'iwi
Channel
Moloka'i
Ranch
THE
WEST END
Maunaloa
46
48
Ho'olehua
47
46
Kaunakakai
Makanalua
Kalaupapa
Kalawao
Kamakou
KAUNAKAKAI
Ualapue
Kamalo
Hālawa
Valley
45
Pailolo
Channel
Kalohi Channel
N
0
10 mi
0
10 km

islandfacts

Population: 7,345 (2010)

Principal city: Kaunakakai

Flower: White kukui blossom

Color: Green

private property to boot. Most visitors will be content to spend a day or so exploring the roadside attractions in each direction. ***Alamo*** (808-597-6381; alamo.com) rents cars at the airport; reserve early for weekends. For a less corporate alternative, ***Island Kine Auto Rental*** (808-553-3535; molokai-car-rental.com) has a mixed fleet of quality used cars, which they rent out of Kaunakakai town. Free airport pickup and personalized advice are included. Island Kine also rents a limited number of four-wheel-drive vehicles. For those who want to see more, ***Moloka'i Action Adventures*** (808-558-8184) has a number of guiding services, including hiking. Their specialty is snorkeling, though, as you can be guided through Moloka'i's reef environment, roust an octopus for you to play with, and, if you wish, spear fish for your dinner.

While planning your stay, contact the ***Moloka'i Visitor Association*** (808-553-5221; 800-800-6367; gohawaii.com/islands/molokai).

Kaunakakai and Things East

Begin your sightseeing on Moloka'i by heading into town. Located midway along the island's south shore just off Route 45, the single-block business district of Kaunakakai comes as close to urban clutter as Moloka'i gets. Walking the strip along Ala Malama, the main drag, will put the rest of the island in perspective and get you in the right frame of mind.

You will find most of the island's nonhotel restaurants here. All offer down-home local cooking at budget prices. Dining atmosphere not included. ***Big Daddy's*** (808-553-5841) offers a selection of authentic Filipino dishes, such as pork adobo, as well as traditional Hawaiian lau lau. Open every day 9 a.m. to 5 p.m. ***Kanemitsu Bakery*** (808-553-5855) produces a repertoire of island-flavored breads famous throughout the state. The bakery is open Sat, Sun, Mon, and Wed 6 a.m. to 2 p.m., and Thurs and Fri 6 a.m. to noon.

Nearby, ***Paddlers Restaurant and Bar*** (808-553-3300; paddlersrestaurant.com) serves casual sandwiches, signature burgers, and steaks, plus dancing most nights. Open Tues to Sat 11 a.m. to 8 p.m. Moderate. ***Maka's Korner*** (808-553-8058) offers local saimin, plates, all-day pancakes, and popular mahimahi. Sit at picnic tables or the small counter. Open Mon to Fri 7 a.m. to 8:30 p.m., and Sat and Sun 8 a.m. to 2 p.m. Inexpensive.

Meanwhile, across the highway on Wharf Road, ***Moloka'i Pizza Cafe*** (808-553-3288) fills another vital niche in the island repertoire; they also serve pasta, fish, and chicken. Open Sun to Wed 11 a.m. to 9 p.m., and Fri and Sat 11 a.m. to 10 p.m. ***Paddler's Inn*** (808-553-3350; 10 Mohala St.) features standard American fare. The restaurant is open daily except Sun and Mon, 11 a.m. to 8 p.m. Live entertainment on the weekends.

While in town, be sure to stop by the ***Moloka'i Art from the Heart*** (808-553-8018) on Ala Malama Ave.; it showcases the work of more than 130 Moloka'i artists, who turn out everything from handmade *pahu* (drums) to Hawaiian quilts. Open Mon through Fri 10 a.m. to 5 p.m., and Sat 9 a.m. to 2 p.m.

And if you're here on a Saturday, don't miss the early-morning farmers' market for fresh produce, arts and crafts, and plenty of local color. It's held at the corner of Ala Malama Avenue and Kamehameha V Highway.

At the end of Ala Malama, across from the baseball diamond, stands the ***Mitchell Pauole Center*** (808-553-3204), where you can get camping permits to tent in county parks. For state camping permits for Pālā'au State Park, contact the Maui office (808-984-8109) or call the park caretaker directly (808-567-6083).

It is worth driving to the end of ***Kaunakakai Wharf,*** where barges unload supplies from O'ahu but no longer head out laden with pineapples. The wharf extends almost a half mile offshore due to the shallow mudflats along this coast. As you savor the view of Moloka'i's southern shoreline and its three neighbors across the Kalohi Channel, you'll see why Mark Twain called Hawai'i "the loveliest fleet of islands anchored in any ocean." From left to right are Maui, Kaho'olawe, and Lāna'i. You may also see O'ahu rising in the distance above West Moloka'i. At the base of the wharf, the stone foundation behind the canoe club was the site of King Kamehameha V's summer retreat.

Geography of Moloka'i

The fifth largest of the Hawaiian Islands, Moloka'i has an elongated shape that represents the union of two volcanoes with a third. Reaching a summit of 4,970 feet at Kamakou, the mountains of eastern Moloka'i are much taller and greener than those in arid western Moloka'i, whose highest point barely tops 1,000 feet. The cliffs along Moloka'i's largely inaccessible northern coast, from Kalaupapa east, soar to more than 3,000 feet in elevation, rising directly above the ocean. They are held to be the tallest sea cliffs in the world.

The ***Hawai'i Ocean Project*** (808-280-0873; hawaiioceanproject.com), whose mission is to educate visitors about Hawai'i's marine life and ecosystem, does so through ocean excursions, such as whale-watching and dolphin snorkeling tours, dinner cruises, and more. Moderate to expensive.

About 1.5 miles east of Kaunakakai, the Polynesian rooftops of the ***Hotel Moloka'i*** (877-553-5347; hotelmolokai.com) appear on a cluster of low-rise, open-air bungalows facing the ocean. The simple but recently refurbished rooms here start at $190.50, with rates rising to $258 for ocean views and $216.75 for kitchenettes. The real charmer of the property is the hotel restaurant, ***Hiro's 'Ohana Grill*** (808-658-1757). Decorated in the nostalgic style of old Hawai'i, the dining area spreads across a large oceanfront lānai with carved tiki pillars, rattan paneling, and lava-rock sidewalls. Plop yourself down in an oversize patio chair and gaze out through the palm trees to views across the Pailolo Channel. At night, tiki torches flicker in the ocean breeze as locals gather to hear live music from island performers. Menu choices here embrace an eclectic mix of steak, pastas, and seafood, with lunchtime sandwich choices. Preparations are simple but tasty, and prices moderate. Open daily except Monday 11:30 a.m. to 8:30 p.m., with a limited menu from 5:30 to 8:30 p.m.

Four miles east of town is ***One Ali'i Beach Park.*** The beach here is still muddy and flat, but it's a nice spot with coconut trees and the remains of a fishpond. These shallow, protected waters were ideal for such ponds, and more than 60 of them ring the coastline, some dating from as early as the 13th century. The Hawaiians were the only Polynesian people to practice aquaculture, building saltwater enclosures as big as football fields from coral and lava rock, with intricate sluice gates. Some of the ponds have been restored, and aquaculture is again becoming an industry on the island, restoring Moloka'i's reputation as the "land of the fat fish." Another thing being restored on the island is its population of native geese. If you call in advance, a visit to nearby ***Nene O Moloka'i*** (808-553-5992) will put you face to feather with Hawai'i's state bird. This captive propagation site also has a collection of native plants and displays on migratory birds, but the stars of the show are the nene, "the most endangered goose in the world." Open weekday mornings at 9 a.m. by appointment; call a week in advance.

For an aerial view, take the next left up to ***Kawela Plantation,*** a hillside housing development. As you climb, vistas extend along the south shore, revealing the outlines of several more fishponds fronting the deep cobalt blue of the channel seas.

The road ahead is rich in Hawaiian history in other ways as well. Kamehameha I landed on this coast near Kawela with an invasion force of canoes that was said to stretch more than 4 miles. Slingshot stones from the fierce battle still litter the scrub-covered foothills. The conqueror's prize was a child bride. Keōpūolani, one of Maui's highest-born chieftesses, had fled during Kamehameha's invasion of that island. By capturing and later marrying her, Kamehameha assured his heirs of the mana necessary to rule.

hawai'itrivia

The water reservoir in Kualapu'u holds 1.4 billion gallons and is the largest rubber-lined reservoir in the world.

Just after the 10-mile marker, where the highway veers sharply to the left, take a dirt road turnoff to the right and drive out to the abandoned wharf at Kamalo. Absorb the views of the coast and the islands offshore, then gaze up at the mountains behind you. ***Mount Kamakou,*** the highest peak directly above, forms the pinnacle of the island at 4,961 feet.

Around the bend from ***Kamalo Wharf,*** on the ocean side, stands ***St. Joseph's Church.*** Built in 1876 by Father Damien, the celebrated priest of Kalaupapa, it is the second-oldest church on the island. An often lei-draped statue of Damien greets visitors in front of the chapel. The door is rarely locked, so be sure to take a peek inside.

Continuing east on Kamehameha V Highway, you will pass (in addition to many more fishponds) a wooden sign on the right indicating the site of ***Smith and Bronte's Landing.*** In 1927 these pioneering aviators abruptly ended the first civilian flight from the United States mainland to Honolulu when they ran

Brief History of Moloka'i

While ancient Moloka'i has legends of powerful sorcerers that protected the island from marauders, the people of Moloka'i were skilled in other arts as well. This island is considered by some to be the birthplace of the hula (along with Hawai'i Island), and both men and women excel at this traditional dance form. Aquaculture was also practiced here to a greater extent than on other islands. Fishponds all along the south shore of the island ensured a reliable source of sustenance.

Modern history has been less kind to the island. The establishment of a leprosy settlement at Kalaupapa in 1864 made the island a byword for the horrors of that disease. The closing of the pineapple plantations on the island in recent decades has left a legacy of economic hardship. Today almost 20 percent of the island's population remains unemployed, the highest rate in the state. Moloka'i residents remain stoic about their island's future. Having seen the social and economic dislocation caused by development on the neighboring islands, many prefer to keep Moloka'i the way it is.

out of fuel here after 25 hours in the air. Both survived the crash. A few miles farther on, a large wooden cross on the left marks the barnlike ruins of ***Kalua'aha Church.*** This first outpost of Christianity on Moloka'i was built by the original missionary congregation in 1844. The mission's location here reflects the original population center around the lusher east and north coasts. Two hundred yards farther, Damien's second church, ***Our Lady of Seven Sorrows,*** built in 1874, stands in much better repair at mile 14.6.

Moloka'i's eastern shore remains the population center for island bed-and-breakfasts and vacation rentals. Most of these keep fairly full, so book early. One of the nicest was originally built in 1927: ***Banyan Tree Bed and Breakfast Retreat Center*** (808-757-3171), which is down the road across from St. Joseph's Church. Seven cottages and suites can be rented separately or together. There's also a shared pool and Jacuzzi. Prices start at $190. Other rental options on the east end include ***Dunbar Beachfront Cottages*** (808-336-0761; molokaibeachfrontcottages.com) and ***Moloka'i Vacation Properties*** (molokai-vacation-rental.net). Both have several properties, some oceanfront. Finally, ***Pu'u o Hoku Ranch*** (808-558-8109; puuohoku.com) rents both a two- and a four-bedroom cottage, about 25 miles out, surrounded by acres of open ranch land and forest, both with great hillside views. The simply furnished but fully equipped rentals go for decent rates. Please direct all inquiries to info@puuohoku.com.

Past the 15-mile marker, the highway passes a giant mango grove. Reputedly the world's largest, the patch features 32 different varieties of this prolific fruit tree spread across 49 acres. It was planted in the 1930s by Hawaiian Sugar as an experimental venture.

On the other side of the highway lies the entrance to ***'Ili'iliōpae Heiau,*** Moloka'i's most impressive ancient temple. Look for the gate immediately after the bridge. Don your safari camouflage (and mosquito repellent) and strike out on the jeep trail into the jungle. At the end of the road, cross the streambed. Hidden in the vegetation on the far side, 'Ili'iliōpae makes a dramatic and mysterious appearance. Legend—backed by geology—holds that the lava rock used in this heiau originated in Wailau Valley on the island's North Shore and was carried across the mountains by a human chain.

The heiau is much bigger than it appears, extending almost 300 feet across the valley. It was once even larger, but according to legend a flood washed away half the structure. The story goes that a father whose sons had been sacrificed by an evil kahuna as temple offerings had petitioned the shark god for vengeance. The floodwaters carried the evil priest and his attendants out into the ocean, where a gathering of sharks waited. What you see today is just the foundation of a once elaborately designed complex that used to be visible for miles. Unfortunately, it has become quite overgrown in recent years.

Continuing on the highway, you'll pass the ***Mana'e Goodz n Grindz*** (808-558-8498), your last chance to stop for supplies or take-out lunch. The store is open Mon through Fri 8 a.m. to 3:30 p.m. Closed Wed. As you drive onward, look for the ubiquitous *hala* (pandanus) trees, whose knotted fruits are often called "tourist pineapples." The tuft-tipped "nuts" made serviceable paintbrushes, and the lauhala, the long fibrous leaves, were woven into mats. The trees along this shoreline are said to derive from an ancestral tree whose stiltlike roots upset the fire goddess Pele's canoe. The enraged goddess tore the tree to bits, sending splinters flying in every direction. They took root in the fertile soil. Of course, almost every rock in Hawai'i has its story to tell, but here on Moloka'i, more people remember.

As you continue east, the highway narrows to a single lane, and the scenery grows more and more dramatic as the road curves around one spectacular cove after another. The tiny beaches nestled along the coast, beginning at the 20-mile marker, are all superb for snorkeling or fishing, but they can get rough, especially in winter. ***Kumimi Beach,*** at 21 miles, has facilities. From here you get the first glimpse of an offshore island used for bombing practice in World War II. The West Maui Mountains loom across ***Pailolo Channel*** as if it were a mere puddle. The highway then makes an abrupt turn inland, winding around—and through—some interesting rock formations before climbing to the lush pastures of ***Pu'u o Hoku Ranch*** (808-558-8109; puuohoku.com). In addition to its bread-and-butter cattle business, the ranch has diversified into niche crops such as *'awa* (also known as kava), a Polynesian medicinal plant and mild stimulant used in traditional therapeutic, ceremonial (and sometimes recreational) rituals and now a popular ingredient for alternative medicines.

On top of the hill, just seaward of the ranch headquarters, the sacred ***Lanikāula Kukui Grove*** grows on the spot where a powerful 16th-century kahuna lies buried. Lanikāula's influence pervaded Hawai'i and made Moloka'i, an island dedicated to spiritual pursuits, off-limits to warfare. Lanikāula died as a result of being betrayed by a visiting kahuna from Lāna'i. His sons planted these light green kukui trees to conceal their father's final resting place. Moloka'i's isolation continued in the 17th century, belligerently enforced by the Kalaipahoa, whose magic poisonwood led other islands to give Moloka'i a wide berth. As these legends testify, Moloka'i's "Lonely Island" reputation long predated leprosy. You can feel some of that loneliness today as you approach the North Shore. Once populous, it is now largely deserted due to lack of road access.

Somehow, after leaving the main ranch, the highway manages to lurch around even wilder turns, and the vistas across lush canyons leading to the ocean become ever more stunning. Just as the scenery reaches its climax, a wide turn allows space to pull over and absorb your first lingering view into ***Hālawa Valley.*** A pair of waterfalls topple over cliffs at the back of the steep-walled valley. Hālawa Stream descends from there through a thousand shades of green to emerge at an estuary at the mouth of a horseshoe-shaped bay complete with black-sand beach. As soon as you can tear yourself away from the lookout, maneuver the last hairpin turns to the valley floor, where you can enjoy Hālawa up close.

One of the oldest settled valleys in Hawai'i, ***Hālawa*** continued to support a thriving community that supplied most of the island's taro long after the more remote North Shore valleys had been deserted. Then tragedy struck, beginning with a 1946 tidal wave that devastated the valley. Today only a handful of die-hards remain in this Shangri-la. Some have begun to farm taro again, as well as tropical flowers and fruit. Unfortunately, valley residents are now claiming that the main hiking trail to the waterfalls passes through their private property and are demanding that visitors pay to take a guided tour. For the time being, there appears no alternative. Call ***Halawa Valley Falls Cultural Hike*** (808-542-1855; halawavalleymolokai.com) to reserve. The trail to the falls begins at the dirt road leading into the valley, past the photogenic green Hālawa Church. It takes an hour or two of hiking to reach ***Moa'ula Falls,*** the lower of the two falls visible from the lookout. Hawaiians used to drop a ti leaf in the pool below before swimming to see if the *mo'o* lizard for whom the falls are named was prowling underwater. The cautious of mind can continue up the streambed to the larger ***Hipuapua Falls*** and bathe in its pool, sans mo'o.

There are showers back at the park pavilion to wash off any mud collected on your descent, and the bay itself stays sufficiently sheltered to permit swimming in all but the roughest weather. Camping at the pavilion is not permitted, but Pu'u o Hoku Ranch allows tenters on its land by the south shore of the bay. Campers can obtain a permit at the Pu'u o Hoku Ranch office (808-558-8109).

Beyond Hālawa, inaccessible by land, begins the spectacular Moloka'i North Shore, where a 1,750-foot waterfall (the state's highest) topples from the slopes of the world's highest sea cliffs. The stormy weather and winter surf that pummel this rugged coastline are such that even boat traffic to the North Shore is largely restricted to the summer months.

Central Moloka'i and Kalaupapa

One and a half miles west of Kaunakakai, the hundreds of coconut trees swaying in the ocean breezes make up ***Kapuāiwa Grove,*** a royal coconut grove planted for Kamehameha V (whose nickname was Kapuāiwa, "mysterious taboo") on the site of seven sacred ponds. It was once much larger, but adjacent construction, an encroaching coastline, and basic neglect have all taken their toll. Unfortunately, the site is closed to the public now—maybe for risk of falling coconuts.

Strung like a cordon against temptation, eight different congregations of Moloka'i worshippers gather on Sunday at ***Church Row*** across the street. Any denomination with Hawaiian members can build here. Some of the services are still conducted in Hawaiian, and visitors are welcome. Locals boast that the only traffic jams on the island occur here on Sunday morning.

After Kapuāiwa, the highway climbs inland past a plumeria flower farm (808-553-3391; molokaiplumerias.com). Just shy of the 4-mile mark (a half mile before the junction between Routes 46 and 47 and immediately preceding the white concrete bridge), an unmarked forest preserve road on the right leads the intrepid explorer 10 miles through the island's lush interior to the ***Waikolu Lookout.*** The road quickly becomes unpaved and in all but the driest weather will require a four-wheel-drive vehicle. Ignore the many turnoffs to smaller hunting trails.

About 9 miles in, you pass a famous ***sandalwood pit,*** dug in the shape of a ship's hold to measure an exact cargo of the fragrant wood for export to China. Run as an exclusive monopoly of Kamehameha I, the business exchanged a full cargo of sandalwood for the brig that carried it. The king amassed a fair-sized fleet in this fashion. You aren't likely to see any sandalwood near the pit today, or anywhere else in Hawai'i, either. After Kamehameha's death, greedy chieftains inherited the franchise and led long forays into the mountains, eventually harvesting Hawai'i's sandalwood to virtual extinction. Some credit the tree's demise to commoners who, tired of being forced on these expeditions away from their fields and fishing, deliberately pulled out saplings by the roots.

> **hawai'itrivia**
>
> The first Hawaiian fossils were discovered on Moloka'i, lodged in sandstone at the Mo'omomi Dunes.

A mile farther, the road ends at a picture-perfect view of ***Waikolu*** ("three waters") ***Valley,*** one of the three major valleys of Moloka'i's virtually inaccessible North Shore. Stretched out 3,000 feet below, furrowed by waterfalls and carpeted in lush vegetation, this valley supplies much of the island's water. Try to arrive in the morning before the clouds move in. Beyond Waikolu lies the entrance to the 2,774-acre ***Kamakou Preserve,*** a fragile parcel of native rain forest managed by the Nature Conservancy of Hawai'i. The preserve protects more than 250 plant species of which at least 219 are found nowhere else in the world. You can hike along a boardwalk trail through Pepeopae Bog to an overlook into Pelekunu Valley, yet another inaccessible North Shore valley. The stunted, rain-drenched native vegetation in this summit "cloud forest" makes the trip one of Moloka'i's most interesting experiences. The only problem is getting there. Be sure to call the ***Nature Conservancy*** (808-537-4508; nature.org) office in Kualapu'u before entering the preserve because the area is subject to violent weather changes. If possible, contact them months in advance to reserve a spot on either of their all-day excursions into the preserves at Kamakou and Mo'omomi, a 92-acre coastal ecosystem and a nesting site for the endangered green sea turtle. The excursions are staged monthly and are offered for the cost of a donation.

To get to ***Kualapu'u,*** take the turnoff north on Route 47 and head uphill 2 miles until the intersection with Farrington Highway (Route 48). The plantation village of Kualapu'u stretches to the left, behind the now-derelict pineapple factory on the corner. On the right, across the road from the factory, is the former headquarters building for Del Monte Pineapple. Kualapu'u's claim to fame rests in its reservoir, which houses irrigation water piped from the rain-drenched North Shore via a 5-mile tunnel bored through the mountains. You can dine here in the renovated ***Kualapu'u Cookhouse*** (808-567-9655). The country Hawaiian decor complements the tasty, local American specialties (burgers, steak, and seafood) served here at moderate to expensive prices. Open Mon 9 a.m. to 2 p.m., and Tues through Sat 9 a.m. to 8 p.m.

Head west on Farrington Highway and enter Ho'olehua, a larger community engaged in diversified agriculture. In 1921, after Congress passed the Hawaiian Homelands Act, the homestead program began here on Moloka'i. At first Hawaiian farmers struggled on the tiny lots they received. Most ended up leasing their land to the pineapple companies. Since pineapple's demise in 1982 and with today's better capital and water allocation, the homestead program is at last reaping some successes.

After passing the island's high school, turn right up Lihi Pali Drive and look for the sign outside ***Purdy's Nut Farm*** (808-567-6601; molokai-aloha.com/macnuts). Visit this 5-acre orchard on Hawaiian homestead land Mon through Fri 9:30 a.m. to 3:30 p.m., and Sat 10 a.m. to 2 p.m.; you can also visit Sat and Sun by appointment. One of the Purdys will tell you everything you want to know about macadamia-nut farming and provide hands-on demonstrations. You can also try or buy their home-roasted nuts, which taste much better than the commercially packaged version.

Speaking of nuts, while in Ho'olehua, you might also take advantage of the unique ***"post-a-nut"*** service offered by the local post office (808-567-6144). Postmaster Gary Lam keeps a supply of coconuts on hand that await your inscription with a felt marker pen to mail as mementos to friends and family back home. All you have to pay is postage (around $12 to $20 for a coconut). Gary stocks his basket with unhusked brown nuts. Green coconuts contain water and are thus much heavier. Both are edible if you strip off the outer husk and crack the inner nut. The post office is located at the corner of Farrington Highway and Pu'u Pele'ula. Open Mon through Fri 8:30 a.m. to noon and 12:30 to 4 p.m.

hawai'itrivia

Meyer Sugar Mill on Moloka'i was built in 1878; it is the oldest mill still standing in Hawai'i.

Farrington Highway turns to dirt a couple of miles outside town, but the road is usually in good condition. If you're game, follow it as far west as you can go to beautiful ***Mo'omomi Beach.*** It's popular with locals for unofficial camping. Turnoffs along the way lead to other nice locales; the whole coastline is studded with tiny strands of deserted beaches hidden between rocky outcrops. The land west of Mo'omomi, Keonelele, "the flying sands," belongs to the Nature Conservancy and consists of windswept sand dunes covered with native vegetation. Entrance by road requires permission, but you can follow a coastal trail on foot from Mo'omomi to take in the rugged isolation of the terrain. The first Hawaiian fossils were found lodged in sandstone here, and the cliffside sea caves harbor ancient burial sites.

Return to Kualapu'u and continue north on Route 47. About 2 miles up the road, a wooden signpost announces the ***Moloka'i Museum & Cultural Center*** (808-567-6436) on the left. One of the first sugar mills in the islands and the oldest left standing, the ***Meyer Sugar Mill,*** the museum's principal attraction, has been restored to working order. Rudolf Meyer left his native Hamburg to seek his fortune in the California Gold Rush. His ship detoured in the Pacific, however, and he ended up taking a surveying position on Moloka'i during the Hawaiian kingdom's land reform of 1848. Meyer married a Hawaiian chieftess and stayed on as an overseer, managing what has become Moloka'i Ranch, while wearing many different hats as a government official. His venture into sugar, beginning in 1878, was never entirely successful.

Almost all the original machinery of the mill—a mule-driven crusher, copper clarifiers, redwood evaporating pans—survives in working condition. The adjacent cultural center focuses on Hawaiian crafts, including lauhala weaving, woodcarving, lei stringing, and quilting. While on the premises, take the time to inspect the Meyer family cemetery nearby and unwind in its shade and solitude.

Priapic Geology

Precontact Hawaiians believed various stones were inhabited by spirits and held magical powers. Among the more famous of these stones is Moloka'i's Phallic Rock, located in Pālā'au State Park. The legend is that the male fertility god Nanahoa lived nearby and was caught staring at a beautiful young girl who was admiring her own reflection in a pool. Nanahoa's wife, Kawahuna, saw her husband leering and in a storm of jealousy attacked the young girl by yanking on her hair. Nanahoa became outraged in turn and struck his wife, who rolled over a nearby cliff and turned to stone. Nanahoa also turned to stone, appropriately enough, some might say, in a phallic shape. According to legend, he still sits there today. Barren women make the pilgrimage to this rock, where it's said if they spend the night and pray for fertility, they could be blessed with a child.

There was once a female stone (the wife) that stood next to the male. As the legend suggests, this stone has since fallen down the hillside.

Visible on the hill above the parking area is the original Meyer family home. It has a reputation for being haunted and is closed to the public. Meyer Sugar Mill receives visitors Mon and Tues 10 a.m. to 2 p.m. Admission is $5.

Farther uphill through green fields of grazing bovines, you reach the former home of ***Kalae Stables,*** the home base for the once "world-famous Moloka'i mule ride" to ***Kalaupapa*** ("flat leaf") ***Peninsula.*** Unfortunately, this tour is no longer in operation, but descent to Kalaupapa began at the UNAUTHORIZED PERSONS KEEP OUT sign just ahead, where the highway turns left. The trail drops 1,600 feet over a mere 3 miles and has 26 switchbacks. Manuel Farinha, a Portuguese immigrant, carved the trail while hanging from ropes over the cliff; but it's named for Jack London, who descended it in 1907 and wrote of his experience. (There's a lesson here.) The views along the trail by foot are predictably stunning, but you need to make special arrangements to enter the Kalaupapa settlement (keep reading for details). At the time of this book's publication, access to the Kalaupapa Trail was restricted to residents and visitors with approved permits issued by the Hawaii State Department of Heath. To avoid fines or, worse, being arrested, please refer to the Superintendent's Compendium, 36 CFR1.5(a)(1). Check nps.gov/kala/planyourvisit/conditions.htm regularly for situation updates.

Continue by car into Pālā'au State Park (808-567-6083; nps.gov/kala/planyourvisit) around the corner. The road ends at the official ***Kalaupapa Overlook,*** where you can take in the unearthly view of the leaflike peninsula jutting out into the Pacific from beneath the impossibly steep cliffs of Moloka'i's North Shore. From the same parking lot you can take a short hike through ironwood

Land of Powerful Prayer

Ancient Hawaiian name chants record that Moloka'i was known in olden times as Moloka'i *pule o'o,* "land of powerful prayer." Legends of sorcery on the island abound. Some of this magic was benevolent. The island's most powerful kahuna, Lanikāula, became famous throughout Hawai'i for his wisdom and learning. Chiefs from all of the islands would travel to his home on the island's east end to seek his counsel. During Lanikāula's lifetime, Moloka'i became a spiritual haven, off-limits to warfare. Unfortunately, Lanikāula was betrayed by a visiting fellow kahuna from Lāna'i named Kawelo, who stole a stool sample from the sage and used it to work a magic death-by-constipation on his erstwhile colleague.

The west side of the island became equally famous for a more ferocious style of magic. Discovered in a dream by the chief Kaneiakama, a miraculous stand of trees suddenly appeared on the slopes of Maunaloa, into which the Kalaipahoa, or "poisonwood gods," entered. Birds flying over the trees would drop dead out of the sky, and chips sent flying from an ax blow would poison woodcutters sent to harvest the timber of these magical trees. Under the guidance of Kaneiakama, the Moloka'i priests finally learned how to harness the power of the Kalaipahoa through ritual offerings. From the wood of the trees, they carved fearsome *ki'i,* whose magic rendered the island immune to attack from its neighbors. Traveling war canoes gave the western coastline of Moloka'i a wide berth. Also at Maunaloa lived Kapo, an early master of the hula and legendary relative of the volcano goddess Pele. Embittered at her younger sister Laka for her greater fame as a hula dancer, Kapo is reputed to have turned to *ana'ana* (black magic) in her old age.

pines to ***Phallic Rock,*** which, when seen, needs no explanation. Barren women spent the night in this forest in order to conceive, and offerings are placed on the rock to this day. Camping in Pālā'au (at a safe distance from phallic effects) is allowed by state permit. Call (808) 567-6923.

A visit to ***Kalaupapa National Historic Park*** (567-6802; nps.gov/kala) will almost certainly provide the highlight of any Moloka'i experience. It is essential if you are to comprehend the emotional scars of this onetime "Lonely Island." Leprosy (Hansen's disease) was first observed in Hawai'i in 1835 and soon grew to epidemic proportions. The biblical stigma (and physical repulsiveness) of the disease moved missionary doctors to push for drastic quarantine measures. The physical isolation of Makanalua ("the given grave") Peninsula made it a natural place to exile leprosy patients, a process that began in 1866.

Flows from ***Kauhako Crater*** (nps.gov/places/crater) created the 2-mile peninsula as a geologic afterthought, long after the rest of Moloka'i had taken shape. As a natural viewing platform from which to marvel at Moloka'i's stunning northern coastline, the peninsula provides a serene counterpoint to the saga of its troubled past. A visit to Kalaupapa, however, does not wallow in the misery caused by man's inhumanity to man as much as it celebrates the redemptive qualities of human compassion and altruism. You will learn of the ***kokua*** (helpers) who volunteered to follow their loved ones into exile and who lived out their lives among the diseased. You will pay homage to the courage of Father (technically Saint, as of October 2009) Damien, a Catholic priest who came here alone to minister to the afflicted and helped transform their lawless purgatory into a life of newfound dignity.

Damien eventually contracted leprosy and died among those he had come to serve. His work did not lack controversy. During Damien's lifetime, his plight attracted headlines around the world, and soon others came to labor alongside him. The original settlement at rainy Kalawao was moved to more hospitable Kalaupapa, a fishing village on the other side of the peninsula. Bit by bit, the suffering of leprosy patients abated, and the advent of sulfone drugs in the 1940s offered a permanent cure to the progress of the disease. Despite this, the isolation laws governing the settlement were not rescinded until 1969. Children younger than age 16 remain barred from entry even today. Please note that at the time of this book's publication, Kalawao County was closed to the general public and for commercial tours under HRS 326 in alignment with CDC and Hawaii State Department of Heath jurisdiction until further notice. As mentioned above, access to the Kalaupapa Trail was restricted to residents and visitors with approved permits issued by the Hawaii State Department of Heath. To avoid fines or, worse, being arrested, please refer to the Superintendent's Compendium, 36 CFR1.5(a)(1). Check nps.gov/kala/planyourvisit/conditions .htm regularly for situation updates.

Before current restrictions, the classic way to get to Kalaupapa was to take the ***Moloka'i Mule Ride*** out of Kalae Stables. Bumper stickers on O'ahu advertise "I'd rather be riding a mule on Moloka'i." But due to restrictions, this offer is currently on pause. Check with the local tourism authority upon arrival to see if the situation has changed. The other options are flying and hiking, with direct flights from Ho'olehua ("topside"), Kahului (Maui), or Honolulu available. However you get there, to enter you need a permit, which you can only get by registering for a tour. Please check the National Park Service Provider for current tour options and availability, as Kalaupapa park, county, and trail are restricted to visitors with a permit. Find more information online: nps.gov/kala/planyourvisit/index.htm. Richard Marks, the former owner of Damien Tours, which has sadly closed, moonlighted as the sheriff of Kalawao County (distinct from the rest of Moloka'i, which is part of Maui). He was a self-taught authority on leprosy and former patient himself, who had audiences with the Pope and Mother Teresa.

If you are lucky, your tour will cover the basic fixtures and monuments of the Kalaupapa settlement, where about 14 of the original patients still reside. You then cross the peninsula to the earlier settlement at Kalawao. Here you visit ***St. Philomena Church***. Note the square holes he cut in the wooden floor so that ailing worshippers could spit without feeling self-conscious. Nearby you can stop for a picnic lunch at a stunningly beautiful site overlooking the mouth of Waikolu Valley and Mokapu Island. (Those who hike or fly in should bring their own food.) If time permits, ask to take a short hike to the rim of ***Kauhako Crater*** (400 feet) for an awesome view of the entire peninsula. A "bottomless" lake, the habitat for at least one species of shrimp found nowhere else in the world, fills the crater floor.

The West End

Moloka'i's coastline lacks good swimming beaches. The south coast consists of shallow mudflats, and the North Shore is mostly inaccessible. The tiny beaches and coves on the east coast have their charm, but they are peppered with rocks. It is along the west coast that Moloka'i has stationed its major white-sand creations. Not coincidentally, it's also the site of the island's only real tourist resorts.

The Maunaloa Highway (Route 46) heads west past Ho'olehua Airport, where it climbs the gentle slopes of its namesake, the 1,381-foot volcano that formed this half of the island (not to be confused with the vastly bigger Mauna Loa on the Big Island). The slopes of the mountain yielded an ultrahard basalt prized for making adzes and other tools. The name of the older of the two resorts in this region, Kaluakoi, translates to "the adze pit." The other outstanding feature of West Moloka'i is the red volcanic soil that blows in the constant trade winds and sooner or later daubs everything (tree trunks, houses, cars) with its ruddy palette.

To hit the beaches on the other side of the mountain, take the signposted turnoff on the right to ***Kaluakoi Resort.*** The road down traverses extremely dry scrubland, whose rolling hills are covered with thorny *kiawe* (mesquite) trees. Kiawe briquettes make great barbecue, as any native of the American Southwest will testify. What's more, the pollen from the tree's flowers makes great honey. Moloka'i at one time led the world in honey production, before disease struck the hives. Island honey is still sold in stores and is a popular gift item.

Kaluakoi Resort, the hotel and two condominiums, and the scattering of surrounding private estates were only part of an ambitious development plan for the West End, whose unrealized boundaries are indicated by the miles of paved roads leading nowhere. Residents of Moloka'i remain skeptical of these

The Birth of Hula

The graceful movements of this traditional dance have long been synonymous with the romantic image of the Hawaiian Islands around the world. Although the story of the hula's creation varies greatly among sources, many accounts credit an early hula school established at Ka'ana as the progenitor of the art form. The demand for hula soon exceeded the limited capacity of the school. Accordingly, Laka, a *kumu hula* (dance teacher), left Ka'ana to travel to the other islands, spreading the art of hula throughout Hawai'i. Today Laka is revered as a goddess and patroness of the dance. Every year, Moloka'i celebrates Ka Hula Piko ("the birth of hula") through offerings at Ka'ana and an island-wide hula festival held at Pāpōhaku Beach Park. The annual celebration takes place on the third Sat of May. If you plan to attend, book your Moloka'i stay early, as island accommodations fill up.

plans, and limited water allocation (largely controlled by the Hawaiian Home Lands Commission) has proved an effective obstacle to further development. For now, the focus of West End development has shifted to Maunaloa. Kaluakoi Hotel itself has been closed for several years. However, the condominiums at ***Kepuhi Beach Resort*** (kepuhibeach.net) are open for rental vacations by owner now.

Kepuhi Beach fronting the hotel is rocky and often unsuitable for swimming. Instead, walk a few hundred yards north to reach ***Pōhaku Mauliuli,*** a patchy sand beach sheltered beneath the eroded face of blackened cinder cone. Known as Make ("dead") Horse to locals after an unfortunate equine fell from the cliffs, the beach's deep waters offer exciting terrain for experienced snorkelers. Almost a mile farther north, tucked inside tiny coves along the rocky shoreline, the determined beachgoer can enjoy the island's finest strands at ***Kawakiuniu and Kawakiuiki*** ("big and little Kawakiu," also known as Kawakiu Beach) ***Bays.*** To get there, you must choose between hiking along the coast or bumping along the badly eroded jeep road that splits from the road to the Paniolo Hale condos. Stay on the left fork to follow the coastline. The two coves are sheltered from the elements, but in winter the waters may be too rough for swimming.

Immediately south of Kepuhi Beach and Kaluakoi Resort, ***Pu'u o Kaiaka,*** or ***Kaiaka Rock,*** a massive basalt outcrop, juts into the ocean. Of spiritual significance to the ancient Hawaiians, Pu'u o Kaiaka was the site of a heiau that was demolished by army bulldozers in the 1960s. If you scramble up the short jeep trail leading from Kaiaka Road to the top, you will, in addition to having breathtaking views of the western coastline, come upon some curious concrete-block structures that resemble a modernistic rendition of the heiau the army destroyed. In fact, the blocks are the forgotten remains of a cable-car winch erected by Libby Pineapple Company to lower its fruit to ships anchored offshore. The pineapple offerings ceased flowing from this sacred spot when Kolo Wharf was built.

On the other side of Kai'aka Rock, the vast windswept sands of Pāpōhaku Beach extend for 2 miles of white powder, accessible through several turnoffs from Kaluakoi Road. Sand from the beach was for years illegally mined to replenish Waikīkī's own diminishing strands. ***Pāpōhaku Beach Park*** offers attractive facilities maintained by Kaluakoi Resort. WARNING: Offshore currents make the waters unsafe at times, and the wind can generate a fierce sandblast. Every May, a festival at the beach park commemorates the legendary birth of the hula on Moloka'i. Turnoffs farther along Kaluakoi Road lead to additional beaches, most of them unblemished by human footprints. ***Kapukahehu,*** the last beach before the paved road ends, is known to locals as ***Dixie Maru,*** after a Japanese fishing boat that shipwrecked offshore. The beach's tiny cove may be more sheltered than those before it.

To escape the coastal heat, follow the Maunaloa Highway for another 2 miles past the turnoff into Maunaloa town, a tiny former plantation community nestled among cool pine trees. After Dole Pineapple pulled out of the island in 1975, Maunaloa became a virtual ghost town that nobody visited. Jonathan

Moloka'i Nightlife

Folks in Honolulu will tell you nothing happens on the island of Moloka'i after dark. But as with most places, the truth is you just have to know where to go. In Kaunakakai the hot place to be (literally) is the alley in back of Kanemitsu Bakery, where locals gather for fresh-baked bread, hot out of the oven starting around 9 p.m. Fri, Sat, and Sun. Here's how it works. You enter the alley to the right of the bakery storefront and head for the light at the end. Most nights you'll find a line already formed there. If not, knock on the door under the light. You have to knock hard to be heard. Eventually, footsteps will approach, and the door will open about 8 inches wide, no more. A voice will ask you what kind of bread you want. You counter by asking what they have. You may have a choice of toppings, either butter with cinnamon sugar or cream cheese with guava jelly. Once your order is placed, the door slams shut again and the footsteps disappear. You wait in the alley, inhaling the aroma of fresh-baked bread, impatient with anticipation. Eventually, the door cracks open once more, and a hand extends your order to you. You pay and wait for change, clutching the piping hot bread. The loaves are cut lengthwise down the middle, with the toppings slathered inside. You may just have to take a bite right there.

Socher's ***Big Wind Kite Factory*** (808-552-2364; bigwindkites.com) almost single-handedly put Maunaloa back on the map. Jonathan's elaborate designs translate the artistic visions of his wife, Daphne, into airborne motion. The tiny front-room shop comes alive with colorful kite fantasies, from dancing hula girls to pineapple windsocks. Tour the factory in back, where the Sochers happily demonstrate the finer points of kite making. Big Wind also imports high-performance stunt kites, for which Jonathan gives free lessons. In an adjacent room, the Sochers operate ***Plantation Gallery*** to showcase the craftwork of local artists as well as carefully chosen imports from Bali, where the Sochers vacation. Open Mon through Sat 10 a.m. to 2 p.m.

In October competitors launch from Hale o Lono for the annual Moloka'i-to-O'ahu canoe races, a 40-mile paddle through monstrous swells and fierce channel currents. Camping is permitted at both Hale o Lono and Kawakiu Bay.

Places to Stay on Moloka'i

KAUNAKAKAI

Dunbar Beachfront Cottages
9962 Kamehameha V Hwy.
(808) 558-8153
molokaibeachfront cottages.com
The name says it all. dunbarbeachfront cottages@gmail.com, three-night minimum.

Hotel Moloka'i
1300 Kamehameha V Hwy.
(808) 660-3408 or (877) 553-5347
hotelmolokai.com
Has rooms by the sea from $190.

Moloka'i Vacation Properties
130 Kamehameha V Hwy.
(800) 367-2984
molokai-vacation-rental.net

Pu'u o Hoku Ranch
Mm 25
(808) 558-8109
puuohoku.com
Offers two secluded cottages on the far eastern tip of Moloka'i. More information at info@ puuohoku.com.

FOR MORE INFORMATION ABOUT MOLOKA'I

gohawaii.com/islands/molokai

visitmolokai.com

Places to Eat on Moloka'i

KAUNAKAKAI

Hotel Moloka'i
1300 Kamehameha V Hwy.
(877) 553-5347
hotelmolokai.com
Charming oceanfront dining in a nostalgic old Hawai'i setting. Moderate to expensive.

Kanemitsu Bakery
79 Ala Malama Ave.
(808) 553-5855
An impressive selection of breads that is coveted statewide. Inexpensive.

Maka's Korner
35 Mohala St.
(808) 553-8058
All-day pancakes, saimin, fresh fish, and other local favorites served counter-side or outside. Inexpensive to moderate.

Moloka'i Pizza Cafe
15 Kaunakakai Place
(808) 553-3288
A menu full of variety and casual fare. Inexpensive.

KUALAPU'U

Kualapu'u Cookhouse
102 Farrington Ave.
(808) 567-9655
A renovated plantation eatery. Good, casual fare. Moderate to expensive.

Lāna'i

For a small island, Lāna'i has seen a lot of changes. In a legendary past, Hawaiians shunned the island, believing it to be inhabited by a nasty breed of akua. Kaulula'au, the mischievous son of a Maui chieftain, was banished here for chopping down his father's breadfruit trees. He defeated the akua and opened Lāna'i to human habitation. Mormon settlers came here beginning in 1853, hoping to build a "City of Joseph" as a model of earthly peace. The mission folded when the settlers discovered that their leader, Walter Gibson, had secretly registered title to the land in his own name. The Mormon Church promptly excommunicated him and relocated to Lā'ie on Oah'u. Undeterred, Gibson brought in new settlers and converted the entire island into an open cattle range, which he managed until King Kalākaua appointed him prime minister.

Unrestricted grazing turned the already dry landscape into a barren wasteland. The arrival of New Zealand naturalist George Munro, who was called in to manage the ranch, helped reverse some of the damage. Munro literally replanted a forest with introduced flora, including the Norfolk Island pines that have become a local trademark. While Munro worked to undo the excesses of ranching, Jim Dole introduced a different type of

LĀNA'I

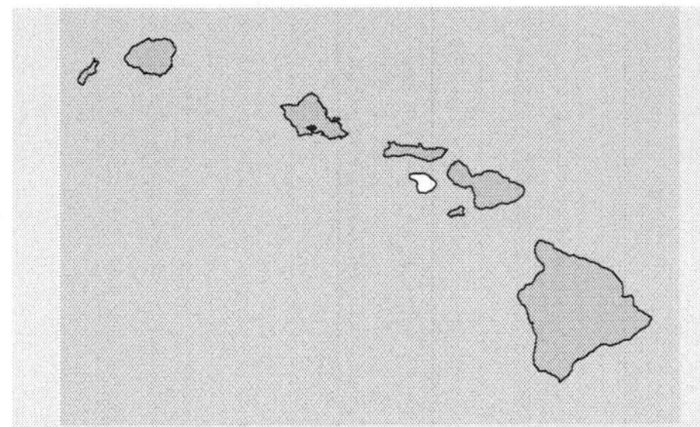

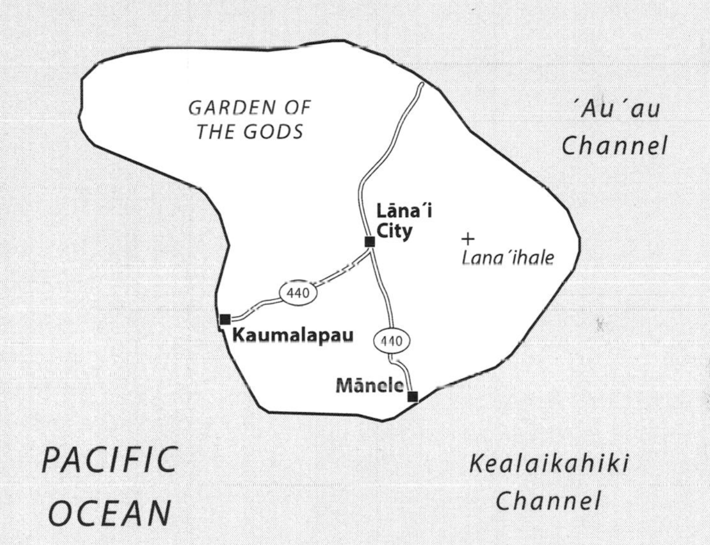
Kalohi Channel
GARDEN OF THE GODS
'Au 'au Channel
Lāna'i City
Lana'ihale
440
Kaumalapau
440
Mānele
PACIFIC OCEAN
Kealaikahiki Channel

N

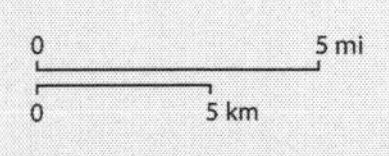
0
5 mi
0
5 km

pine as ranching's replacement, purchasing the entire island in 1922 to begin the world's largest pineapple plantation. Castle & Cooke, the island's former owner, has phased out pineapple production in recent years, shifting workers from agriculture to hotel work in two resorts. The erstwhile "Pineapple Isle" is now being promoted to well-heeled vacationers as "Hawai'i's Private Island." Contact the Lāna'i Visitors Bureau (800-947-4774; gohawaii.com/islands/lanai) for more information. And thanks to Larry Ellison's purchasing of the island from Castle & Cooke in 2012, via a private entity of his Oracle Corp., the island's tourism has certainly increased, following his investment.

These changes mean less than they might sound. The substitution of tourists for pineapples might seem like a backward step, but less than one-fifth of the island ever grew pineapples to begin with. Shaped roughly like a kidney, Lāna'i measures 18 miles long by 12 miles across. Adventurous travelers will have no difficulty losing themselves amid untamed wilderness and hidden locales. As you explore, you cannot help but stumble upon a variety of wildlife. Axis deer and mouflon sheep mingle with countless game fowl that flourish here in the absence of the mongoose found on other islands. You probably will want to rent a jeep to get around. Be prepared for unchivalrous bumps and thick red clouds of dust. Be warned that landmarks might change as fields are abandoned, and with them the access roads cleared through the bush. Get good directions and advice on weather and road conditions before setting out anywhere away from pavement. To secure a ride, try ***Lāna'i Cheap Jeeps*** (808-489-2296; lanaicheapjeeps.com). If you want to let someone else do the driving, contact ***Adventure Lāna'i EcoCentre*** (808-565-7373; adventurelanai.com). This tropical adventure outpost offers guided four-by-four treks, kayaking and snorkeling trips, and surfing safaris. They also offer safari-style vehicles (Jeep Wranglers and Land Rovers) if you want to head off the beaten path on your own.

islandfacts

Nickname: Pineapple Isle

Dimensions: 18 x 12 miles

Highest elevation: Lānaihale (3,370 feet)

Population: 3,367 (2020)

Principal city: Lāna'i City

Flower: Kauna'oa

Color: Orange

Lāna'i City

Though a small island, Lāna'i has always thought big. Its tiny town has been optimistically named Lāna'i City and is situated in the center of the island with plenty of room to grow. An elevation of 1,650 feet keeps cool breezes blowing through Lāna'i City even during summer. Most of the houses here date from the town's origins in 1922. Their brightly colored iron roofs punctuate the green of the ubiquitous pines. Almost all of Lāna'i's inhabitants live here in town, the majority of them of Filipino extraction. More by tradition than function, the plantation horn still sounds every evening, although thankfully the 4:30 a.m. wake-up calls have ceased. Sunday cockfights, although illegal, remain a fixture of island social life.

Dole Park, a grassy square shaded by rows of Norfolk Island pines, occupies the town center. Lāna'i's few commercial buildings mostly cluster around the park. Visit the ***Lāna'i Art Center*** (808-565-7503; 339 7th St.; lac@lanaiart.org) to view the work of local artists and take classes to create your own. Stop by ***Pele's Other Garden*** (808-565-9628; pelesothergarden.com) to munch New York–style deli grub for breakfast and lunch or Italian fare at dinner. Open Mon through Fri 11 a.m. to 2 p.m. and 4:30 to 8:30 p.m. The ***Blue Ginger Café and Bakery*** (808-565-6363) serves local-style meals Mon, Thurs, and Fri 6 a.m. to 8 p.m., Tues and Wed 6 a.m. to 2 p.m., and Sat and Sun 6:30 a.m. to 8 p.m. It doubles as a bakery. Inexpensive. ***Ganotisi's Pacific Rim Cuisine*** (808-565-7120; 408 8th St.) serves Asian- and Hawaiian-inspired plate lunches every day with tasty burgers and fries. Open 7 a.m. to 8 p.m. daily. ***No Ka 'Oi Grindz Lāna'i*** (808-565-9413), which translates to a phrase basically meaning "the best food," offers kimchi fried rice and big *loco moco* (an egg over easy on a hamburger patty on a bed of rice and covered with brown gravy). Open Mon to Sun 10:30 a.m. to 1 p.m. Inexpensive. ***Lāna'i City Bar & Grill*** in the ***Hotel Lāna'i*** (808-565-7212; 828 Lāna'i Ave.; hotellanai.com; lanaicitybarandgrill.com) serves moderately priced dinners featuring seafood, steaks, and rotisserie chicken. Open Tues to Sat 5 to 10 p.m., happy hour 4 to 6 p.m., and extended happy hour Fri and Sat 9 to 11 p.m. Live music every night. Reservations recommended. Built in 1925 as a clubhouse for Dole executives, the hotel has 10 rooms and a separate cottage that start at $330, less than half the rates charged by its upmarket sisters, the ***Four Seasons Resort Lāna'i*** and the ***Lodge at Kō'ele*** resorts. Call (800) 321-4666 for centralized reservations for the latter. ***Dreams Come True*** (808-565-6961 or 800-566-6961; dreamscometruelanai.com) offers bed-and-breakfast rooms with private sky-lit baths, whirlpool tubs, and some four-poster beds in a restored plantation house with kitchen access for $200, $234.82 after tax. You might contact statewide bed-and-breakfast agencies for alternatives (see the Introduction).

Camping at Hulopoe Bay is private, scenic, and peaceful and even offers solar-heated showers. The bay is a marine life conservation area, so while there's no three-prong fishing allowed, you can snorkel to your heart's content. Permits are issued for a three-night maximum stay, and the fee is $15 per person per night and a 30-percent fee. For more information, contact ***Castle and Cooke Resorts*** at PO Box 630310, Lāna'i City 96763, or phone (808) 565-2695. It is advised to check ahead on hawaii.gov or nps.gov to ensure that camping permits are still permitted for non-residents.

Branching Out

From Lāna'i City, paved roads cut across an inland plateau and drop sharply to the coast on each of Lāna'i's three sides; hunting tracks climb the slopes of the central mountain and, together with the former pineapple field roads, partition the island's interior. Begin by heading west on Kaumalapau Highway, the only road truly deserving the designation of highway. As the main access road to the airport and harbor, it is wide, well graded, and smoothly paved. Thus, as you might expect, it has little of interest lying along it. Drive down to the harbor anyway. The transition from the flat tableland to the steep slope down the coast offers some vistas over the craggy gulches, sheer cliffs, and rocky sea stacks that characterize Lāna'i's western shore. The very industrial-looking harbor squats beneath the rocky cliff from which it was blasted. It may no longer buzz with its previous pineapple-related activity, but it and the airport are still Lāna'i's main gateway to the outside world.

A side trip from Kaumalapau to Kaunolu, however, demonstrates the reverse trade-off and offers a fascinating destination—an ancient village that was Kamehameha I's favorite fishing retreat—at the price of a hellishly difficult access. Definitely get current directions for this one: As empty pineapple fields are converted

Brief History of Lāna'i

Pineapple King James Dole, who purchased Lāna'i in 1922, combined innovative methods of mass production with mass marketing to make the pineapple synonymous with Hawai'i the world over. But in Hawai'i, he made pineapple synonymous with Lāna'i, transforming the island's population and economy in the process. Lāna'i became the world's largest pineapple plantation, although it was not the first place in Hawai'i that pineapple (not a native fruit) was grown.

Ironically, Lāna'i claims distinction for another "first" regarding a different crop: sugar. The Polynesians grew sugarcane but never produced refined sugar. In 1802 a Chinese man on Lāna'i is believed to have been the first to have done so. Sugar would go on to transform Hawai'i, becoming the dominant crop in the islands, but not on Lāna'i.

to pastures, new fences might arise. For one possible route, turn left at the stop sign onto Kaupili Road, just past the airport turnoff as you are coming down the highway. The road deteriorates to gravel and then dirt as it winds through some curves and then follows a fenced border along the former pineapple fields. You soon will see the island of Kaho'olawe ahead on the horizon. As you drive, scan the southwestern tip of the island, on your right, for a tiny lighthouse; this is your destination. You should find the road down to Kaunolu 2.1 miles from the highway, where the fencing ends at a runoff ditch. The 3-mile descent is incredibly steep and rocky. Do not attempt this unless you are experienced at handling a four-wheel-drive vehicle.

A bruising half-hour ride down the left side of a gully brings you to ***Kaunolu Bay,*** whose archaeological treasures constitute a National Historic Landmark. The stone foundations of more than a hundred Hawaiian homes cling to the slopes above this tiny cove. Tufts of pili grass used for thatching grow wild in the rocky terrain. If you wet the wispy seeds of the pili, they will rotate—a unique self-planting mechanism adapted to intermittent rainfall. Just to the right of the kiawe tree at the end of the trail, on a bluff overlooking the dry streambed of the gully, you can find the terraced foundation believed to be the site of King Kamehameha's house. Facing Kamehameha's house, on the bluffs across the gully on the right side of the bay, stands ***Halulu Heiau;*** and on the far side of this bluff, a small gap in the rocky rim marks the entrance to ***Kahekili's Leap,*** named for Kamehameha's greatest rival, the High Chief of Maui, who excelled at cliff diving.

Climb down the slope to the base of the bay, then walk up the streambed. On your left you will pass a narrow rock wall enclosure that formed part of a shelter for repairing canoes. Above on your right you can now clearly see the terracing of Kamehameha's house site. Climb up the opposite wall of the gully to reach the heiau. Kamehameha rebuilt the temple after he conquered Lāna'i, making it one of the last monuments to the old gods. Its carefully fitted rock walls stand in excellent repair. (Please take care that they remain so.) Walk over to Kahekili's Leap for a dramatic view of ***Puli Kabolo,*** Lāna'i's tallest sea cliff,

Geography of Lāna'i

The sixth largest of the Hawaiian Islands, Lāna'i is the smallest island open to visitors. Formed from a single central volcano, it has 47 miles of coastline, two resort hotels, few roads, no traffic lights, and only a handful of swimming beaches. The island summit at Lana'ihale reaches 3,370 feet, and the widest point of the island spans 18 miles.

which rises 1,000 feet above deep blue ocean. At the base of the cliff, the pounding surf echoes inside a large sea cave like rolling thunder. Kamehameha's warriors used to dive from the ledge you are standing on to prove their loyalty and courage. Merely imagining the 62-foot plunge into the Pacific—with a 15-foot rock outcrop to clear at the base—should be enough to give most visitors a jolt of vertigo.

Your next excursion takes you south on Mānele Road, descending from Lāna'i City through the historic Palawai Basin. Once the caldera of the volcano that formed Lāna'i, the basin became the site of the short-lived Mormon settlement and later cradled Dole's first pineapple fields. The foothills east of the Palawai hold some of the best-preserved petroglyphs in the state. To probe their secrets, look for the large water tower on the hillside above the basin. On the right of the water tower is a wide gulch, and to the right of the gulch grows a stand of trees where the ***petroglyphs*** lurk. To get there, turn left onto Hō'ike Road, a former pineapple road marked by a yield sign (facing south). Turn left at the second irrigation ditch and follow the water pipe to the third power pole, where a no trespassing sign marks the beginning of the trail up to the petroglyphs. The petroglyph-laden rocks are located at the far lower edge of the trees amid a clump of rich green sisal plants with spiky leaves and tall central stalks. A jeep trail leads up the hill to the first carved boulder. Proving that on Lāna'i nothing comes easily, the better-preserved, more intricate carvings lie on rocks farther up the slope. Patterned images of canoes, warriors, and animals abound. One shows a man on horseback, dating its origin to after the arrival of Western ships, but no one today can explain why these carvings were made or what they signify. Please be respectful of their fragile condition.

Continue along Mānele Road as it rises out of Palawai Basin and then descends steeply to the coast. You will see Kaho'olawe again across Kealaikahiki ("the way to Tahiti") Channel and maybe the twin towers of the Big Island beyond. Two beautiful bays await you at the end of the road. Both are marine-life conservation zones offering excellent snorkeling. ***Mānele Bay*** arrives first on your left, its former black-sand beach now converted to a small-boat harbor. Guarded by fortresslike cliffs, the cove offers views of Maui's ***Mount Haleakalā*** rising above the clouds on the horizon. ***Expeditions*** (808-661-3756; 800-695-2624; go-lanai.com) offers ferry service to and from Lahaina Harbor on Maui five times daily. The fee is $30 one way.

An extension of Mānele Road curves west to ***Hulopoe Bay*** around the point. Hulopoe Beach, often called Mānele as well, dazzles visitors with its wide crescent of snowy white sand edging a lovely bay. The shore break can be rough in summer, suitable for bodysurfing. A pod of spinner dolphins frequents the waters offshore. (Federal law prohibits harassment of this endangered species.)

Pele's Other Garden operates a small sandwich stand. Unfortunately, this idyllic location has not gone unnoticed. Day-trippers from Maui now come daily, and the 213-room ***Four Seasons Resort Lāna'i*** hotel (808-565-2000; 800-321-4666; fourseasons.com/lanai) perches on the bluffs above the bay.

For seclusion, walk around the left side of the bay, past some enormous tide pools, to the cove at ***Pu'u Pehe.*** Also known as ***Sweetheart Rock,*** it was named for a legendary beauty who drowned in a nearby sea cave, where her jealous husband had confined her, and was buried on this giant sea stack. You can sun yourself on the hidden beach below, although the water is too rocky for good swimming. Walk to the far edge of the bluffs facing Sweetheart Rock for a sweeping view of Lāna'i's southern coast, with the mountains of Maui and Kaho'olawe, and sometimes even the Big Island, visible across the sea.

Keomuku Road, Lāna'i's third paved road, departs north past the Lodge at Kō'ele. ***Kalokahi o Ka Malamalama,*** the tiny church next to the lodge, survives from the ranch days. You can attend Sunday services in Hawaiian here. The road then climbs past guava trees and curves right toward Lāna'i's eastern shore. Just beyond the bend, a small paved road on the right leads to the old Koele cemetery and the start of Lāna'i's famous ***Munro Trail.*** This 9-mile-long jeep path showcases much of the exotic vegetation that Munro introduced to reestablish a viable watershed in the island's upcountry. The trail climbs the summit of 3,370-foot ***Lāna'ihale*** ("house of Lāna'i"), which resembles a second-story addition to the island. Rising steeply above the surrounding tableland, the Hale, as locals call it, presents panoramic views of Lāna'i and up to five other islands in the chain. Look for guavas and thimbleberries along the trail. Do not attempt the ascent if it has been raining or looks like it will start.

hawai'itrivia

Luahiwa Petroglyphs are among the best preserved in all the islands.

From the cemetery, bear left and look for a small sign marking the Munro Trail's entrance into the forest proper. If you are traveling on foot, it might be easier to take the ***Koloiki Ridge Trail,*** which begins behind Koele Lodge and joins the Munro Trail halfway along. After descending through forest for the first few miles, the trail then climbs to reach a telephone relay station overlooking the steep walls of Maunalei ("mountain lei") Gulch, named for the wreathlike clouds so often draped around the mountain here. In 1778, Kalani'ōpu'u's invasion force from the Big Island laid siege to Lāna'i's last defenders in this valley. The trail continues along the ridgeline above the upper valley to overlook a lower middle ridge, Ho'okio, where keen eyes can still discern the ***Ho'okio Notches,*** carved by the stalwart Lāna'i warriors to fortify their stronghold. Kalani'ōpu'u eventually starved them out and then proceeded to massacre and pillage the entire island.

At 4.7 miles, just before the summit, a side trail heads left through eucalyptus trees for a view of ***Hauola Gulch,*** a 2,000-foot gash in the mountain's side, the deepest on the island. From the windswept, rain-soaked summit, you get the island's best views, provided the Hale breaks free from its cloud cover. The trail then descends steeply down the drier back side of the mountain to link up with Hoike Road, the main jeep access from Palawai Basin.

Keomuku Road continues northeast and begins another bumpy, winding descent to the coast. The stacks of rocks you see along the highway here and elsewhere are not ancient Hawaiian monuments but rather a form of graffiti. While Hawaiians did use such cairns as trail markers, these were built by latter-day visitors to "ward off the ghosts." Game abounds in this area, and if you're not careful, you could violate hunting regulations by running over a few wild turkeys with your car.

The paved road ends at the bottom of the hill. An unpaved extension on the left, fairly easy going, leads north to ***Shipwreck*** or ***Kaiolohia Beach.*** Situated equally between the islands of Maui and Moloka'i offshore, this long, desolate beach gets battered by fierce trade winds and ocean swells funneling through the Pailolo Channel. Littered with debris that drifts across its protective outer reef, the beach has witnessed countless shipwrecks and intentional groundings since the days when flotillas of whalers laid anchor in the famous Lahaina waters off Maui. Although swimming is less than ideal, beachcombers will have a field day. As you drive farther, notice the dwellings of "Federation Camp," built from driftwood and salvaged wreckage. Filipino fishermen built these as weekend shelters during the 1930s. At the end of the drivable road, a path leads to the site of a former lighthouse. Offshore, an abandoned World War II Liberty Ship lists just beyond the reef, stubbornly holding out against the punishing waves.

Heading in the other direction from the end of paved Keomuku Road requires a jeep to reach Keomuku itself and points beyond. To navigate the 12-odd miles to Naha on the southeastern coast takes at least an hour. Four miles along you reach the ghost town of ***Keomuku,*** headquarters of the hapless Maunalei Sugar Company. Gibson's daughter started this short-lived venture at the turn of the century. The plantation was visited by the plague in its first year and was forced to fold after the second year, when the sweet well water mysteriously turned brackish.

Ka Lanakila o Ka Malamalama, a picturesque and abandoned wooden church nestled in a coconut grove, remains the only intact building in Keomuku. It remains closed to the public. Behind the church, three large whaleboats rot on land that was shoreline in 1935. Soil runoff has added the new land. Less than a mile farther south, you'll pass ***Kahea Heiau,*** whose stones were pilfered to line the plantation rail bed. Hawaiians believe such desecration led to Maunalei Sugar's demise.

Beyond the heiau lies the old sugar dock, ***Kahalepalaoa Landing.*** Queen Ka'ahumanu came from Maui near the end of her life to preach to Lāna'i's people on this spot and convert them to Christian ways. Today Maui day-trippers follow in her footsteps to indulge in more hedonistic pursuits at Club Lāna'i. The road turns inland from here, with the coast hidden behind a forest of kiawe trees, and emerges a few miles farther along at Lopa, where the beach is somewhat more sheltered than the windswept coast farther north. Traveling an additional 2 miles brings you to Naha and the end of your jeep trail. Another abandoned fishing village, ***Naha*** had one of the island's few fishponds, and its walls can still be traced offshore. According to legend, after outwitting all the akua on the island, Kaulula'au built a huge bonfire here to signal his victory to the people of Maui. Beyond Naha an ancient paved trail built by the Hawaiians leads over the mountains to Palawai; for now, however, you will do better to backtrack on Keomuku Road.

The last compass direction accessible from Lāna'i City by road is northwest. Your route follows what Lāna'i maps euphemistically label Kanepu'u Highway. In reality, it's a dirt extension of Fraser Avenue from town. Follow this road as it curves to the left, then take the first right. After passing through former pineapple fields for the first few miles, you reach the lowland forest of ***Kanepu'u.*** Munro recognized the value of this pristine habitat of native plants and trees and planted a surrounding rectangle of eucalyptus trees and sisal plants as a windbreak. Today the Nature Conservancy continues to preserve this bastion of native vegetation, which includes rare Lāna'i sandalwood and Hawaiian gardenia. Interpretive signposts line a short nature walk.

The edge of the forest brings an abrupt transition to a now-barren landscape, weakened first by overgrazing and then stripped entirely of vegetation by the punishing winds that sweep across the north coast. At about 7 miles in, you come to a series of bizarre rock formations covering a rugged landscape of peaks and canyons. Welcome to the ***Garden of the Gods.*** The beauty of this bleak terrain lies in the burning mineral colors of its soil and eroded rock. The changing hues at sunset become dramatic. Not far from here is where legend says the treacherous kahuna Kawelo engineered the death-by-constipation of Moloka'i's sage, Lanikāula, by burning his rival's stool in a magic fire.

hawai'itrivia

The temperature of the sand in which turtle eggs incubate determines the sex of the hatchlings.

Beyond the Garden of the Gods, the road deteriorates as it drops steeply to the coast. WARNING: Do NOT continue if it has been raining here or looks likely to start. If you do go all the way, you will reach beautiful ***Polihua*** ("bosom of eggs") ***Beach,*** a former haven for green sea turtles coming to deposit their eggs. Lāna'i chants tell of Pele's love for turtle meat. Perhaps the goddess has been especially hungry, as the species is now endangered; nest sites should not be disturbed. Offshore currents make swimming risky, but it is a quiet spot to look for whales passing through Kalohi Channel and to watch the clouds blow across Moloka'i. Ka'ena Point to the west served as a penal colony for women between 1837 and 1850; thieves and adulteresses were forced ashore here to fend for themselves. In fact, the concept of adultery did not exist in old Hawai'i. Missionaries had to make do with translating the seventh commandment as "Thou shalt not sleep mischievously." Apparently, the exile system was no more successful than the commandment. Male convicts from Kaho'olawe swam ashore to Maui and stole canoes, which they promptly used to liberate the women on Lāna'i.

Farther around the point, at Ka'ena Iki, lies Lāna'i's largest heiau. This ancient temple is difficult to find and hard to reach, but as you survey this lonely corner of the island, just knowing it exists adds a touch of mystery.

Places to Stay on Lāna'i

LĀNA'I CITY

Dreams Come True
1168 Lāna'i Ave.
(808) 565-6961 or (800) 566-6961
Three-room bed-and-breakfast for $200 per night, before tax.

Four Seasons Resort Lāna'i at Mānele Bay
1 Mānele Bay Rd.
(808) 565-2000 or (800) 321-4666
fourseasons.com/lanai
This upscale resort has a Mediterranean feel and sits on bluffs overlooking Lāna'i's best beach. Rooms from over $1,000.

Hotel Lāna'i
828 Lāna'i Ave.
(808) 565-7211 or (800) 795-7211
hotellanai.com
A quaint 10-room structure that's been accommodating guests since 1925. Rooms from $330.

Places to Eat on Lāna'i

LĀNA'I CITY

Blue Ginger Café and Bakery
409 7th St.
(808) 565-6363
Inexpensive local-style meals in Lāna'i City. Inexpensive.

Ganotisi's Pacific Rim Cuisine
408 8th St.
(808) 565-7120
Pacific plate lunches, tasty burgers, casual outdoor seating. Inexpensive.

Lāna'i City Bar & Grill
828 Lāna'i Ave.
(808) 565-7212
lanaicitybarandgrill.com
Located in Hotel Lāna'i, Lana'i City Bar & Grill serves dinner Tues through Sat, and Sun brunch. Moderate.

No Ka 'Oi Grindz Lāna'i
335 9th St. Ste. C
(808) 565-9413
Try the kimchi fried rice or the giant loco moco. Inexpensive.

Pele's Other Garden
811 Houston St.
(808) 565-9628
pelesothergarden.com/peles
Serves New York–style deli and Italian food. Moderate.

Maui

Sailboarders come from around the world to frolic at the beaches of Maui's windy central isthmus. Humpback whales also make Maui their winter destination of choice. Although they visit all the Hawaiian Islands, the biggest groups gather in sight of Maui's coastline. The island has much to recommend to other visitors as well. Within an area not much bigger than O'ahu, Maui boasts a 10,000-foot volcano, a historic whaling town, a rain forest laced with countless waterfalls, and miles of beach colored with white, red, and black sands.

The island of Maui takes its name from a demigod, Maui of a Thousand Tricks, whose exploits form legends across Polynesia. Maui's magic fishhook pulled up the first islands from the Pacific floor, so that man could have a place to live. Maui pushed up the sky so that man could stand erect. Maui stole fire to warm man's hearth. It was on the island of Maui that the demigod performed his most celebrated feat: slowing the passage of the sun. Some say that the shape of the island resembles the trickster's body. The West Maui Mountains are the demigod's head, with Haleakalā's girth a limbless torso to the east. A narrow isthmus forms the neck between these mighty mountains, fetching Maui its nickname of the Valley Isle.

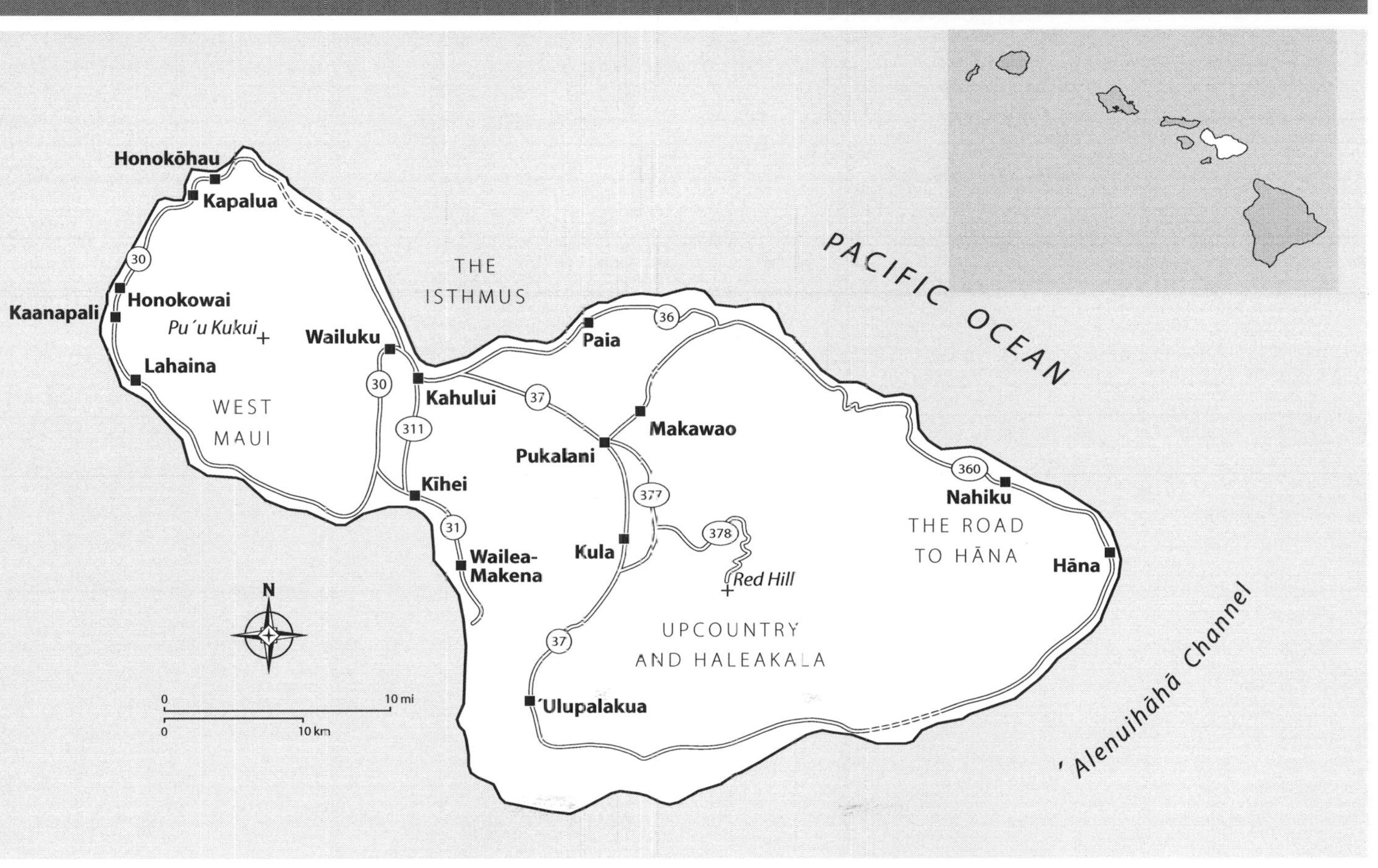
MAUI
Honokōhau
Kapalua
Honokowai
Kaanapali
Pu´u Kukui
Lahaina
WEST
MAUI
Wailuku
Kahului
Kīhei
Wailea-
Makena
THE
ISTHMUS
Paia
Makawao
Pukalani
Kula
Red Hill
UPCOUNTRY
AND HALEAKALA
´Ulupalakua
Nahiku
THE ROAD
TO HĀNA
Hāna
PACIFIC OCEAN
´Alenuihāhā Channel
30
311
31
37
36
377
378
360
N
0
10 mi
0
10 km

Those seeking a guided hiking experience on Maui have several choices. Ken Schmitt earned his naturalist spurs living off the land for three years in the Maui jungle. While he has retired since, he recruited a team of kindred spirits to serve as ***Hike Maui*** (808-879-5270; hikemaui.com) guides. Prices start at $109 for a 3-hour trip. They also do a unique kayak, snorkel, and waterfall hike in West Maui for $199.

The Isthmus and Points South

Maui's population centers on the northern edge of the central isthmus, the nape of Maui's neck. Modern Kahului has the main airport and harbor. In the foothills to the west, its older brother, Wailuku, retains prominence as the seat of Maui County and has the historical flavor Kahului lacks. As Ka'ahumanu Avenue heads west from Kahului, it slopes uphill to become Main Street in Wailuku. At the top of Main Street, begin your tour at the ***Bailey House Museum*** (808-244-3326; mauimuseum.org). This restored mission station portrays both the lifestyle of the early missionaries and the Hawaiian culture that preceded them. The Wailuku mission began in 1837 under the Reverend Jonathan Green, who established a young women's seminary on the property. The main goal was to instruct them in "employments suited to their sex," primarily to produce suitable companions for the graduates of the boys' school across the mountains in Lahaina.

islandfacts

Nickname: The Valley Isle

Dimensions: 48 x 26 miles

Highest elevation: Haleakalā (10,023 feet)

Population: 164,351 (2022 census.gov estimate)

Largest city: Kahului

County seat: Wailuku

Flower: Lokelani (a rose)

Color: Pink

Reverend and Mrs. Green were joined and eventually replaced by the Baileys, who converted the adobe building to coral stone in 1841. Young women in the seminary donated their hair as the binding agent for the plaster. Edward Bailey was a multitalented man who later founded a sugar plantation when the seminary closed in 1849. An accomplished artist, he gifted posterity with oil paintings of 19th-century Maui, many of which are displayed in the museum gallery.

The upstairs rooms of the Bailey home feature missionary-period furnishings, including some beautifully patterned Hawaiian quilts in the bedroom. You'll also find hand-operated spinning wheels and looms, sewing having been one of the principal employments taught at the seminary. The rooms below are devoted to Hawaiiana. Jewelry junkies will marvel at the variety of materials Hawaiians used for necklaces. Instead of perishable flower leis, the well-dressed Hawaiian might wear a strand of shells, kukui nuts, feathers, teeth, or even human hair. The museum also offers rare examples of Hawaiian *kapa,* some of the most beautiful bark cloth produced in Polynesia. Another room displays the enormous *ipu,* or gourds, decorated to be used as containers, musical instruments, or lamps. Open Tues through Fri 10 a.m. to 2 p.m.; modest admission charge. The garden in front displays plants found during the missionary era, with the back garden devoted to precontact botany. Ask about the self-guided ***walking tour*** if you wish to explore other historic buildings in Wailuku.

Walk a block downhill to High Street, where ***Ka'ahumanu Church*** sits in Honoli'i Park. Its weighty steeple points heavenward in classic New England style, while the white walls and green roof invert the colors of the cloud-draped West Maui Mountains behind. Named for Queen Ka'ahumanu, an early convert to Christianity, the present structure dates from 1876, but its predecessors go back to the earliest missionaries. Wailuku's government buildings huddle under

Brief History of Maui

As they lived on the second-largest island in Hawai'i, Maui chieftains long rivaled those of the Big Island in the bid for preeminence. In the mid-18th century, a Maui warrior by the name of Kahekili embarked on a bold mission of conquest, uniting O'ahu, Moloka'i, and Lāna'i under his rule. Had his conquests continued, we might today know the archipelago as the Maui Islands instead of Hawai'i. Instead, Kahekili was eclipsed by a younger warrior from the Big Island named Kamehameha, who eventually succeeded in unifying the entire island chain under his rule.

Maui's most enduring legacy in the newly unified Kingdom of Hawai'i was wrought by two women. Keōpūolani, a Maui princess of the highest rank, became Kamehameha's "sacred" wife. Her royal lineage (superior to his own) ensured that his heirs would have the mana to rule and became the foundation for the Kamehameha dynasty.

But Kamehameha's favorite wife, Ka'ahumanu, played an even greater role in Hawaiian history. Ka'ahumanu, also from Maui, had a stormy relationship with Kamehameha during their marriage. After his death, Ka'ahumanu served as regent, sharing power with Liholiho, Kamehameha's heir. To consolidate her position, Ka'ahumanu convinced Liholiho into overthrowing the kapu system of checks and balances that ordered relationships between peoples, gods, and chiefs; she later encouraged the advent of Christian missionaries. Ka'ahumanu also succeeded where even Kamehameha I had failed in "conquering" the northernmost island, Kaua'i. She accomplished this by the novel stratagem of abducting and then simultaneously marrying both Kaua'i's former king, Kamuali'i, and his eldest son.

shady trees nearby. The State Building at 54 S. High St. issues state camping permits, dispenses free hiking guides, and books cabins; call well in advance for the latter (808-984-8109; mauicounty.gov). Open Mon through Fri 8 a.m. to 4 p.m. Camping in the county's Kanaha Beach Park is not recommended.

So much for religion and power. Now for shopping. Stroll north on Market Street, 2 blocks below High Street, to explore the stores and galleries along ***Antique Row.*** You never know what treasures you might discover as you sift through Asian and Pacific artifacts, genuine antiques, and various arts and crafts. Locals all over Maui rave about the Vietnamese cuisine at the ***A Saigon Cafe*** (808-243-9560; 1792 Main St.). (The steaks on the menu are holdovers from the venue's former incarnation as Naokee Steak House.) The sign for the cafe is not visible from Main Street itself. You'll find it near the bridge where Ka'ahumanu Avenue crosses over Lower Main Street, at the corner of Kaniela and Main Streets. Open every day 11 a.m. to 8:30 p.m.

Ichiban Okazuya Hawai'i (808-244-7276; 2133 Kaohu St.) serves plate lunches, stir-fry noodles, and chicken katsu. Open Mon to Fri 10 a.m. to 7 p.m. Inexpensive. ***Tasty Crust*** (808-244-0845) is the no-frills joint where the locals go for plate lunches and amazing banana pancakes. Open every day except Mon 6 a.m. to 8 p.m. Inexpensive.

Heading north (downhill) on Market across the Iao Stream bridge leads you into Happy Valley for more dining options. You won't find the "action" this former red-light district once attracted, though all 11 of Maui's hostess bars hover nearby. Just before the bridge, Mill Street leads east off Market Street into Wailuku's industrial sector along Lower Main Street. ***Tokyo Tei*** (808-242-9630; 1063 Lower Main St.), ensconced in an ugly two-story office complex, has served tasty Japanese fare since 1935. Open Mon through Sat 10:30 a.m. to 1:30 p.m. and 4:30 to 8:30 p.m. Another longtime local diner is ***Sam Sato's*** (808-244-7124; 1750 Wili Pa Loop), famous for its *manju* (rice flour pastry filled with sweetened adzuki beans) and tropical fruit turnovers. To find it, turn left off Lower Main Street, opposite the school. Open Tues through Sat 7 a.m. to 2 p.m. (with take-out service until 4 p.m.).

For late-night dining, you have to go to Kahului. Visit ***Koho's Grill and Bar*** (808-877-5588) in Kahului's Ka'ahumanu Shopping Center for local diner fare. Open daily 7 a.m. to 10 p.m.; Fri and Sat until 11 p.m. Inexpensive. Worth a visit is ***Brigit & Bernard's Garden Café*** (808-877-6000) for their surf-and-turf menu plus draft beers on a spacious patio. Open Tues to Wed 8 a.m. to 8 p.m., Thurs to Sat 8 a.m. to 9 p.m., and Sun 8 a.m. to 4 p.m. Inexpensive.

Wailuku sleeps as cheaply as it eats, with a number of flophouses catering to transients and workers. The influx of sailboarders to Maui's North Shore has led some to upgrade. The best of the bunch is the ***Banana Bungalow***

Geography of Maui

Maui is the second largest of the Hawaiian Islands. Built from the overlapping flows of two volcanoes that meet along a narrow isthmus, this natural wind tunnel makes the "Valley Isle" a mecca for windsurfers. Of the two landmasses, the western Maui mountains are older and more heavily eroded. Their summit at Pu'u Kukui reaches 5,788 feet. Haleakalā, the volcano that forms eastern Maui, rises gently to a 10,023-foot summit and harbors an enormous erosive crater within.

(808-244-5090; 800-846-7835; 310 N. Market St.; mauihostel.com). It offers doubles for $159.47 and dorm beds for $63.12, as well as daily tours and activities, many of which are free to guests.

Wailuku does offer one luxury accommodation option in ***The Old Wailuku Inn at Ulupono*** (808-244-5897; 2199 Kaho'okele St.; mauiinn.com). Built in 1924 by a wealthy island banker as a wedding gift for his daughter-in-law, the inn has been lovingly restored to evoke the grandeur of that earlier era. Woven lauhala mats rest on hardwood floors, while full-size Hawaiian quilts drape the beds. A variety of Hawaiian heirlooms and antique furniture from Asia enhance the period look. The inn also pays tribute to Hawai'i's earlier poet laureate, Don Blanding, and contains several features inspired by his poems. Views from the breakfast room encompass Haleakalā, while the front porch faces Iao Valley. The 10 rooms start at $276 and include a full breakfast; two-night minimum.

To visit a far older shrine than Ka'ahumanu Church, continue down the hill on Lower Main and turn left onto Waiehu Beach Road. Cross Iao Stream and turn left at Kūhiō Place, then left again up Hea Place to ***Haleki'i Heiau.*** Built atop a massive sand dune overlooking Kahului Bay, the temple was partially reconstructed in 1958, but the carved wooden images *(ki'i)* that presumably stood there to deter invaders no longer exist.

While in Wailuku, every Maui visitor must undertake the pilgrimage into ***'Iao Valley,*** which at the time of this book's publication was temporarily closed until mid-April 2023 for slope restabilization, which is by far the largest, steepest, and deepest cleft in the West Maui

hawai'itrivia

Haleakalā is the world's largest dormant volcano.

Built in 1801, the Brick Palace in Lahaina is Hawai'i's first Western-style building.

Piilani Heiau, Hawai'i's largest temple, was built in 1400 AD near Hāna.

Mosquitoes first arrived in the islands in 1872, as stowaways aboard the *Wellington,* a merchant ship.

Mountains. The head of the valley opens onto the ancient crater that formed this half of the island. Its rear wall rises 5,788 feet to ***Pu'u Kukui,*** West Maui's highest peak. Because of this western mountain screen, darkness comes early to the valley. Mornings can be memorable as the sunlight descends the ridgetops probing through the mist. Equally dramatic are late afternoons, when the clouds that crowd into the narrow valley opening reflect ethereal bolts of sunlight that backlight the stage.

To get there, take Main Street west past the Bailey House and bear left onto 'Iao Valley Road. Drive into the steep-walled canyon entrance and watch the scenery unfold. The valley gradually widens as its walls grow taller, serrated by narrow side canyons and hanging valleys. Waterfalls concealed in these dark crevasses often spray mist that the sun's probing rays transmute into rainbows.

Kepaniwai, a clearing halfway up the valley, literally means "damming of the waters." The name has its gruesome origins in a battle in which Kamehameha's Western cannons massacred Maui defenders in a carnage that left 'Iao Stream literally dammed by piles of corpses. Today, ***Kepaniwai Heritage Gardens*** on the bank of 'Iao Stream celebrate Hawai'i's diverse ethnic heritage. As you roam the grounds, try to puzzle out the different motifs, from a Japanese sculpture of cane workers to a traditional Filipino bamboo house. Local kids of all ethnic groups come here to splash in the stream and fish for tadpoles in the ponds. Free. The ***Hawai'i Nature Center*** (808-244-6500; hawaiinaturecenter.org) next door showcases a different facet of Hawai'i's diversity, with hands-on, interactive exhibits focused on 'Iao Valley's ecology. You'll meet such Hawai'i originals as the world's only carnivorous caterpillar, and the *o'opu,* Hawai'i's "sucker fish," with the unique ability to climb its way upstream. The center also offers rain-forest hikes and other interpretive activities.

The road continues deeper into the valley through a winding gorge. Pause to squint at the ***JFK Profile,*** a natural rock formation noticed only after President Kennedy's death. Ahead is ***'Iao Valley State Park.*** Check the Division of State Parks for the latest updates, as the park was temporarily closed at the time of this book's publication. See dlnr.hawaii.gov for more information. Various paved paths crisscross the valley floor, and hiking trails lead up the different tributary branches of 'Iao Stream as well as up a central ridge to the tableland above the upper valley floor. Wherever you roam in the park, your eyes are drawn toward ***'Iao Needle,*** a basalt spire jutting 1,320 feet above the valley floor. A narrow ridge actually connects the Needle to the valley wall, but its freestanding illusion is maintained until you walk behind it.

South of Wailuku, the Honoapi'ilani Highway (Route 30) continues out of High Street to reach the small pineapple plantation town of Waikapu, home of ***Maui Tropical Plantation*** (808-244-7643; mauitropicalplantation.com). This

60-acre "working farm" showcases Hawai'i's agricultural history and diversity. It's worth visiting but would seem less of a tourist trap if the gift shop did not sit firmly athwart the entrance. If you skip the narrated ride, admission is free. Open daily 8 a.m. to 9 p.m., with tours from 10 a.m. to 4 p.m., and the store is open 9 a.m to 5 p.m.

Don't let the sedate pineapple fields around Waikapu fool you; the rest of the isthmus "raises cane." Surrounded by tall, waving cane fields, the tiny town of Pu'unene sits southeast of Kahului at the intersection of Pu'unene Avenue (Route 350) and Hansen Road. Pu'unene centers around its sugar mill, a monster of hissing pipes and ducts and throbbing machinery, one of the few working mills left in Hawai'i; visitors are barred for safety reasons. Instead, the curious can learn the sugar story—and even see a working scale model of a mill—by visiting the ***Alexander & Baldwin Sugar Mill Museum*** (808-871-8058; sugarmuseum.com) right across the street.

Housed in a 1902 plantation superintendent's residence, the museum brings to life the people and events that created Hawai'i's once dominant industry. Begin by mastering Arithmetic Lesson Number 1: Constant Sunshine Plus a Ton of Water Equals a Pound of Sugar. Maui's isthmus gets plenty of sunshine, but the water comes from irrigation. In 1878 Samuel Alexander and Henry Baldwin, children of Lahaina missionaries, began the Hāmākua Ditch, a 50-mile engineering miracle that tunneled and bridged its way across Haleakalā's rainy windward gulches to tap millions of gallons of water. You can see remnants of it on the drive to Hāna. In addition to its inherent difficulties, the project became a race against time. If they didn't finish in a year, the water rights and all their work would go to their rival, Claus Spreckels, who held financial strings on King Kalākaua. They made it—barely.

With the increase in irrigated lands under production, a labor shortage arose. Different immigrant groups were brought in to work the fields and were housed in separate camps with names like Ah Fong for the Chinese and Codfish for the Portuguese. Such segregation helped new arrivals adjust to the culture shock of relocation and also prevented a united labor front from forming. Photo murals illustrate the different pastimes these plantation workers indulged in: sumo wrestling for the Japanese, cockfights for the Filipinos, with baseball serving as the one "melting pot" sport. The museum is open Mon to Thurs 10 a.m. to 2 p.m.; $7 admission.

South of Waikapu, Route 30 leads to Ma'alaea Bay on the isthmus's southern shore. The ***Maui Ocean Center*** (808-270-7000; mauioceancenter.com) here presents a fascinating introduction to Hawai'i's underwater environment. Grasp a squishy sea cucumber in the "touch pool." Test your knowledge of cetacean trivia by playing the Humpback Dating Game. Stroll through a glass tunnel that leads into a 750,000-gallon "open-ocean" tank, with sharks and other colorful fish swimming overhead. Naturalist talks/feedings are scheduled at different tanks throughout the day. Open daily 9 a.m. to 5 p.m.; $44.11 admission.

If your ocean center visit has inspired you to do some marine explorations of your own, stop by the nearby ***Pacific Whale Foundation***'s (808-249-8811; 800-942-5311; pacificwhale.org) marine resource center for free reef and whale-watching guides and helpful advice. Open daily 9:30 a.m. to 2:30 p.m. (They have another location in Lahaina, at 612 Front St.) The foundation also operates a coral reef information station at Ulua Beach in Wailea (with a second station in Kā'anapali during summer), which offers free reef tours; call for schedule. They also run educational whale- and dolphin-watching boat trips, with all profits donated to conservation research. If you'd rather do your whale watching from dry land, the foundation mans a free information station at McGregor Point (on the road to West Maui) during winter months.

Further information on whales and marine life generally can be found at the ***National Marine Sanctuary*** (808-879-2818; 800-831-4888; hawaiihumpbackwhale.noaa.gov) headquarters, just around the bay at 726 S. Kīhei Rd. Scientists monitor Hawai'i's whale population from here. Visitors can use free telescopes to do a little monitoring of their own as well as peruse exhibits on marine ecology and its importance to Native Hawaiian culture. Open Mon through Fri 9:30 a.m. to 2:30 p.m.

If looking at so many fish has made you hungry to eat some, wander over from the ocean center to ***Tante's Fishmarket Restaurant & Bar*** (808-868-2148; tantesfishmarket.com) for upscale seafood fine dining. Try the daily catch prepared with your choice of lemon butter, panang curry, furikake-crusted, or even stuffed with lobster and crab. Open daily 10:30 a.m. to 9 p.m. Expensive to investment-caliber.

Moving from fishes to birds, you pass ***Kealia Pond National Wildlife Refuge*** (808-875-1582; fws.gov/refuge/kealia-pond), a wetland bird sanctuary, heading southeast around the bay toward Kīhei. Ornithology enthusiasts can stop at the visitor office located on the inland side of the pond at the 6-mile marker along the Mokulele Highway (Route 311) for a free brochure. Open Mon through Fri 7:30 a.m. to 5 p.m.

The rest of Kīhei is cluttered with condos and holds little of interest to the off-the-beaten-path traveler. Instead, take advantage of the Pi'ilani Highway to bypass them and fast-forward to the less-traveled territory that begins farther south at Makena. Turn left (south) from Wailea Alanui Drive and then right (seaward) at the second juncture with Old Makena Road to swing past historic ***Keawalai Congregational Church*** (808-879-5557). Sunday services, at 10 a.m., are conducted half in English, half in Hawaiian. Churchgoers might

Humpback Heaven

Like many species, humpbacks head south for the winter as Arctic ice packs encroach on their summer feeding grounds off Alaska. Fashionable humpbacks gather in Hawai'i; roughly 3,000 whales, more than two-thirds of the North Pacific population, winter in island waters. The whales begin arriving in November, reach peak numbers by February, and stick around until about May. They do not eat while in Hawaiian waters, as their preferred food, krill (a tiny shrimp), is not found in tropical oceans. Instead, the humpbacks live off stores of blubber accumulated during the summer and devote their time to other pursuits.

Topping their list of vacation activities is reproduction. Whales breed and then give birth a year later in the warm, sheltered waters offshore from all the major Hawaiian islands, with the largest numbers gathering around Maui. Female humpbacks calve every two or three years, with a 10- to 12-month gestation period. Their newborns measure 12 to 14 feet and weigh 2 tons. Drinking 50 to 100 gallons of milk, the newborns will grow as much as 100 pounds per day, reaching up to 40 tons and 50 feet long by maturity.

Humpbacks communicate through unusually complex whale songs, haunting rhythmic melodies that extend from the subsonic range to high-pitched whistles and can travel hundreds of miles of open ocean. Only male humpback whales sing complete songs; the tunes they use vary by region in the Pacific and evolve over time.

Humpbacks are also known for their playful acrobatics, often leaping from the water or splashing with their flukes and fins. The purpose of this behavior is not well understood, but it makes for fascinating whale watching. Any number of whale-watching tours operate during the season from Lahaina or Malaia harbors.

To learn more about humpbacks on dry land, visit the National Marine Sanctuary in Kīhei or the Pacific Whale Foundation's Ma'alaea, Lahaina, or McGregor Point locations.

also appreciate open-air services farther north in Kīhei, held (weather permitting) in the ruins of a church built by David Malo, Hawai'i's first native ordained minister. Look for ***Trinity-by-the-Sea Church*** (808-879-0161) off South Kīhei Road on Kulanihako'i Street, 1 block south of Kalepolepo Beach Park.

On the horizon you can see all the islands of Maui County floating in an inland sea. From left to right, they are Kaho'olawe, Lāna'i, and Moloka'i. During the Ice Age, a drop in the sea level welded these lands together into a single mass. Molokini Islet, in the middle of Alalakeiki Channel, formed during this period as a tuff cone on a once-larger Haleakalā.

Continue about a mile past the Maui Prince Hotel to the parking lot for ***Oneloa*** ("long sands") ***Beach.*** The last undeveloped beach on the coast, Oneloa glories in a half mile of wide, white sand bordering azure waters. Rising from the northern edge of the beach, ***Pu'u Olai,*** a 360-foot cinder cone, resembles a pimple on the slope of Haleakalā. Climb over its seaward edge to reach ***Little Beach,*** a popular (and illegal) nudist enclave. Dangerous conditions arise during high surf at both beaches.

As you move south from Oneloa, you enter the ***'Āhihi-Kīna'u Natural Area Reserve.*** A glance up the slope of Haleakalā reveals a dark scar on the volcano's green flank. This black, congealed mass of lava came from the unexpected 1790 ***Paea Flow,*** the last eruption on Maui. Scientists ascribe the flow to an isolated pocket of lava trapped underground after its source had dried up. Hawaiian legend interprets it as the wrath of Pele consuming Paea, a young man who had spurned her affections. The eruption formed the massive Cape Kīna'u south of Ahihi Bay and has left the entire coastline rocky and barren. If you're feeling adventurous, a little more than a half mile across the lava-covered cape you can follow the paint splotches on the trail that starts between telephone poles 17 and 18; it crosses the lava for about a mile to reach ***Fishbowl,*** a sandy snorkeling spot.

Another mile south across the flow brings you to ***La Perouse Bay,*** named for an early French explorer who claimed it for his country, sailed off, and was never heard from again. Drivable road ends here, but remnants of the ancient ***King's Highway*** continue closer to the shore. Oral histories testify that this stone-paved pathway, built in the 15th century by the great chief Pi'ilani, once girded the island. Part of the conservation zone, the waters here are a snorkeler's paradise, although the center of the bay can be murky. Make your way to the rocky coves to the right (north). Dolphins often frequent La Perouse Bay in the morning. To the south, rock foundations and walls from Hawaiian houses are readily discernible, haunting the desolate lava with vestiges of a once-flourishing settlement.

For those wanting to explore more of this desolate coast, ***Blue Water Rafting*** (808-879-7238; bluewaterrafting.com) weaves its way in and out of sea caves, with snorkeling stops and historical narratives. The daily 4-hour Sea Caves & La Perouse Snorkel tour costs $189.

Finally, to explore some more of the isthmus's north shore, head east from Kahului along the Hāna Highway (Route 36). As you leave Kahului, you pass ***Kanaha Pond Waterfowl Refuge,*** once a freshwater fishpond sacred to royalty and now the nesting site for migratory waterfowl as well as native birds such as the Hawaiian heron, stilt, and coot. Bird-watchers can walk a perimeter trail accessed from the airport road. The highway continues through sugarcane and passes some of the world's most famous sailboarding beaches.

Trade winds sweeping across Maui's northern shoreline funnel into the central valley isthmus. As the sun heats the land, cooler air is sucked in from the ocean, and by afternoon the winds whip to a fury. Incoming swells generate constant surf, creating the perfect terrain for acrobatic jumps and rides. When the wind is blowing, beaches all along Maui's North Shore glisten with the butterfly wings of neon-colored sails. A popular fad here is kite surfing, a variant that is basically windsurfing with a detachable sail tethered to a pair of ropes. ***Kanaha Beach,*** by the airport, offers the best learning conditions for windsurfing. Most of the windsurf shops offering rentals and lessons cluster nearby on Dairy Road (straight ahead as you exit the airport). Many can also arrange beachfront accommodations. Try ***Maui Vacation Advisors*** (800-736-6284; mauivacation advisors.com) for "off-the-beaten-path" accommodations and custom packages.

Five miles east, Pā'ia once had the largest population on Maui clustered around its now-closed sugar mill. When the new "dream city" built in Kahului lured workers around the bay, Pā'ia dwindled to a virtual ghost town. In the '60s, the town acquired a hippie tinge that it has not entirely shed, but Pā'ia's revival dates from the advent of windsurfing. Hordes of mostly European sailboard fanatics have descended upon the town environs, renting beach bungalows and filling the streets with rental cars laden with windsurfing gear.

Pā'ia's ramshackle plantation buildings spread along the T formed by the Hāna Highway and Baldwin Avenue. They house an incongruous mix of surf shops, old-style markets, and clothing boutiques ranging from aloha wear kitsch to hemp chic. Near the western entrance to town, the ***Maui Crafts Guild*** (808-579-9697; mauicraftsguild.com) offers a sampling of Maui artistry in media from raku pottery to handpainted silks. A cooperative society of artists stocks and staffs the yellow two-story home, allowing you to meet creator and creations under the same roof. Open daily 10 a.m. to 6 p.m. You'll find a different kind of artistry at ***Hawaiian Fish Printers*** (808-575-2734; 375 W. Kuiaha Rd.), which showcases the ancient Japanese art of *gyotaku* (fish printing). This art form offers an alternative to taxidermy in commemorating the trophy catches of sport fishermen; instead of being mounted on a wall, the fish can leave behind a colorful imprint before making their way to a supper plate. For art-as-exercise, you could try ***Maui Yoga Shala's*** (808-495-3133) hula and Tahitian dance workouts, part of a global menu of classes at 381 Baldwin Ave. Call for schedule.

Pā'ia boasts a number of funky restaurants. The more affluent sailboarder crowds gather at ***NyloS Restaurant*** (808-579-3354; nylosmaui.com), Maui's only chef's table restaurant that has no set menu. Instead, guests get to try a nightly rotating three-course meal by chef Jeremy Solyn—who is also a certified sommelier, resulting in superb entree and wine pairings that are unmatched on the island. Try a gastronomic adventure out, whose past incarnations have included an organic mirepoix purée, curried jumbo white shrimp from Kaua'i, and housemade pastries with fresh Kula strawberries brushed with organic chocolate "paint." Open Wed to Sat 5 to 10 p.m. Investment-caliber for sure.

If you're feeling more Mexican than fusion, ***Milagros*** (808-579-8755), at the foot of Baldwin, takes seafood south of the border from ono enchiladas to ahi/spinach chimichangas. Open daily 11 a.m. to 9 p.m. Expensive. Another good bet for day-trippers bound for Upcountry or Hāna is vibrantly colored ***Café Mambo*** (808-579-8021; cafemambohawaii.com), where you can enjoy gourmet box lunches, a mix of Moroccan stews, crispy-skin duck, burgers, and fajitas with locally sourced Hāna ingredients, all served fresh in this fun and funky eatery. Open daily 11 a.m. to 8 p.m. Inexpensive to moderate.

Even more eclectic is the crepe and curry combo across the street at ***Cafe des Amis*** (808-579-6323). Open daily 11 a.m. to 8:30 p.m. Inexpensive to moderate.

A mile and a half east of town, in a romantic beach shack just off the highway in Kuau Cove, ***Mama's Fish House*** (808-579-8488; mamasfishhouse .com) serves seafood as fresh as its oceanside views. Mama buys only from local fishers; the menu tells who caught each fish where and how. It's up to you whether the end product comes grilled, seared, sautéed, or baked. Open daily 11 a.m. to 9 p.m., with happy hour pūpū served in between. Investment-caliber prices. Reservations recommended.

Mama's also rents well-equipped, albeit pricey, cottages, clustered on the same lot, starting at $595. Call (808) 579-9764.

As you head east of town, take a look at ***Mantokuji Buddhist Temple.*** The huge gong sounds daily at dawn and dusk. The windsurfing faithful worship 2 miles farther at ***Ho'okipa*** ("hospitality") ***Beach Park.*** Their mecca, a small rocky beach with less-than-hospitable currents and surf, offers experts unbeatable windsurfing terrain. When conditions are right, you can watch the world's top talents launch themselves into aerial loops off the face of mountainous waves, then jibe to surf the next breaker in.

The Road to Hāna

The road to Hāna is perhaps the most famous off-the-beaten-path adventure in Hawai'i. A constant stream of rental cars embarks on this 52-mile odyssey, negotiating 59 bridges and more than 620 curves. You should, too—but if at all possible, break up the trip by stopping overnight; it'll take the pressure off your drive. The road to Hāna is like life: It's not the destination that counts but what you do along the way.

The ***Hāna Highway*** (Route 360) traverses Maui's shoulders, the rainy northeast slopes of Haleakalā. You pass isolated valleys, hidden (and not-so-hidden) waterfalls, and stunning seascapes. Along the way grow tropical plants of every description. Roll down your windows and smell the flowers—there's always something in bloom. Do, however, check the weather before leaving (866-944-5025; weather.gov/hfo/). Heavy rains along this windward coast can cause landslides and close the highway entirely. Beyond Hāna, the southern route to ʻUlupalakua Ranch (Route 31) is poorly maintained and sometimes impassable.

Stock up before you leave Pāʻia because it's a long, empty road ahead. East of Hoʻokipa Beach Park, Route 36 winds around ***Maliko Gulch.*** This was the last obstacle in building the Hāmākua Ditch, an early irrigation channel bringing water to the isthmus sugar fields, and weary workers balked when they saw its steep walls. To rally his troops, Henry Baldwin—who had lost an arm in a mill accident only months before—grabbed a rope and lowered himself into the ravine using his one good hand. He repeated this feat every day until the gulch was spanned.

After leaving Maliko, the highway climbs inland past pineapple fields and smaller gulches before reaching Haʻikū, a semirural community once anchored by a pair of pineapple canneries. The canneries closed long ago and have been converted to commercial space. To explore the area, turn inland onto Haʻikū Road; it's the second right past the 11-mile marker. Stay on Haʻikū for about a mile until you reach the first cannery building. Instead of pineapples, part of the cannery now processes *noni,* a traditional Polynesian medicinal plant used to stimulate the immune system. Another part of the erstwhile cannery is devoted to taro, the traditional Hawaiian staple crop. You'll find the taro burgers produced here on the menu at ***Veg Out*** (808-575–5320; veg-out.com), a cafe across the street that also bakes a mean peanut butter cookie. Open daily Mon through Fri 11 a.m. to 7:30 p.m., and Sat noon to 7:30 p.m. Nonveggies could grab a $3 fresh fish, chicken, or steak taco from the ***Island Taco*** stand in the cannery lot; open daily 11 a.m. to 8 p.m.

For a more substantial meal, try ***Ka Haku Smoke Shack*** (529-535 Hāna Hwy.), cooking up a heap of food in big outdoor grills that you can't miss. For not much over $20, you can score the "chef's choice" platter: with tender ribs, seasoned chicken, glazed pork belly, a vegetable relish of onion, tomato, and *pohole* (fiddleneck) fern, plus coconut rice and cinnamon-and-brown sugar caramelized sweet plantains with whipped cream—all served in a banana leaf–lined hollow bamboo stalk. Everything's locally sourced, with zero waste, and the kitchen only closes when the food runs out. Amazing.

If you continue to follow Haʻikū Road (turning left at the cannery) as it wends its meandering bucolic path, you'll rejoin the Hāna Highway a couple of miles farther east. Or turn left onto West Kuiaha Road a half mile along Haʻikū Road, and you'll arrive at Cannery Number 2, now used by surfboard manufacturers.

Cave Legends

Near Hāna, a well-marked trail in ***Wai'ānapanapa State Park*** (808-587-0300; dlnr.hawaii.gov/dsp/parks/maui/waianapanapa-state-park) leads to two caves formed from ancient lava tubes and now partially filled with water. An old Hawaiian legend tells of beautiful Popo'alaea, who ran away from her cruel husband, Kakae, and hid with her handmaiden in the first of these caves on a dry inner ledge not visible from the opening. Kakae came after her, furious at Popo'alaea's betrayal. Although her tracks led to the cave, Kakae could not at first tell where she had vanished and started to move away. Unfortunately, just then the torchlight he carried revealed the bright colors of the princess's feather *kāhili* (a standard of royalty) mirrored on the clear water of the cave. Venting his anger with savage strokes of his dagger, Kakae slew the women there on the spot, their blood spilling into the pool. The tiny Ōpaeka'a shrimp that live in this pool annually recall this act of cruelty. In spawning every spring, they turn the water red, supposedly in deference to the slain princess. Adventurous travelers today can swim to the inner ledge where Popo'alaea hid, equipped with a flashlight wrapped in a resealable plastic bag. Those interested in more extended spelunking should contact Maui Cave Adventures (808-248-7308; mauicave.com) for 40-minute self-guided tours through the much larger Ka'eleku Caverns nearby. Open 10:30 a.m. to 4 p.m. Admission $15.

Get the jump on the drive to Hāna by lodging in Ha'ikū at ***Adventure in Paradise/Maui Tradewinds*** (808-573-0066; 4322 Une Pl.; mauitradewinds .com), which offers two private units with an ocean view and private hot tub. Contact for the latest prices.

The Hāna Highway officially begins after the 16-mile marker at the intersection with Route 400. Route 36 changes to Route 360, for whatever reason, and the mileage markers begin at zero. As if to justify this symbolism, the road immediately launches into wild turns through lush jungle. Continue to the first bridge (Ho'olawanui Stream) past the 2-mile marker. A trail leads from a gate on the near side of the bridge a quarter mile inland to ***Twin Falls,*** the first of many to come. You can swing from a rope into the swimming hole below the falls. A larger falls waits a half mile upstream; bear left along the irrigation ditch. Daredevils leap from the top of this one as well. WARNING: As with all streams on the Hāna Coast, beware of flash flooding. Heavy rain on the mountainside and swollen, mud-gorged water are warning signs.

A mile farther, roughly one-third of the way to Hāna, ***Huelo Point*** boasts a couple of old churches and some modern, splashy vacation rentals in a tropical jungle setting. The most extravagant of these, ***Hale Akua Garden Farm & Eco-Retreat Center*** (808-572-9300; haleakua.org) offers all the opulence and privacy of a sultan's pleasure palace. Its perch on the edge of a 300-foot cliff affords a dramatic view of a waterfall toppling into an oceanfront gorge, with the Hāna coastline and Haleakalā Crater framed in the background, a view you can admire from the Jacuzzi decks. The sumptuous decor includes private, landscaped gardens, Balinese statuary, Javanese textiles, a marble kitchen, and a private pool for each rental. The one-and-a-half-bedroom ***Waterfall House*** consists of six glass-sided, skylit octagons, with a marble fireplace and a baby grand piano. The one-bedroom Cliffhouse has its own marvels, such as the garden shower that pours from inside an urn held by a 10-foot Balinese stone maiden. Both rentals have a three-day minimum stay and require a security deposit. Hale Akua Garden Farm & Eco-Retreat Center has a lot going on, between managing an organic farm, hosting educational tours and retreats, holding weekly yoga classes, and offering fresh farm produce. Rooms here range from large suites to cozy bedrooms, with views of waterfalls and cliffs. This multifaceted facility is worth a visit. WARNING: Whales splashing offshore at night might disturb your slumber. Other distinctive rentals are offered by ***Huelo Point Lookout*** (808-463-7062; maui-vacationrentals.com).

Kailua Village, at 5.5 miles, is the headquarters of the East Maui Irrigation Company, Alexander & Baldwin's irrigation arm. All along the Hāna Highway, you will see E.M.I. CO. signs, and portions of the original 19th-century stone aqueducts shadow the road, funneling water to the island's dry side. Rainbow and robusta eucalyptus trees planted for lumber at the turn of the last century predominate for the next few miles.

At 9.6 miles, a wide pullout space marks the start of the short ***Waikamoi Ridge Trail,*** a half-mile nature walk with scenic overlooks with picnic tables at beginning and end. A variety of plants along the trail, including mahogany, paperback, and tree ferns, are labeled. The trail also passes through a "musical" forest of bamboo; the slightest wind sets these hollow trees creaking and sighing cacophonously. A sign at the trailhead reads QUIET, TREES AT WORK.

Waikamoi Stream, at the next bridge, has a small pool for swimming, but most people stop here for the springwater that runs from a metal pipe in the rock wall just past the bridge. For splashier aquatic antics, continue to ***Puohokamoa,*** the next stream at the 11-mile marker. There are three waterfalls here, involving hikes of graduated difficulty. A leisurely stroll on a paved pathway leads past picnic tables to the nearest falls and swimming hole below. *Laua'e,* a multilobed, spore-studded fern that was a symbol of romantic love in old Hawai'i, grows here. For a bit more seclusion, cross the stream and hike up the steep (often slippery) left bank to a larger pool and falls upstream. The really adventurous hiker can rock-hop a half mile downstream (there is no trail) and peer over the edge of a 200-foot cascade that tumbles into a narrow gorge below. A tamer alternative is to walk back 100 yards on the highway to glimpse the lower falls peeking through the rain-forest canopy. A trail from behind the telephone pole at the bend descends to even better views.

The next stream after Puohokamoa, ***Haipua'ena,*** has two less well-known falls with swimming pools to enjoy. A white cross painted on a rock marks the start of the trail upstream along the left bank past coconuts, ti leaves, and heliconia flowers. The first pool and falls are pleasant, but they are really only a false front for the true beauty upstream. Getting there requires a short but treacherous climb.

Past the 12-mile marker, ***Kaumahina State Wayside Park*** has restrooms and a picnic area that serves up coastal views stretching to Ke'anae Peninsula and beyond. African tulip trees flame with frilly orange blossoms. The heart-stopping scenery continues as the highway winds along a narrow ledge above the ocean to descend into ***Honomanu Valley,*** one of the few ancient valleys not flattened by subsequent flows from Haleakalā. A side road just past the bridge follows the stream down to a gravel-sanded bay, with views up valley.

Just past the 15-mile marker, the YMCA's ***Camp Ke'anae*** (808-248-8355; ymca.org/camps/camp-keanae) perches on an isolated headland in a lush garden setting with spectacular coastal views. Run as a sanctioned American Youth Hostel, the camp offers both dorm berths and camping; contact for the latest rates. Bring your own bedding. Just around the bend on the inland side, ***Ke'anae Arboretum*** spreads across 6 acres of labeled botanical specimens, although it's not always well maintained. Amble up Piinaau Stream past ginger and banana to enter the arboretum grounds. There are three main sections. In the first, you encounter native trees, huge sheaths of bamboo, and all manner of palms. The second showcases taro and other Hawaiian crops. A tougher trail forges through the last section, a mile of rain forest. Free.

Beyond the arboretum, a turnoff on the left provides a bumpy but scenic detour onto ***Ke'anae Peninsula.*** Lava from Haleakalā's last crater eruption funneled through the Ko'olau Gap, filling Ke'anae Valley to form this flat, crusted appendage. Horses roam the grassy pastures, and an old stone church poses impassively. As you circle the perimeter road, savoring the coastal views in either direction, please respect the privacy of residents who cling to the rustic lifestyle here. The road dead-ends short of a full loop in front of extensive taro fields. Oral histories tell of the transformation of this barren peninsula into rich farmland by a thousand loads of topsoil hand-carried from the hills.

The highway, meanwhile, climbs above the peninsula and offers a lookout point near the 17-mile marker. Ke'anae marks the halfway point to Hāna; a series of roadside food vendors lies ahead.

At 18 miles, a left turn onto Wailua Village Road takes you into this isolated taro-farming community. ***St. Gabriel's Catholic Church*** and the ***Miracle of Fatima Shrine*** stand on the ocean side of the road. The church features an attractive altar draped in kapa cloth, but the story behind the shrine is what merits a visit here. In 1860, when the Catholic community set out to construct this tiny chapel (the original St. Gabriel's church), they lacked adequate building materials. Harvesting underwater coral blocks required enormous time and effort until, answering their prayers, an ocean storm miraculously washed abundant chunks of coral onto the shore. When the grateful Catholics had taken all they needed, a second storm washed the remainder back to sea—or so the story goes.

The highway climbs on above the village. The ***Wailua Wayside Lookout,*** a half mile up on the right, should not be missed. Steps tunneled through a thicket of *hau* lead to a panoramic view of the patchwork taro paddies below, and inland up the broad slopes Wailua Valley rises to Haleakalā Crater. A half mile farther, the spectacular ***Waikani Falls*** plunges forcefully from cliffs above the highway.

Near 22 miles, you pass the smaller ***Kopiliula Falls,*** and a half mile farther, you can pause for a breather at ***Pua'a Ka'a*** ("rolling pigs") ***State Wayside Park.*** Spread along the banks of a stream, the park has picnic tables in a pleasant setting overlooking a small waterfall.

The next 3 miles of highway break into stretches of open country in between overgrown streams and waterfalls. Roadside ginger grows along this section of the road; be sure to inhale the natural perfume. Rainfall in the hills above the highway here averages an inch a day. For a coastal detour, take Nahiku Road, near the 25-mile marker, which descends through 2 miles of lush greenery to the sea. Nahiku was the site of an early-1900s rubber plantation; you'll pass rubber trees along the way. Coastal views at the shoreline extend back to Ke'anae. A trail to the left leads to a small, freshwater pool.

The road breaks clear again into pastureland at the 27-mile point, with ocean and crater views. Notice the cluster of giant travelers' palms by the upcoming ranch house on the left. These fantastic fan-shaped specimens can store up to a quart of water at the base of their leaves for thirsty travelers to access. ***Nahiku Tī Gallery & Coffee Shop*** (808-248-8800), just ahead, is the largest of the many roadside stands spaced along the Hāna Coast. The smoked fish tacos sold here, eaten with steamed breadfruit, a starchy Hawaiian staple (add lots of salt), make for a tasty picnic lunch. The fish can be dry so ask for plenty of lemon juice or eat it with your favorite tropical fruit. Inexpensive. Other island products sold here include 'awa tea and noni fruit, two traditional Polynesian medicinals. The gallery is open Mon to Fri 11 a.m. to 5 p.m., and Sat and Sun 11 a.m. to 3 p.m., although the food stand is closed on Thurs.

Around 30 miles, the road descends to the flat expanses of the Hāna Coast. Past the 31-mile point, turn left and bump your way seaward on

'Ulaino Road. About 1.5 miles in, a sign points to ***Kahanu Gardens*** (808-240-1301 ext. 321; ntbg.org/gardens/kahanu). You drive in past dense groves of coconut, hala, kukui, hau, and breadfruit trees, all of which played key roles in the ethnobotany of ancient Hawai'i. Even plant haters should come here, if only to gaze in awe at ***Pi'ilanihale Heiau,*** the largest such temple in the state. Built by the Pi'ilani chiefs in the 15th century, this massive stone complex rises 40 feet above the ground and spreads across more than an acre. The gardens are open for self-guided tours Mon through Sat between 9 a.m. and 3 p.m. Admission is $18.

If Kahanu's schedule does not match yours, you might stop at ***Hāna Maui Botanical Gardens*** (808-248-7725; ecoclub.com/hanamaui), 1 mile back up 'Ulaino Road. This 27-acre fruit and flower farm owned by a Native Hawaiian family offers its own self-guided "botanical walk."

If it has not rained recently and the road is passable, you can follow 'Ulaino Road as it curves around left past Kahauu Gardens, ending up near the ocean; continue walking across the stream straight ahead to reach the waterfall-fed ***Blue Pool,*** a tropical vision, at the ocean's edge.

Back on the highway, the next crossroad leads to Hāna's tiny airport (808-872-3830; airports.hawaii.gov/hnm), currently served only by ***Mokulele Airlines*** (866-260-7070; mokuleleairlines.com). But with no car rentals available in Hāna, and no public transportation, it might be better to fly in from Kahului, get your car there, and drive in. (Guests of the Hāna-Maui Resort have access to the resort's shuttle.) Continue past the 32-mile point before turning seaward to ***Wai'ānapanapa*** ("glistening water") ***State Park*** (808-984-8109; dlnr.hawaii.gov/dsp/parks/maui/waianapanapa-state-park). Notice the many breadfruit trees on the way in. The bowling ball–size fruit provided a starchy Hawaiian staple, and the sticky tree sap was used to trap birds. Pass the housekeeping cabins at the park office (book at least six months in advance for these) and drive on to the second parking lot to explore the park's caves and beach.

A lovely nature trail loops around the lava-tube caves. Begin on the left fork and descend to the first water-filled cavern, where according to legend, a Hawaiian princess hid from a jealous husband. With a flashlight in a plastic bag, you can swim a short distance to the ledge of a dry inner chamber where she hid. The trail continues past other caves, then returns through a tunnel-like thicket of hau trees.

Another short trail descends to the black "sand" beach, actually composed of fine lava gravel. A rugged sea arch juts from the mouth of the bay, and seabirds nest in the rock islands offshore. Swimming becomes dangerous during periods of high surf. Coastal footpaths follow remnants of the ancient ***King's Highway*** for miles in either direction past burial mounds and heiau. The stark vegetation, composed predominantly of beach naupaka and hala trees, evokes images of a much older Hawai'i.

Just ahead, a fork in the road marks the entrance to Hāna proper. Forty-eight percent of the almost 2,000 inhabitants here claim native ancestry. To explore this cultural heritage, veer left from the highway onto Uakea Road and continue a half mile to the ***Hāna Cultural Center*** (808-446-2967; hanaculturalcenter.org). Begin at the museum building, Hāna Waiwai. The treasures here resemble family heirlooms, which many of them are. The late Coila Eade started the museum as a retirement project, and it blossomed with community support. She carved the beautiful koa doors at the entrance as well as the busts inside of prominent Hāna residents. Hawaiian artifacts on display include a century-old *olonā* fish-net, coconut-frond brooms, and all manner of specialized stones used by a Stone Age people. The center also includes a restored 1871 courthouse, which still sees occasional use, and a replica of a traditional Hawaiian village, complete with eth-nobotanical gardens and authentic thatched hale. Museum open daily 10 a.m. to 4 p.m. At the time of the publishing of this book, the cultural center museum and gift shop were temporarily closed; please check online or call before visiting.

Past the museum, turn left onto Keawa Place to unwind at peaceful ***Hāna Beach Park,*** a pleasant, dark-sand swimming beach on the right side of Hāna Bay. Rising above the beach, tree-covered ***Ka'uiki Head*** blushes with oxidized iron. Ka'uiki dominates its surroundings, as it does Hāna history. The extinct cinder cone served as a natural fortress guarding Hāna during invasions to and from the Big Island. In 1773 two decades of clashes between Maui's Kahekili and Big Island invaders led by Kalani'ōpu'u culminated in a dramatic siege in which the Maui forces surrounded the hill and, by cutting off his water supply, forced Kalani'ōpu'u to withdraw. Polished sling stones thrown in the battle litter Ka'uiki's slopes.

From the wharf at the mouth of the bay, you can follow the narrow trail around Ka'uiki's red flank. A 5-minute walk brings you to the tip of the head-land, where a small copper plaque marks the cave in which Queen Ka'ahumanu was born to exiled ali'i and hid during Kalani'ōpu'u's first invasion. She was almost lost as an infant when, unbeknownst to her parents, she fell off a canoe. While Hāna remained under Big Island rule, Ka'ahumanu met and married the up-and-coming Kamehameha, and her fortune began to shift. She became his favorite wife, but although he placed a kapu on her body, she tormented him by sleeping with other men. Visiting British Captain Vancouver helped reconcile the couple, and upon Kamehameha's death she became queen regent.

Just inland of the bay, a traditional hale akule stands on a rise at the edge of Ka'uiki, built from ironwood beams joined by traditional rope lashings (no nails), with a thatched roof of loulu palm leaves. Old-timers frequent this fish-spotting station, keeping an eye on the bay below to alert local fishermen when the akule is running, but always happy to talk with visitors in the meantime. You may have noticed other such hale on the highway leading into Hāna, opposite the high school and elsewhere around town. They were built by local Hawaiians as an expression of their cultural heritage, under the guidance of Hāna resident Francis Senensee, a world expert on native architecture.

Continue on Uakea Road until it ends at the beach cottages of Travassa. From here, another trail winds around the opposite flank of Ka'uiki to ***Kaihalulu*** or ***Red Sand Beach.*** Erosive cinders along the path make the footing treacherous, and the hotel keeps the trailhead deliberately obscure to discourage its use. The reward for the fleet of foot is a gorgeous pocket of red cinder sand enveloped in a secluded cove. The crystalline waters are a vision of blue on red. A protective wall of jagged lava rock just offshore keeps swimming conditions safe. The near side of the beach is less rocky. Clothing optional.

Backtrack a block on Uakea Road and turn left onto Hau'oli Street. At the corner of the Hāna Highway is ***Wananalua Church,*** dating from 1842. Hāna's first missionaries deliberately built this coral block temple over the site of a pagan heiau. A white cross atop nearby ***Lyon's Hill*** honors the memory of Paul Fagan, who introduced ranching to Hāna after sugar died out. Fagan later opened the Hotel Hāna Maui in 1946 as a guesthouse for his millionaire friends.

Today, that hotel is ***Hāna-Maui Resort*** (808-400-1234; hanamauiresort .com), consisting of more than 60 guest rooms housed in single-story bungalows spread across 65-plus acres of bay-front property, right in the center of town. The humble exterior of the plantation-style cottages in which guests are housed sets the tone for the understated elegance within. Cross-ventilating windows let you savor the island breeze and the sound of the surf. The main hotel building, also low-rise, has a similarly relaxed, open-air ambience. (Be sure to look at the "Hawaiian weather stone" at the lobby entrance.) Cows grazing in a paddock across the street show that the resort has not strayed too far from its ranching roots. Most employees are descendants of former ranch or plantation workers, and almost all are local. They welcome guests in an easygoing manner that is both warm and professional. Rooms here start at $829.

Nonmillionaires who wish to stay overnight in Hāna have several choices. For those who prefer lodging with a Balinese motif, ***Hāmoa Bay House & Bungalow*** (808-248-7884; hamoabay.com) sits on 4 acres of tropical splendor complete with its own herb garden and myriad tropical fruit trees, all within walking distance of Hāmoa Beach. Decorated with a mix of Balinese charm and old Hawai'i nostalgia, including a (decorative) mosquito net above the beds, the studio cottage also includes a Jacuzzi tub and outdoor shower and rents for $310 and up, with a three-night minimum. The two-bedroom main house features an outdoor shower and indoor *furo* (steeping tub). It goes for $325 and up, also with a three-night minimum. Both have full kitchens. If you'd rather be above it all, ***Ekena*** (808-248-7047; ekenamaui.com) offers more conventional comforts in a spacious, modern, hilltop pole home, with sweeping coastal views. It has two levels but rents to only a single party at a time, as anything from a one- to four-bedroom unit with full kitchen; rates start at $335, with a three-day minimum stay.

Back in town, ***Hāna Kai Maui Resort*** (808-248-8426; 800-346-2772; hanakaimaui.com) offers far more modest studio and one-bedroom condos with functional, motel-style amenities (including a kitchen) in a pair of drab, two-story buildings. Why bother? Location, location, location. The bay-front perch is even better than the hotel's, and some units have fabulous ocean views. Rates range from $380 to $525.

Simpler quarters in town can be found at ***Aloha Cottages*** (808-572-9820; Haiku/Huelo). Almost all of the cottages have full kitchens and rent from $75. Bargain-basement rooms await at ***Hana Inn*** (808-248-7033; 4870 Uakea Rd.; hanainn.com) around the block. Rooms with communal bathrooms and kitchens start at $130.

Kitchen facilities may come in handy because dinner options are limited to the hotel and ***Hāna Ranch Restaurant*** (808-270-5280), uphill from Hāna Highway on Mill Road. The restaurant offers moderately priced lunches and dinner, served daily from 11 a.m. to 9 p.m.

If you've got a taste for outdoorsy fun, try ***Braddah Hutts BBQ Grill*** (808-264-5582)—just look for the open-air tents and BBQ setup right off Hāna Highway. Braddah Hutts might not have a fancy dining room (unless you count picnic tables and plastic chairs), which it more than makes up for with oversize barbecue plate lunches, freshly shredded coconuts, and fresh-catch ahi to enjoy seared or raw, poke-style.

Otherwise, for do-it-yourself options, the ***Hāna Ranch Store*** (808-270-5295) sells groceries and fresh seafood. Open daily 7 a.m. to 5 p.m. Hāna's most famous retail establishment—celebrated in bumper stickers and in song—is nearby ***Hasegawa General Store*** (808-248-7079). Occupying the former Hāna theater building, it stocks an amazing hodgepodge of goods crammed under one roof. Open daily 9:30 a.m. to 6 p.m. The ***Hāna Coast Gallery*** (808-248-8636) at the hotel also has an excellent collection of higher-end pieces. Open daily 9 a.m. to 5 p.m.

One and a half miles south of town on what has now become Route 31, a county road, you reach another prominent cinder hill, ***Ka Iwi o Pele*** ("the bones of Pele"). According to the legend, "the bones" are an anatomical monument from the fire goddess's defeat by her older sister, the ocean. Turn onto

Haneo'o Road to loop around the coast. The multicolored sands of ***Koki Beach Park,*** to the left of Ka Iwi, face Alau Island offshore. To the right of the beach park are some ancient fishponds. On the far side of the loop, Haneo'o Road passes ***Hāmoa Beach,*** a pearly strand in a semicircular cove encased by tall cliffs and shaded by tropical almond (false Kamani) trees. Body surfing is excellent here; stick to the middle of the beach, as currents sweep outward to the sides. The Hāna-Maui guests get shuttled in, but the beach belongs to everyone to enjoy.

The highway continues through pastureland, and white-faced Herefords return your stares as you drive past. Just past the 48-mile marker, follow the trail on the near side of the bridge toward the ocean. A 5-minute walk brings you to ***Waioka Pond,*** commonly called Venus Pool, an enormous pool of azure freshwater surrounded by black lava rock, with a waterfall at one end and the ocean at the other. The beauty of the spot is almost surreal. Another name for this gulch is Waihonu ("turtle water"); algae flourish in the brackish water offshore, and guess what feeds on them? The road narrows and begins to wind as the pavement deteriorates and lush jungle returns. About 7 miles from Hāna, you will see ***Helio's Cross*** marking his grave on a hill just ahead. Helio Koa'eloa left this valley of his birth to learn the forbidden faith of Catholicism and returned to win converts by the thousands. He died in 1848.

Around the bend comes ***Kanahuali'i Falls,*** followed shortly by ***Wailua Falls.*** You can descend a half-mile trail opposite the former to the valley floor and take a dip in the secluded pools where the river meets the rocky shoreline. Around you lie the ruins of an abandoned village. The road winds on past the ***Virgin by the Roadside*** shrine, cut into the cliffside. Ocean vistas alternate with stream-fed jungle. Near the 10-mile point, you enter Haleakalā National Park's ***Kipahulu District*** at Oheo Gulch (808-572-4400; nps.gov/hale/contacts). Tourist crowds come here to see the "seven sacred pools," formed as Pipiwai Stream spills down a watery staircase of hollowed-out lava basins. The pools actually number more than 20 and never were sacred. You have a choice of trekking a few hundred yards down to the lower pools or hiking a half mile uphill to ***Makahiku Falls*** and an optional 2 miles farther to ***Waimoku Falls.*** The descent to the lowest pools takes you near the ocean past some archaeological remains of Hawaiian house sites. You can see the Big Island offshore on a clear day. Sharks and currents make ocean swimming a bad idea. Instead, try a dip in one or all of the pools, working your way upstream where the crowds thin out. Currents are gentle, but heed warning signs of flash flooding. Look for the reddish conical flowers of the *'awapuhi* (ginger) plants that grow here. The Hawaiians crushed these bulbous hand grenades to extract a natural shampoo. Lather up and rinse in a waterfall!

If you choose the hike, you get a great overlook of Makahiku Falls cascading 200 feet below. From here, an old irrigation ditch allows you to detour to more secluded pools above the falls. The main trail continues through pastures studded with guava trees and then meanders through darkened thickets of dense bamboo that creak and rattle in the wind. The trail gets muddy at stages, but the Park Service has placed boardwalk planks across the worst spots. The trail ends beneath 400-foot cliffs, from which the threadlike fingers of Waimoku Falls descend in shimmering rivulets.

Park rangers lead regular hikes and conduct other interpretive activities. The Park Service has also formed a partnership with Kipahulu ʻOhana, a local Hawaiian group, to offer cultural demonstrations, exhibits, and other activities, from canoe carving to taro farming. Call (808) 248-8558 to check the current schedule. Primitive camping facilities are also available on a first-come, first-served basis. There is a parking fee for visitors.

A mile past Oheo, aviation buffs and old-timers make the pilgrimage to ***Lindbergh's Grave*** at Hoʻomau Church, on the ocean side of the road. Here "the Lone Eagle" chose to die, enveloped in the remote beauty of the land. His epitaph reads from Psalm 139: "If I take the wings of the morning and dwell in the uttermost parts of the sea."

As you continue onward, you enter Haleakalā's rain shadows; *wiliwili* trees give way to patchy scrub, opening up stunning coastal views. The next 6 miles of road reach an axle-grinding low and may constitute forbidden territory for rental cars. The worst patches have been paved, but the road is still occasionally washed out in stormy weather. The reward for those who persevere is a rugged coastline whose desolate beauty forms a striking contrast with the lush rain forest on the road to Hāna. Call the Hāna Public Works Office at 248-8254 to check road conditions before you chance it. As you wind your way along the coast, you'll see the 1857 ***Huialoha Church*** on a barren windswept point. To reach it, angle back on the side road, marked by mailboxes 192 and 193. It's a tranquil spot enveloped in the beauty of the sea and land around it. From here peer uphill into Kaupo Gap, through which ancient lava flows once poured from Haleakalā Crater; today hikers follow the same route via an overnight trail.

A few miles farther, the road edges back toward the shoreline at ***Nuʻu Bay,*** the best swimming beach on the coast. It's the first of the two bays here, reached by a short walk down from the highway. The road then begins to climb slowly inland through the barren landscape along Maui's hairless underbelly. Remains of ancient villages haunt the lava, and the endless miles of parched terrain overlook wide horizons of ocean. Above it all, the Haleakalā Crater dominates the landscape, its steep slopes etched by erosive gullies. The road crosses a few steep ravines and dips a final time before climbing high above Popowai sea arch. Kaho'olawe appears on the horizon, and the slopes below are pockmarked by cinder cones and scarred by lava. Twenty-one miles after leaving the Kaupo Store, the cool eucalyptus forest surrounding Maui Wine signals your arrival in Upcountry.

Upcountry and Haleakalā

Unlike Vesuvius, St. Helens, Fuji-san, and Kilimanjaro, ***Haleakalā*** ("the house of the sun") lacks the classic upsloping shape and explosive pedigree of its volcanic peers. Hawaiian volcanoes form through comparatively gentle eruptions that spread layer upon layer of viscous lava over a broad area. The flattened appearance of the "shield volcanoes" that result can be deceiving. Haleakalā does not look 10,000 feet tall because it is so wide—it spreads across most of the island. In mass, its concave dome packs more solid rock than a dozen of the world's more visually impressive "tall" volcanoes put together.

Wrapped around Haleakalā's gentle western slopes, a loosely defined agricultural zone known as Upcountry takes advantage of the temperate climate and fertile volcanic soil. Truck farmers grow a variety of vegetable crops, floral nurseries cover hillsides with tropical blooms, and two of Hawai'i's largest ranches herd cattle along Haleakalā's upper slopes. Upcountry residents are an easygoing lot. Comforted by cool breezes and chilly nights, they boast that their sunset views across West Maui can't be beat.

The many different routes to Upcountry all climb through pineapple-covered foothills planted in countered rows like the whorl of a fingerprint. The Haleakalā Highway from Kahului passes through Pukalani, the largest settlement. Two "back door" routes lead first through Makawao, an Upcountry outpost with far more character. These roads, Baldwin Avenue, which climbs from Pā'ia, and Route 400, which starts farther along the Hāna Highway and turns into Makawao Avenue, intersect each other at right angles in the center of Makawao town.

If you take Baldwin Avenue up, stop at the ***Holy Rosary Church*** on the right past the sugar mill to see Maurice Felbier's rendition of Father Damien comforting a leper. Three miles farther, look for the sign to ***Hui No'eau*** (808-572-6560; 2841 Baldwin Ave.; huinoeau.com). A beautiful lawn drive lined with trees leads to a tile-roofed Mediterranean mansion, built by noted architect C. W. Dickey for Harry and Ethel Baldwin in 1917. Ethel helped found Hui No'eau, the oldest art society on Maui, and today the *hui* (club or association) maintains the home as a workshop center for the benefit of its membership and visiting artists. Although it is not set up as a commercial gallery, various artists exhibit their works here and frequent shows and art classes are held. Wander around the garden courtyard and peek into the stables where potters manipulate their wheels. Open Tues to Sat 9 a.m. to 4 p.m.

Two miles farther, Makawao, Maui's cowboy town, keeps up its "Macho-wao" image through periodic rodeos. Maui's own Ikua Purdy stunned the mainland cowboy establishment when he won the 1908 world championship in steer roping—the first time Hawaiian *paniolo* (cowboy) had competed in a mainland event. While the ranchhands twirled their lariats, their bosses played polo with the plantation aristocracy, a tradition also maintained in Makawao. Most cowpokes work at the surrounding ranches during the week, leaving Makawao to a more precious set. No longer selling rawhide and rope, many of Makawao's shops have gone yuppie, stimulated not only by a boost in tourism but also by a rash of Upcountry subdivisions. The main streets are choked with fashionable boutiques and art galleries. Note the store selling fireplaces and chimneys—an indication of Upcountry's chilly nights.

Start your browsing amid the former Makawao Theater complex at the lower end of Baldwin Avenue. Yet another artists' collective exhibits here, and in back, ***Hot Island Glass*** (808-572-4527; hotislandglass.com) displays its own form of artistry. Watch colored lumps of glass being shaped in the 2,000-degree furnace. Open daily 9 a.m. to 5 p.m., with glassblowing starting at 10:30 a.m. (except on Sat), but call to confirm there will be glassblowing during your visit. The complex also has a very pleasant courtyard cafe.

A number of alternative-lifestyle people live here, too, close to the spiritual "power source" of Haleakalā Crater. Seekers, or those merely curious, can enter ***The Dragon's Den*** (808-572-2424), at the corner of Baldwin and Makawao Avenues. This Asian lair has shelves filled with jars of restorative herbs, teas, and medicines. William Malik grew up in China and acquired a formal education in Chinese healing. He opened this shop as the pharmaceutical wing of his adjacent practice. Other alternative practitioners have joined him. Open Mon through Sat 10 a.m. to 6 p.m., and Sun 11 a.m. to 4 p.m.

As for restaurants, Makawao has plenty. Old-timers favor the cream puffs from ***Komoda Bakery*** (808-572-7261) and head to ***Polli's*** (808-572-7808), at the top of Baldwin, for their Mexican fix. Across the street ***Casanova's Italian Deli*** (808-572-0220; casanovamaui.com) embodies Makawao's new upscale persona. The deli was established by four Italian school friends from Milan who moved to Makawao because they heard it had horses. Casanova's has expanded into an adjacent property to operate a *ristorante* and *discoteca,* but it's cheaper to order from the deli counter. Park yourself on the front porch and watch life in Makawao pass by. The restaurant is open daily from 5 to 9 p.m.

Above Makawao Avenue, Baldwin Avenue becomes Olinda Road, which leads past the 1843 coral-block ***Po'okela Church*** and climbs steeply through lush hills. Eucalyptuses line the narrow road, along which designer homes alternate with rustic farmhouses. Gaps in the tree cover offer dramatic vistas of the coast far below. Higher up, you'll pass the state's Captive Rearing Project for endangered *'alala* crows and nene geese. To stretch your legs at the top of Olinda, follow the dirt road that continues from the gate through rolling pastures. If you take the left fork, you can follow a large irrigation pipe east through several miles of variegated forest to end up in Haleakalā's moss-covered watershed.

Just before it dead-ends, Olinda connects with Pi'iholo Road, which winds through a pine forest to loop back to Makawao. On the way down, look for ***Aloha o Ka Aina,*** a plant nursery that specializes in ferns. Turn left at the bottom of Pi'iholo to return to town.

Makawao Avenue continues southwest as Route 365 to Pukalani. Here, amid this elevated wasteland of shopping malls and suburban homes, one of Maui's few authentic Hawaiian kitchens lurks in an unlikely place, the Pukalani Country Club. To reach it, go a half mile downhill on Haleakalā Highway from Makawao Avenue, turn left onto Pukalani Street past the shopping center, and follow the street to its end. The ***Pukalani Country Club*** (808-572-1325; pukalanigolf.com) serves all your local favorites, such as squid in coconut milk. Large picture windows overlook the golf course with views of West Maui beyond. Open Tues through Sat 8 a.m. to 7 p.m., and Sun and Mon 8 a.m. to 5 p.m. Inexpensive.

Ever since its opening in a forgotten plantation camp, a stampede of savvy locals have flocked to the ***Hāli'imaile General Store*** (808-572-2666; hgsmaui.com). To follow their footprints, turn from Haleakalā Highway onto Hāli'imaile Road, just south of Pukalani. Beverly Gannon left behind a background in show business to team up with two local chefs and convert this 1929-vintage plantation store into a gourmet restaurant. The result is an ever-changing menu of eclectically blended dishes based around "fish, pasta, duck, lamb, and a smoked something." Delicatessen-style lunches command moderate prices, while dinners approach the investment-caliber range. Open Tues through Sat 11 a.m. to 2:30 p.m. and 5 to 8:30 p.m.

Beyond Pukalani, the Haleakalā Highway splits off to the left as Route 377, while Route 37 continues south as the Kula Highway. These parallel routes traverse the Kula District, some of Maui's most fertile farmland. Kula onions are prized throughout the state for their sweet, mild flavor. Kula potatoes, first planted to feed hungry forty-niners during the California Gold Rush, now appear in island markets as Maui-style potato chips. Kula's flower farms have blossomed into a multimillion-dollar business, thanks largely to the commercial success of the South African protea. Like the Greek god Proteus, for whom they are named, these striking flowers take many forms; dressed in metallic hues, they have a texture ranging between feathers and stiff felt and form eclectic bouquets that retain their beauty fresh or dry. There are five major types: the regal powder-puffs of the king protea, the spiky bristles of pincushions, the featherlike minks, the silvery foliage of leucadendrons, and the odd-looking banksias, resembling an acorn on a stick. Although primarily a winter crop, some varieties bloom year-round. Many of Kula's flower nurseries post signs welcoming visitors and will sell retail.

Most of the farms lie alongside roads running between the two highways. Plot your own course on these steep country lanes, perfect for a lazy Sunday drive. If you take Copp Road, one such connector, uphill from the Kula Highway, turn left onto Mauna Place two intersections up to reach ***Proteas of Hawai'i*** (808-878-2533; 800-367-7768; proteasofhawaii.com), at the north end of Mauna Place. More than 100 shape-morphing varieties await your inspection here Mon through Thurs 8 a.m. to 2 p.m., and Fri 8 a.m. to noon. To see new varieties in the making, you can also visit the experimental ***University of Hawai'i Maui Agricultural Research Center*** (808-878-1213; ctahr.hawaii.edu/site/LocationDetails.aspx?ID=ER-MMAUI), across the street. There's a self-guiding map you can follow, or call ahead and someone may be able to escort you.

This area is home to a number of farms growing carnations, protea, and other flora, including ***Napualani Farms*** (808-878-3185; 486 Upper Kimo Dr.), ***Pōhaku'aina Farms Inc*** (808-878-6075; 165 Alanuilili Place), and ***Maui Carnation Farm*** (808-878-2800; 945 Upper Kimo Dr.) with various hours depending on the farmhands working.

Immediately before Copp Road, on your way down the Hula Highway, look for the silver roof of the ***Holy Ghost Church*** on the uphill side of the Kula Highway. Portuguese Azores islanders built this unusual octagonal structure in 1894. To reach it, turn left from Copp onto confusingly named Lower Kula Road, which runs above and parallel to the highway. Inside the church, you'll find a lovely gilded altar and bas-relief sculptures depicting the Stations of the Cross. Notice the statue of Saint Antoine with a pig underfoot. Volunteers bake *pao doce* (Portuguese sweetbread) every Monday and Thursday morning for sale in the adjacent hall. Church members also throw an annual free luau in a tradition stemming from the old country. Their ancestral village had faced a severe drought, and the villagers had vowed that if God brought forth rain, they would feed the entire island. Centuries later, on a new island, in a faraway land, this vow is still remembered.

If you took Copp Road to reach Lower Kula Road, on the way you'll pass ***Kula Bistro*** (808-871-2960), offering a medley of breakfast options plus pizza, pasta, and panini in a casual atmosphere. Carry out to enjoy the sumptuous hilltop views outside. Open Mon 11 a.m. to 8 p.m., and Tues through Sun 7:30 to 10:30 a.m. and 11 a.m. to 8 p.m. Inexpensive.

The high road is worth taking, too, either coming or going, not for moral reasons, but because the scenery's better. Chrysanthemum and carnation farms decorate the surrounding hillside. In spring the jacaranda trees erupt in a blaze of lavender/periwinkle blossoms. A mile farther, the Haleakalā Highway turns uphill again, becoming Route 378, while Route 377 continues as Kekaulike Avenue and soon begins to descend. About 2.5 miles along and just after the Copp Road junction, the ***Kula Botanical Garden*** (808-878-1715; kulabotanicalgarden.com) on the left might merit a visit. In case you're planning a vendetta, the "taboo garden" near the top features an assortment of some of the world's most poisonous plants. Open daily 9 a.m. to 4 p.m.; admission $10.

The next left is Waipoli Road, which narrows to a single lane as it climbs 10 miles of switchbacks through cattle land to reach ***Polipoli Spring State Recreation Area*** (808-984-8109; dlnr.hawaii.gov/dsp/parks/maui/polipoli-spring-state-recreation-area). The last few miles are unpaved and require four-wheel drive. If you can make it to the top, the combination of serenity and scenery can't be beat. Tall stands of redwood mingle in an experimental forest composed of trees from around the world. A variety of hiking trails beckon, and campers can enjoy the park's unearthly views overnight by booking the state-owned cabin (808-984-8109) well in advance. Immediately past Waipoli Road, Route 377 rejoins the Kula Highway. The cabin is $100 a night and books up fast.

As you continue south along the Kula Highway, moving farther around the volcano's flank, Moloka'i disappears from the north and reappears behind the south end of West Maui. Every mile brings you farther into Haleakalā's rain shadow. In contrast with the lush hills of Olinda, *panini* (prickly pear) cactus carpets the lower elevations. A couple of miles south from the second junction of Routes 37 and 377, you reach tiny Keokea, a onetime community of Chinese immigrants. Downtown Keokea has four stores, two of them rival gas stations. ***Keokea Gallery*** (808-283-7925) takes its ties to local art seriously; many of the paintings depict scenes in or around town, while owner Sheldon Wallau paints new ones in the back of the room. Contact for open hours. A real treat awaits you in ***Grandma's Coffee*** (808-878-2140; grandmascoffee.com), where late owner Alfred Franco roasted his homegrown beans just like Grandma taught him, using a century-old roaster that her family may have brought when they fled Puerto Rico after the Spanish-American War. Peek through the counter window to see the original machinery. Grandma's also serves breakfast and lunch, with local specials such as sweet-and-sour spareribs. Paintings of Upcountry rodeos by local artist Sharon Shigekawa decorate the walls. Open daily from 7 a.m. to 2 p.m.

To tour Keokea's "Chinatown," backtrack to Cross Road, near the town entrance, which angles above the park. A half mile uphill, the ***Kwock Hing Society Building*** serves as a solitary reminder of the immigrant farmers who flocked to the area. Among the village's early residents was Sun Yat-sen's brother. The future Chinese leader often visited Keokea while studying in Honolulu. He sent his family here for safety while plotting his revolution and was funded heavily by Hawaiian Chinese through societies such as Kwock Hing. A mile and a half past Keokea town on the highway, look for ***Dr. Sun Yat-sen Memorial Park.*** Two enormous mock-stone lions face off in opposing corners, while a statue of him gazes down the hill to the site of his brother's former home.

From here, Route 37 begins a gradual, bumpy descent as it continues south across miles of cactus-studded pastureland partitioned by crumbling walls of lava stone. Most of Moloka'i swings out of view as the island of Lāna'i seizes center stage on the horizon. Farther along, uninhabited Kaho'olawe appears with tiny Molokini in midchannel. Five miles out of Keokea, the highway reaches the headquarters of the vast 'Ulupalakua Ranch. James Makee, a whaling captain turned gentleman planter, founded the ranch in 1856 to complement his sugar ventures. Makee's lavish social life included the entertainment of royalty; King Kalākaua was a frequent visitor.

Across the street, the ***Ranch Store*** boasts the oldest Levi Strauss account in the world. Bags of swine and horse feed have yielded shelf space to tourist bric-a-brac as well as a deli. Sitting on a porch in front of the store, two life-size sculptures impersonate a pair of old-timers who actually hung out on this very porch. 'Ulupalakua former resident Reems Mitchell immortalized the duo in his trademark caricature style. The cowpoke standing next to them is Ikua Purdy, a world-champion roper from the ranch's early history. Mitchell's better-known works on exhibit elsewhere include the "old salts" fronting the Pioneer Inn in Lahaina. While he has passed, his unique legacy remains.

Across the street from the mill, you can visit ***Maui Wine's vineyards*** (808-878-6058; mauiwine.com) and reward yourself with a glass of bubbly for coming this far. Emil Tedeschi has brought family know-how from Napa Valley to open Hawai'i's first vineyard and winery, in cooperation with 'Ulupalakua Ranch. You can take a free tour of the winery to learn the painstaking steps through which grapes and pineapples become bottled wines and champagne. Almost everything gets done by manual labor according to traditional methods. Despite its founder's credentials, the winery likes to boast that "this is not Napa Valley." After the tour, stop at the visitor center to sample the final product. It is housed in a cottage built for King Kalākaua's use during his visits. An adjacent gallery filled with historic photos chronicles a century of ranching life. Open Tues to Sun 11 a.m. to 5 p.m. Private tastings and tours are available by reservation.

Beyond the winery, the highway deteriorates further. A narrow, winding road rattles its way east to Kaupo across 22 miles of old lava flows covered by scrub bushes that barely sustain the scattered cattle that graze here. Consider going at least the first couple of miles to experience the bleak solitude of the landscape. As you round the corner to Haleakalā's southern slopes, the ink-black path of the Cape Kīnaʻu lava flow below draws the eye, in vivid contrast with the tree-covered cinder cones higher up.

Those who wish to devote more than a day to Upcountry or position themselves midway to Haleakalā's summit for a predawn ascent have several options. ***G & Z UpCountry Bed & Breakfast*** (808-224-6824) in lower Kula is surrounded by a 6-acre fruit farm and Haleakalā views at 3,000 feet. Amenities include free parking, fully equipped kitchen, and a large deck with BBQ grill. Plus, a complimentary continental breakfast every morning with island fruit, mango scones, cinnamon rolls, and other goodies.

Other Upcountry bed-and-breakfast cottages with hilltop views include rustic ***Kula Lodge*** (808-878-1535) with fresh flowers blooming and scenic vistas.

Located just below Makawao, the ***Banyan Tree Bed & Breakfast*** (808-866-6225) offers historical charm and leafy tranquillity in lieu of unobstructed views. Built in the 1920s as a plantation manager's home abutting the pineapple fields, the property became the residence of Ethel Baldwin, one of Maui's early patrons of the arts. Ethel painted here daily and even got her chauffeur to join her. Cottages and suites start at $190. A swimming pool is on-site.

The voyage to the top of ***Haleakalā Crater*** provides in every way the crowning experience of a Maui visit. After driving to the volcano's 10,023-foot summit, you peer over the rim of the 3,000-foot-deep crater inside. Measuring 7.5 miles long by 2.5 miles across, this mind-boggling space could swallow Manhattan, skyscrapers and all. Erosive stream action cut the original basin during a lull between eruptions, after which subsequent flows filled in the floor and restored the crater's volcanic appearance. Rust-streaked colors paint a lunar landscape of cinder cones and crusted lava flows. Mark Twain called it "the sublimest spectacle" he had ever seen.

To receive the quintessential Haleakalā experience, purists insist you must arrive at the mountain early enough to watch the sun rise above the far rim of the summit wall—but you need reservations now (recreation.gov/ticket/facility/253731). Shadows creep along the crater-pocked floor as the first rays ignite the smoldering embers of the volcano in a blaze of colorful light. Such a vision entertained the demigod Maui, who waited here in ambush and used a magic lasso to snare the sun's legs as they poked above the crater rim. Threatened with its life, the sun promised to travel across the sky more slowly, giving Maui's mother time to dry her kapa cloth. Almost as impressive as the show itself is the

The Art of Maui

The unsurpassed beauty of the Hawaiian Islands has always attracted a steady stream of artists. Maui has made a cottage industry out of "art tourism" as a means of exploiting the synergy between local talent and tourist pocketbooks. The hotbed of such activity is undoubtedly Lahaina, which claims more art galleries per capita than any other American city. Local galleries promote Friday night as Art Night, with special shows, featured artists-in-residence, and free refreshments offered from 6:30 to 9:30 p.m. The weekend outdoor showings of the Lahaina Arts Society beneath the central banyan tree provide another chance to get acquainted with local artists. The art on Maui should not be dismissed as only made-for-tourists kitsch. The many artist cooperatives scattered around the island nurture some genuine talents. Moreover, the Maui Arts and Cultural Center in Kahului showcases rotating exhibits and performances from throughout the world. Call 808-242-2787 or 808-242-7469 for details or visit mauiarts.org. Please call or check ahead to verify changes following the 2023 Maui fires.

number of pilgrims willing to brave frigid early-morning temperatures to follow in Maui's footsteps.

Those preferring to rise at a more civilized hour will be pleased to know that Haleakalā's sunsets claim a following of their own, even though clouds that descend into the crater during the day sometimes linger after dark, obscuring the view. Call (808) 877-5111 for the exact times of sunrise and sunset and general weather conditions. Allow an hour and a half for the drive up. Please note that the Haleakalā Visitor Center at 9,740 feet was temporarily closed for a building improvement project. Call ahead and reserve tickets online to ensure access.

From the junction of Routes 377 and 378, a series of switchbacks ascends 6,800 feet over 20 miles, reaching the summit a total distance of 38 miles from Kahului. You'll pass a number of biking groups cruising "the world's steepest downhill ride." If that sounds impressive, how about the autumn Run to the Sun, an annual footrace going up! The road quickly climbs above the tree line through open cattle land. Signs advise you to turn on lights in clouds. The ***Haleakalā National Park*** boundary and turnoff to the ***Hosmer Grove*** campground arrive at roughly the halfway mark. A brochure available at the campground will guide you along the quarter-mile nature trail nearby. Just ahead you can pay the $30 entrance fee and proceed to the ***Park Headquarters*** building. Inquire here about the morning schedule of ranger-led talks and hikes, and collect camping permits, if desired. Call (808) 572-4459 for live bodies 8 a.m. to 4 p.m. A small collection of displays chronicles the natural history of the park. You can learn about the campaign to restore the nene

Hawai'i Storytelling

The closest most tourists come to experiencing Hawaiian culture is at a commercial luau, where a "Polynesian Revue" blurs Hawaiian hula with other Polynesian dancing in an elaborate showbiz production that is more Vegas than Hawai'i.

In South Maui, the ***Fairmont Kea Lani*** in Wailea (866-540-4456; fairmont-kea-lani .com) offers visitors the chance to paddle a Hawaiian canoe. Canoes were the automobiles of ancient Hawai'i: the fastest way to get from point A to point B and a symbol of personal freedom. Giant voyaging canoes carried the first Polynesians to Hawai'i, perhaps refugees from political strife or simply overcrowded islanders seeking a brighter future across the horizon. Canoes also enabled fishermen to access the ocean's bounty and kept communities connected before modern means of communication. Today most boating activity aimed at visitors involves modern powered craft, and chances are if a tourist paddles anything during his or her Maui visit, it'll be a kayak. The Fairmont teaches visitors the basics of canoe paddling, as well as its cultural significance, in part through native chants associated with canoe travel. Weather permitting, canoe trips depart Mon to Fri at 7, 8, 9, and 10 a.m. The whole experience lasts about 45 minutes and costs $65; reservations are required; call the hotel concierge at 808-875-4100, ext. 290.

Finally, for your Hawaiian cultural fix in East Maui, check out the ***Kipahulu 'Ohana***'s ongoing programs of cultural activities at the Kipahulu District of Haleakalā National Park (kipahulu.org). Under the guidance of their kupuna, Native Hawaiians who reside locally provide demonstrations and hands-on activities for visitors. Call for a schedule: (808) 248-8673.

goose, Hawai'i's state bird, to the unique habitats of Hawai'i's tall volcanoes. Somewhat-tame nene often hang out in the parking lot; don't encourage them with food.

As you continue zigzagging up the barren rubble that covers Haleakalā's upper slopes, you will come to two crater overlooks that deserve a stop on the way up or down. ***Leleiwi Overlook,*** at 8,800 feet, offers the chance to view the elusive "specter of the brocken." During late afternoon on cloudy days, you may see your own rainbow-shrouded shadow reflected in the mist. ***Kalahaku Overlook,*** at 9,320 feet, features a patch of silversword plants, which thrive atop Hawai'i's highest volcanoes. These peculiar bushes resemble metallic porcupines. After growing for 5 to 20 years, they erupt once in a spectacular display of tiny flowers and then wither and die. Because silverswords have fragile, shallow roots adapted to the volcanic soil, take care not to walk within 6 feet of any plant.

Near the summit, the Park Service operates another visitor center, open from sunrise to noon daily. In addition to natural history exhibits, the center houses a much-reproduced painting by Paul Rockwood depicting Maui's encounter with the sun god, La. The metallic domes of Science City, an off-limits research center, gleam nearby. From the visitor center, the road climbs a half mile to ***Red Hill***, the actual summit. Most people watch the sunrise from the small shelter here. The 360-degree windowpanes allow you to view every island except Kaua'i on a clear day.

No one with the legs to carry them should pass up the chance to explore Haleakalā Crater on foot. Short of space flight, it's the closest thing to walking on another planet. The ***Sliding Sands Trail*** from the visitor center provides the main access to the crater floor. The trail gets its name from the loose cinders it traverses, so watch your footing. As you descend, you pass a procession of cinder cones, some of which rise as high as 700 feet; when clouds roll in, they poke through the mist like islands in a sea. The crater floor below is wracked by crevices and lava caves. Hawaiians threw the umbilical cords of their newborns into one such pit called ***Keanawilinau.*** This practice prevented rodents from making off with the cords, which would have given the grown child ratlike qualities.

The Sliding Sands Trail connects midway with the ***Halemau'u Trail***, which loops back up the crater walls, emerging near the highway at the 8,000-foot level for a hardy 11-mile daylong hike. A third trail allows backpackers an overnight route through the ***Kaupo Gap***, descending to Maui's remote southeastern coast. Hawaiians often made such a trek as a shortcut across the island. Except for kāhuna in training, Hawaiians did not live in the crater itself. If you're not a kahuna, camping in the crater's two campgrounds requires a permit. Address requests to recreation.gov or call (877) 444-6797.

In a hurry to get back to the beach? ***Paraglide Maui*** (808-563-4667; paraglidemaui.com) launches tandem flights from atop Haleakalā, weather permitting; more often they'll leave from the 6,000-foot level, where you may see other para/hang gliders launching as well. Prices vary by flight time.

West Maui

The West Maui Mountains are older, lusher, and more scenically eroded than Haleakalā. Good highway rings the entire landmass. Departing southwest from the isthmus, the Hanoapi'ilani Highway climbs high bluffs overlooking the ocean. As you round Maui's chin, the island of Lāna'i joins Kaho'olawe on the horizon, rising from the ocean like a giant humpback whale. People stop at the marked lookout here at ***Papawai Point*** to watch for real humpbacks in the Au'au Channel. The sight of a 40-ton leviathan breaching offshore has caused more than one traffic accident along this highway.

You can admire these same views (and better) by hiking the 5-mile ***Lahaina Pali Trail,*** which crosses the West Maui Mountains to reach a 1,600-foot elevation before emerging south of Olowalu at the highway's 11-mile marker. Numbered posts along the way are keyed to a free hiking guide you can get from the state parks office in Wailuku, which narrates features of the area's history and ecology. The trail starts at the highway's 5-mile point. It's best to start the hike from this side and if possible arrange a ride back from the other end.

The highway continues to carve and burrow its way through the mountain slope and eventually descends through cane fields on the other side. A row of monkeypod trees and a drop in the speed limit signal your arrival at Olowalu. Snorkeling is good here at the 14-mile marker; head to the offshore reef 100 yards out.

The ***Olowalu*** region is steeped in history. In 1790 an American captain, Simon Metcalf, opened fire on native canoes he lured into range, killing more than 80 Hawaiians to avenge the theft of his longboat and the murder of a Western sailor. The Hawaiians retaliated by seizing a companion ship captained by Metcalf's son and slaughtering most of the crew. Two English survivors from this bloodshed, Isaac Davis and John Young, became prisoners of Kamehameha, then an ambitious Big Island chieftain. Combining their expertise with the firepower of the cannons also acquired in the incident, Kamehameha won his bloody victory later that year in the alluvial 'Iao Valley above Olowalu. An ancient trail through a now-blocked mountain pass once connected Olowalu with 'Iao Valley. Refugees from Kamehameha's triumph at Kepaniwai escaped over this trail, bringing events full circle.

Hidden in the cane fields here is an impressive collection of ***petroglyphs.*** Because of vandalism, the site is no longer advertised to the general public. If you take the paved cane road that parallels the highway and turn right at the water tower a few hundred yards west of the Olowalu Store, an unpaved cane road leads a half mile to these markings. The petroglyphs are carved into a cliff face just after the road forks. Look for the former viewing platform.

Five miles northwest of Olowalu, a flotilla of yachts anchored offshore signals your arrival at the town of ***Lahaina.*** More than any other place in the islands, Lahaina embodies a feeling of old and new superimposed. The town has gone through many incarnations over the years: a center of royalty, then a raucous whaling port, then a sleepy sugar settlement. Although thriving today as a tourist center, Lahaina has retained its sense of romance and history. However, much

editor's note

Please double-check any of the Lahaina listings before visiting, as the 2023 fire sadly left much of the town destroyed.

of Lahaina was destroyed in the 2023 Maui fire. Please double-check before visiting any of the locations. The ***Lahaina Restoration Foundation*** (808-661-3262; lahainarestoration.org) moved early to preserve many of the historic sites, and building codes keep new developments in line with the old. As many of Lahania's historic sites were destroyed in the August 2023 fire, the foundation is working to restore many of them. Also good is the *Lahaina Historical Guide,* which you can pick up for free at any of the commercial centers in town to read more about the town's former landmarks. Again, we cannot stress enough to please check the situation ahead of time before visiting.

Front Street stood as the town's main drag, with a boardwalk strip running partway along the ocean. At the corner of Front and Dickenson stands the ***Baldwin Home*** (808-661-3262), Lahaina's oldest building, which served as a museum before the fires destroyed it. In 1838 newlywed missionaries Edwin and Charlotte Baldwin moved into this home after a 161-day honeymoon trip around stormy Cape Horn. The museum displayed some of their possessions, among them Charlotte's sewing kit and china brought from Connecticut. Mosquito nets over the four-poster beds reflect the arrival in 1872 of the winged parasites, carried unwittingly aboard the *Wellington,* a merchant ship docked at Lahaina.

The Reverend Edwin Baldwin ran a medical clinic in an adjacent room and serviced three islands in addition to his pastoral duties. His medical instruments fill the shelves of his study. Notice the hilarious English translation of his official posted rates. Licensed native doctors in 1865 could levy charges ranging from $50 for "very great sickness" to $3 for "incantation to find out disease" and could even assess a $10 fee for "refusal by patient to pay."

Lahaina's first missionaries, the Richardses, used to live in a house next door. In 1827 these stubborn crusaders had to crouch in their cellar while cannonballs

Fright Night

If you frighten easily, stay away from Front Street on October 31. Monsters, witches, and an assortment of scary creatures will be on the prowl during the annual Halloween festivities. No one is really sure how the tradition started, but Halloween in Lahaina has grown into an event of mythic proportion. Lahaina hotels now charge special Halloween rates. No costume is too bizarre, far-out, or ghoulish. In fact, the weirder the better.

Festivities begin with the children's parade at 4 p.m. down Front Street, followed by dancing in the streets, as hundreds of weird-looking people vie for thousands of dollars worth of prizes in a costume contest. Please check to assure this is still happening when you visit, following the 2023 fire.

whistled overhead, fired by a sea captain furious at the edicts by the ali'i, who placed a kapu on prostitution. Rallying to the motto "No God West of the Horn," the lusty sailors rioted to win back their grog and women, but as whaling gradually died as an industry, the ali'i won by default.

Walk a block seaward to the waterfront, where you'll see the stone foundations from Kamehameha I's 1802 ***Brick Palace,*** the first Western building in the islands, which is closed for restoration after the fire. Kamehameha never lived here because his wife, Ka'ahumanu, refused to move in. Kamehameha III later tended a wetland taro patch nearby to demonstrate "the dignity of labor." He also built the harbor lighthouse in 1840, reputedly the oldest of its kind in the Pacific. Walk to the seawall at the edge of the lot. The ***Hauola Stone,*** just below, is shaped like a reclining chair. You're supposed to sit here with legs dangling in the surf to activate the stone's curative powers.

Inland from the harbor entrance stood the historic ***Pioneer Inn*** (808-661-3636; 800-457-5457; 658 Wharf St.; pioneerinnmaui.com). George Freeland, a Canadian Mountie, tracked a notorious criminal to Lahaina and stayed to open in 1901 what for many years was the only hotel in town. Now a Best Western, its raucous atmosphere has tamed considerably. To get a sense of the inn's former clientele, ask for a copy of the inn's original house rules warning against drunkenness, written in pidgin English. Rooms start at $304. At the time of publication, the inn was temporarily closed for fire restoration. Please check ahead before booking.

Next to the Pioneer Inn, Lahaina's massive ***Banyan Tree*** shades almost an acre of the central courthouse square. Planted in 1873, the tree has aerial roots that have grown into twelve major trunks, giving it the appearance of a small forest. While damaged during the fire, the tree appears to continue to thrive. The ***Courthouse*** next to the tree, built in 1859, served as a center of Maui government. Inside, the ***Lahaina Art Society*** (808-661-0111; facebook.com/LahainaArtsSocietyMaui/) exhibits its members' works. Check out the Old Jail Gallery in the basement, where iron-barred cells now imprison painted canvas. You will find works from some of the island's top talents in mediums ranging from *sfumato* (smoke painting) to basket weaving. On weekends, member artists gather to display additional works under the Banyan Tree outside. Open daily 10 a.m. to 4 p.m. In the corner of the square, you will notice "ruins" of the original waterfront fort built in the 1830s to intimidate rowdy sailors. The fort was actually torn down completely in 1854. Rather than damage the Banyan Tree, the Restoration Society settled on this partial reconstruction.

Farther south on Front Street, take a peek inside the ***Episcopal Church*** to see the painting by DeLos Blackmar of a Hawaiian Madonna. Temporarily closed for restoration.

The area around here overflowed with sites of royalty. ***Malu'ulu o Lele Park*** once held a 17-acre fishpond called Mokuhinia, home of Kihawahine, a legendary mo'o. Maui's royal ali'i lived on Moku'ula, an island in this sacred pond, protected by the mo'o, and Kamehameha's heirs enjoyed its seclusion while growing up. The island even housed a royal mausoleum for a time. In 1918 the pond was filled in and the ground leveled. Today all you see is an ordinary ball field. The legacy of Moku'ula has not been forgotten, however. In 1995 the erstwhile royal residence was entered on the National Historic Registry. Teams from O'ahu's Bishop Museum have twice surveyed the site to locate buried features. Plans to excavate and restore the complex are still in talks.

Turn inland up Shaw Street to the corner of Waine'e Street and ***Waiola Church.*** Formerly named ***Waine'e Church,*** the original 1832 edifice here could seat 3,000 people and was the first stone church in the islands. In 1858 a whirlwind funneled out of Kaua'ula Valley and tore off the roof, and in 1894 royalists protesting Hawai'i's annexation burned the church to the ground. Rebuilt, it burned down again in 1947 and was restored, only to be demolished by another Kaua'ula windstorm. Reoriented with its front door facing Kaua'ula Valley and renamed Waiola, the church has remained standing . . . so far. In the old cemetery next door, elaborate tombstones designate the likes of Queens Ka'ahumanu and Keōpūolani and Maui governor Hoapili. Next to Ka'ahumanu lies Kamuali'i, the husband she kidnapped from Kaua'i, thus consolidating the united Hawaiian kingdom. This closed following the fire, so you may just see its remains. Please check ahead before visiting.

Return north on Waine'e Street past the Indian-style ***Hongwanji Mission.*** A block further, you'll find what remains of ***Hale Pa'ahao*** ("stuck in irons house"). The wall and wooden jailhouse that once stood here were built by the prisoners themselves, most of whom were jailed for disorderly conduct. Before being destroyed in the fire, you could peer inside one of the cells where prisoners were locked up at night and listen to a recorded account of prison life. Most interesting perhaps was the list of crime statistics from the period. It seems that 1857 was a big year for "giving birth to bastard children," "violating fish taboos," and "felonious branding."

The ***US Seamen's Hospital,*** farther north, remained closed until further notice at the time of this book's publication. It was originally built as a bachelor pad by Kamehameha III. Here he could escape his missionary advisers' watchful eyes to drink, gamble, and even meet for clandestine trysts with his sister, Princess Nahienaena. Such incestuous unions between high-ranking ali'i had been a sacred duty in the old days, to assure offspring of the purest bloodlines. The new Christian morality of the missionaries condemned incest. Distraught by the strain of these conflicting moralities, Nahienaena suffered an early

Heavenly Maui

For an off-the-beaten-path experience that's literally out of this world, try stargazing from the top of 10,000-foot Mount Haleakalā. The elevation and isolation ensure some of the clearest night skies on earth. Even without a telescope, you'll see more stars than you've ever dreamed of. Jan Roberson's ***Maui Stargazing*** (808-298-8254; mauistargazing.com) stages summit astronomy viewings after dark. Roberson provides the telescope, warm clothing, and a picnic meal, and JD Armstrong, PhD, provides celestial know-how to narrate a tour of the evening sky. He points out heavenly highlights such as planets, nebulae, galaxies, and star clusters—the content varies with the changing sky. He charges about $225 for the experience, which lasts five hours, depending on interest and weather permitting.

If you'd rather do your stargazing from the comfort of a luxury hotel, try the Grand Wailea Resort (808-875-1234; grandwailea.com) and the Kā'anapali Beach Club (808-661-2000); both have numerous pools, balconies, and plenty of outdoor space perfect for lounging under the stars. The sky isn't as clear, and weather's more iffy, but it's a whole lot warmer than a windy mountaintop. For guests only, the Hyatt Regency (808-661-1234; maui.hyatt.com) in Kā'anapali, named one of the world's top hotels for stargazing by CNN, holds its own nightly shows for $30 and offers a "champagne special" for couples. Ask the reception for further details.

death. A special path was cleared through the breadfruit trees of Lahaina for her body to be carried to Maluulu o Lele; the path existed as Luakini Street. The word *luakini* describes temples where human sacrifices were performed. To the grieving Hawaiians, Nahienaena was a sacrifice to the new morality of the missionaries. The United States later leased the building as a home for destitute and disabled American sailors. Consular officials in charge of the hospital ran a profitable racket, charging the US government inflated prices and even billing for "patients" interred in the nearby seamen's cemetery.

Continue north along Front Street, and you used to be able to meditate under the giant Buddha of ***Lahaina Jodo Mission.*** The Mission remains in restoration, following the 2023 fire, at the time of publication.

Lahaina means "merciless sun." If you're ready to holler uncle, take to the cooler hills. Lahainaluna Road leads uphill past the once operational Pioneer Sugar Mill to ***Lahainaluna*** ("above Lahaina") ***School.*** Founded by missionaries in 1831, it's the oldest school west of the Rockies. Boarding students from as far away as California once enrolled here. On the campus you will find ***Hale Pa'i*** (808-662-0560; lahainarestoration.org), the old mission printing house. The printery's hand press cranked out Hawaiian translations of the Bible as well as an early newspaper, paper money, and even drafts of the Hawaiian constitution.

Hale Pa'i is open Mon to Wed 10 a.m. to 4 p.m. Call to confirm they are open when you're planning to visit.

Among Lahainaluna's first students was David Malo, a brilliant scholar whose book *Hawaiian Antiquities* forms the basis for much of our knowledge of precontact Hawaiian culture. A Christian minister himself, Malo respected the missionaries for their spiritual exertions. At the same time, he saw clearly the devastating impact of Western contact on Hawaiian society. He died a bitter man, asking to be buried "above the tide of foreign invasion." His grave rests on top of Mount Ball, near the giant L cut into the forest above the school.

To many people, Lahaina doesn't mean history but shopping. Rows of Western-style arcades lined Front Street creating a carnival atmosphere. Art is a major commodity here. Notice how many galleries carry works showing dual underwater/surface landscapes in the "two worlds" style pioneered by Robert Lyn Nelson. Every Friday evening, local galleries hosted special Art Night receptions prior to the 2023 fire. For those who like their art aged, ***Lahaina Printsellers*** (808-667-5815; printsellers.com) has amassed an amazing collection of antique maps and prints. They specialize in drawings made by early Pacific explorers, with a selection from Captain Cook's voyages second only to that in the British Museum. Their Lahaina store, located at 764 Front St., is open Mon to Fri 10 a.m. to 9 p.m., and Sat and Sun 11 a.m. to 6 p.m. Temporarily closed at publication time. Call ahead before visiting.

For gift items, browse ***Totally Hawaiian Gift Gallery*** (808-667-4070; totallyhawaiian.com), at the Whalers Village. Open daily 9 a.m. to 9 p.m. Temporarily closed at publication time. Call ahead. You used to be able to stop in at ***Lahaina Scrimshaw*** to browse and learn about scrimshaw. Sailors of old started the tradition of engraving ivory teeth from sperm whales to while away the hours at sea. Upon returning to their home port, they would present the completed work to their sweethearts as a testament to their undying ardor and constancy. In fact, stores like Lahaina Scrimshaw were cottage industries even in those days. Lazy sailors could purchase mass-produced art from these early precursors of the airport gift shop. But due to recent legislation, many merchants selling and showcasing centuries-old scrimshaw (like Lahaina Scrimshaw) have been forced to close to dissuade poaching merchants; local bills were passed banning the sale of wildlife parts, including elephant ivory and rhino horn. The ***Crazy Shirts*** outlet (808-661-4775; crazyshirts.com), two doors down, has a wall devoted to whaling memorabilia. Temporarily closed. Call ahead.

Restaurants rival shops in Lahaina in variety, number, and mutability. Popular standbys overlooking the waterfront on the 800 block of Front Street include ***Kimo's*** (808-661-4811; kimosmaui.com) for seafood and ***Longhi's***

(808-667-2288; longhis.com) for hip Italian; both expensive. Kimo's was temporarily closed at publication time; please call ahead.

Farther south at 505 Front St., ***Pacific 'O*** (808-667-4341; pacificomaui .com) features trendy Pacific Rim creations, such as prawn and basil wontons and shiso spicy tuna, served right on the beach, with live jazz on weekend nights. Open Mon to Sat 5 to 9 p.m. Investment-caliber prices. You'll also find casual options like the ***Paia Fishmarket Front Street Restaurant*** (808-662-3456; 632 Front St.; paiafishmarket.com). This laid-back seafood restaurant offers up fish and burgers in a relaxed setting with a nice terrace. Both of these restaurants were temporarily closed at publication time, so please call ahead.

If all you want is a quick bite for lunch, ***The Bakery, Lahaina*** (808-667-9062), hidden behind the train station at 991C Limahana Place, prepares made-to-order sandwiches and scrumptious pastries. Open Tues through Sat 6 to 11:30 a.m. If you prefer your sandwiches with a Eurasian twist, make your way to ***Ba-Le*** (808-661-5566), in the Lahaina Cannery on the north edge of town. They also have fresh Vietnamese salads and summer rolls. Open Mon through Sat. Call ahead. Temporarily closed at publication time.

But for West Maui's best meal deal, you have to go all the way north to Honokowai, past Kā'anapali. Turn left off the highway at Times Supermarket and descend Lower Honoapi'ilani Road until you see the 5-A Rent-A-Space shopping plaza at 3608. The somewhat redundantly named ***Honokowai Okazu & Deli*** (808-665-0512) (*okazuyas* are the Japanese equivalent of delis) may be a bare-bones hole-in-the-wall serving local ethnic staples, but the food, prepared by former chefs of Mama's Fish House, is first rate. Their *ono* (wahoo, a fish) dinner special is usually fresh-caught and costs less than $13. They do a mostly take-out trade, but there is limited table and counter space. Open Mon through Sat 11 a.m. to 2:30 p.m. and 4:30 to 8:30 p.m.

The ***Plantation Inn*** (808-667-9225; 800-433-6815; 174 Lahainaluna Rd.; theplantationinn.com) has its own faux-Victorian look going; it was built that way. A white balustrade surrounds the two-story building. The interior features lavish use of natural woods, stained-glass windows, and polished brass. Floral wallpaper, lace curtains, and Persian rugs add to the indulgent feel. The rooms have authentic period furniture, from pull-chain toilets to four-poster beds; a few have ceilings with faux paintings; and suites include whirlpool baths and kitchenettes. Modern conveniences are discreetly concealed. Rates start at $387 and include a full breakfast.

A block north of Lahainaluna Road on the highway is the Lahaina terminal of the ***Lahaina-Kā'anapali Railroad,*** also known as the Sugar Cane Train (808-667-6851; sugarcanetrain.com). The islands' only remaining steam locomotives now haul tourists instead of sugarcane along the 6-mile track. The train was temporarily closed at the time of publication, so please call or check ahead before going.

Kā'anapali, north of Lahaina, was the first planned resort in the Hawaiian Islands. In the middle of 3-mile-long Kā'anapali Beach, ***Pu'u Keka'a,*** commonly called Black Rock, is an eroded black cinder cone that rises from the ocean. Hawaiians believed that spirits of the dead leaped from this rocky bluff to enter the world beyond. Maui's powerful 18th-century ruler, Kahekili, inspired his men by diving into the ocean alongside the invisible spirits. Today the Sheraton-Maui sprawls across Black Rock, and during its nightly torch-lighting ceremony, this leap is dramatically reenacted.

hawai'itrivia

Early whalers didn't go after humpbacks because they sink upon death.

To explore more Kā'anapali history and legends, reserve in advance for the ***Kā'anapali Resort Association***'s (808-661-3271) free 90-minute walking tours. Talk to the front desk for more info.

If Lahaina has piqued your interest in whaling, be sure to visit ***The Whale Center of Hawai'i*** (808-661-4567; whalersvillage.com), in the Kā'anapali shopping complex of the same name. James Campbell, who founded Pioneer Sugar Mill, began his career as a carpenter on a whaling ship. The displays, formerly the Whalers Village Museum, are funded by his estate in his memory and do a good job of conveying the story of whaling in Hawai'i. Relive the drama of the chase as tiny whaleboats row stealthily into battle with "the enemy." Learn how the economic factors governing whaling's rise and fall included women's fashions in hoopskirts and the discovery of petroleum in Pennsylvania. You can even see a life-size model of a forecastle where common sailors slept.

A separate gallery focuses on the whales themselves. Extensive interactive displays include videos of humpbacks at play accompanied by recorded whale songs. In fact, Lahaina's whalers of old didn't hunt humpbacks. Lahaina merely served as a central staging ground for the North Pacific fleet's pursuit of sperm whales off Japan and Alaska. With modern technology, humpbacks were indeed hunted to near extinction, but this happened long after the last whale ships left Hawaiian waters. Open daily 10 a.m. to 6 p.m. Free. Check to assure operating hours following the Maui fire.

Newer resort developments, alternating with abandoned cane fields, have sprouted north of Kā'anapali. Now that King Cane has shut down, the scent of "West Maui incense" from burning cane (the most efficient method of harvesting) no longer wafts through the luxury hotels. After Napili, the fields switch to pineapple cultivation, which holds better long-term prospects, as pineapple is a higher-value crop. To learn more about these spiky icons of the Hawaiian Islands, sign up for Maui Pineapple Company's tour. Other islands fade from view as East Moloka'i looms across the channel. Kapalua, the last tourist enclave on this coast, ends at the 30-mile marker. The demons of development have left three beautiful beaches beyond. WARNING: These northern strands can become dangerous for swimming, especially during winter.

At 31 miles, a side road leads to ***D. T. Fleming Beach Park*** in Honokahua Bay. The facilities here are the last you will find before Wailuku. To the left of the beach park, the northern edge of Makaluapuna Point has some curious lava formations whose unusually light color and vertical, thrusting shape have earned them the nickname "dragon's teeth." You can get to them most easily by turning off the highway onto Office Road just before the beach park, following it to its end, then walking across the edge of the golf course.

A half mile past the 32-mile marker, the road winds above ***Mokulēia Bay.*** Beachgoers descend very steep trails from either side to the secluded beach below; locals call this Slaughterhouse because such a facility once stood on the cliffs above. The bay belongs to a marine-life conservation zone. ***Honolua Bay,*** the northern limit of the conservation zone, awaits a half mile farther at the mouth of a lushly tropical valley. The beach here, accessed by several trails down from the highway, suffers seasonal depletions of its sand and can be quite rocky during winter. The right side of the bay receives the best winter surf on the island, rivaling O'ahu's North Shore. In calmer months snorkelers take advantage of the abundance of marine life in the conservation zone. The inner bay can be murky, but excellent coral formations farther out await exploration.

The road continues through pineapple fields and open forest. Near the 36-mile point, it rounds a sharp corner and begins a dramatic descent into Honokōhau Bay. The Honoapi'ilani Highway ends here at the last of six hono *(bays)* claimed by the 15th-century chief Pi'ilani. As you curve around the bend, glimpses of the rugged coastline beyond beckon. Route 340, a narrow county road, continues up the other side of the bay, with mile markers enumerated in the reverse direction descending from 22. Don't miss this road. It wriggles through the mountains, passing remote farms and villages. The tiny town of Kahakuloa is the epitome of small-town Hawai'i, where lazy dogs sleep in the middle of the road, the air is fragrant with sweet ginger, the cobalt blue ocean laps at the shoreline, and the neighbors are welcoming.

About a mile along Route 340, a white Coast Guard beacon marks ***Nakalele Point.*** Bizarre rock formations spewed from a volcanic spatter cone close to the shoreline give this region its nickname of Hobbitland, after author J. R. R. Tolkien's fantasy world. To the right of Nakalele Point, a blowhole

Tours and Tales

Pineapples appear on many a Maui restaurant menu, and although not endemic to the islands, the fruit is a symbol of Hawai'i known around the world. But very few visitors actually know how these spiky bromeliads grow. Mischievous tour guides have been known to prey on this ignorance by pointing to similar-looking fruit on hala (pandanus) trees, which they call "tourist pineapples." Maui Land & Pineapple Company's 2-hour plantation tours remedy this gap by bringing visitors up close and personal with Hawai'i's famous fruit. You'll learn the history behind Hawaiian pineapples, see how they are cultivated today, and visit fields currently being harvested to pick your own edible souvenir. Tours are offered daily 9:30 a.m. to 3:30 p.m. at their location in Kapalua; cost is $75. (808) 665-5491; mauipineappletour.com.

Another Kapalua event happens only once a year and is far from being free. The Nature Society of Hawai'i manages much of the West Maui Mountains, including the summit of 5,877-foot Pu'u Kukui. Usually inaccessible, the summit area is opened to 12 visitors once a year, ferried by helicopter for a tour of this unique, cloud-forest habitat of native birds and plant life. A boardwalk enables visitors to move across the boglike terrain, whose rain-soaked soil reduces vegetation to stunted growth. A lottery is held to choose the lucky 12; to enter visit puukukui.org. The only catch is the cost: $1,200, which helps to fund native forest conservation.

powered by this coast's constant surf sends ocean sprays wafting through the air. To explore this unearthly terrain, take the ***Ohai Trail,*** which starts between the 40- and 41-mile markers and continues about half a mile along the seashore. The trail is named for the silver-leaved native shrubs with red flowers that you pass on the way in.

As you continue along the highway, signs warn of falling rocks. Hidden hands have stacked many of these rocks into cairns that line the road like sentinels. Clinging to the edge of cliffs, the road winds through knobby green hills and past remote valleys with abandoned settlements. The tree cover fades as the scenery grows more and more dramatic, and almost every turn begs you to pull over. Below the highway, the blue vastness of the Pacific Ocean hisses and seethes, crashing in fury and then retreating in restless agitation.

Just shy of the 16-mile point, near the top of a hill, ***Pōhaku Kani,*** an enormous solitary boulder, squats above the highway on the inland side. Now marred by graffiti, the rock once served as a bell stone, struck by ancient Hawaiians to produce a resonant, bell-like tone. Immediately after the bell stone, the road crosses a cement culvert. On the right, a gate blocks a road inland. To explore a section of this coast that you can't see from the highway, turn onto the dirt road opposite the gate, heading toward the ocean and parking when the going gets rough. From here you can scramble down a short, rocky headland slope to reach a spectacular cliffside ledge roughly 100 feet up, with the ocean almost directly below, coastal views in both directions, and Moloka'i on the horizon. Below you lies a patchwork of small pools on a low lava shelf. After watching to be sure that the biggest breaking waves do not engulf this shelf, you can clamber down to swim in the pools' brackish, partly spring-fed water.

A mile and a half farther, the road narrows to a single lane as it climbs around the twin valleys of Kahakuloa Bay. ***Kahakuloa*** ("the tall lord") ***Head*** towers above the far edge of the bay. Visible for miles along this coast, this green volcanic knoll shelters a tiny Hawaiian settlement in the valley floor below. Residents of Kahakuloa Village tend taro fields and fish in the traditional manner. As you begin to head up the far side of the valley, there's a roadside stand that sells very yummy banana bread. Notice the irrigation channel bringing water under the highway to the taro fields below. This water comes from centuries-old irrigation works built upvalley by Hawaiians of yore and managed communally by the village.

From here, the road turns uphill through mountain pastures past the Honolua Ranch headquarters. The contortions of this single-lane road reach a climax as it winds in and out of deserted valleys high above the coast. By the 10-mile point, the road begins a slow descent with views along the coast and across the isthmus to East Maui. The ***Turnbull Studios & Sculpture Garden*** (808-244-0101; turnbullfineart.com) is worth a stop. Bruce Turnbull's imaginatively shaped wood and bronze creations have an uplifting, almost mythical quality. Open daily 10 a.m. to 5 p.m. Just beyond the 7-mile marker, a side road leads to Maluhia Boy Scout Camp. A mile up this road, just before it curves into the camp, is the start of the ***Waihe'e Ridge Trail.*** Hardy hikers can climb 1,563 feet (a little less than 3 miles) to reach scenic Lanilili Peak. For a less strenuous hiking option, continue 1.5 miles to Waihe'e Valley Road, across the bridge on the far side of the valley. Follow the road past taro patches until the pavement ends at a T junction with a former cane road. Take this road to the right for a stroll up the valley, past streamside taro patches, across a hanging footbridge, to reach a natural pool 2 miles in. Enjoy the pristine beauty while you can. The road soon improves, and before you know it, you're on a two-lane highway, speeding back to civilization.

FOR MORE INFORMATION ABOUT MAUI

gohawaii.com/islands/maui

visitmaui.com

Places to Stay on Maui

HA'IKŪ

Adventure in Paradise/ Maui Tradewinds
4322 Une Pl.
(808) 573-0066
mauitradewinds.com
Contact for latest pricing.

HĀNA

Hale Akua Garden Farm & Eco-Retreat Center
110 Door of Faith Rd.
(808) 572-9300
haleakuagardenfarm.com
Organic farm, educational tours, weekly yoga classes. Expensive.

Hāmoa Bay House & Bungalow
(808) 248-7884
hamoabay.com
Bali charm, tropical fruit on property, and walking distance to Hāmoa Beach. $310 and up.
Contact to inquire about reservations and availability.

LAHAINA

Plantation Inn
174 Lahainaluna Rd.
(808) 667-9225
(800) 433-6815
theplantationinn.com
Charming faux Victorian lodging.
Rates start at $387 and include a full breakfast.

WAILUKU

The Old Wailuku Inn at Ulupono
2199 Kaho'okele St.
(808) 244-5897 or (800) 305-4899
mauiinn.com
Offers gracious hospitality in a nostalgic old Hawai'i setting. Rates start at $276.

Places to Eat on Maui

KAPALUA

Plantation House Restaurant
200 Plantation Club Dr.
(808) 669-6299
kapalua.com/dining/plantation-house
Romantic hilltop dining with views across three islands. Expensive.

Sansei Kapalua
600 Office Rd.
(808) 669-6286
sanseihawaii.com
Top-rated sushi venue thrives on East-West culinary fusion. Expensive.

LAHAINA

Roy's
2290 Kā'anapali Pkwy.
(808) 669-6999
royyamaguchi.com
Hawai'i superchef Roy Yamaguchi opened these twin venues to cope with the demand for his inventive Pacific Rim cuisine. Expensive.

MAKAWAO

Hali'imaile General Store
900 Hali'imaile Rd.
(808) 572-2666
hgsmaui.com
Neither "general" nor a "store." Offers a wide-ranging selection of great regional dishes and wines. Expensive but worth it.

Makawao Garden Cafe
9546, 3669 Baldwin Ave. #1101
(808) 573-9065
For lunch only; innovative island cuisine. Inexpensive.

PĀ'IA

Mama's Fish House
799 Poho Place
(808) 579-8488
mamasfishhouse.com
Offers fresh seafood in a romantic oceanfront setting. Investment-caliber.

WAILUKU

A Saigon Cafe
1792 Main St.
(808) 243-9560
Serves delicious Vietnamese fare in a no-nonsense setting. Moderate.

Tasty Crust
1770 Mill St.
(808) 244-0845
Two words: banana pancakes. Inexpensive.

Hawai'i Island

Anchoring the archipelago on its southeastern end, the island of Hawai'i represents the volcano goddess Pele's latest and greatest creation. Built on the overlapping flows of five volcanoes, the island covers almost twice the area of all its northern neighbors put together. Mauna Kea ("white mountain"), at 13,796 feet, not only tops all rival peaks in the Pacific but, viewed from its base on the ocean floor, would be the tallest mountain on earth. A smidgen below Mauna Kea in height, its neighbor, Mauna Loa ("long mountain"), covers half the island with its massive girth. It's the world's largest volcano, weighing more than the entire Sierra Nevada range, and it's still growing.

Ever vigilant, Pele continues to add to her domain, sending rivers of molten rock flowing down the hillside to form new land. The goddess makes her principal abode inside Kīlauea, the pygmy of the Big Island volcanoes at 4,000 feet. Kīlauea ("spewing") has spewed the hot stuff almost daily since 1983, averaging 300,000 cubic yards per day, making it the world's most active volcano. The steady pattern of these "drive-in" eruptions has delighted tourists but brought woe to homeowners in lava-inundated areas. Still, each acre of expanded shoreline buys Pele added security against the encroachments of her archrival, the ocean.

HAWAI'I ISLAND

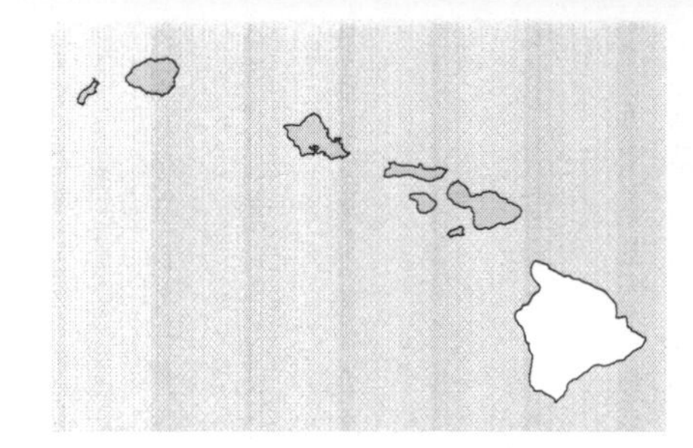

Geography of the Big Island

The youngest island in the chain, the Big Island of Hawai'i is by far the largest, and it is the only one still growing. Its 266 miles of coastline have relatively few beaches. Except for a remote northern section, most of the island is encircled by the Hawai'i Belt Highway; the name it goes by varies between segments. The Big Island has five main volcanoes, two of which top 13,000 feet. Kīlauea, the pygmy of the bunch, has the distinction of being the most active volcano on the planet. Its current eruption has continued almost daily since 1983, much of the time allowing visitors to witness one of nature's most awesome and spectacular forces in action. The Big Island's terrain varies enormously from dry, barren lava fields to lush tropical jungle to snowcapped peaks. The many state-of-the-art telescopes atop 13,796-foot Mauna Kea take advantage of the world's clearest night skies.

Thanks to the conquests of Kamehameha I, another famous Big Island resident, the island of Hawai'i came to bestow its name on the entire chain. Today locals distinguish the island from the state by referring to the former simply as the Big Island. It's big not just in size. The variety of terrain rivals that of a continent. Mark Twain, gazing from the desert of Ka'u to the rain forest of Hāmākua, from the snowcapped peak of Mauna Kea to the beaches of Kona, boasted that he "could see all the climes of the world at a single glance of the eye." Hilo and Kona, the two population centers, spread over opposite coasts, 95 or 124 miles apart, by the northern or southern route.

For guided exploration of the island's natural splendor, consider ***Wasabi Tours Hawai'i*** (808-238-5222; wasabitourshawaii.com), offering adventures ranging from snorkeling with manta rays to helicopter tours and ziplining, and Rob Pacheco's ***Hawai'i Forest & Trail*** (808-331-8505; hawaii-forest.com); both have access to private land not otherwise accessible. But not all of Hawai'i Forest's trips involve hiking; they range from stargazing atop Mauna Kea to caving in a lava tube, plus two trips of special interest to birders. The vertiginous hike behind North Kohala's Kapoloa Falls will wow even jaded waterfall connoisseurs. Half-day outings that include a snack cost $175. Both companies are based in West Hawai'i, and both companies also offer longer outings.

For personalized attention, call Warren Costa of ***Native Guide Hawai'i*** (808-982-7575). Costa, a Native Hawaiian born in Hilo, leads his own customized all-day tours, taking no more than four guests at a time on activities ranging from early-morning red-lava hikes to nighttime stargazing on Mauna Kea. Contact warren@nativeguidehawaii.com for current prices and offerings. Check local newspapers for free hikes offered by other island groups. Finally, for those who'd rather pedal than walk, the ***Hilo Bike Hub*** provides excellent trail information. Call (808) 961-4452.

Hilo and Environs

The Big Island is unique in that its principal settlement lies on the lush windward coast. More than 100,000 people make their homes around north-facing Hilo Bay, making Hilo the largest town outside O'ahu. Its 130 inches of annual rainfall nourish all the greenery of a rain forest. The visitors' bureau may tell you that Hilo's rainfall arrives mostly at night, but expect passing showers any time of day. You shouldn't let these bouts of precipitation discourage you from enjoying Hilo's offerings. It keeps things cool and makes the flowers grow—to the tune of a $20 million orchid-anthurium industry. Hilo has survived two devastating tidal waves, at least four close calls from advancing lava flows (most recently in 2022), and countless earthquakes. Residents of this indomitable city by the bay are not about to let a little rain dampen their lifestyle. And neither should you. (If it does rain, visit one of Hilo's first-rate museums.)

Route 11 passes Hilo's airport as it approaches from the south. The highway ends at the junction of Kamehameha and Kalaniana'ole Avenues, which reach west and east, respectively, around the bay. Instead, continue straight onto ***Banyan Drive*** to loop around Waiākea Peninsula in the center of the bay. Rows two and three thick of mammoth banyan trees, planted by celebrities, line the drive.

Brief History of the Big Island

The Big Island's pivotal role in Hawaiian history centers around the life and death of Kamehameha I, its most famous native son. Kamehameha's inheritance of the family war god, Kūka'ilimoku ("Ku the devourer of lands"), gave him a psychic edge in warfare. When an army belonging to Keōua Kū'ahu'ula, Kamehameha's cousin and principal rival on the Big Island, was destroyed by an erupting volcano in 1790, it was taken as a sign that the volcano goddess, Pele, favored Kamehameha. Kamehameha's victories on the battlefield owed as much to the modern weapons and training that he received from his Western advisers as they did to the gods of ancient Hawai'i, however. By conquering the other islands, Kamehameha gave the name of his home island, Hawai'i, to the unified kingdom he created. But this victory came at a price. The old gods died with him at Kailua-Kona, where his heirs abolished the system of kapu just in time for the arrival of the first missionaires in 1820. Moreover, Western ships, which continued to come in ever greater numbers, avoided the Big Island because it lacked a protected harbor. As the center of trade and commerce shifted to Lahaina and then Honolulu, the preeminence of the Big Island became steadily undermined.

Search for those planted by your favorite public figures, from Amelia Earhart to Richard Nixon.

At the end of a strip of hotels, Keli'ipio Place detours to the footbridge to Coconut Island. The Hawaiians called this island Mokuola ("healing island") because underwater springs supposedly gave curative properties to waters around it. In addition to affording vistas across the bay, this palm-covered plot provides an excellent vantage point from which to view the Big Island's twin peaks, Mauna Kea and Mauna Loa. Come in the early morning before the clouds roll in.

Next, take a stroll in nearby ***Lili'uokalani Gardens***. While this attractive park bears the name of Hawai'i's deposed queen, it exhibits Japanese motifs in its miniature stone pagodas, pavilions, teahouse, and footbridge over reflecting ponds. On the far side of the gardens, ***Suisan Fish Market*** stages a daily morning sale. Night fishers bring in their catches beginning at 6 a.m., and local vendors gather to inspect the colorful platters of fish and core samples cut from giant tuna. Visitors welcome; please note that the market officially opens at 9 a.m. On the other side of Lihiwai Street, the extension from Banyan Drive, the ***Waiākea Memorial Clock*** remains frozen at 1:05 a.m., the time at which the 1960 tsunami hit.

hawai'itrivia

Ka Lae is the southernmost point in the 50 United States.

Hawai'i is the worldwide leader in harvesting macadamia nuts and orchids.

Parker Ranch was formerly the largest privately held ranch in the United States.

Mauna Kea is the tallest mountain in the world (measured from its base at the ocean floor).

Turn right from Lihiwai Street and follow Kamehameha Avenue across the Wailoa River and the estuarine waters of ***Waiākea*** (or Wailoa) ***Pond.*** On the west bank, inland from the highway, Hilo's ***King Kamehameha Statue*** gazes out across the bay that he loved to surf. This is a replica of two statues originally cast in 1880, which stand in Kapa'au and Honolulu, respectively. This modern-day duplicate was commissioned by the Princeville Resort on Kaua'i, but community elements there opposed its display on the one island that the great conqueror had failed to subdue. Instead, the statue ended up here at Waiākea, the staging grounds for many of his war fleets. Almost 150 million gallons of freshwater empty daily into the spring-fed pond to the right of the statue. Hilo's original downtown once centered around this former Hawaiian fishpond. The area was devastated by the 1946 and 1960 tidal waves that funneled into Hilo Bay with deadly force. The area has been converted into a public park as a kind of buffer zone. Near the statue, the ***Shinmachi Tsunami Memorial*** stands in front of the ***Wailoa Information Center***

(808-933-0416). The center itself houses rotating exhibits as well as a photo history of the tsunami. Open Mon through Fri 8:30 a.m. to 4:30 p.m.

Above the center, on Aupuni Street, stand Hilo's county and state buildings. Their controversial location in this flood-ravaged tsunami zone was designed to reinspire confidence in the city's renewal. You can get the scoop on camping in the county or state parks around the island by applying to the appropriate agency. Some county parks have pavilion shelters, and a few state parks have well-maintained housekeeping cabins at affordable rates. Call (808) 961-8311 for county parks (open weekdays; hawaiicounty.ehawaii.gov) or (808) 974-6200 for state parks (weekday mornings; hawaiistateparks.org). Satellite county offices can also be found in Waimea, Captain Cook, and Kailua-Kona.

To get a more complete picture of the awesome destruction wreaked by tsunamis, continue a mile farther around the bay to the ***Pacific Tsunami Museum*** (808-935-0926; 130 Kamehameha Ave.; tsunami.org). Here you will learn how tsunamis can cross the Pacific as fast as a jet airplane and form waves as tall as 100 feet. The tsunamis that twice struck Hilo this century moved houses and scattered boulders around town "like a giant hand shooting marbles." Hundreds drowned, but you can also read amazing accounts of survivors swept out to sea for days as well as a legendary Hawaiian said to have surfed an 1868 tsunami in to safety (not recommended). The museum occupies the space of the former First Hawaiian Bank, a 1930 edifice that itself withstood both recent tsunamis. The bank vaults serve as theaters for video screenings. Open Tues through Sat 10 a.m. to 4 p.m. Admission is $10.

Another nearby Hilo museum explores islands at the other end of the Hawaiian archipelago. The ***Mokupapapa Discovery Center*** (808-498-4709; 76 Kamehameha Ave.) tells the story of the 124 islands, reefs, and shoals that lie northwest of Kaua'i, stretching across more than 1,000 miles. Although currently uninhabited and little known even to Hawai'i residents, two of the islands were in fact settled by Polynesians for more than a thousand years, albeit abandoned before Western explorers arrived. Run by the National Oceanic and Atmospheric Administration, the center relies on interactive, flat-panel technology and life-size dioramas to bring to life these delicate marine ecosystems, whose denizens range from nesting

islandfacts

Nickname: The Big Island or Orchid Isle

Dimensions: 93 x 76 miles

Highest elevation: Mauna Kea (13,796 feet)

Population: 200,381 (2018)

Principal city: Hilo

Flower: Red lehua

Color: Red

albatrosses to Hawaiian monk seals. Visitors can view an artist's animated rendition of the "hot spot" life cycle in which Hawaiian islands are created and eventually destroyed; take a virtual scuba dive off the Pearl Hermes atoll; and enter a cockpit mock-up of the Pisces 5 submersible and manipulate its robot arm to collect rock specimens from a simulated ocean floor 1,000 feet below. Open Tues through Sat 9 a.m. to 4 p.m. Check the calendar for evening lectures and special events. There is no admission fee.

The buildings around here constitute Hilo's new downtown and its (surviving) historic center. Note the dark gray sidewalks, a consequence of pouring concrete mixed with black sand from Hilo's bay front. The Census Bureau may call Hilo a city, but it still feels like a small town. Strangers greet each other in the street, and parking is free all day. Things move slowly here. You'll find remnants of earlier parking methods—hitching rings—still embedded in downtown sidewalks. (One is on Haili Street, a few yards inland from Kamehameha.)

To explore more Hilo history, you can pick up a self-guided tour map (and other visitor information) from the ***Downtown Improvement Association***'s website at downtownhilo.org/home/walking-tour, or the ***Big Island Visitors Bureau*** (808-961-5797; 101 Aupuni St., #238). You may find it just as nice to wander at random.

A few highlights to look for: The majestic 1925 ***Palace Theater*** (808-934-7010; 38 Haili St.; hilopalace.com) has been restored. Its 1936 carbon-arc projector beams art-house films on weekends, with periodic live concerts as well as hula and Hawaiian-language classes. Guided tours available. A couple of blocks away, at the corner of Kalakaua and Kino'ole Streets, ***Kalākaua Park*** honors Hawai'i's last king, "the Merrie Monarch," who helped popularize traditional Hawaiian culture. Hilo's annual Merrie Monarch Festival (808-935-9168; merriemonarch.com) in April is the biggest hula competition in the state and the one time of year Hilo hotels are filled to overflowing. A statue of Kalākaua by Henry Bianchini kneels in the park in front of the banyan tree he planted. The king is depicted in military dress, balancing in his right hand an *ipu hula,* a gourd instrument symbolic of the culture he helped revive. The buildings around the park once served as Hilo's center of government. On the other side of Kalākaua Street stands the Old Police Station, now home to the ***East Hawai'i Cultural Center*** (808-961-5711; ehcc.org). Rotating exhibits can be viewed Tues through Fri 10 a.m. to 4 p.m, and Sat from 10 a.m. to 2 p.m. Admission is free. Continue your sightseeing on Haili Street, 1 block off Kino'ole, past a trio of vintage church buildings. The oldest, Haili Church, was founded by the original missionaries.

To see the secular trappings of these soul seekers, follow Haili Street uphill to the adjacent buildings of the ***Lyman Museum and Mission House***

(808-935-5021; lymanmuseum.org). Mission House admission times are 10 a.m. to noon, 12:15 to 2:15 p.m., and 2:30 to 4:30 p.m. The mission home was built in stages by David and Sarah Lyman beginning in 1839. The four-poster beds have mattresses stuffed with wood shingles, handy chamber pots sit in the corners, and whale-oil lamps illuminate the desks. A curio shelf displays toys brought by whaling captains as well as autumn leaves that Mrs. Lyman obtained to illustrate to her children the meaning of seasons. Because of fire hazards, cooking had to be done in an outdoor oven. The house doubled as a mission school, with boarders lodged upstairs.

Besides saving souls, the Lymans made at least two unwitting contributions to science. Mrs. Lyman's diary remains of interest to geologists for its detailed record of earthquakes and eruptions. Her son Frederick collected hundreds of land snails, all of which are now extinct, in a drawer. It is fitting that these items in the home should stand beside a museum of science that houses the world's first and only known specimen of olymanite, a mineral discovered by a Lyman descendant.

You can explore the museum while waiting for your tour of the mission house. The ground floor displays Hawai'i's cultural heritage, while the upstairs exhibits focus on the natural history of the islands. The collection of Hawaiian artifacts includes a full-scale *hale pili* (grass hut). Representations from other ethnic groups range eclectically from the altar of a Chinese Taoist temple salvaged after a Hilo tidal wave to a formal wedding kimono shared by brides in Miyazaki, Japan, that was sold to finance a village son's education in America. Upstairs, glow-in-the-dark natural fluorescents highlight a top-notch mineralogy collection, and an astronomy exhibit contrasts the stargazing of the ancient Hawaiians with the cutting-edge research performed at the Mauna Kea observatories. The museum and mission house are open Mon through Sat 10 a.m. to 4:30 p.m. Admission varies dependent on the tour; check the museum.

Walk back a block to Waianuenue Avenue and the ***Hilo Public Library*** (808-933-8890; hilopubliclibrary.org). Two mammoth boulders lie out front. The larger one, lying horizontally, is the ***Naha Stone,*** brought from the Pinao Temple on Kaua'i in days of yore. A kind of Hawaiian Excalibur, the Naha Stone reputedly could reveal male descendants of its royal house. By moving the 3.5 ton stone, Kamehameha symbolically "overthrew a mountain" and proved his worthiness to conquer the islands. Visitors are welcome to try to duplicate this feat.

In addition to its historic attractions, downtown Hilo boasts a wealth of mom-and-pop shops perfect for browsing. Fashion textiles seem a particular strength, with several noted Big Island designers represented here. The following are popular (but all are worth a visit): ***Sig Zane*** (808-935-7077; sigzane designs.com) has a bay-front roost at 122 Kamehameha Ave., near the corner of Kalākaua. Sig's aloha-wear designs are patterned around the indigenous flora of Hawai'i. His knowledge of native plants draws on a lifelong involvement in the art of hula. Open Mon to Sat. 10 a.m. to 4 p.m. ***Na Makua*** (808-969-7985; 107 Waianuenue Ave.; namakua.com) showcases the graphic designs of father-and-son duo Nelson and Kainoa Makua in a range of casual Hawai'i wear. Nelson's vivid depictions of Hawaiian mythology have been featured on Merrie Monarch Festival posters. Open Mon to Fri 10 a.m. to 5 p.m. It's also worth popping into ***Hawaiian Arts*** (808-935-1860; 284 Kamehameha Ave.; hawaiian arts.com) to watch the staff mixing colors on the eight-arm *tako* (octopus) silk-screening machine in back as it prints T-shirt designs by Eddie Yamamoto. Open Mon to Fri. 9 a.m. to 5 p.m. Fabric hounds, meanwhile, will flock to ***Dragon Mama*** (808-934-9081; 266 Kamehameha Ave.; dragonmama.com) for gorgeous Japanese textiles. Pick out a yard or two or have owner Utae Arai Suzuki create you a pillow or futon cover.

Those with a literary bent will enjoy ***Basically Books*** (808-961-0144; 334 Kilauea Ave.; basicallybooks.com). Its excellent selection of Hawaiiana includes an impressive publishing line of Hawaiian folklore anthologies. The bookstore is open Mon through Sat 10 a.m. to 5 p.m. Nearby on Kamehameha Highway, ***Joy's Gift Shop*** (808-969-7970) carries a mix of clothing, vintage collectibles, and ukuleles. Open Mon to Sat 9 a.m. to 6 p.m., and Sun 10 a.m. to 5 p.m.

If you're in Hilo on a Wednesday or Saturday morning, don't miss the colorful ***farmers' market*** (hilofarmersmarket.com), staged near the corner of Kamehameha and Mamo Street a few blocks over. Look for bright tropical fruits like rambutan and cherimoya. Open daily, but the biggest days are Wed and Sat. (Remember to wash all raw greens thoroughly before eating; in recent years, cases of rat lungworm disease have increased, especially on Hawai'i Island and particularly at farmers' markets.)

The Wailuku River serves as the northern boundary of downtown Hilo and harbors scenic attractions of its own. Straddling the river near its mouth, between the second and third bridges, is ***Maui's Canoe,*** a low rock island. According to legend, the outrigger canoe was beached here in a flood unleashed when the demigod Maui rescued his mother, Hina, from Rainbow Falls. To this day, foam from the falls accumulates alongside the canoe.

To see the other half of the legend, head upstream on Waianuenue Avenue (1 block in from the river) and bear right at the fork. Turn right again to ***Rainbow Falls,*** where the Wailuku River cascades down a drop of 200 feet. After rains, the waters crash with thunderous volume and send up clouds of mist that produce the falls' trademark rainbows in the sunlight. When a rebuffed suitor trapped Hina in the hollow cavern behind the falls, sealing the entrance with dammed waters, her dutiful son smashed the dam with his canoe paddle. Walk to the upper platform above the falls for a view up and down the river. Bananas, red ginger, mango trees, and other tropicals festoon the park with rich lushness.

Continue 1.5 miles to ***Pe'epe'e Falls*** for a glimpse of this smaller falls upstream. Directly below the overlook, the river spills its way over a series of lava pools. The bubbling rapids thus produced give the pools their nickname, ***Boiling Pots.*** Some say the body of the mo'o dragon Kuna, slain by Maui, snakes along the river bottom, churning the waters. Despite the warning signs, locals take a path down to the river and swim in these natural (cold) Jacuzzis during low-water periods. If you follow them, beware of underwater sinkholes and flash floods. It's not for nothing that *wailuku* means "waters of destruction." A third cascade, ***Wai'ale Falls,*** waits just up the road at the bridge over the river.

For a different outdoor experience, return to the first fork at Waianuenue Avenue and take the other branch 3 miles up Kaumana Drive to ***Kaumana Caves County Park.*** The "caves" are actually two ends of a lava tube whose ceiling collapsed. Such tubes form as surface rocks cool around an underground river of swiftly flowing magma. When the current of molten rock dwindles, the empty tunnels often remain. Sightless insects found nowhere else in the world have evolved inside these dark chambers. The tube at Kaumana formed during Mauna Loa's 1881 eruption and stretches for miles underground. Surface lavas came within a mile of the then-smaller city limits and stopped only when Princess Ruth came overland from Kona to appease Pele with traditional prayers and offerings—much to the missionaries' chagrin.

A steep stairway descends into a tropical pit of green, speckled with impatiens. Continued collapses make the upper cave unsafe, but with a flashlight you can explore the lower tunnel as far as you dare. Tree roots hang from the 20-foot-high ceiling, the walls are smooth, and the hardened lava floor resembles rippled fudge. In this damp, mossy environment, it's hard to picture the torrent of glowing molten rock that flowed here more than a century ago. Kaumana Drive continues as Route 200, or the Saddle Road, running across the center of the island.

If one of Hilo's passing showers has caught up with you by now, seek refuge in one of the city's newest museums. Turn onto Komohana Street just before the fork on Waianuenue Avenue (about a mile in from the bay) and continue 1.8 miles to Nowelo Street, where you turn left and take the second left onto 'Imiloa Place to reach the ***'Imiloa Astronomy Center of Hawai'i*** (808-932-8901; imiloahawaii.org). This state-of-the-art museum/planetarium sprawls across 9 acres on the slopes of Mauna Kea above the University of Hawai'i's Hilo campus, overlooking Hilo Bay. Three titanium-covered cones tower above the complex, just as the volcanoes of Mauna Kea, Mauna Loa, and Hualalai dominate the Big Island. The surrounding gardens showcase native Hawaiian vegetation, planted in four sections that correspond to elevation changes ascending from shoreline to the upland "gardens of the gods." Funded primarily by NASA, 'Imiloa represents a unique collaboration between Mauna Kea's cultural and scientific communities. Native Hawaiian groups have often clashed with astronomers over their conflicting claims to the mountain summit. 'Imiloa's exhibits blend both perspectives: A scaled-down replica of a double-hulled sailing canoe is paired with a 3-D tour of space, courtesy of the Subaru Telescope, drawing parallels between the voyages of discovery by ancient Polynesian mariners navigating by starlight and the modern-day discoveries of astronomers who peer across time and space. (All exhibits are bilingual in English and Hawaiian.) Open Thurs through Sun 9 a.m. to 4:30 p.m. Admission $19.

For beaches in Hilo, folks head to the east rim of the bay along Kalaniana'ole Avenue. The Big Island's young age means most of its shoreline is bare, but prevailing currents have hidden strands of white and black sand in between the rocky tide pools along this coast. ***Onekahakaha Beach Park*** just off Kalaniana'ole, 2 miles in, has the best swimming, with its wide, sand bottomed pools protected by lava-rock barriers. Farther on, as you approach Kealoha Beach Park, look for the large fishponds on the inland side of the road, many of which still function.

Continue on to ***Richardson Ocean Center*** at the far end of Leleiwi Beach Park. The center has beautiful gardens surrounding it, as well as a former fishpond. Ask for a trail guide pamphlet detailing the many interesting plants on the property. Open daily 7:30 a.m. to 7:30 p.m. Just offshore, turtles feed on algae in the brackish spring-fed water, and spinner dolphins frequent this stretch of current-free coast.

Restaurants in Hilo are mostly simple, family-run operations serving homegrown ethnic fare at unbeatable values. Everyone has his or her favorite, and it's hard to go very wrong. The food court on Kamehameha by the farmers' market features everything from an 'awa/kava bar to a Samoan cafeteria.

For upscale dining downtown, ***Cafe Pesto*** (808-969-6640; 308 Kamehameha Ave.; cafepesto.com) wins kudos for Pacific Rim designer pizzas; the rest of the menu can be mixed. Open daily 11 a.m. to 8:30 p.m. ***Jackie Rey's 'Ohana Grill*** (808-961-2572; 64 Keawe St.; jackiereys.com/hilo) offers an imaginative menu ranging from Hawaiian specialities to Pacific Rim cuisine. It's located in a majestic, century-old building, decorated with Murano glass chandeliers and avant-garde art. Open daily 4 to 8:30 p.m. Expensive.

A more original choice is ***The Seaside Restaurant*** (808-935-8825; 1790 Kalaniana'ole Ave.) on the east side of the bay. Despite its name, the restaurant is actually across the street from the ocean, but it overlooks Loko Waka, an enormous freshwater fishpond. Colin Nakagawa tends the pond by day and cooks fresh fish dinners by night from its stocks of mullet, rainbow trout, golden perch, and *aholehole* (a type of bass). The menu also includes ocean-caught fish bought fresh at market (plus a handful of nonseafood choices). The rest of the Nakagawa family pitches in to help, as they have since 1926; the friendly service more than compensates for the somewhat primitive decor. As for the food, you can choose fish in a number of preparations. Drawing on traditional island recipes, the techniques, such as steaming in ti leaves, emphasize simple, natural flavors in lieu of gourmet high-concept creations. Considering that the entrees come as complete dinners, the prices are quite moderate. Open Thurs to Sun 4 to 8 p.m. For another lakeside venue, you might try ***Miyo's*** (808-935-2273; 564 Hinaro St.) for moderately priced Japanese meals served in an idyllic garden setting. Open Mon through Sat 11 a.m. to 2 p.m. for lunch, and 5 to 8:30 p.m. for dinner.

The ***Hilo Bay Café*** (808-935-4939; 123 Lihiwai St.; hilobaycafe.com) has won quite the foodie following with its eclectic menu. It's open Tues through Sat 11 a.m. to 2:30 p.m. and 5 to 8:30 p.m. Reservations are recommended. Moderate.

Those in search of a late-night feed after an evening of lava viewing can slurp hot saimin and other local fare at ***Nori's*** (808-935-9133; 688 Kinoole St.) in the Kukui Plaza. Open Fri through Sun 10:30 a.m. to 6 p.m. Or stop by ***Ken's House of Pancakes*** (808-935-8711; kenshouseofpancakes.com), at the main highway junction heading into town from the airport. Sink into one of the orange booths at this classic diner, and gracious aunties, with flowers in their hair, will whisk you out a hot, golden stack of macadamia-nut pancakes. Enjoy them with tropical fruit syrups, freshly made in house from guava, coconut, and liliko'i (so good you may want to take a bottle home). Ken's also serves a full menu of local favorites. Open daily 6 a.m. to 9 p.m.

A block in from Ken's, on Route 11, is ***Sombats*** (808-969-9336; 88 Kanoelehua Ave.; sombats.com), the top Thai choice in town. Open Mon through Sat for dinner 5 to 8 p.m.

Finally, no discussion of Hilo eateries can be complete without a mention of plate lunch. These quintessentially local meals revolve around ethnic entrees, from teriyaki chicken to kalua pork, accompanied by a standard two scoops of rice and macaroni salad. In a city where plate lunch is king, ***Cafe 100*** (808-935-8683), Hilo's first drive-in, presides as grand poobah. The menu includes Hawaiian and local staples, including several variations on the loco moco. Reputedly invented in Hilo, this dish revolves around rice, a fried egg, a hamburger patty, and ample gravy. In case you wondered, the cafe takes its name from the 100th Infantry Battalion, the all-Japanese-American unit in which founder Richard Miyashiro fought during World War II. Miyashiro learned to cook in the foxholes of Italy and returned to open the restaurant after the war—just in time for the 1946 tsunami. A second newly built restaurant opened in 1960—to be demolished just as promptly by the tsunami of that year. Rebuilt safely inland, at 969 Kīlauea Ave., the cafe has thrived ever since and remains in the family. Open Mon through Fri 11 a.m. to 7 p.m.

As for lodging, Hilo has many fine choices. If it's an ocean view you want, ***Hale Kai Hawai'i B&B*** (808-935-6330; 111 Honoli'i Pali; halekaihawaii.com) is hard to beat. It sits on a bluff directly above Honoli'i Cove, Hilo's premier surfing spot, with sweeping views stretching across the entire bay. All five rooms face the ocean. Rooms cost around $190 and include a full breakfast. Their individually themed decor features inn owner Ricardo's photography. He moonlights as a geologist—ask him about volcanoes. Wife Maria, a landscape designer, tends to the garden outside.

Even though it's closed to visitors and guests, the historical Shipman House Bed and Breakfast, also known as "The Castle," is certainly a sight that cannot be missed at 131 Kaiulani St. Almost every piece has a story in this 1900 Queen Anne Victorian mansion. Queen Lili'uokalani was also a frequent guest in her day. The Shipman family has an interesting history itself (to which a book placed in each room is devoted). The first Shipmans came to Hawai'i as a missionary couple destined for Micronesia. The wife's pregnancy prevented them from continuing any farther. A grandson, Herbert, made two notable contributions to Hawai'i: He's credited with saving the native nene goose and introducing the first orchids to the Big Island, which now bears the nickname of Orchid Isle. Indeed, the family boasted several ardent horticulturists, and the sumptuous 5-acre grounds surrounding the mansion form a large part of its appeal. Royal palms line the driveway, and unique flowers abound, several of which bear the Shipman name. In addition to the streambed, the house overlooks a sunken gulch where Cecil B. DeMille filmed *Four Frightened People* in 1933; its wild jungle foliage has yet to be explored since then.

Also on the east side of the bay, near Onekahakaha Beach Park, budgeteers will rejoice in ***Arnott's Lodge*** (808-969-7097; 98 Apapane Rd.; arnottslodge.com), tucked away on a side street. This congenial backpacker's haven offers simple studios for $189 a night with a private bath. The lodge also runs excellent daily ***Hiking Adventures*** using four-wheel-drive vans to tour remote regions of the island. The expeditions cater to an adventurous clientele.

For those preferring hotels, the ***Dolphin Bay*** (808-935-1466; 333 Iliahi St.; dolphinbayhotel.com) stands out for its friendly, ever-helpful staff. Located in a quiet residential area north of downtown, the hotel has 18 rooms, each with a full kitchen and private bath. Rates start at $139 for a double and include pastries and fresh-picked fruit from the garden.

Finally, for those longing for the serenity of a private waterfall, the ***Inn at Kulani'iapia*** (808-935-6789; waterfall.net) offers $259 bed-and-breakfast rooms that overlook a 120-foot cascade on a very remote macadamia farm above Hilo.

South of Hilo, Route 11 becomes the Mamalahoa Highway. The name means "law of splintered paddle," commemorating an event that happened not far from here. As a young chief on a raiding party, Kamehameha impetuously attacked an old fisherman but tripped and fell in the act. The fisherman promptly brained him with a canoe paddle and ran away. Later, when the man was brought to him, instead of seeking revenge for this affront to his chiefly dignity, Kamehameha admitted he was in the wrong. His "law of the splintered paddle" instructs that the elderly and infirm should not be molested.

Many people consider Hilo's nicest attractions to be its gardens, most of which lie south of the city along Route 11, on the way to Volcano. The rainfall here transforms almost any residential street into a tropical wonderland, and commercial plant nurseries have grown from cottage industries to major moneymakers. Some of these cater to the tour-bus set, while others just tolerate visitors.

hawai'itrivia

It takes 345 pounds of pressure to crack the macadamia's outer nutshell; no wonder the trees were long thought of as purely ornamental.

For a different kind of garden with more dynamic life-forms, turn west onto Mamaki Road, just past the 4-mile point. You pass the Rainbow Tropicals Nursery before reaching Stainbach Highway and ***Pana'ewa Rainforest Zoo & Gardens*** (808-959-7224; hilozoo.org). This county-run facility takes full advantage of its lush setting. Enter through a wire tunnel "cage" crossing the middle of the first animal enclosure. Tiny monkeys clamber along the wire above, following you as you walk and making you wonder who's on display. Elsewhere, peacocks and guinea fowl roam the grounds amid native Hawaiian birds, pygmy hippos, and tigers penned in natural-style enclosures. There is a petting zoo every Sat 1:30 to 2:30 p.m. and an alligator feeding every Sun, Tues, and Thurs at 1:30 p.m. Open daily 10 a.m. to 4 p.m. Free.

Much of the former sugar land south of here and throughout the island has switched to macadamia-nut orchards, a mainstay of the Big Island's move toward diversified agriculture. If you want to learn more about this local export industry, a sign guides you to the ***Mauna Loa Macadamia Nuts Visitors Center*** (808-966-8618) just ahead. Open daily 9 a.m. to 4 p.m.

The Puna Coast

Two miles farther south, you reach Kea'au, an aging sugar settlement, now the site of a daily farmers' market, at the crossroads of Route 11 and Route 130. In front of the Kea'au Village Market stands a statue of a Filipino cane worker, machete in hand, unveiled in 2006 to celebrate the arrival a century earlier of Hawai'i's first Filipino migrants, who came to work at a mill not far from here. Sculptor Fred Soriono, himself a son of Filipino immigrants, carved the 600-pound statue from a 2-ton slab of solid lava rock, deliberately choosing this hard-to-cut material to represent the struggle and determination with which his forebears built a new life in this faraway land.

Now that the ongoing eruptions have cut Route 130's coastal link with the Chain of Craters Road, few tourists head this way, yet the Puna Coast has attractions of its own that you shouldn't miss. The region has one of the fastest-growing populations in the United States, a substantial portion of whom live alternative lifestyles "off the grid."

In addition to its flower children, Puna bills itself as the anthurium capital of the world. The many plant nurseries around here specialize in these elegant waxy blossoms. While anthuriums are native to Latin America, ***Hi'iaka's Herbal Garden*** (808-966-5956) specializes in native Hawaiian botanicals, including several endangered species such as the *'uhi'uhi* gourd plant and yellow hibiscus. Master gardener Barbara Fahs offers self-guided tours for $5 or more in-depth personally guided tours for $15. In addition, visitors can purchase a variety of herbal products, including Pele's Passion, a secret Hawaiian aphrodisiac. Open by appointment.

Four miles in from Kea'au, you'll reach the town of ***Pāhoa,*** which Route 130 bypasses but you should not. It takes only a few moments to detour through Pāhoa's colorful strip of vintage false-front shops. Unlike the other towns in the Puna area, Pāhoa predates the sugar industry, having begun as a logging town. The golden spike linking the transcontinental railroad was driven into an 'ōhi'a wood tie milled in Pāhoa. The town's Akebono Theater claims to be the oldest in the state. Stroll down Pāhoa's wooden sidewalks to absorb the multiple personalities of Puna's main town. Parked pickup trucks display bumper stickers calling for the legalization of marijuana, one of Puna's principal cash crops. ***Island Naturals*** (808-965-8322) serves as a social center for the many alternative-lifestyle people inhabiting the region. Dreadlocks and tie-dye clothes predominate here. But you'll find the biggest crowds at the bar at Luquin's.

Pāhoa also offers an impressive array of inexpensive ethnic restaurants. In addition to its bar, ***Luquin's Mexican Restaurant*** (808-333-3390) serves a tasty tortilla. Open daily 10 a.m. to 9 p.m. ***Ning's Thai*** (808-934-7540), across the street, caters to curry lovers in town. Open Mon through Sun 11 a.m. to 8:30 p.m. Enjoy kava at ***La Hiki Ola Kava Bar*** (808-965-0615), open daily 2 to 8 p.m.

As you leave Pāhoa's commercial section, look for ***Sacred Heart Church*** ahead on the left and you'll be seeing double. A miniature replica flanks the church building on its left. Originally built as a parade float, the model now sees its use from juvenile churchgoers. Continue on the main road out of Pāhoa until it becomes Route 132, after it crosses Route 130. The road leads into a tunnel of tall albezia trees drenched in philodendron vines. Two miles along, be sure to stop at ***Lava Tree State Monument*** (808-961-9540; dlnr.hawaii.gov/dsp/parks/hawaii/lava-tree-state-monument/) to view some unique monuments to Madame Pele's destruction. As lava from a 1790 flow engulfed the ʻōhiʻa forest in this area, moisture from the trees caused the molten rock to harden around their trunks. As the trees rotted away, a hollow shell of lava rock remained. A 1-hour nature loop takes you through the park, but plenty of examples of these "lava tree" pillars stand near the entrance. The same eruption also left deep crevices in the surrounding terrain, so this is one place not to stray off the beaten path.

Scuba Spectacular

Readers of Rodale's *Scuba Diving* voted the Big Island the world's best overall diving destination in 1998. Given the diversity of dive sites around the island, it's not hard to see why. Moreover, as a young island, Hawai'i has steep drop-offs along its coast that permit divers to come into contact with a variety of open-ocean marine life that doesn't normally come in close to shore. In addition, the extensive system of lava tubes all along the island makes for interesting cave diving.

One of the unique diving experiences on the island is the nightly manta ray dives off the Kona Coast. Divers shine lights from below, attracting plankton on which the mantas feed. These enormous (up to 15-foot wingspan) yet harmless creatures sail in graceful arcs through the column of light, spiraling from top to bottom. (Snorkelers can watch the action from the surface.) A number of companies offer manta ray dives; try Manta Ray Dives of Hawai'i (808-325-1687; mantaraydiveshawaii.com). About one in every three nights, the mantas don't show; there are no guarantees.

Perhaps the most exciting dives the Big Island offers—and probably the most dangerous, too—are the hot lava dives offshore from the volcano. Because water is such a great conductor of heat, it's possible for divers to get close to a zone of active lava intrusion and watch the red molten stuff ooze and billow into unique formations known as "pillow lava." Eruption sites are unstable areas, and conditions have to be right for the dive to happen, but it's a once-in-a-lifetime experience for advanced divers only. Nautilus also provides free underwater maps to island dive spots.

Continuing on Pohoiki Road bypasses part of the Puna Coast scenery, so if you have time, backtrack and take the left fork on Route 132. As you descend to the coast, you emerge from low 'ōhi'a forest to cross the undulating terrain of the 1955 lava flow. As the road descends to a lower basin, you pass through vast papaya fields. No one will object if you pick up a fruit or two from the ground. Route 132 intersects Route 137 just past ***Pu'u Laimana*** ("Lyon's Hill") on the left. A 1960 eruption from this cone destroyed the once-large settlement of Kapoho.

You can continue east along the cinder road extension of Route 132 for 1.7 miles across the crusty 1960 flow almost to the tip of ***Cape Kumukahi*** ("first beginning"), which ends a few hundred yards farther. As the easternmost point of the island, this is where the sun's first rays greet the Aloha State. From here, take the four-wheel-drive road that angles back to the right just before the main road ends and hug the coastline, heading for the angled cove where the first houses begin at the southern base of the cape.

Backtrack to Route 137 and turn left. A mile south brings you to the Kapoho Kai/Vacationland subdivision on the ocean side and the older Kapoho Cone inland. To climb the cone for a coastal panorama, take the jeep road across from the first subdivision turnoff and follow it into the crater for a moderate, 2-mile ascent up the slopes on the left side.

Just less than a mile farther, the highway turns sharply inland at the entrance to ***Isaac Hale Beach Park*** on the eastern edge of Pohoiki Bay. Visitors used to come here to bathe in a small lava-rock basin whose clear springwaters were warmed by volcanic heat. The basin was destroyed due to eruptions in 2018—but they were replaced with a new black sand beach. The powers that be may taketh away, but it seems this time they giveth, too.

Just beyond Isaac Hale, Route 137 meets the other end of Pahoiki Road. From here the coastal highway, dubbed the "red road" after its tinted asphalt mixed with volcanic ash from the 1960 Kapoho eruption, narrows as it continues south. Two miles down the red road, ***MacKenzie State Recreation Area*** (808-587-0300; dlnr.hawaii.gov/dsp/parks/hawaii/mackenzie-state-recreation-area) provides a peaceful picnic spot amid a grove of ironwood trees, reopened as of September 2018. The park borders low sea cliffs, and waves crashing below send saline mists billowing through the trees. A sign by the parking lot marks the site of the old King's Highway, a traditional Hawaiian trail improved in the 1850s by convict labor. Follow the trail a few hundred yards north (left, when facing the ocean) to enter an exposed lava tube. Halfway along, a collapsed "skylight" helps you find your footing. The tunnel exits just across the highway. Camping here is allowed by state permit, but MacKenzie has a bad reputation.

Not only have thefts occurred, but the park sits athwart a notorious route of the "night marchers," a ghostly train of ancient Hawaiians who walk the earth under the new moon. If you see them, you should fall to the ground and not look up until they've passed.

Another 1.6 miles brings you to Opihikao junction, where Kamaili Road climbs 5 miles uphill to meet Route 130. Just less than a mile from the top, you come to a runaway truck ramp. Locals call the stretch of road immediately preceding the ramp ***Pu'u Lapu*** ("haunted hill"). If you put your car in neutral, you coast in reverse and get the illusion of rolling uphill.

Just past the (partly obscured) 19-mile marker, turn onto the overlook above ***Kehena Beach***. This black-sand beauty splits into two sections. The staircase leading to the section beneath the overlook collapsed in a 1975 earthquake, but a rough trail closer to the mile marker allows you to scramble down to the clothing-optional beach on the north side. Coconut and ironwood trees provide some shade. Dolphins often frequent the waters offshore, but heavy surf can make swimming dangerous.

Route 137 ends 3 miles past Kehena, closed by a 1990 lava flow that engulfed the town of Kalapana, destroying 103 houses as well as two of the island's most famous black-sand beaches. The black, steaming crust of lava piled across the highway provides a vivid portrait of man's powerlessness against the forces of nature. It's hard to imagine that almost all the land on the ocean side of the road was created in a few fiery months. Charred trunks of coconut palms that once grew along Kaimu Beach lie toppled on the lava. Yet as the molten rock continues to pour into the Pacific, deposits of black sand have formed anew at the flow's edge. Like the Hindu god Shiva, Pele must destroy in order to create. Local residents have done their part, planting hundreds of baby coconuts along the shore.

The current eruption, which began in 1983, has shifted its active zone farther south, with hot lava flows generally better accessed from the national park's Chain of Craters Road at the other end of the coastal highway's broken circuit. If this should change, be sure to read the safety information in the following section before approaching active flows.

A junction links Routes 130 and 137. The famous ***Star of the Sea Painted Church*** from Kalapana was "evacuated" using a flatbed truck and saved from advancing lava flow in 1990. It now rests by the roadside just around the bend on Route 130. A wooden statue of Moloka'i's Father Damien stands in front. As you return on Route 130, stop at the scenic turnout a half mile north of the top junction of Opihikao/Kamaili Road, at the 15-mile marker. If you follow the narrow trail that leads through 'ōhi'a forest, you will pass a series of volcanic steam vents. The fifth and last crater, about a quarter mile in, was known to provide a natural steam bath that ran the risk of being scalding (before recent eruptions in lower Puna).

For a commercial version of the same experience, the adjacent ***Kingdom of Heaven in Hawai'i*** (808-965-2112) is as Puna as Puna gets. Enthusiastic owner Dr. Leonard Horowitz has tapped into the energy of the multiple steam vents on his 29-acre property to create a New Age spa, cloaked in alternative spirituality (clothing optional). Although still a work in progress, the resort offers outdoor soaking tubs, an aloha pool, natural steam saunas, blue-mud facials, and a "rainbow therapy" walk past multicolored steam vents. You can also book a room here and further enjoy the property; learn more on heavenlykingdom.net.

In the Bosom of a Volcano

Moving southwest from Kea'au, Route 11 passes a series of former sugar camps as it climbs a gentle 4,000 feet over 21 miles to the summit of Kīlauea volcano. Macadamia-nut orchards are muscling their way into cropland that sugar has vacated, and flower nurseries also abound. One that accepts visitors is ***Akatsuka Orchid Gardens*** (808-967-8234; akatsukaorchid.com), at the 22.5-mile point, past Glenwood. Open Wed and Fri 10 a.m. to noon and 12:30 to 3 p.m.

For a different sort of plant nursery, visit the ***Fuku-Bonsai Cultural Center*** (808-982-9880; fukubonsai.com) in Kurtistown, on Ōla'a Road between the 9- and 10-mile markers, to learn about the Asian art of growing miniature trees. Open Mon through Sat 8 a.m. to 4 p.m. Closed on Wed.

Continuing uphill on Route 11, you enter an impressive rain forest, and temperatures cool as you gain elevation (it's an average of 15°F cooler at the summit than along the coast). As you approach the summit of Kīlauea, don't expect any lofty peak. Viewed from the air, the mountain appears as but a faint swelling on the flank of the far larger Mauna Loa. Kīlauea's flattened dome shape reflects the gently oozing flows from which it arose. Don't get the impression that Hawaiian volcanoes are pussycats. It's just that they lack the pent-up gases that cause their continental cousins to blow their tops. Instead, the frequent and controlled nature of their eruptions makes the Big Island one of the few places in the world where people run to—not from—a live volcano.

Hawai'i Volcanoes National Park (808-985-6000; nps.gov/havo) encompasses some of the wildest terrain on earth. Extending from sea level to 13,667 feet, the park covers a range of habitats, from desert to rain forest to the subarctic summit of Mauna Loa. Two of the most active volcanoes in the world lie within its boundaries, which makes this one of the most volatile areas on earth. If Pele truly lives here, she's been a busy deity of late.

Kīlauea volcano has been continuously erupting since 1983 but on May 3, 2018, a substantial increase in volcanic and seismic activity changed Puna forever. First, a 6.9 magnitude earthquake hit Puna on May 4. Within days, two dozen fissures erupted lava in or near the subdivisions of Leilani Estates and Lanipuna Gardens, overrunning Hawai'i Route 132 by the end of May and reaching the ocean in early June. The lava evaporated Green Lake in Pu'u Kapoho crater, the largest national freshwater lake in Hawai'i and filled in the interconnected tide pools of Kapolo and Kapoho Bay.

An estimated 875 acres of new land had been created in the ocean as a result of the lava flow but at some great cost to the people of lower Puna. Over 700 homes were destroyed, nearly 2,000 people in the area had to be evacuated, and recovery efforts were estimated in December 2018 to cost more than $800 million dollars. The 2018 lower Puna eruption was the most destructive volcanic incident in the United States since Mount St. Helens erupted in 1980. For many local residents, though, it was simply Madame Pele exercising her right to reclaim what she wants.

Seismic rumbles register constantly in the park. Most go unfelt by humans, but they do build to violent earthquakes every now and then. New phases of eruptions often open with spectacular fountains of lava that drain into glowing ponds of red-hot rock. As these lavas flow down the mountain slopes and into the sea, they recontour the landscape and often create geologic formations of rare beauty. A word of warning: Taking rocks as souvenirs violates federal law. The Park Service gets packages every day from visitors who want to return things they took to rid themselves of lingering bad luck.

From the park entrance at the highway's 29-mile point, the 11-mile Crater Rim Road loops around Kīlauea Caldera, doling out a crash course in volcanology. Pay your $30 per vehicle admission (valid for a week's reentry) and proceed first to the visitor center to get oriented. You can take in some natural history exhibits, get information on hiking trails and camping, and watch some stellar footage of past eruptions while getting the scoop on current volcanic activity. The park staff runs various interpretive programs mostly during the summer months; check the schedule. The Kīlauea Visitor Center is open daily 9 a.m. to 8 p.m.

Take a moment to browse in the ***Volcano Art Center*** (808-967-8222; volcanoartcenter.org) next door, which occupies the original Volcano House lodge built in 1877. This nonprofit venture showcases the work of local artists, including some striking eruption photography. The administrative office is in Volcano Village. Open daily 9 a.m. to 5 p.m. Across the street sits the ***Volcano House*** (866-756-9625; hawaiivolcanohouse.com), perched right on the rim of Kīlauea

Caldera. Four hundred feet below, the volcano's gaping maw measures almost 3 miles across, textured by lava flows and craters of varying ages. To appreciate the violent collapses that formed this sunken pit, walk left from the Volcano House along Waldron's Ledge. Until 1983 the Crater Rim Road ran this way. On November 16 of that year, a 6.6-magnitude earthquake shredded the road and tore away part of the ledge.

As you walk, pay attention to the rain forest around you. Reaching heights up to 30 feet, the many *hapu'u* tree ferns evoke a primeval atmosphere. Look for the red-tinged amaumau ferns, sacred to Pele. And keep your eyes peeled for the wild orchids that thrive in these misty uplands. Towering above this lush undergrowth, 'ōhi'a trees grow here as they do throughout the park, from the coastal desert to the 9,000-foot elevation level. This versatile tree is one of the first life-forms to inhabit a new lava flow and begin its revegetation, and it can be identified by its red, tassel-like lehua blossoms (sacred to Pele's sister, Hi'iaka). In Hawaiian tradition the *'ōhi'a-lehua* represents the male-female essence, a yin-yang duality that legend traces to a pair of lovers, transformed by the gods. Picking the lehua blossoms parts the lovers and supposedly brings rain (divine tears). Judging by the weather, it seems to happen quite often here.

Start your driving tour around the Crater Rim, moving counterclockwise. Just around the bend from the visitor center, a side jog leads to ***Sulphur Banks,*** where some of the park's most active fumaroles emit noxious fumes that reek of rotten eggs. Yellow sulfur streaks paint the landscape and oxidize iron in the lava to create striking colors. As Mark Twain joked, "The smell of sulfur is strong, but not unpleasant to a sinner." Nonsulfuric ***steam vents*** are also nearby. In the early-morning cool, the "steaming bluff" from trailside vents along this section of the crater rim makes an impressive sight.

As you continue past the Kīlauea Military Center, look for 'ōhelo berry bushes along the road. Sacred to Pele, the pale red fruits resemble cranberries and ripen year-round. (Any clue yet what the goddess's favorite color is?) To indulge, you are supposed to toss the first handful toward the caldera as an offering. Next up at Uwēkahuna Bluff, the ***Hawai'i Volcano Observatory*** (808-967-7328; usgs.gov/observatories/hvo) overlooks Halemaumau Crater. Awestruck Hawaiians left offerings at a heiau here, cringing before the sight of their fearful deity. Today's scientists are more clinical as they monitor Pele's vital signs to try to predict eruptions.

Before the 2018 eruptions forced its evacuation and closure, the Thomas A. Jaggar Museum explained the dangers and difficulties of studying an active volcano. Working seismographs monitored the constant shifting in the area while displays taught visitors to distinguish the two main types of lava: *A'a* lava travels as rough piles of slow-moving clinkers and hardens the same way. The hotter *pahoehoe* flows in streams or seeps out in narrow fingers; it hardens in smooth, wavy surfaces, or curls into ropy formations. The determining factors as to which type emerges include rate of extrusion, temperature, chemical composition, and gaseous mix of the magma. Other oddities strike your eye, such as Pele's "hair" and "tears," as well as pumice, cinder, and "lava bombs." You can find examples of all these in the park. At the time of publication, it was uncertain whether the Jaggar Museum would reopen, but locals were exploring options to make the exhibits available to the public once again. According to nps.gov, the current plan is to replace the old functions of the Jaggar Museum with the Kilauea Visitor Center and demolish the three structures damaged in the 2018 eruption: Jaggar Museum, the Okamura Building, and the Geochemistry Annex. Visit nps.gov/havo/learn/management/jaggar-museum for details.

As you continue around the crater drive, the vegetation becomes stunted, then almost barren. This is the dry side of the mountain, and below stretches the stark wasteland of the Ka'u Desert. What little rain falls here is full of sulfur from the eruptions, a naturally occurring version of "acid rain." Some of that sulfur hits you in fumes as you round the southwest corner of the caldera and heralds your approach to ***Halemaumau Crater,*** Pele's fire pit. This "crater within a crater" measures 3,000 feet across and drops 280 feet to a smoothly paved lava floor. The goddess maintained a more formidable presence here before 1924, when the crater bubbled with a constant lake of molten lava. Subsequent lava flows have "ponded" the crater, with the last summit eruption in 1982. The following year a new eruption started at Pu'u 'Ō'ō along the east rift zone, and lava has flowed from there ever since; today only wisps of steam reveal the presence of magma beneath the surface of Halemaumau. An early Christian convert, Princess Kapi'olani won followers by defying Pele here in her own home. But locals in the area sometimes still purchase "lava insurance" through offerings of gin and other commodities favored by the goddess.

Continuing from Halemaumau, you'll pass the turnoff to Chain of Craters Road, which descends to the coast. Stay on Crater Rim Road for now to complete the last leg of the loop. The crater around which you are looping at this stage is ***Kīlauea 'Iki*** ("little Kīlauea"). This kid brother of the main caldera erupted in 1959 with fountains of lava that towered as high as 1,900 feet! Two overlooks allow you to peer into this yawning fissure, a mile long and almost 400 feet deep. As with Halemaumau, a smooth tarmac of jet black lava covers the floor where a molten lake once churned. You can see traces of the "bathtub ring" left on the walls by the high-water mark of the ponded lava.

Near the first overlook is ***Pu'u Pua'i*** ("gushing hill"), formed on the southwest crater rim from trade winds carrying pumice, cinder ash, and lava splatter from the eruption. Running alongside the hill (beginning at the overlook) is the popular half-mile "Devastation Trail," which passes through an 'ōhi'a forest caught in the firestorm.

Between the two Kīlauea 'Iki overlooks is another must-see, the ***Thurston Lava Tube.*** A 300-yard loop descends through gorgeous rain forest into a sunken crater, where the entrance to the lava tube drips with ferns. The inside is well lighted and smoothly hollowed. (Souvenir collectors stripped all the stalactites from the ceiling—the curse of Pele be upon them.) The sound of birdsongs greets you on the other side.

Those for whom the Thurston tube sounds too tame may want to sign up for the Park Service's free weekly hike through ***Pua Po'o Lava Tube,*** a pristine lava tube only accessible on this guided tour. The trip involves 4 miles of hiking and takes about 4 hours (with an hour spent in the tube itself). Some climbing/crouching is required, and you must bring your own flashlight. The trip size is limited, so reserve ahead. The trip is currently offered on Wednesday afternoon. The Park Service starts its sign-up list on the Wednesday of the week prior. Call (808) 985-7373.

Your loop completed, it's time to head to the coast. Branching off Crater Rim Road from the southeast corner of the caldera, the Chain of Craters Road descends 24 miles downslope to the site of the recent eruptions. As its name implies, the road passes a series of impressive craters along Kīlauea's east rift zone. The constant eruptions since 1983 have all flowed from points east of this road.

The seldom-traveled Hilina Pali Road, 2 miles long, detours right to ***Kulanaokuaiki Campground,*** a pali overlook and the start of several backcountry trails. The main road descends an impressive pali of its own, with several pull-offs overlooking the blackened shelf of Hawai'i's newest lands. The perennially overcast skies reflect "vog" formed by lava entering the ocean. At the bottom of the hill, about 17 miles along, look for the sign to the ***Pu'u Loa Petroglyphs.*** A 1-mile trail leads to one of Hawai'i's largest concentrations of stone carvings. Some are recognizable images, others abstract symbols. *Pu'u Loa* translates to "long hill," but the Hawaiians read this as "long life." The top of the hill is pocked with thousands of tiny holes drilled by Hawaiian parents of old in the belief that burying a *piko* (umbilical cord) in a puka would ensure a long life for the child.

The road continues toward the sea and then travels about 5 more miles along the coast. Several turnoffs allow you to walk to the edge of rugged lava cliffs overlooking the deep blue of the open ocean. Driven by the sea goddess's fury, constant waves rip against the land, battering against Pele's island stronghold. The eroded shoreline reveals striking sea arches and rock islands. Farther north, Pele has struck back, pouring her lava into the sea to build new land. Towers of steam rise above this epic battle between two great forces of nature. Underwater, the superheated lava cools explosively, splintering into glassy fragments that ocean currents collect and deposit to form black-sand beaches. Most of these fledgling strands get covered by encroaching flows, but just as steadily new ones form down current.

Since 1983, the start of the current eruption, Kīlauea volcano has paved more than 43 square miles with fresh lava, while adding 544 acres of new land. This is the longest eruption in 600 years, with no end in sight. Call (808) 985-6011 to inquire about any eruption update.

The road ends somewhere short of the park's eastern border at Waha'ula, where a visitor center, campground, and 1,000-year-old heiau have all been consumed by recent flows. If lava is still flowing in the area, you will probably have to walk to see it. Conditions change daily. There are generally three places where hot lava may be seen: coming down the pali, in the flat coastal plain, and entering the ocean. (The summit vent at Pu'u 'Ō'ō is too dangerous to approach except by air.) Surface flows in the flatlands generally present the best viewing opportunities. Slow-moving pahoehoe flows sometime extend molten fingers that allow visitors to safely approach close enough to roast marshmallows in the 2,000°F heat. Viewing pali flows requires a long walk inland; these tend to be jagged a'a flows, as pahoehoe breaks apart as it slides down the sleep slopes. As you trudge across the hardened coastal flows that undulate like a frozen ocean, you may notice that some of the lava has a glassy, refractive sheen, gilded in the sunlight; in other places a white or silvery powder lines the crevices. Both are signs of fresh lava caused by mineral deposits that will be gone in weeks. Heat and smoke are signs of fire: You may be crossing active flows carried in underground lava tubes. Needless to say, keep away from any openings. At times, the flows funnel entirely underground through lava tubes extending to the water's edge. Spectators watching from a distance catch glimpses of the red stuff as it drips over a ledge into the ocean amid clouds of steam.

Ocean flows present special dangers, including the collapse of unstable "benches" jutting out to sea that the lava often builds without adequate foundation. Other hazards include tephra jets, littoral fountains, and scalding steam created when hot lava enters the sea with explosive force, sending debris flying hundreds of yards inland, along with acid fumes. However, approaching lava anywhere can be dangerous. Unstable surfaces, toxic fumes, and exposure to heat make extreme caution imperative. Carry extra water and never venture out in heavy rains; small children, pregnant women, and those with respiratory or heart problems should keep their distance. The Park Service does what it can to regulate access, marking a "safety path" with reflectors. Yet conditions change constantly, and rangers are not always available. Be sure to review the detailed handouts and displays on lava hazards at park headquarters (and posted on its website). Lava is a force of nature that yields to no one.

The radiant glow of the red-hot rock often provides the best spectacle when viewed at night. Many people hike in at sundown. The park stays open 24 hours a day, but unless you know where you're going and are adequately prepared, it's easy to stumble in the jagged, irregular pathways or get lost in the dark.

Return up Chain of Craters Road and turn right to return to the visitor center; if you are still game, there's more to see in the park off Route 11. (If you are headed to Kona, you can make these stops on the way.) Take the second right 2 miles from the park entrance onto Mauna Loa Road. Immediately after turning, take another right along the loop road to the ***Lava Tree Molds.*** These manhole-size oddities formed in a manner similar to the "lava trees" in Puna: Lava inundated a forest and crusted around the water-laden trunks of large trees. In this case, the flow raised the surrounding ground level. The hollow molds left after the wood burned or rotted away indicate the depth of the new lava cover. The width of the molds indicates that the trees were koa, the largest of the native trees. Plenty of smaller koas grow nearby. The young saplings have fernlike leaves that change to sickle-shaped leaf stalks as the trees mature.

Two miles farther, Mauna Loa Road reaches ***Kīpuka Puaulu***, also known as Kīpukapuaulu ("bird park"). A *kipuka* forms when lava flows bypass a section of forest, leaving an island of vegetation surrounded by devastation. Studies of insect species cut off from the mainstream population by kipuka formed at a known date have shown that evolutionary changes can occur much more quickly than biologists had previously thought possible. The flow that created this kipuka happened about 400 years ago, but a visible difference remains between the old growth and the new scrubland around it. Wildlife appreciates the difference as well. Bird-watchers can walk the 1-mile loop around the forest to see and hear many native and foreign species. The bright red 'i'iwi and *'apapane* have black-tipped wings and curved beaks to suck nectar from treetop blossoms. The *'elepaio* has an onomatopoeic name resembling its song. It has brown feathers and a white rump. Mauna Loa Road continues 10 more miles to the mountain's 6,650-foot elevation, a launching point for the 18-mile, two-day ascent to Moku'aweoweo Caldera at the 13,679-foot summit of Mauna Loa. It's worth driving up on a clear day for the view over Kīlauea. Please note that at the time of the publishing of this book Mauna Loa Trail is closed above Red Hill cabin due to hazards from the recent eruption. Check nps.gov/havo/planyourvisit/hike_day_kipukapuaulu.htm or call (808) 985-6011 for further details.

Six miles farther on the highway, past the 37-mile point, look for the sign for the ***Ka'u Desert Trailhead*** near the western border of the national park. An easy 0.8-mile walk across lava fields brings you to some literal footprints of history from a pivotal event in Hawai'i's past. The violent eruptions of 1790 spewed clouds of volcanic ash that trapped an army belonging to Keōua Kū'ahu'ula, Kamehameha's cousin and main rival. The victims suffocated in the noxious fumes, leaving their footprints preserved in hardened deposits of ash. Such Pompeii-like destruction is unusual for Hawaiian eruptions, and both factions interpreted the disaster as a sign that Pele favored Kamehameha. A protective shelter on the trail encases a section of these footprints.

One final attraction has nothing to do with volcanoes. Take the golf course turnoff between Mauna Loa Road and the park entrance and continue to ***Volcano Winery*** (808-967-7772; volcanowinery.com) at the end of the road. The winery produces white wines from the Symphony grapes it grows on surrounding vineyards as well as a range of novelty wines from tropical fruits and honeys. A tasting room is open to visitors daily from 10 a.m. to 5:30 p.m.

Restaurant options in Volcano Village are limited, so you may want to pack a picnic. The Volcano House has the best views but suffers from tour-bus crowds. You're better off leaving the park to seek nourishment in nearby Volcano Village. Backtrack 1 mile on the highway toward Hilo, and turn left onto Old Volcano Road, where you might eat at ***Lava Rock Cafe*** (808-967-8526) for local plate lunch. Open Tues through Sat 7:30 a.m. to 8 p.m., Sun until 2 p.m. Or try the golf course clubhouse (on the way to the winery) for local American fare; it closes at 3 p.m.

Probably your best bet in the evening is ***Kīlauea Lodge and Restaurant*** (808-967-7366; kilauealodge.com), which serves gourmet continental dinners in the lofty central hall of a renovated 1938 YWCA retreat. Albert Jeyte, the owner-chef, won an Emmy for makeup work in the television series *Magnum P.I.* The hearty central European flavors match the cozy warmth of the fireplace. Open Tues 5 to 9 p.m., and Wed to Sun 9 a.m. to 9 p.m. Expensive. Another solid option is ***Thai Thai*** (808-967-7969) for Thai food. Open daily 11:30 a.m. to 3 p.m. and 4 to 9 p.m. Moderate. Nestled in a lush Hawaiian garden is ***Café Ono*** (808-985-8979; cafeono.net), the culinary wing of Volcano Garden Arts, farmhouse-turned-gallery now recognized as a World Heritage Site owned and lovingly manicured and maintained by dancer, painter, and sculptor Ira Ono. Open Thurs to Sun, 11 a.m. to 2 p.m. Moderate. Call ahead. For those who just want to fill their bellies with decent grub at a modest price, the ***Kīlauea Military Camp*** (808-967-8333; kilaueamilitarycamp.com) canteen serves an a la carte menu nightly (except Fri), which features a mixed plate buffet of Hawaiian specialties for as low at $15.95. It's located on the Chain of Craters Road, just past the steam vents. Open daily 7 to 9:30 a.m., and Fri and Sat 5 to 9 p.m. Inexpensive.

Given all there is to see in the park, plus the possibility of nighttime lava viewing, you should consider staying overnight. Fortunately, the volcano has proven to be fertile soil for bed-and-breakfasts. ***Aloha Happy Place*** (808-989-5050; facebook.com/alohahappyranch) is not nearly as kitschy as the name would imply. This rustic mission-style home on Old Volcano Road, built in 1928, is located on a green, early 20th century–esque ranch and farmstead. Original works of art line the walls and an extensive library, complete with a lava rock fireplace, offers a selection of priceless books to (carefully) peruse. Contact for availability and prices.

Although later to enter the bed-and-breakfast market, Lisha and Brian Crawford's ***Chalet Kīlauea Collection*** has become the dominant player in town, with bed-and-breakfast and vacation rental options spanning the gamut from budget to luxury, all managed with corporate efficiency. The Crawfords' upscale ***Volcano Inn*** features international theme rooms decorated with objects that Lisha and Brian collected during their world travels. All have private whirlpool baths, with tariffs that run starting at $159 a night and include a formal candlelit breakfast. Their ***Volcano Hale*** offers simple rooms with shared baths in a renovated 1912 home for $70 to $80. For central reservations, call (808) 967-7786 or visit volcano-hawaii.com.

For a more intimate abode, consider either of the following: ***Volcano Rainforest Retreat*** (808-985-8696 or 800-550-8696; volcanoretreat.com) offers four unique hideaway cabins created by owner-architect Peter Golden, who seems mildly obsessed with polygonal shapes. Nestled within a mossy, tree-fern forest, the smaller two cabins have central skylights and floor-length picture windows; their tightly efficient design includes a tiny kitchenette. Two larger units offer a full kitchen. All units have private entrances and access to an outdoor hot tub. Breakfast included. Prices range from $300 to $555, with discounts for longer stays. Even more private is ***Volcano Teapot Cottage*** (808-937-4976; volcanoteapot.com), a two-bedroom bungalow built in the early 1900s on its own 2.5 acre plot. It's painted a cheery red with white trim on the outside. The interior displays such Victorian touches as a four-poster bed and an original claw-foot tub. Owner Antoinette Bullough leaves daily breakfast fixings, and naturally there is plenty of tea. $215 per night, two-night minimum.

Volcano Village Estates (808-967-7986; volcanovillageestates.com) features lodging on the sumptuous grounds of the 1931 Dillingham family summer estate at similar prices. Other good choices include ***Volcano Places***

(808-967-7990; volcanoplaces.com) and the aforementioned ***Kīlauea Lodge and Restaurant*** (808-967-7366; kilauealodge.com). Finally, for those on a bare-bones budget, Satoshi Yabuki's ***Holo Holo In*** (808-967-7950; volcano-hostel.com) offers dorm beds for $30, and private rooms for $80. Call after 4:30 p.m. Tent space at the two national park campgrounds costs $10 a night per suite. Not bad.

Ka'u District

Route 11 descends south from the volcano through miles of scrubland followed by macadamia-nut orchards and coffee grown amidst former cane fields. There is more to this placid landscape than meets the eye. The coastline here is a major nesting ground for the endangered hawksbill turtle, while underground lies a vast network of lava tubes formed during eruptions of Mauna Loa centuries ago. Caveman wannabes can explore the latter and the mysteries they conceal (bug colonies, bat skeletons, archaeological remains) by contacting ***Kula Kai Caverns*** (808-929-9725; kulakaicaverns.com). They charge $28 for a 60-minute tour (two-person minimum); longer trips are also available. Tour times are negotiable, with evening visits possible. At about the 51-mile marker, you reach Pahāla, the largest settlement in the area. The town began as a sisal plantation, switched to sugar, then macnuts, and is now moving into coffee. Stop by the ***Plantation Store*** (808-928-9811; pahala-hawaii.com), on Maile Street just inland of the highway, for locally made crafts, coffee tasting, and other island goods. If you call ahead, you can arrange visits to local coffee farms. Julia Neal, the store owner, is a great resource on local happenings; she moonlights as the publisher of the community paper, fighting to preserve Ka'u's undeveloped coastline. Her involvement in conservation also has a personal dimension: She and her partner refurbish historic plantation–era cottages, often rescued from bulldozers and transferred from their original sites. Available as vacation rentals, they cost from $175 for a two-bedroom cottage to $850 for a seven-bedroom plantation manager's manse. If you're here on a Saturday, you can also take part in the 10:30 a.m. hula class held down the road. Nearby ***Waikapu on 30*** (808-242-1130) offers no-frill local takeout of Hawaiian plates and local fare (the lau lau's especially good here.) Open Mon to Fri, 9 a.m. to 2 p.m. Inexpensive to moderate.

Punalu'u, 4.5 miles farther, boasts the most famous ***black-sand beach*** left on the island. Turn left down the beach road and park by the coconut trees at the bottom. The rhythmic ebb and flow of the surf create mesmerizing patterns of white foam on the black beach. *Punaluu* means "diving springs"; early Hawaiians would dive into the bay to fill stoppered containers with freshwater from the underwater springs that empty into the ocean here. You can find one such spring near the shoreline to the left of the boat ramp. Turtles gather offshore to feed on algae that flourish in the brackish waters and occasionally haul out to bask on the sand (look, but don't touch). The north side of the bay guards the ruins of a heiau, which should not be entered. The more recent set of ruins you see bordering the old fishpond, inland of the beach, formerly housed a restaurant/cultural center.

The beach road loops uphill to rejoin Route 11. The ***Sea Mountain Resort*** (808-928-6200; 95-788 Ninole Loop Rd.) along the way takes its name from Lō'ihi Seamount, the heir apparent in the Hawaiian Island chain, located 20 miles offshore. Fueled by a very active sea volcano, Lō'ihi has risen to within 3,000 feet of the surface. Geologists estimate the new island could appear within a mere 10,000 years. Stay tuned.

As you continue along Route 11, you can alleviate the monotony of its flat, linear course by gazing uphill at a series of interesting flat-topped craters clinging to the slopes of Mauna Loa. At 60.5 miles you pass the turnoff to ***Whittington Beach Park,*** which has a swimming pond but no beach. The crumbling pier offshore once served to load sugar for shipping. The road begins to climb inland

Wood Valley

Five miles inland from Pahāla, a sleepy cane village on the sparsely populated south side of the Big Island, lies Wood Valley, a largely inconspicuous indentation in the slopes of Mauna Loa. This misty valley is one of the most remote places on the island, its onetime plantation camp now abandoned, as are the sugarcane fields that line the road leading into it. The cane gives way to tall trees once you reach the valley, and the bright gaudy colors of ***Wood Valley Temple*** (808-928-8539; nechung.org) come into view. This improbable sanctuary was built by Japanese cane workers as a Nichiren Mission, with its upper level later taken from a Japanese Shingon shrine in Pahāla. The temple now belongs to Tibetan Buddhists and was inaugurated by the Dalai Lama himself in 1973 as Nechung Dorje Drayang Ling ("Immutable Island of Melodious Sound"), a spiritual retreat center affiliated with two other temples in Tibet and India. Visiting Buddhist scholars, monks, and lamas often host lectures and workshops here, and anyone is welcome to attend the daily services at 8 a.m. and 6 p.m., to participate in meditation practice on Sunday at 10:30 a.m., or to stop by for quiet meditation alone during the day. The 25-acre grounds include many tropical fruits and other botanicals. You can also find lodging here for $115 for a double with shared bath and kitchen, or $85 for a single. To get to the temple, turn off the highway at Pahāla and take Pikake Street 5 miles north into Wood Valley. Because this is a place for spiritual contemplation, casual tourists are discouraged. Donation requested.

through dairy pastures with great coastal vistas. Like everything in this area, the tree-lined town of Na'ālehu, at 64 miles, bills itself as "the southernmost in the USA."

Try a meal in the country's southernmost restaurant, ***Hana Hou Restaurant*** (808-929-9717). The large dining room has vintage Hawaiiana decor. The monstrous flat-top diesel stove you see in the kitchen came off a military ship, brought to this 1941 restaurant courtesy of the US Army. Fresh fish caught daily at South Point tops the moderately priced menu. Open Sun through Thurs 11 a.m. to 5 p.m., and Fri and Sat until 7 p.m. Closed Tues and Wed. If they're closed, try ***Shaka's*** (808-929-7404) down the road, with a similar menu and live music on Friday nights. Open daily 8 a.m. to 9 p.m. The nearby ***Punalu'u Bake Shop and Visitors Center*** (808-929-7343; bakeshophawaii.com), open 8:30 a.m. to 5 p.m. daily, tempts visitors with samples of island-flavored sweetbread, as well as simple cafe fare. You can picnic in back in a garden gazebo surrounded by Hawaiian botanicals, while enjoying a pair of eye-catching murals depicting island life.

Na'ālehu has a roadside bed-and-breakfast, but for interesting alternatives, check out ***Patty's Motel*** (808-929-8426), minimal yet elegant studio apartments that start at $125 a night on Airbnb. Two-night minimum stay. Not too far away on Kamaoa Road, the simply named ***Hawai'i Island Resort*** (808-785-6456; experiencealohahere.com) offers lodging in a large, rural house. A tennis court and macadamia nut orchard more than make up for low-key rooms.

From Waiohinu, Route 11 climbs out of a broad valley onto a forested plateau. The turnoff to South Point arrives at the 70-mile marker. Although rental car companies often forbid the drive, the 12 miles of single-lane road are in good drivable condition. You pass an orange grove near the top of the road, then continue through open cattle pasture. A wind farm of sleek, three-armed windmills towers above the savannah, another alternative energy project. Near the end of the road, take the right fork and park by the fishing platforms built onto the cliffs. As you look back, the panoramic sweep of the cliff bordering the western edge of the peninsula illustrates in relief the elevated plateau from which you have descended.

A Coast Guard beacon a quarter-mile along the coast marks ***Ka Lae*** ("the point"), as Hawaiians call the southernmost border of the 50 states. Beneath the beacon stands ***Kalalea Heiau,*** a small rock enclosure with a wooden *ahalele* (offering stand) inside. Archaeological remains litter the area, many carbon-dated to the 5th century, if not earlier. Oral traditions hold that the first Polynesian voyagers landed here. In the rocks below the heiau, holes drilled with Stone Age tools served as ancient canoe moorings, allowing Hawaiians to fish in the often stormy, current-swept waters below. In calmer periods, daredevils sometimes take the plunge. The left fork of South Point Road leads to the headquarters of ***Ka 'Ohana o Kalae,*** a grassroots organization that works to protect the island's natural and cultural sites. The *Hawaiian-in-Chains* statue outside speaks to the native sovereignty movement. From the end of the pavement, a hot and dry 3-mile hike along a jeep road leads to ***Green Sand*** (or Papakolea) ***Beach.*** Olivine grains eroded from the base of a cinder cone behind the beach give the sand its distinctive green tint. The path down to the beach can be treacherous, and swimming conditions are often unsafe. There is a $5 charge to park at the trailhead, or you can take the shuttle for $20 to $30 per person.

West of South Point, Route 11 begins to cross a series of ancient lava flows. The only other accessible beaches in Ka'u lie at the end of the ***Road to the Sea.*** This unmarked cinder road departs from the highway 0.4 mile north of the 79-mile point, between 'Iolani Lane and Aloha Drive but on the opposite side of the road. Two-wheel-drive vehicles can handle all but the very last section of the 7-mile descent. Park and hike down to a string of green- and black-sand beaches tucked beneath Humuhumu Point and extending west about a mile. The striking littoral cones along this coast were formed from spattering ash thrown back by blasts of steam as lava entered the ocean. Two miles farther along the highway, the road-weary can rest at ***Manukā State Wayside Park*** and bask in the tranquillity of its arboretum.

The Kona Coast

The Mamalahoa Highway continues around the west slopes of Mauna Loa to enter the Kona District. As the highway climbs higher, broad vistas open up over the ocean below. Rainfall here varies by elevation, from a parched dry coast to rain forest in the uplands. Coffee bushes thrive on the middle slopes of South Kona, shaded by the afternoon cloud cover. Kona coffee, the oldest commercial beans grown in the islands, has gained worldwide recognition. North Kona reaps its own growing crop in tourism. Heeding pressure from Hawaiian activists, many of the new hotels preserve the historical sites on their properties as mini-museums.

At the 89-mile point, you pass the turnoff to ***Miloli'i,*** a traditional Hawaiian fishing village. Local fishermen still use traditional outrigger canoes (powered by nontraditional outboard motors) to net *ōpelu* (mackerel) that have been tamed and fattened by repeated feedings. It's a steep 5-mile descent to the village. From the end of the road, a 15-minute hike south leads to a secluded black-sand beach at Honomalino Bay.

One and a half miles past the 100-mile point, a narrow, bumpy road descends 2 miles to ***Ho'okena Beach Park.*** Shaded by coconut palms, the gray-sand beach faces cliffs across Kauhako Bay. The bay's protective arms make Ho'okena an excellent swimming beach. ***Kealia Beach,*** a short walk to the north, has smaller pockets of white sand and offers good snorkeling.

Continue on Route 11 for another 2.5 miles and turn seaward to ***Hōnaunau Place of Refuge***. A sign halfway down directs you on a short detour right to ***St. Benedict's Painted Church*** (808-328-2227; thepaintedchurchhawaii.org). A Belgian priest, Father John Velghe, took four years and a healthy dose of imagination to paint the interior. Biblical scenes decorate the side panels for the benefit of illiterate churchgoers. The wall behind the altar gives the illusion of being in the Cathedral of Burgos in Spain. For a tropical touch, Father Velghe made the interior pillars sprout palm fronds curving onto the painted ceiling.

Eating options in this stretch of South Kona cluster along the highway, ensconced in vintage plantation buildings, all on the ocean side. Open for breakfast and lunch, the ***Coffee Shack*** (808-328-9555; coffeeshack.com) offers decent grub, but the real reason to stop here is its sweeping views of the coastline below. Open every day except Wed 7 a.m. to 3:30 p.m. ***Super J's*** (808-328-9566) serves authentic Hawaiian food Mon through Sat 10 a.m. to 3 p.m. Closed Sun and Tues. Farther on, the ***Manago Hotel Restaurant*** (808-323-2642; managohotel.com/restaurant) commands a loyal following with a variety of local favorites, from fried *opelu* to pork chops. It also claims its fame as the island's oldest restaurant. Open daily except Mon 7 to 9 a.m., 11 a.m. to 2 p.m., and 5 to 7:30 p.m.

The ***Manago Hotel*** (808-323-2642; managohotel.com) is an equally fine choice for lodging. Run by the third generation of Managos, the 1917 hotel's roadside rooms are backed up by a plush wing overlooking the ocean. A Japanese garden and carp pond enhance the courtyard in between. Rates vary by wing and floor, from $91 to $103 for doubles. For a touch of Asian luxury, ask for the Japanese suite, which rents for $116 for doubles. Furnished in memory of Kinzo and Osame, the hotel's immigrant founders, the room features *ofuro* tubs, tatami mats, and futons.

Several bed-and-breakfasts also operate in the area, many on working farms. Marianna Schrepfer, a delightfully warm German earth mama, presides over the eclectic accommodations at ***Rainbow Plantation Bed and Breakfast*** (808-323-2393 or 800-494-2829, which include a cozy twin-bed berth in a converted 34-foot fishing boat. Guests enjoy a homemade breakfast of freshly squeezed liliko'i juice, farm-fresh eggs, and homemade banana bread; have access to a communal kitchen; and are free to roam 7 sprawling acres of tree farm/botanical garden/animal menagerie. Please check hotels.com, expedia.com, trip.com, and other sites for the latest rates and specials. Coffee is the crop on the various acreage surrounding ***Kona Palace in Captain Cook*** (303-946-3010) perched

Coffee Tourism

The rich, mellow taste of ***Kona*** coffee has earned it an elite status among world coffees. But until recently, visitors to Kona never actually saw coffee growing. This $6 million crop is scattered among more than 500 small farms in South Kona. Many of these are now promoting tourism much the same way that vineyards in wine-producing regions do, by opening visitor centers and tasting rooms.

The Kona coffee belt spans roughly 20 miles of coastline between Honaunau and Holualoa. It begins about 2 miles inland at 800-foot elevation and extends about another mile upward to the 1,700-foot level. Sheltered beneath the slopes of giant Mauna Loa, the coffee belt has a unique climate: It's one of the few places in Hawai'i that gets more rain in summer than in winter. The typical weather pattern of morning sun followed by afternoon clouds and rain has proven ideal for coffee to thrive. From March to May, coffee bushes in Kona erupt in a cloud of fragrant white blossoms known as "Kona snow." From the blossoms grow "cherries," which ripen to a brilliant red when ready for harvest in the fall. Harvest times vary by elevation, and the clusters of cherries on each bush ripen individually, requiring harvesting to be done by hand in several rounds. Stripped of pulp, the cherry pits become "green" (unroasted) coffee beans. Usually there are two beans per cherry, but about 5 percent of cherries yield only one bean, called a peaberry. Many coffee farms produce a special peaberry coffee, which has a distinctive taste.

The first coffee was planted in Kona around 1828 by Samuel Ruggles, a missionary. Although commercial coffee was once grown on all the islands (a trend that is now reviving), a collapse in the world coffee market in 1898 put the large-scale plantations out of business. In Kona, small 5-acre plots were instead leased as crop-shares to Japanese farmers, who carried on the coffee-growing tradition (sometimes harvesting fields at night to escape the watchful eyes of their creditors). For many years, Kona coffee remained the only commercial coffee crop grown in the United States.

To learn more about coffee growing firsthand (and sample some of the house product), plan to visit at least one coffee farm while in Kona. For a complete guide to coffee tourism, look for the free brochure/map entitled "Kona Coffee Country Driving Tour," distributed at various visitor centers. Besides the Greenwell Farms and Kona Historical Society tours mentioned in the text, other places welcoming visitors include ***Kona Le'a Plantation*** (808-322-9937; konalea.com), at the 2-mile marker on the Mamalahoa Highway (Route 180), which is home to the Holualoa Coffee Company and ***Kona Joe's*** (808-322-2100; konajoe.com), between the 113- and 114-mile marker on the main highway (Route 11). Kona Le'a offers tours from tree to cup on weekdays from 8 a.m. to 3 p.m. Kona Joe's tours take place daily from 8 a.m. to 5 p.m. Its patented trellis farming method borrows the technique of vineyards to string out coffee branches like grapevines for optimal yields.

high atop the Kona coffee hills on Napoopoo Road. A long drive up is the price you pay for sweeping coastal views. Spacious one- or two-bedroom suites rent for around $300 a night, with buffet breakfast, including unlimited cups of the homegrown brew. ***Affordable Hawai'i at Pōmaika'i*** ("Lucky") ***Farms*** (808-328-2112) has 4 acres in coffee and macadamia nuts. The most unusual of the four rooms here is the coffee barn, a seriously rustic private shack with huge screen windows and an outdoor shower. Even funkier lodging can be had at the ***Dragonfly Ranch*** (808-328-2159; dragonflyranch.com), a New Age center of sorts. The "designer hippie" lodgings have a tree-house feel. They range from a room with a private bath for $180 to the Ali'i suite, complete with an outdoor feather bed, for $275. The suites all have private outdoor showers, and most have views of the coast. Breakfast fixings are supplied, and snorkeling gear is available. Host Barbara can provide Hawaiian *lomilomi* massage and other homeopathic treatments on request.

At the bottom of Honaunau Road, you will find ***Pu'uhonua o Honaunau National Historic Park*** (808-328-2326; nps.gov/puho). Remember, life in ancient Hawai'i was governed by a system of rigid kapu. Women couldn't eat bananas; commoners had to keep their shadows off the pathway of a chief; fish remained off-limits during spawning. Transgressions of any kapu, however minor, offended the gods and could provoke a natural disaster, such as a tidal wave. To protect the community, offenders had to be killed immediately—unless they could reach a *pu'uhonua* ("hill of sanctuary"), such as the one here at Honaunau, to receive spiritual cleansing within. Defeated warriors and noncombatants also took sanctuary here.

The National Park Service has worked to restore the area sites to the way they appeared in the late 1700s. You enter through the palace grounds of the ruling chief of the area, whose courtyard adjoined the pu'uhonua. Numbered coconuts designate points of interest as you stroll through the living compound and canoe landing. Ask at the visitor counter for a copy of the rules for *konane* (Hawaiian checkers). A stone *papamu* (playing board) with light and dark pebbles sits in a shaded spot awaiting players. The "Great Wall"—an impressive mortarless construction 10 feet high, 17 feet thick, and 1,000 feet long—separates the palace grounds from the sanctuary itself. At the far edge of the wall, ***Hale o Keawe Heiau*** features a reconstructed thatched building, a *lele* stand for offerings, and ferocious carved tikis standing vigil around the perimeter. Buried bones of 23 high chiefs imbue the 17th-century temple with its sacred mana. Two older heiau remain unreconstructed. Look for the Ka'ahumanu Stone, under which Kamehameha's favorite wife hid until her pet dog gave her away. Ka'ahumanu swam to this sanctuary to escape her husband's jealous wrath. Only the intercession of British Captain George Vancouver persuaded the couple to make up. Coconut and noni trees are the only vegetation within the pu'uhonua grounds. Other native plants grow around the periphery. The park visitor center is open daily from 8:30 a.m. to 4:30 p.m., but the grounds are open from 8:15 a.m. to sunset. You can enjoy excellent snorkeling on the north side of the bay or follow a hiking trail a half mile south along the coast through the ruins of an ancient Hawaiian fishing village to find an exposed lava tube overlooking the sea. Admission is $20 per vehicle for seven days.

If the pu'uhonua at Honaunau Bay preserves something of the old system, the next bay to the north bears witness to the coming of the new. To get to ***Kealakekua Bay,*** where Captain Cook landed, you can either drive 4 miles along the coast through barren scrub-covered lava fields past Ke'ei Beach or backtrack uphill and take either the middle road past the Painted Church through scenic coffee country or the main highway farther up; then turn down Napo'opo'o Road. On the way down, at the junction with Middle Ke'ei Road, you might stop to smell the flowers at ***SYK Enterprises*** (808-328-9301), Hawai'i's largest plumeria tree farm. Look for the warehouse on the left (south) side of the road and stop by anytime before 5:30 p.m. to purchase a freshly strung lei.

Just shy of the highway's 110-mile marker on the uphill side, the ***Amy B. H. Greenwell Ethnobotanical Garden*** (808-323-3318) spreads across 12 acres of hillside. Designed as a microcosm of Kona agriculture in ancient times, with plantings varying by elevation from ocean to mountain, the gardens have helpful labels throughout as well as a series of interpretive panels along a short nature walk. Open Thurs through Sun 9 a.m. to 2 p.m. Donation requested. Opposite the 110-mile marker, the ***Kona Coffee Living History Farm*** (808-323-3222) has been restored by the Kona Historical Society to its circa-1920s condition, using vintage equipment and authentic replicas. The museum is self-guided with entrance from 10 a.m. to 2 p.m. Tues through Fri. Admission $20.

Just past the Manago Hotel, Napo'opo'o Road descends from the highway to Kealakekua Bay, with sweeping views of the coast fanning out below. Whichever route you choose to get here, you end up at ***Napo'opo'o Beach Park,*** one corner of which edges against the bay. A famous heiau dedicated to the harvest god, Lono, once stood here. Contrary to common belief, however, it was separated from ***Hikiau Heiau,*** the terraced platform you see today. When Captain Cook sailed into Kealakekua Bay, the Makahiki Festival honoring Lono was in full swing. American anthropologist Marshall Sahlins perpetuated a myth that Cook was taken for Lono and welcomed as a god. In reality, the Hawaiians were most likely fascinated by the European ships and the sailors' use of iron.

When Cook returned a month later to repair storm damage, the Makahiki was ending and the season for war and battle had begun. This time the welcome was more grudging. According to American John Ledyard, the only citizen aboard Cook's ship not loyal to the British crown, relations had become strained due to Cook having forcibly stolen materials he needed on his first visit. A skirmish erupted over a stolen lifeboat; Cook attempted to hold Kalaniʻōpuʻu, the ruling chief of Hawaiʻi Island, hostage in exchange for the vessel, which ultimately led to Cook's death.

A plaque in front of Hikiau Heiau commemorates the first Christian service in Hawaiʻi, a burial ceremony performed by Captain Cook on temple grounds. Another plaque salutes Henry Opukahaia, a young Hawaiian apprenticed at the heiau who turned his back on the old gods and sailed to New England to receive a Christian education. His passionate pleas would inspire the first missionaries to come to Hawaiʻi to lead his people away from idolatry.

Across the bay, steep bluffs descend from the hillside and slope down to a peninsula at the far mouth of the bay. At the base of this peninsula, a white marble obelisk stands near the spot where Captain Cook fell. To get there, you can hike down, starting at the jeep road turnoff on the right off Napoʻopoʻo Road, just below its junction with the highway. It takes about 2 hours. A number of roadside shops also rent kayaks. It's a 1-mile paddle to reach the monument. Technically, this is British soil you'll be standing on—ceded land akin to a consulate. An Australian ship still comes annually to tend to the monument's upkeep. The waters offshore are a popular snorkeling spot; a pod of spinner dolphins frequents the bay as well as others to the south.

Just south of Kealakekua Bay, a turnoff from the coastal road to Honaunau leads to the white sands of ***Keʻei Beach,*** which has a place in history all its own. Kamehameha fought his first battle to subdue the Big Island here, defeating his cousin Kiwalao, the son of former ruling chief Kalaniʻōpuʻu. Luckily, the losers had a puʻuhonua nearby.

Return up Napoʻopoʻo Road to Route 11 and the town of Captain Cook and continue north on the highway 1 mile to the H. N. Greenwell Store, which is run as a museum by the ***Kona Historical Society Museum*** (808-323-3222), just outside Kealakekua Village. Built in 1875 by rancher Henry Nicholas Greenwell, the museum features photographs, memorabilia, and artifacts from Kona's past. Open Mon through Fri 10 a.m. to 2 p.m. Admission is $7. An Englishman by birth, Greenwell came to Kona in 1850, one of the first haole settlers on the coast. The ruins of his family homestead lie adjacent to the store; those interested can get a self-guiding tour sheet from the museum, as well as a separate guide to historic stores in the area. In addition, the society offers a lecture series; call for schedule or visit konahistorical.org. Reservations must be made up to a week in advance. Please contact the museum ahead of time to check open hours, as, at the publication of this book, Kona Historical Society was temporarily closed.

Among H. N. Greenwell's many ventures was the export of coffee. He began selling beans harvested by Native Hawaiian farmers; his wife later had many acres of their own land planted with coffee trees. Her great-grandchildren still tend some of those trees on the 35-acre ***Greenwell Farms Coffee Estate*** (808-323-2295 or 888-592-5662; greenwellfarms.com). Although not connected to the historical society, a driveway down to the farm extends from the museum parking lot. You can sample a variety of house brews, including a rare peaberry coffee, at a tasting booth and take a brief tour of the farm. Open daily 8:30 a.m. to 5 p.m.

Continue on Route 11 to the tiny town of Kainaliu. The highway strip here has a number of interesting shops and galleries. ***Kimura Fabrics*** (808-322-3771) inhabits a 1926-vintage general store. Inside, Hawaiian checkered *palaka* and barkcloth tapa prints hang alongside hand-batiked silks. Open Mon through Sat 9 a.m. to 5 p.m. The nearby 1932 Aloha Theatre still functions as an art-house cinema and concert venue.

For tasty grub nearby, swing by ***Rebel Kitchen*** (808-322-0616; rebel kitchen.com) on Hawai'i Belt Road. This reggae, punk-y hotspot offers Cuban- and Cajun-inspired cuisine like jambayala, jerk chicken, and blackened ahi sandwiches.

Perhaps the best eating option in South Kona, however, remains nearby ***Ke'ei Café*** (808-322-9992). Located in an airy second-story loft space with wooden rafters crisscrossing overhead, the cafe's eclectic mix of New American cuisine has won a devoted following. Nightly fresh catch comes pan-seared with caramelized onions and lemon caper butter sauce or sauced in a Thai green curry. Dinner is offered Tues through Sat 5 to 8 p.m. Moderate. Next up on Route 11 comes Honalo, where ***Teshima's*** (808-322-9140), a long-standing local favorite, serves Japanese meals at honest prices. The wood-paneled mock-*shoji* decor showcases paintings by the Teshimas' grandson Jason. Open daily 7 a.m. to 2 p.m. and 5 to 9 p.m.

Next door to Teshima's, take a moment to peek inside ***Daifukuji Soto Mission*** (808-322-3524; daifukuji.org). (Remove your shoes before entering.) This large wooden complex, painted red with a silver corrugated roof, has several rooms and a Japanese garden in back. The main entrance opens onto a lovely altar embellished in gold and silver brocade. Giant ceremonial drums fill an adjacent side room.

Just outside town, Route 180 splits off on an uphill route to Holualoa. If you stay on the main highway, 3 miles farther, Kamehameha III Road crosses Route 11 and plunges down toward the coast, intersecting Ali'i Drive, a lower coastal road, just above Keauhou Bay. Turn left (south) onto Ali'i Drive and take the next right down to the bay. Kamehameha III was born here. An interpretive garden trail follows the cliff line leading to the birth site. The story goes that the royal prince was delivered stillborn but was revived miraculously in a nearby spring by an attending kahuna. In gratitude, his father, Kamehameha I, built a 1-mile-long *holua* ("sledding") track on the hillside above the bay. An HVCB marker designates the royal birth site, and a bronze plaque on a nearby boulder notes where the resuscitation took place. Golf course development has destroyed most of the holua course, but if you look uphill from Ali'i Drive, you might make out the parallel walls of the ramp where wet leaves greased the original course. You can see one of the long, incredibly narrow sleds used for the sport at Hulihe'e Palace in Kailua.

Ali'i Drive ends a short distance farther south at the sacred burial ground of ***Kuamo'o Battlefield.*** A pivotal battle was fought here in 1819, pitting Liholiho, Kamehameha's heir, against his cousin Kekuaokalani. The pretext for the clash was Liholiho's abolishment of the kapu system, which traditionalists opposed. As keeper of the war god, Kekuaokalani's challenge threatened Liholiho's authority. In similar circumstances, Kamehameha himself had overthrown Kalani'ōpu'u's heirs using Western weapons, but this time the overwhelming weight of musketry favored Liholiho. The death of the old guard and their gods was assured, and the way was paved for the Christianization of the islands. Today a rough trail leads across the barren lava field to the Lekeleke burial grounds, where more than 300 warriors lie entombed beneath rocky cairns. The golf course across the road provides an almost surreal contrast to the stark surroundings.

Perched on a spectacular lava bluff overlooking Keauhou Bay, the ***Outrigger Kona Resort and Spa*** (808-930-4900; outrigger.com/hawaii/hawaii-big-island/outrigger-kona-resort-and-spa) is one of the few places on earth where you can watch nightly manta ray feedings right offshore. Powerful searchlights shone from the hotel attract tiny plankton on which the mantas feed. These distant relatives of the shark family have wingspans up to 20 feet and weigh as much as 3,000 pounds. Equipped with neither bones nor teeth, mantas hoover in plankton by the gallon through their perpetually gaping maws and filter them through the same gills with which they breathe. Grab a seat at the hotel's oceanfront bar for a chance to glimpse these enormous, graceful animals after dark. Rooms here start at $249.

The more adventurous can also book passage on nightly dive and snorkel excursions that launch from the nearby harbor; prices start at $130. Call ***Sea Paradise*** at (808) 322-2500; seaparadise.com. The divers shine lights from below, creating columns of light in which the mantas feed, spiraling gracefully from top to bottom, while snorkelers watch from above. The mantas are most reliable from March to November; during winter they often do not show. (Other dive companies offer manta trips farther north that involve a longer boat ride out and less reliable mantas, but you'll see greater numbers when they do come, and there's more interesting terrain to explore if they don't.) If you're looking for your own, pre-manta feed, ***Kenichi Pacific Restaurant*** (808-322-6400; kenichipacific.com), located in the Keauhou Shopping Center, serves a creative Japanese fusion menu centered on sushi and seafood. Open Tues through Sun 4:30 to 9 p.m. Expensive.

Going north, Ali'i Drive hugs the coastline for 6 miles to Kailua, past various hotels and unusual vegetation draped in a dense curtain of vines. About a mile north, Kahalu'u Bay is a popular snorkeling spot. On the north end of the bay sits ***St. Peter's Catholic Church,*** a tiny vision in blue built on the grounds of an old *heiau.* ***Magic Sands Beach,*** just up the road, gets its name from its seasonally varying deposits of white sand.

Back on the highway, heading north from Route 11's junction with Kamehameha III Road, the Kuakini Highway splits off Route 11 and descends to meet Ali'i Drive in Kailua. Just below the intersection, a driveway leads to the ***Sadie Seymour Botanical Gardens*** (808-329-7286), headquarters of the Kona Outdoor Circle and named after its founding president, who helped introduce the now ubiquitous bougainvillea to the Kona Coast. Designed by Sadie's son, the garden is arranged according to world region, each on a separate terrace. A self-guiding tour brochure is available, and guided visits can be arranged (best to call ahead). Botany buffs may appreciate the horticultural library housed in the Outdoor Circle building. The garden grounds also contain the 17th-century ***Kealakouwa'a Heiau,*** which served as both canoe-building drydock and spiritual center to bless the finished product. The botanical garden is open daily during daylight hours; the Kona Outdoor Circle building is open weekdays 9 a.m. to 1 p.m. Free. The Outdoor Circle also organizes botany classes as well as excursions to other local gardens, both commercial and private; call for a schedule.

Another 2 miles north brings you into the town of Kailua (often referred to as Kona and officially hyphenated as Kailua-Kona). Tourist dollars and rampant development have transformed the town into an endless strip mall, with nasty traffic snarled along poorly laid-out streets. The main points of interest cluster around the harbor at the north end of Ali'i Drive.

Begin your tour at ***Hulihe'e Palace*** (808-329-1877; daughtersofhawaii .org/hulihee palace), a two-story stone structure built in 1838 by John Kuakini, the Big Island's first governor. His daughter-in-law, Princess Ruth, inherited the building, but at 6 feet, 10 inches, and 410 pounds, she couldn't fit up the stairs and preferred to sleep in a grass house she built outside. Various members of the Hawaiian royalty used Hulihe'e as a vacation home until 1914, when Prince Kūhiō sold the property and auctioned off all its contents. By 1924 the empty palace had fallen into disrepair, and the Daughters of Hawai'i acquired an easement over the property to restore it as a museum. Fortunately, the Daughters were able to recover many of the original palace possessions. The ensemble of beautiful furniture and historical artifacts spans the entire century of the Hawaiian monarchy.

As you enter the building, a marble bust of King Kalākaua flanked by feather kāhili, the standards of royalty, greets you at the foot of the stairs. An adjacent room contains possessions belonging to Kamehameha I, including his 'awa pipe and his stone exercise ball weighing 200 pounds. Upstairs, you'll find some of the gifts received by King Kalākaua on his travels around the world, including the busts of Grecian gods that inspired him to commission his own. Pause to read an original copy of a poem written by Robert Louis Stevenson to Princess Kai'ulani, and then enter the bedrooms to admire the sumptuous furniture. Finally, step onto the balcony for a refreshing view across Kailua Bay.

Before you leave, take a look at ***Kiope Pond*** behind the gift shop. This spring-fed pool was the original water source for the palace. Later, when pipes supplied freshwater throughout Kailua, the well was enclosed and converted to a small fishpond, which still functions today. Hulihe'e Palace opens its doors Wed, Thurs, and Sat 10 a.m. to 3:30 p.m., and Fri 10 a.m. to 2:30 p.m. Admission $22.

Across the street, ***Mokuaikaua Church*** (808-329-0655; mokuaikaua.com) has a rich history of its own. When the first 23-member troop of missionaries came to Hawai'i in 1820, they landed in Kailua for an audience with Kamehameha II. The king granted the missionaries a one-year probationary stay and ceded them land in Kailua. The brethren immediately broke ground for the islands' first church, leaving Asa Thurston as its minister. Governor Kuakini built the current building in 1838. It took 4,000 workers to erect the 3.5-foot-thick walls, incorporating lava stones from a 15th-century heiau built on the site by Chief Umi and a lime mortar prepared from burned coral. Beautiful stained-glass windows, the gift of a church member in 1970, grace the interior. Behind the pews, a koa wood panel separates the royal section, which is backdropped by four kāhili colored to represent the four major islands.

Browse among the exhibits in the rear of the church to learn more about the church and missionary history. A model of the brig *Thaddeus,* "Hawai'i's Mayflower," which carried the first missionaries on their 164-day voyage around Cape Horn, occupies a prominent place. Also intriguing is the Micronesian navigation stick chart obtained from a sister church on Kwajalein Island. The carefully shaped latticework of crossed sticks schematically represents the currents, swell patterns, and flotsam drift lines learned for a given region through prolonged observation. Such an intimate relationship with the environment around them enabled Polynesian navigators to conquer the Pacific.

Walk along the harbor seawall. As you approach the pier, note the marked finish line for Kona's annual Ironman Triathlon (ironman.com), held in October, the original and most famous race of its kind. Competitors must survive a 2.4-mile rough-water swim, cycle a hilly 112 miles, and run 26.2 miles to earn the right to cross this line. Across the bay, ***Kailua Pier*** becomes a popular hangout at the end of the day when the charter fishing boats weigh in their prize catches. Kona waters are world famous for their game fish, so if someone's been lucky, you might see a 1,000-pound marlin dangling from the scales. (If not, the King Kamehameha Hotel has several stuffed giants in its lobby.) The International Billfish Tournament (hibtfishing.com) in late July/early August brings a circus-like atmosphere to town as competitors from around the world compete to land the big ones. Other tournaments happen throughout the year.

To the right of the pier, ***Kamakahonu Beach*** cozies up inside a small cove fronting the King Kamehameha Hotel. Kamehameha I spent his last days here, enjoying the peace and prosperity of his reign. A mortuary platform marks the spot where the king was buried, but his bones were removed and secretly hidden according to ancient custom. After Kamehameha's death in 1819, his son and heir, Kamehameha II, overthrew the kapu system when he shared a meal with his mother Queen Keōpūolani and Kamehameha I's other queen Ka'ahumanu at his table here at Kamakahonu. This left a void that the arrival of the missionaries and their new god, Jehovah, would fill in the following year. ***Ahu'ena Heiau,*** a relic of the gods Liholiho forsook, sits at the mouth of the cove. Restored by the Bishop Museum, the small complex includes a thatched *hale mana* (main prayer house), a *hale pahu* (house of drums), an *'anu'u* (oracle tower), and several beautifully carved ki'i akua. The adjacent ***Hale Mahina*** ("House of the Moon") has a thatched roof of sugarcane leaves. Kamehameha came here to relax and gaze along the fertile expanse of the Kona Coast. He himself tended a taro plot on the slopes of 8,000-foot Mount Hualalai.

In addition to the heiau on its grounds, the lobby of ***King Kamehameha Kona Beach Hotel*** (808-329-2911 or 800 367-2111; marriott.com/en-us/hotels/koacy-courtyard-king-kamehamehas-kona-beach-hotel/overview) constitutes a quasi-museum. Display cases house artifacts from ancient Hawai'i, ranging from feather capes to hula instruments. Ask the concierge for an informative brochure on the collection. A prominent mural by Herb Kāne portrays King Kamehameha's court at Kamakahonu with the same view toward Ahu'ena Heiau as the hotel's side entrance affords today. Rooms start at $429.

Restaurants in Kailua-Kona cater mostly to tourist tastes and wallets, but there are a few good bets. For tasty, albeit pricey, Hawaiian fare, look for ***Kanaka Kava Bar*** (808-327-1660), located in the Ali'i Sunset Plaza off Ali'i Drive toward the south end of Kailua-Kona. Kava is the main attraction at this open-air cafe; you can sample it plain or mixed with fruit juices. You'll also find authentic Hawaiian specials like squid *luau* (steamed taro leaves with squid and coconut milk) and *'opihi* (limpet—a type of shellfish) on the menu. Open daily 3 to 10 p.m. Moderate. For inexpensive, do-it-yourself sushi, follow the locals to ***You Make the Roll*** (808-326-1322), at the corner of Ali'i Drive and Sarona, just north of Hualalai Road. Open Mon through Sat 11 a.m. to 4:30 p.m. Finally, for a more elegant dinner, head 3 miles south on Route 11 to ***La Bourgogne*** (808-329-6711) for classic French and Italian cuisine in an intimate 14-table space. Open Wed through Sat 5 to 10 p.m. Book in advance. Investment-caliber.

When Kailua's heat and crowds begin to press, Hualalai Road offers an escape up inland to the cool coffee country of Holualoa. As you climb the 4 miles up the slopes of Mount Hualalai, the vegetation grows more lush with every foot of elevation. At the intersection with Route 180, stop for a moment at the ***Kimura Lauhala Shop*** (808-324-0053) to browse among handcrafted creations woven from the fibrous leaves of the hala tree. Open Wed to Fri 10 a.m. to 4:30 p.m., and Sat til 4 p.m. The store has been run by the Kimura family since 1915.

Turn left onto Route 180 and continue uphill a half mile, enjoying coastal views over Keahole Peninsula as you enter the town of Holualoa ("long sled run"). This former coffee town has gone artsy, with galleries galore showcasing everything from fine arts to ukuleles and Hawaiian gourds. Most are open Tues through Sat 10 a.m. to 4 p.m.

The oldest gallery in town, and one of the nicest, is ***Studio 7*** (808-324-1335). This was owner Hiroki Morinoue's parents' store, which they ran as a pool hall and laundry business. He has transformed it into a gallery that is a work of art itself, with pebble paths and wooden partitions. Hiroki and his wife, Setsuko, display their work and that of a few others, including their daughter Miho. Open Tues through Fri 11 a.m. to 5 p.m. Owners sometimes shut down early, so call for an appointment.

Another vibrant player in the Holualoa art scene waits 3 miles south (downhill) on Route 180. The ***Donkey Mill Art Center*** (808-322-3362; donkeymill artcenter.org) occupies a 1954 mill that formerly housed Kona's first coffee growers' cooperative. Renovated, it now hosts workshops, lectures, and exhibitions by local artists. Open Wed through Sat 10 a.m. to 6 p.m.

Accommodations in Holualoa come in two forms, economy and deluxe. Deluxe is the ***Holualoa Inn*** (808-324-1121; holualoainn.com), built as a mountain retreat by former *Honolulu Advertiser* publisher Thurston Twigg-Smith and now run as a bed-and-breakfast by the family. Eucalyptus wood milled on Maui covers the floors, while the walls inside and out luxuriate in natural cedar. Creature comforts include a pool, game room, library, wet bar, and hot tub. The entire property overlooks a 40-acre coffee plantation with captivating views of the Kona Coast. Prices for the six rooms range from $595 to $760 and include full breakfast with Kona coffee grown on the premises as well as afternoon pūpū. Three-night minimum. Children should be age 13 or older. The more budget-friendly option in town is the venerable ***Royal Kona Resort*** (808-774-5662), which rents rooms from $183 for a deluxe double.

North to Kohala

To enjoy Kona's legendary blue waters in relative seclusion, head north from Kailua. Kuakini Highway (the middle road between Ali'i Drive and Route 11) runs through the town's industrial section and ends a mile farther along at the ***Old Kona Airport State Park*** (808-587-0300; dlnr.hawaii.gov/dar/marine-managed-areas/hawaii-marine-life-conservation-districts/hawaii-old-kona-airport/). The broad swath of white sand here stretches along the coast for almost a mile. A sandy inlet on the south end offers the best shelter for swimming during periods of surf. You won't have to worry about parking—there is an entire runway left from the old airport. To reach other beaches, take Route 19, the extension of Route 11, a straight, flat road that crosses lava flows of varying vintage. The turnoff to Honokōhau Harbor comes 3 miles up the coast. The marine vessels here seem to float in a sea of lava, but in fact the harbor connects to the ocean through an artificial channel. This is another great place to watch charter fishing boats weigh in their catch. Most people take the right fork of the harbor road and park where the road becomes private property. Cross the lava barrier on the right to follow a paved trail through a half mile of kiawe scrub to ***Honokōhau Beach,*** which used to be a popular nude beach until the feds started cracking down. Kukui trees border the salt-and-pepper sands, and a low lava shelf dogs the waterline for much of the beach. The central portion offers the best swimming and has a good snorkeling reef offshore.

The archaeologically rich land bordering the beach has been purchased by the federal government for ***Kaloko-Honokōhau National Historical Park*** (808 329-6881; nps.gov/kaho). Although the Park Service is still developing interpretive materials for the park, there is quite a lot that can be seen already. At the southern end of the park, just beyond the harbor mouth, the 'Ai'opio Fishtrap was built to trap fish that entered with the tide. Next to it stands the remains of a large heiau fronted by a wooden lele and a replica of a traditional canoe shed built from 'ōhi'a logs and pili grass. Smaller anchialine pools nearby contain brackish, spring-fed waters that rise and ebb with the tide. Found throughout the park, these pools host several native species, including the *'opae 'ula* (Hawaiian red shrimp) and the orange-black damselfly. Swimming is permitted in 'Ai'opio, but not in the other pools in the park.

The rest of the park is better accessed from the highway. The main entrance to the park lies a half mile north of the harbor road, and admission is free. From there, visitors can follow the three-quarter-mile Mauka-Makai Trail past a number of archaeological sites, including house platforms, animal enclosures, and a large tiered monument of uncertain purpose. A thriving community of several hundred inhabitants once lived here, fishing, farming, and tending livestock: pigs, dogs, and . . . fish. Spread across 20 acres near the shoreline, Aimakapa Fishpond served as a storehouse of ready protein to provision armies, feed visiting chieftains, and ward off famine. The pond now provides an important refuge for endangered waterfowl, including the *ae'o* (Hawaiian black-necked stilt) and *'alae ke'oke'o* (Hawaiian coot).

A small sandy beach fronts Aimakapa, where swimming is possible. The waters here are popular with turtles, which sometimes come onshore (and should not be disturbed). A little more than a mile north lies the massive Kaloko Fishpond, which, in addition to being infested with spiny bristleworms, reputedly guards the bones of King Kamehameha I in a secret underwater cave. (The bones of Hawaiian ali'i were hidden to prevent their mana from falling into enemy hands.) Built from carefully fitted lava rock, the seawall of Kaloko is by far the largest in the islands and demonstrates impressive engineering skill. The angle and alignment of the rock wall is designed to absorb and deflect the energy of incoming waves. The Park Service is working on restoring the fishpond to functioning capacity. You can walk to Kaloko from Aimakapa or access it directly via an unpaved road entered from the highway north of the main entrance, opposite Kaloko Industrial Park. The visitor center is open daily 8:30 a.m. to 4 p.m.

A few miles up the coast, near the 94-mile marker, another turnoff leads past Wawaloli Beach Park to the ***Natural Energy Lab of Hawai'i*** (808-327-9585; nelha.hawaii.gov), at Keahole Point. Part of the lab's research focuses on ocean thermal energy conversion (OTEC), which exploits differences in ocean temperatures at varying depths to generate electricity. This experimental technology holds the promise of a renewable, environmentally safe energy source. In the meantime, the nutrient-rich cold water that the lab pumps up from the ocean depths allows for successful aquaculture of black-pearl oysters, Japanese flounder, and Maine lobster. The park is open to the public daily from 5 a.m. to 8 p.m. Contact for tour and admission information. ***Ocean Rider*** (808-329-6840; seahorse.com), an on-site seahorse farm, offers its own hour-long tours Mon through Fri for $74; reserve ahead.

Up until 2017, Keahole Airport shared space with the ***Onizuka Space Center***, which was dedicated to the memory of Holualoa-born astronaut Ellison Onizuka, who perished in the 1986 *Challenger* space shuttle disaster. Various space-themed exhibits, interactive displays, and NASA paraphernalia were on display. The center has since closed. Two miles north of the airport, look uphill to spot a gaping lava tube. All the lava here came from Hualalai's last flow in 1801. A mile farther, a sign marks the turnoff to the beachfront ***Kona Coast (Kekaha Kai) State Park*** (808-587-0300; dlnr.hawaii.gov/dsp/parks/hawaii/kekaha-kai-kona-coast-state-park) at Mahai'ula Bay. Open daily 8 a.m. to 6:45 p.m. For a more secluded strand, continue on the highway. As you drive, look for Pu'u Kuili, a grassy 341-foot cinder cone on the downhill slope. Just north of the cone, immediately after the 88-mile marker, you can rattle your way down to Kua Bay on a jeep road. Passenger cars can make the drive almost to the end; alternatively, the walk takes only about 25 minutes. Rock-hop across the final yards of lava field between the road and ***Maniniowali Beach,*** the bay's hidden gem. Turquoise waters and a gently sloping sandy bottom make for perfect swimming conditions, although winter surf can create hazards and deplete the sand.

Just past Maniniowali, you will pass the turnoff to the Four Seasons Hualalai at the 87-mile marker, home to the ***Ka'upulehu Cultural Center*** (808-325-8000; fourseasons.com/hualalai). Ka'upulehu is the name of the original ahupua'a of this area, the traditional land division running from the top of Hualalai Volcano down to the sea. The center displays a specially commissioned series of 11 paintings by artist/historian Herb Kāne that portray the inhabitants of Ka'upulehu in ancient times engaged in activities of daily life: farming, fishing, and so on. Kane was a leading member of the Polynesian Voyaging Society, which has retraced ancient migration paths across thousands of miles of open ocean in traditional double-hulled canoes, navigating by starlight. A wood-inlaid map illustrates the "Polynesian Triangle" of settlement that such voyages made possible. Throughout the day, elderly master craftsmen demonstrate traditional Hawaiian art forms ranging from feather lei making to celestial navigation. Call for a schedule. Open daily 8:30 a.m. to 4 p.m. Free.

The nearby ***Kona Village Resort*** (808-325-5555 or 800-367-5290; rosewoodhotels.com/en/kona-village)—known for delivering a tame version of the great Gauguin getaway with individual palm-thatched roof hale bordering a picturesque bay and fishpond, as conceptualized by Johnno Jackson in the early 1960s—is no doubt equally spectacular after its recent renovation à la Rosewood Hotels. The former fishing village was given a sustainable elevation fit for 21st-century tastes.

As you continue north on the highway, note the yellow donkey-crossing signs. The donkeys, known as "Kona nightingales," run wild in the hills and come down at night to drink from coastal springs. Stop at the lookout near the 82-mile point and let your gaze travel the barren lava coast below until it strikes the bright cobalt blue of ***Kīholo Bay.*** If you pull off the highway at the wide shoulder just south of the 81-mile marker, you can hike down a jeep trail to reach this picturesque oasis. A half hour's exertion brings you to the north end of the bay, where sea turtles nest by the brackish 5-acre lagoon, the remains of an ancient fishpond, rebuilt by King Kamehameha in 1820 and then destroyed by an 1859 eruption. Patches of black-sand beach line the rocky shore, and a few shade trees cluster about, backed by private homes. To the south stands the enormous yellow compound of Earl Bakken, inventor of the portable pacemaker in 1957. Bakken became a beneficiary of his own invention four decades later after experiencing an irregular heartbeat while en route to receive an engineering award for the device. A little farther, you'll spot the striking curved gables of the "Bali House," which was built in Bali and reassembled on-site by the owner of Paul Mitchell hair products. If you continue another 100 yards south, you can rinse off the salt just inland of the beach in a delightful freshwater pond called Luahinewai, formed from rainwater collected in a lava tube. You enter through a collapsed "skylight." Please be sure to remove any suntan lotion before going in. Just past the pond, a jeep road provides an alternative route back to the highway, emerging between the 82- and 83-mile markers.

Past Kīholo, on a clear day, you can see all of the island's volcanoes except Kīlauea. Note the gelatin-mold shape of Pu'u Wa'awa'a, a pumice cone, on Hualalai's northern flank. The highway passes through more lava flows that came mostly from distant Mauna Loa. Luxury resorts sprout along the arid South Kohala coast. Two of the hotels here (listed below) have developed extensive "historical parks" on their grounds. Interpretive trails lead past a variety of archaeological sites. Both employ a "court historian" to lead tours and staff mini-museums. Call for the current schedule.

The turnoff to the ***Waikoloa Beach Marriott Resort*** (808-886-6789; marriott.com/en-us/hotels/koamc-waikoloa-beach-marriott-resort-and-spa/overview), at Anaeho'omalu Bay, comes first at the 76-mile point. Petroglyphs fill a two-acre lava field by the golf course. Two large fishponds that Kamehameha I claimed for his own front a narrow coconut-fringed beach strip edging the bay. If you walk to the far south end of the beach and continue across ancient lava flows from Mauna Kea, you reach, after about a mile, a beautiful spring-fed pond at Weliweli Point. Locals call this hidden oasis One Coconut. What do you think grows here?

The ***Mauna Lani Hotel*** (808-885-6622 or 855-201-3179; aubergeresorts.com/maunalani), 2 miles up the highway, has even more elaborate sites to explore. You can pick up an excellent brochure from the concierge. A historical trail starts through an underground "city" of interconnecting lava tubes in an old pahoehoe lava flow. The trail then meanders around the two picturesque fishponds that the resort maintains in working condition. Watch as the large captive fish inside wiggle and splash on the surface to shake off parasites. On the ocean side, *makaha* ("sluice gates") help circulate the water and let small fish enter while keeping big fish from getting out. You can walk south along the coast to find more interesting sites. Most of the area remains undeveloped and separate from the resort.

At Holoholokai Beach Park, north of the Orchid Hotel end of the Mauna Lani resort, a public access trail leads to the ***Puako Petroglyphs,*** one of the finest petroglyph fields in all of Polynesia, with more than 3,000 rock carvings in all. You can take rubbings from fake petroglyphs placed here to spare the originals. Scattered in an old cracking pahoehoe flow overgrown with kiawe, stick-figure images of warriors and canoes float in the frozen lava sea. Part of the fun is trying to make out the different images and symbols. Were they ritual markings or prehistoric doodles? Their mystery reaches across time.

Tucked in a quiet residential corner of Puako across the road from the ocean, ***Makai Hale*** (808-880-1012; makaihale.com) offers beautiful accommodations with an even more beautiful view of the ocean from a sprawling pool deck plus a Jacuzzi that could rival any nearby 4-star hotels. The 500-foot elevation up here is also perfect for whale-watching season, from Dec to Mar. Owners Jerry and Audrey Maluo have seemingly spared no expense in creating resortlike accomodations. Call for prices and availability.

A mile to the north, ***Hāpuna State Beach Park*** wins the Big Island popularity poll hands down. This nicely landscaped park has it all. Inviting waters accommodate a variety of recreational activities. The wide expanse of white sand is backdropped by grassy hills equipped with picnic table pavilions. And with less than 10 inches of rain annually, you can count on the sunniest skies on the island. Hāpuna does get dangerous surf in winter, although a shallow cove on the north side offers some protection. Farther up the hill you can rent A-frame cabins that sleep four for $40. Bring your own bedding and kitchen supplies. Visit dlnr.hawaii.gov/dsp/parks/hawaii/hapuna-beach-state-recreation-area for reservations and further information. Please note that at the publication of this book, the water was offline in the park. Please check online ahead of time for any important park notices.

For a more hidden beach, turn south onto an unmarked side road just below the cabins on the Hapuna access road. Look for the dirt-road access to the beach at Waialea Bay, a half mile along. Locals call this Beach 69 because the turnoff comes just before a utility pole with that number.

Back on Route 19, the vegetation picks up near the Kawaihae junction. Most people stay on Route 19 as it climbs inland along the south slopes of the Kohala Mountains to Waimea; instead, turn left to continue along the Kohala coast on Route 270. The North Kohala peninsula is the oldest part of the Big Island geologically and harbors many of the island's most beautiful and historic spots. Just below the junction, turn left again into ***Pu'uokohola Heiau National Historical Site*** (808-882-7218; nps.gov/puhe). Kamehameha I built this last great monument to the gods of old Hawai'i atop Pu'u o Kohola ("the hill of the whale") in response to a prophecy. A famous Kaua'i kahuna had predicted that if Kamehameha built this temple to honor his family war god, Kūka'ilimoku, he would conquer and unify the islands, a feat never before achieved.

Kamehameha's rivals joined forces in 1790 to try to stop the temple's completion, but their attacks failed. That same year, Pele's violent eruption destroyed an army belonging to Keōua Kū'ahu'ula, Kamehameha's main opposition on the Big Island, showing which side the gods favored. By 1791 the temple had been completed, and Kamehameha invited Keōua to the dedication ceremony as guest of honor. Apparently, Keōua knew his fate but came anyway. As he stepped ashore, he and his companions were struck with spears and carried to the temple as the first sacrifices. The prophecy began to be fulfilled. With the death of his rival, Kamehameha reigned supreme on his home island and proceeded to conquer the others. By 1810 Kamehameha had become the first ruler of a unified Hawaiian kingdom.

Stop first at the visitor center to receive an orientation to the park grounds and view Herb Kane's depiction of Keōua's fateful arrival. In addition to Kamehameha's temple, two older heiau occupy the park grounds. ***Mailekini Heiau*** sits in ruins midway down the slope. This temple was converted into a fort and mounted with cannons by John Young, a British sailor who became Kamehameha's confidant and military adviser. ***Haleokapuni Heiau,*** dedicated to the shark gods, once rested on a reef below the hill. The park is open daily 7:30 a.m. to 5 p.m.

Nearby Kawaihae Harbor has heavy industrial overtones complete with cattle-loading docks and a cement plant. Across the highway from the harbor is a cluster of restaurants. For fresh "surf" fish, wander nearby to ***Seafood Bar and Grill*** (808-880-9393), or for fresh "turf," head to ***Kohala Burger & Taco*** (808-880-1923; kohalaburgerandtaco.com) to snag burgers made with Hawai'i grass-fed beef on house-baked bread, plus milkshakes at this chill, Mexican-American venue with a definite '50s flair. Hours vary throughout the week. Please check kohalaburgerandtaco.com/opening-hours before going. Moderate.

Route 270, the Akoni Pule Highway, turns uphill immediately after the restaurant and heads north above the coast. At the 14-mile marker, explore the shadows of the past that haunt ***Lapakahi State Historical Park*** (808-587-0300; dlnr.hawaii.gov/dsp/parks/hawaii/lapakahi-state-historical-park). The rocky remains of an ancient fishing village spread across several acres along

Sailing Hawaiian Style

Five hundred years before the Vikings, when European galleys hugged the coastline of the Mediterranean, afraid to risk the open sea, Polynesian navigators had conquered the Pacific, the largest ocean on earth, making regular crossings from one isolated group of islands to the next across thousands of miles of open ocean. By the late 20th century, however, Polynesian sailing canoes had disappeared from island waters as Western vessels built from modern materials supplanted them. Much of the craft of traditional canoe building was lost and has only recently been revived. The Big Island is fortunate to have an authentic replica of these ancient Polynesian catamarans available to visitors. They offer a unique experience that no one with an interest in sailing should forgo.

For those who don't want to schlep to South Kohala, Capt. Kiko Johnston-Kitazawa (808-895-3743; waakaulua.com), a master waterman and boatbuilder, will bring his 28-foot sailing canoe to a port near you. He provides a similar historical narration on canoe culture, as well as exploring the hidden nooks and crannies of the coastline and the stories they harbor. Kiko's tours are limited to six passengers and offer a personalized experience. Three-hour trips cost $125 per person.

the sea. Scattered among this dry, seemingly inhospitable scrubland are all the essentials needed to sustain life. Pick up a pamphlet at the entrance if no ranger is available to guide you. Marked stations along the way point out the architectural plan of the village as well as the native trees and plants used by its inhabitants. Lapakahi, like every community, had its recreation area. Here you are invited to try your hand at Hawaiian games such as *'ō'ō ihe* (spear throwing) or *'ulu maika,* a version of bowling that requires you to roll stone disks between wooden stakes. Although a few upland fields were tended, the ocean was the focus of village life. Koai'e Cove provided a safe landing for canoes. Fishers congregated on the low bluffs overlooking the sea, mending nets or playing *konane,* but always keeping a watchful eye for signs of fish. Displays show some of the common fishing tools and techniques, like the lift nets used to lure the timid *opelu.* Lapakahi's rich marine life is now protected by conservation statutes. During the calm summer months, the waters offshore offer first-rate snorkeling. Look for whales during winter. Open daily 8 a.m. to 4 p.m.

To visit a pair of sites pivotal in Hawaiian history, turn seaward at the 20-mile point, proceed 2 miles to Upolu Airstrip, and follow a dirt road back along the coast for 1.6 miles and then a few hundred yards uphill to ***Mo'okini Heiau.*** Oral histories date this massive temple to the 5th century, making it one of the oldest and most important in the islands. A human chain is said to have carried the stones from Pololu Valley overnight to build the temple's

30-foot-high walls in an irregular parallelogram covering a quarter acre. If a stone was dropped, it was left where it lay; a trail of scattered stones taken from Pololu can still be found en route. With the arrival of the high priest Pa'ao from Tahiti in the 12th century, the site became one of the first luakini heiau, where human sacrifices were offered to the new, bloodthirsty god that Pa'ao brought with him, Kuwahailo ("Ku of the maggot-dripping mouth").

Walk around to the western entrance, where green lichen tints these leeward walls. Outside the temple an authentic grass hale rests on a stone foundation. Kahuna nui Leimomi Mo'okini Lum, a direct descendant of the Mo'okini line of high priests, lifted the kapu against commoners a decade ago, so feel free to go inside. The main scalloped altar stood at the rear left, flanked by prayer houses.

Continue along the coast another half mile to the ***birthplace of Kamehameha the Great*** at Kokoiki. On a stormy night, sheltered within these concentric walls on a remote windswept plain, the high chieftess Kekuiapoiwa gave birth to the child who would be named "the Lonely One." As Kamehameha's political fortunes rose, the legends surrounding his childhood multiplied. Under missionary influence, two have assumed Christlike parallels. Accounts of a strange light in the heavens on the night of his birth have tempted astronomers to fix the date at 1758, when Halley's Comet returned to view. Another story relates a prophecy that the newborn child would grow to become "a slayer of chiefs." Hearing this, Alapa'i, the ruling chief, supposedly played Herod, ordering the infant to be put to death. Kamehameha spent a lonely childhood in hiding. Initiated into the worship of Ku at Mo'okini, the young warrior became the war god's most dedicated follower. Maui, whose southern face looms directly offshore, would be the first island Kamehameha conquered.

A mile farther east on Route 270 brings you to Hawi, the largest town in North Kohala, and the junction with Route 250, the mountain road. By now you have rounded the point, and the landscape has become lushly tropical. Hawi itself has an interesting collection of Western storefronts now filled with galleries and restaurants. More elaborate meals can be had at ***Bamboo Restaurant & Gallery*** (808-889-5555; bamboorestauranthawaii.com). This cavernous plantation-era building in the center of town began life as a hotel, was converted to a grocery store, and has ended up somewhere between the two as a restaurant-cum-gallery. It serves fresh island cuisine with Pacific Rim accents as well as a famous passion-fruit margarita. The Hawaiian nostalgia decor combines colorful artwork with old Hawai'i kitsch, such as Matson menu covers from the 1950s (on the walls). The oversize wicker chairs come from the old Moana, Waikīkī's first hotel. (Yes, there is bamboo here as well.) On weekends live music plays in the evening, and the waitstaff have been known to dance an impromptu hula when the spirit moves them. Open Sun through Sat 11:30 a.m. to 2:30 p.m., and Thurs through Sat 6 to 7:30 p.m. Closed Mon. Prices verge on investment-caliber; however, half portions are available.

Two miles past Hawi comes Kapa'au, with another row of plantation store-fronts and galleries. Every tourist who wanders into town stops for the obligatory snapshot of the ***King Kamehameha Statue.*** This is the original casting of the statue that stands in Honolulu and Hilo. A plaque on a rock near the statue commemorates Hawai'i's version of *Saving Private Ryan,* the World War II rescue of the "Lost Battalion" trapped behind German lines in Italy. Japanese-American soldiers, recruited primarily from Hawai'i (at a time when their kinsmen were imprisoned in internment camps on the West Coast), fought heroically in the 100/442nd Battalion to liberate the trapped Texan unit. Eight hundred Japanese Americans perished to save 221 Texans.

While here, be sure to peruse the bulletin boards outside the old courthouse building (now converted into a senior citizen center) behind the statue. The billboards contain fascinating snippets and photographs revealing area history with further displays inside. Seniors operate an information table weekdays 9 a.m. to 3 p.m. to dispense travel tips and "talk story" about bygone days.

A half mile east from Kapa'au, just before the 24-mile marker, turn uphill at the sign for the Bond Historic District. The palm-lined drive passes through macadamia orchards. On the right look for the buildings of the ***Bond Historic District***. Arriving in 1841 to take over North Kohala's mission, the Reverend Elias Bond dominated the area's history in his time. Besides building churches and schools and practicing medicine for the mission, he founded a sugar company and served in a variety of government roles. The Bond family home is being restored, but visitors are welcome to wander the compound and view the buildings from the outside as long as they first check in at the office. In addition to the original 1841 home, built from stone and wood with whitewashed stucco walls and a corrugated tin roof, Father Bond built separate quarters for his son, Dr. Bond, where the latter ran a clinic. As the only doctor for miles, Dr. Bond was often in demand. A horse, which a sign labels as "Kohala's first ambulance," was kept at the ready in a special stall for emergencies. When Dr. Bond eventually tried to retire, his patients did not stop coming. One day, the good doctor simply walked away from it all, boarding a ship in Hilo, never to return. The Bond home has remained uninhabited ever since, with the original furnishings intact, just as he left them. A nonprofit foundation backed by a private philanthropist is overseeing its restoration as well as managing the surrounding property. Be sure to walk behind the buildings to enjoy the extensive gardens, which include a lily pond and a citrus orchard, as well as all manner of tropical fruit. Continue up the road to ***Kalahikiola*** ("the day salvation comes") ***Church,*** a somewhat squat stone structure with a square wooden steeple. Father Bond rallied his flock to build the first meetinghouse here. It took three years of toil, hauling timber sawed by hand across the mountains. The church lasted only four years until a storm blew it down. (The carpenter's helper had forgotten to put pins in the tie beams.) Father Bond was not fazed. He decided to build its replacement in stone. Men carried boulders from neighboring gulches on their backs, lime came from coral harvested underwater, and sand was brought in calabashes from Kawaihae. Two years later, the community had built its spiritual home. The church is still used for Sunday services, which are the only opportunity to view the interior.

Past the church, the (often muddy) road continues to the ***Kohala Girls' School,*** the final cluster of buildings within the district. Operating from 1874 until 1955 as a boarding facility, the school primarily taught Christianity and homemaking. It's now a retreat center. A network of three hiking trails is on the landholdings and above the school.

About a mile farther along the highway, the road winds around a gulch. On the far side of the bridge, look for a small boulder on the side of the road. Kamehameha supposedly carried this rock up from the coast to prove his strength. It has remained here ever since. Just around the bend is the ***Tong Wo Society*** building above the road, fronted by a tiny cemetery plot. The building served as a community center/dining hall for Chinese immigrants from 1886 to 1948. At its peak it fed 2,000 Chinese men daily. A temple altar remains intact; however, the gambling/opium den in back has entirely rotted away. Draw your own moral conclusions. The building is usually open on Sunday.

The highway turns farther as you reach the turnoff to ***Keokea Beach Park.*** The road descends past another Buddhist cemetery and then curves into the gulch of Niuliʻi Stream. The beach park at the bottom enjoys a picturesque setting amid rugged coastal bluffs. A boulder breakwater guards a small, sandy swimming hole.

The final 1.5 miles of Route 270 treat you to spectacular countryside as it winds around lush hillsides overlooking the sea. Trees and meadows alternate in harmonious proportion until all of a sudden your scenery gauge blows off the chart as the sheer cliffs of the eastern Kohala Coast confront you straight ahead. Dotted with islands and silhouetted ridge upon ridge, this unpopulated and almost inaccessible terrain stretches for more than 11 miles. The end of the road overlooks ***Pololu Valley,*** the first in a chain of remote valleys that corrugate this coastline. Pololu's taro fields used to yield productive harvests until the Kohala Ditch diverted most of the valley's water supply to leeward sugar fields. Today the valley lies deserted, its taro terraces overgrown by vegetation. A steep 20-minute hike from the lookout takes you to the wide, flat valley floor. The black-sand beach here is *not* recommended for swimming.

Make your return along Route 250, the mountain road, for a scenic counterpoint to the coastal route's historic interest. Climbing swiftly above Hawi, the road curves along the spine of the Kohala Mountains to descend upon Waimea 20 miles south. You wind around knobby hillocks whose timeworn form and lush coating belie their dimpled volcanic tops. Lines of evergreens planted as windbreaks provide a darker contrast to the lime-green cattle and sheep pastures. It's hard to imagine that these hills were covered with sandalwood forest until two centuries ago, when wholesale logging of this fragrant wood left the hills barren. As you climb to nearly 4,000 feet, the views over the southern Kohala coastline and central tableland grow ever more impressive. The road then begins a swift descent from its aerielike perch, dropping 1,000 feet to the already elevated town of Waimea.

Paniolo Country

Surrounded by cattle range in the elevated foothills of Kohala and Mauna Kea, Waimea remains Hawai'i's premier paniolo town. Paniolo was the Hawaiian pronunciation of *español*, the language spoken by Mexican vaqueros brought to help drive cattle in 1832. By extension, the word became the name for island cowboys whose heritage predates their mainland counterparts of the American West by almost four decades. Ranching at Waimea began with John Parker, a young American who jumped ship in 1809 at age 19 and went to work for King Kamehameha, rounding up wild cattle descended from stock brought by Captain Vancouver two decades earlier that had multiplied to the level of a public nuisance. Parker befriended the king and married a royal granddaughter. Combining the land she inherited and the choice cattle stock culled during his prior employment, he started his namesake ranch in 1847—just in time to market beef to the forty-niners of the California Gold Rush.

The ranch now covers 225,000 acres and is the largest independently owned ranch in the United States. It produces 10 million pounds of beef annually, one-third of the amount raised in Hawai'i and one-tenth of the state's consumption. At an elevation of 2,500 feet, Waimea has cool mountain breezes that keep things fresh, so bring a sweater.

Coming down from Route 250, you intersect Route 19 just west of Waimea. Inside town itself, Route 19 makes another junction with Route 190, the inland road from which it split in Kailua. Those with an interest in military history should head south on Route 190 to view the ***Camp Tarawa Monument*** on the outskirts of town. Twenty thousand marines were stationed here during World War II at what became the largest marine training facilty in the Pacific. The green knolls of Parker Ranch served as stand-ins for Pacific atolls to practice a new kind of amphibious warfare that would lead these troops on their tortuous path to Iwo Jima.

To learn more about Waimea history, stop by ***Parker Ranch Shopping Center*** (parkerranchcenter.com) just across the main intersection. The statue of the galloping paniolo lassoing a steer in the parking lot depicts native son, Ikua Purdy, who stunned the mainland rodeo world in 1908 with a world-championship performance in roping.

The ***Parker Ranch visitor center*** is at the historic homes at ***Pu'u o Pelu*** ("folding hills") (808-885-7311; parkerranch.com). Head a half mile south on Route 190 and turn up the tree-lined drive to the main estate. "Colonel" Samuel Parker built his "Hawaiian Victorian" residence here away from the family homestead so that he could entertain in accustomed luxury such guests as King Kalākaua. (Kamuela, the Hawaiian translation of Samuel, is Waimea's alternate name.) Richard Smart, the ranch's sixth-generation owner who died in 1992, renovated the ranch house with European flourishes. French doors open onto a formal rose garden overlooking a lake. Smart also amassed an impressive art collection. Works by Degas, Renoir, and Pissarro, among others, crowd the walls of the house. To complete the illusion of a grand château, a tape of European songs sung in three Romance languages by Richard Smart himself (a Broadway wannabe) plays constantly.

Next door stands a replica of the original Parker residence, ***Mana Hale.*** The interior and contents come from the actual family homestead in the Kohala uplands and are fashioned almost entirely from native koa wood. The wooden saltbox design evokes memories of John Parker's childhood in Massachusetts. Photos and other memorabilia recount Parker family history for those who missed the visitor center. You can visit both historic homes Mon through Fri 8 a.m. to 4 p.m. Free.

If historic homes and wagon rides sound too tame for your cowboy soul, a number of Waimea ranches will put you back in the saddle. Native Hawaiian owned and operated, ***4D Quarter Horses Hawai'i*** (808-987-4872; 4dquarter horses.com) lets guests ride horses across the open range on the slopes of Mauna Kea. Unlike the usual nose-to-tail trail rides offered elsewhere, experienced riders can trot, canter, and even take part in a cattle drive on this working ranch; novices are also welcome. Prices are $110 for a 1.5-hour ride, $200 for a 2.15-hour open ranch ride, and $175 for a 2.5-hour cattle drive. ***Paniolo Riding Adventures*** (808-889-5354; panioloadventures.com) also offers adventurous off-trail riding in the panoramic Kohala Mountains at similar prices. Reservations are required for both.

But Waimea doesn't cater to just cowboys anymore. Many of the observatories atop Mauna Kea have their ground headquarters here. To learn about the groundbreaking research being done at the most powerful among these, stop by the ***Onizuka Visitor Information Station*** (ifa.hawaii.edu) at the ***W. M. Keck Observatory*** (keckobservatory.org) on Route 19, past the second traffic light opposite the hospital. Visitors can watch a 10-minute video, view some displays, and peer through a small telescope pointed to Mauna Kea's summit. Open daily 10 a.m. to 2 p.m.

hawai'itrivia

Mauna Loa mountain is the largest volcano in the world. Its surface area covers almost half the island, and its massive weight—more than the entire Sierra Nevada range—creates a depression in the ocean floor more than 5 miles deep. What's more, it's still growing!

Waimea has no shortage of creative dining places. Accomplished chefs from the luxury hotels of South Kohala have made a steady exodus to Waimea to open their own establishments. Most of them congregate west of the town center on Highway 19 (Kawaihae Road) and serve moderately priced lunches, with dinners in the expensive range.

In the Opelu Plaza, ***Merriman's*** (808-885-6822; merrimanshawaii.com) boasts the culinary wizardry of an ex–Mauna Lani chef. Peter Merriman bases his Pacific Rim concoctions around novel produce grown on the Big Island. Some grumble that the kitchen quality has slipped now that Merriman's has expanded to other venues. However, it remains top dog in town, and some would say on the island. Potted palms and parasols seem to sprout from the floral carpet interior in an exuberance of tropical colors. Moderately priced lunches are served Mon through Fri 11:30 a.m. to 2 p.m.; dinners nightly 5 to 8:30 p.m., with brunches on Sat and Sun from 10:30 a.m. to 1 p.m. Investment-caliber.

Nearby, ***Dom De Luca's Restaurant*** (808-887-1313; domdelucarestaurant.com) in Waimea Center has won praise for classic Italian cuisine with

How Green Is My Island

The Big Island has long been a powerhouse for alternative agriculture, and with the release of thousands of acres of sugar land, its diversification into niche crops has only intensified, as a visit to any of the island's many farmers' markets will confirm. But until recently, such ventures had little connection to the visitor industry. While growers of the major cash crops such as coffee and macnuts can afford slick visitor centers, the smaller players don't have the resources to handle both farming and tourism. Honoka'a Chocolate Co offers something sweet for visitors with a cacao tour on their working farm followed by a chocolate tasting. Please visit honokaachocolateco.com for factory hours and further details.

ingredients farmed nearby, including Waimea-farmed greens, Mo Betta Farms tomatoes, and 'Ano'ano Farms romaine lettuce. Open Thurs to Mon 11 a.m. to 8:30 p.m. Moderate to expensive. This whole area's something of a pizza haven, with ***James Angelo's Underground Pizza*** (808-885-7888) not far, serving big pies or hearty, assorted topping-filled slices for just $5, plus calzones and subs for $10. Open Tues to Sat 10:30 a.m. to 8:45 p.m., and Sun 3 to 8:45 p.m. Inexpensive.

Finally, those seeking a barbecue fix should continue to the east side of town, where ***The Fish and the Hog*** (808-885-6268) is offering slow-cooked pulled pork and brisket as well as fresh seafood (order the chili-dusted calamari) in a colorfully decorated bistro. It's a place so hip and thoughtfully sustainable that it's earned a write-up from Gwyneth Paltrow's lifestyle brand Goop. Now that's some serious BBQ. Open daily 11:30 a.m. to 8:30 p.m. Moderate to expensive. Even more down-home is local favorite ***Hawaiian Style Cafe*** (808-885-4295), next door to Merriman's. The Naugahyde-backed booths and Formica counters recall diners of yore. Open every day 7 a.m. to 2 p.m., and Tues to Thurs 5 to 8:30 p.m., and Fri and Sat until 9 p.m. Come on Friday for authentic Hawaiian food. Inexpensive.

In addition to its restaurants, Waimea offers fertile ground for gallery hopping. In the ***Gallery of Great Things*** (808-885-7706; galleryofgreatthings hawaii.com), you will find works by local artists, such as Marian Berger's portraits of rare native birds, as well as authentic replicas and genuine artifacts from Hawai'i and other Pacific Rim cultures. Open Mon through Sat 9 a.m. to 5:30 p.m., and Sun 10 a.m. to 4 p.m. To meet local artists (mostly amateur), stop by the ***Firehouse Gallery*** (808-887-1052; waimeaartscouncil.org). Located across Lindsey Street from the ranch shopping center, opposite the Chevron station, the gallery occupies Waimea's historic firehouse, as the name suggests, and is freshly renovated in bright red paint and part of a cluster of historic county buildings. Open Fri to Sun 11 a.m. to 3 p.m.

With all Waimea has to offer, you may want to stay overnight. The ***Jacaranda Inn*** (808-557-5068; jacarandainn.com) offers eight semiprivate suites on an 1897 ranch estate built by a Parker Ranch manager and later used by Nelson Rockefeller to entertain dignitaries from Henry Kissinger to Jackie Kennedy. Exquisitely decorated in styles varying from whimsical South American to Victorian elegance, many suites have Oriental rugs, old-fashioned bedposts, Tiffany lamps, and palatial bathrooms. Each suite has its own character, but all exude an intimate luxury that bespeaks wealth and good taste. The rooms are spread among several wings, separated by garden courtyards. The 11-acre grounds feature everything from begonias to birds of paradise—and, of course, jacaranda. From the gazebo in back, a trail leads to a swimming hole and waterfall. Prices start at $169. The three-bedroom, three-bath plantation cottage offers a full kitchen, a private hot tub, and gorgeous views of the Kohala Mountains. Prices start at $250 a night for double occupancy, with a three-night minimum.

For those who prefer a more bucolic setting, Charlie and Barbara Campbell built their original ***Waimea Garden Cottage*** (808-885-8550; waimeagardens .com) as a honeymoon retreat for their daughter. The cottage is built around a washroom from an old Hawaiian homestead. Vintage farming tools and other antiques add a rustic note to the elegant eucalyptus floors, wainscoting, and French doors. A newer unit has been added, with a fireplace and private bath. The cottages rent for $195 to $230. Guests are encouraged to feed the poultry and collect fresh eggs, which they can prepare in a fully equipped kitchen. A stream, which you can follow to a natural waterfall pool, flows outside the cottage. They require a three-day minimum stay.

Before leaving Waimea, pause at "Church Row" on the east side of town. ***'Imiola*** ("seeking life") ***Church,*** the oldest house of worship on the strip, dates from 1838 (rebuilt in 1857). The church has a beautiful koa interior. Lorenzo Lyons, one of the first Waimea missionaries, worked here until 1886, translating hymns into Hawaiian. Music was arguably the most beloved gift brought by the missionaries, as Hawaiian mele previously had consisted of monotonic rhythms. Cherry trees on the grounds were planted by Waimea's Japanese-American community.

Hāmākua and Waipi'o

From Church Row, Route 19 continues east toward the lush Hāmākua Coast. Waimea stands at something of a climactic fault line. Notice how much greener things are here than on the other side of town.

About 2 miles out from the town center, just past the 54-mile marker, a left turn onto White Road ends up at the trailhead for a 40-minute hike to the spectacular rear wall of Waipi'o Valley. The trail winds through 'ōhi'a and bamboo forest, past groves of white and yellow ginger, following a branch of the Kohala ditch system built to irrigate sugar. It's fairly easy going, but it can be treacherous when wet.

Farther along the highway, near the 52-mile point, the old Mamalahoa Highway offers a pleasant detour along a deserted mountain road. Paralleling the highway route east, the road rolls across misty hills and then descends through tall forest that segues into more recent plantings of eucalyptus destined for paper mulch. The two roads meet up at ***Tex Drive-In Hometown Cafe,*** famous for its *malasadas* (Portuguese doughnuts). A half mile below you lies Honoka'a, the main town of the Hāmākua Coast.

Route 240 passes through the center of town as Mamane Street before heading north up the coast to Waipi'o Valley. At the entrance to town, next to the library, the three-legged ***Katsu Goto Monument*** recalls the grisly hanging of a Japanese labor activist in 1889. As you reach the main commercial strip just ahead, all sorts of interesting shops clamor for your attention. ***Honoka'a Trading Company*** (808-775-0808) is a "used goods" store crammed full of antiques. ***Honoka'a Market Place*** (808-775-8255) also has a nice mix of new and old handicrafts. You can check out Manila's latest at the ***Filipino Store*** opposite the People's Theater. The town even has a shirtmaker whose services you can hire, and its vintage theater still shows movies on weekends. Most of these stores operate on irregular hours, so take a stroll and stop wherever you fancy. Local businesses have also commissioned a number of striking murals that add to the sense of timelessness by depicting scenes from bygone days.

Find assorted retail and women's clothing at ***Mary Guava Designs*** (808-775-8255), open Mon to Sat 9:30 a.m. to 5:30 p.m., and Sun 11 a.m. to 3:30 p.m. Plus local art and other handcrafted goods, like seashell jewelry, spa perfumes, organic Hawaiian honey, and locally knitted scarves and cowls, down the street at ***Big Island Grown*** (808-775-9737). Just don't get this gift shop confused for the similarly named Big Island Grown, a recently approved medical cannabis dispensary in Waimea. Open Mon to Sat 9 a.m. to 7 p.m.

Social activity in town seems to converge on ***Hotel Honoka'a Club*** (808-775-0678 or 800-808-0678; hotelhonokaa.com), which occupies a rambling plantation building between the antique shops. The hotel offers two classes of rooms. Beds in the "hostel" section rent from $40 to $50. Standard rooms with private baths go for $99 to $129 and two-bedroom suites for $150 to $175. The nonhostel rooms include a continental breakfast. Dining options in Honoka'a are limited; you may want to drive back to Waimea. ***Cafe Il Mondo*** (808-775-7711), near the hotel, bakes a mean calzone. Make sure to try the macadamia nut pesto. Open Tues to Sat noon to 4 p.m. But the best deal in town is probably still the fresh ahi sandwich at ***Tex Drive-In*** (808-775-0598); to get there you'll need to go back up on the highway. They also serve a range of local ethnic fare. Open daily 6 a.m. to 6 p.m.

Continue north on Route 240 toward Waipi'o. Two miles out of Honoka'a, ***Waipi'o Wayside Bed and Breakfast Inn*** (808-775-0275; waipiowayside.com) hides behind a white picket fence. The ever gracious Jackie Horne rents five rooms in this 1936 sugar plantation manager's home, each individually decorated, many with antique furnishings. A frustrated would-be restaurateur, Jackie works off her culinary energies in the lavish full breakfasts she serves along with helpful travel tips. She also keeps a large selection of teas perfect for sipping in the garden gazebo out back. Double rooms go for $140 to $225 and come with extra amenities more common to a luxury hotel.

Six miles farther, take the turnoff to loop past the aging houses and shops of Kukuihaele, the last settlement topside of Waipi'o Valley. *Kukuihaele* means "traveling light," a reference to the ghostly procession of night marchers who supposedly pass by on their way into Waipi'o Valley.

Continue on to the ***Waipi'o Valley Lookout*** at the end of the highway, perched directly above the valley rim. Almost a mile wide, the valley floor appears virtually flat, flanked on all sides by cliffs rising from 1,000 to 3,000 feet. The characteristic square finish of Waipi'o's far wall is broken by a low, jutting peninsula. A constant waterfall tumbles near its base. Bands of vibrant color flare as your gaze wanders. The blue Pacific presses inward on the bay, separated by a white ribbon of surf from the black-sand beach at the valley mouth. Dark stands of ironwood trees followed by lighter green fields of grass provide the next swaths of color. Taro fields form a patchwork inland, and a meandering river in the center of the valley drains these wetlands into the mouth of the bay. Beyond the taro plots, a tangled mass of jungle defies human cultivation.

A number of vacation rentals perched on the valley rim offer lodging with a view similar to that of the lookout. Kristan Hunt's ***Hāmākua Hideaway*** (808-987-5572) sits out on the rim, along a stream bank, with views of the Kohala cliff line as well as part of the valley. Contact for rates. ***Richard Mastronardo's Cliff House*** (808-385-1702; cliffhousehi.com), a snazzy modern two-bedroom duplex surrounded by rim-side pastureland, goes for $359; two-night minimum.

Another way to see more of the valley from "topside" is to take a rim tour, along privately owned former sugar land. You have a choice of tours on foot or on horseback. For riding, check out ***Wailea Horseback Adventure*** (808-775-1007 or 877-757-1414; waipioridgestables.com). If it's been raining, you will enjoy staggering views of waterfalls along the way—you can even arrange to swim in one of them. Prices average around $145.

But you should not be content to view Waipi'o only from on high. The valley floor holds many secrets for those with time to explore below. Known as the Valley of Kings, Waipi'o was the largest and most important valley in Hawaiian history. As many as 30,000 people once farmed this fertile haven, perhaps a quarter of the island's population. Young Umi came here to claim his inheritance from the High Chief Liloa. Gaining custody of the war god, Kūka'ilimoku ("Ku the devourer of lands"), Umi went on to unify the Big Island, which he ruled from this valley. Also in Waipi'o, Umi's descendant, Kamehameha, inherited control of the fearsome deity from his uncle, the ruling chief Kalani'ōpu'u. With the aid of the war god, Kamehameha became ruler of all the islands. In 1791 a great naval clash between Kamehameha and Maui's Kahekili took place offshore. Known as Kepuwahaulaula ("the battle of the red-mouthed guns"), this bloody but inconclusive conflict saw the first widespread use of Western cannons, mounted on canoes.

Arriving as a cruel April Fools' joke, the 1946 tidal wave wiped out many of the farmers who remained in the valley in the modern age. In the 1960s the Peace Corps used Waipi'o as a training ground to expose recruits to jungle life. Now only a handful of residents remain, far outnumbered by the wild horses that roam the valley floor. Others come from topside to tend their taro plots and reminisce about old times. If you want to join them, you have several options. A paved road does descend from the lookout to the valley floor, but its 26 percent grade requires four-wheel drive. To hoof it takes about a half hour and strong knees. Otherwise, the following outfits will take you down and give you a valley tour for a combined price. They have courtesy phones at the lookout, but you'll do better to call in advance. None operate on Sunday.

Waipi'o Valley Shuttle (808-775-7121) in Kukuihaele offers four-wheel-drive tours for $36.50 to $67 that depend on the destination. ***Waipi'o Valley Wagon Tours*** (808-775-9518) relies on mule power for its tours. Call for tour times and prices. Sheri Hannum's ***Waipi'o Na'alapa*** (808-775-0419; naalapastables.com) gives 2.5-hour trail rides for $115. Tours are offered twice daily at 9 a.m. and 2:30 p.m. Closed Sunday.

For those hiking in on their own, there's plenty to see, but be aware that much of the valley remains private property. Begin by heading toward the beach, the largest black-sand strand on the island. Swimming is not recommended, but you can sometimes watch surfers offshore. Camping here is unofficially tolerated. If you do camp, pick your spot with care. Not only do night marchers patrol the valley, but a *lua milu* ("portal to the next world") reputedly opens at a secret spot along the beach. Other legendary denizens of the valley you might meet include Nenewe, a shark-man, and Pupualenalena, a yellow dog kupua.

From the mouth of the stream, facing back toward the lookout, you'll see Kaluahine Falls dropping 620 feet from the mouth of the valley. Zigzagging above the beach on the other side, a switchback trail climbs the cliffs on Waipi'o's western wall. Continuing along the uninhabited tableland above and crossing a series of gulches, the 9-mile trail eventually reaches Waimanu Valley, a smaller but wilder version of Waipi'o. The often muddy hike takes at least 6 hours and passes a rain shelter midway.

From the beach, Waipi'o Valley stretches almost 5 miles inland. The interlocking Vs of its rear canyons make a stirring sight. To explore Waipi'o's interior, reverse course and take the main dirt road upstream. On the way, besides taro fields, you pass a commercial lily pond from which lotus flowers and roots are harvested. Farther inland you will find all kinds of tropical fruits and flowers blooming. Wild horses graze along the streambank, coming and going as they please.

Sticking to the left side of the valley leads you to a closed canyon from whose rear wall topples ***Hi'ilawe Falls.*** Dropping more than 1,200 feet in free fall, the waters of Hi'ilawe make Hawai'i's longest unbroken descent. Sugar irrigation ditches divert some of the water, so usually only one of the twin falls is flowing. The harvest god, Lono, descended a rainbow to find his bride-to-be bathing at the bottom. Travelers attempting a more conventional trek overland should beware of falling rocks. You need to cross two streams to reach the right side of the valley, where the trails extend farther into the interior. After a rain, any number of waterfalls spill from the cliffs.

When and if you manage to tear yourself away from Waipi'o, backtrack through Honoka'a and strike out south on Route 11 down the Hāmākua Coast. This was one of the last areas on the island still growing sugarcane continuing into the 1990s. The imprints of King Sugar's rule remain visible in side roads leading through abandoned cane fields to isolated plantation camps above and below the highway. Some of the tiny hamlets are only now starting to spring back to life. A series of gulches cuts through the landscape, draining the runoff from Hāmākua's moist climate. The gulches contain spectacular rain forest, often bejeweled with sparkling waterfalls. The early plantations used to send cut cane flowing downslope in elaborate flumes.

For a taste of sylvan splendor, turn inland 3 miles south of Honoka'a to visit ***Kalopa State Recreation Area*** (808-587-0300; dlnr.hawaii.gov/dsp/parks/hawaii/kalopa-state-recreation-area). Follow signs that guide you uphill through 3 miles of pastureland and cane field. The road ends in the park's tall 'ōhi'a forest, where native flora have been making a strong comeback. An easy 0.7-mile nature walk will take you through some excellent examples of endemic foliage. Other more demanding trails beckon adventurous hikers. Four well-maintained cabins with hot showers and linens each accommodate up to eight people, and a communal hall has a fully equipped kitchen and fireplace. You may appreciate the latter at this cool 2,000-foot elevation. To make reservations, call the Hilo office at (808) 974-6200.

About 12 miles farther, near the 28-mile marker, the road winds around a deep gulch. Turn seaward a half mile farther to explore ***Laupahoehoe*** ("leaf of lava") ***Peninsula.*** The road winds 1 mile downhill past an old Jodo Mission temple to the county park on the peninsula. From the point, you can enjoy breathtaking views in both directions along the coast. A small monument in the park commemorates the deaths of 19 children carried away from the former school grounds here by the 1946 tsunami. Past the peninsula, the highway swoops around another deep gulch to reach the current town of Laupahoehoe. At the junction with the highway, the ***Laupahoehoe Train Museum*** (808-962-6300; thetrainmuseum.com) recalls the heritage of the railways that hauled island cane from field to market and linked the isolated plantation camps along this coast long before the first highway was built. The museum displays occupy a former rail employee's home, and a few old stock cars gather rust in back. Open Mon, Wed, and Fri 10 a.m. to 2 p.m. Admission $10.

The highway continues to make its way south across several more deep gulches. Just south of the 20-mile marker, take the signed turnoff for Waikaumalio County Park for a quiet picnic stop with covered tables along a grassy streambed. Hakalau Gulch, at the border of South Hilo District, is still spanned by an original trestle rail bridge.

About a mile south, turn uphill past the decrepit buildings of Wailea and descend into a wildly tropical gulch where ***Kolekole Beach Park*** abuts an icy-but-swimmable river. At the time of this book publishing, the beach park was temporarily closed. Please check ahead before visiting. A waterfall is right at the base of the elevated highway bridge overhead. Continuing on the same road on the other side of the gulch lets you rejoin Route 19. Or continue farther south and treat yourself to baked island goodies at ***Mr. Ed's Bakery*** (808-963-5000), as well as a variety of jams, jellies, and preserves made with tropical local fruit. Open 6 a.m. to 6 p.m. every day but Sun.

Wailea is also home to ***Akiko's Buddhist B&B*** (808-963-6422; akikosbnb.com). The late Akiko Masuda was the first person to buy property here in almost 40 years when this self-described former hippie/dance teacher purchased the ultimate fixer-upper, which she transformed into a place of grace and beauty. A former auto garage serves as the *zendo,* where Sunday yoga classes are held. The wooden floor in the retreat center comes from an Oregon high school's basketball gym. Guests can choose between lodging "Japanese monastery style," in rooms with futons adjacent to the meditation room, or staying in rooms with conventional beds next door. A third option is two open-air cottages, equipped with solar power and a separate shared bathroom and kitchen. These occupy an adjoining property surrounded by nature. Early-morning meditation sessions are held by appointment, and various alternative retreats and cultural events are staged throughout the year. The decor everywhere is sparse, and plenty of rough edges remain, but a genuine sense of aloha permeates the walls. For rates, please contact at (808) 963-6422, or email direct to msakiko@hawaii.rr.com.

To see the same stream you saw at Kolekole farther uphill, turn up Route 220 to get to ***Akaka Falls State Park*** (808-587-0300; dlnr.hawaii.gov/dsp/parks/hawaii/akaka-falls-state-park). On the way you will pass through the town of Honomu, worth a casual stroll. Store hours are mostly a lazy "whenevah." ***Glass from the Past*** (808-963-6449) sells antique bottles and jars that owner David Ackerman digs up from old landfills in the area. The store also has vintage clothing, unique collectibles, and ephemera (just in case you wanted a turn-of-the-last-century laundry receipt written in Tagalog). At the top of the hill, a string of Buddhist temples and Christian churches congregate in ecumenical harmony. The sleepy serenity of the town today belies Honomu's onetime nickname, "Little Chicago," owing to its boozing, gambling past.

Turn right to follow Route 220 another 3 miles uphill through cane fields to the state park. A 0.75-mile trail loops down around the gulch of Upper Kolekole Stream. You first overlook Kahuna Falls, whose beauty gets shown up by the 420-foot unbroken plummet of Akaka Falls farther on. As lovely as these waterfalls are, don't ignore the rest of the park's charm. You pass by prolific growths of bamboo, ferns, orchids, hibiscus, azaleas, gingers, and heliconia.

For those who haven't yet overdosed on scenery, a blue sign 3 miles farther south at Pepe'ekeo designates the scenic detour along the old belt road closer to the ocean. The twisting road leaves the cane fields and macadamia orchards to burrow through 4 miles of tropical jungle with breathtaking views of the coastline. Fruits and flowers litter the road as you cross a series of streams spanned by one-lane bridges. About 2 miles along, a sign announces the cute yellow shack on your right as ***What's Shakin'*** (808-964-3080). What's shakin' inside are blenders whipping up scrumptious fresh fruit smoothies and tropical juices. All of the fruit is grown organically on the 20-acre plot immediately behind the store. Open Tues to Sun 10 a.m. to 3 p.m. A mile farther, the road overlooks the steep-faced walls of spectacular Onomea Bay. The valley bordering the bay belongs to the ***Hawai'i Tropical Botanical Garden*** (808-964-5233; htbg.com), where you can wander gravel paths through labeled plantings of exotic flowers and towering palms, with shrieking macaws flapping overhead. A lovely waterfall awaits at the back of the narrow gulch, while along the coast, sea stacks (pillarlike rock islands) roil a restless sea. Admission to the garden costs $25, plus an extra $10 if you want a ride down to the valley floor. But you can take in much of the scenery along the free public-access shoreline trail, which skirts the edge of the gardens and then winds across the bay before eventually climbing back toward the highway. The signposted trailhead waits a few hundred yards past the garden visitor center.

From the end of the scenic drive, it's about 7 miles to Hilo. You will pass some plots of dryland taro, a new old crop that has taken over former sugar land.

The Saddle Road and Mauna Kea

Crossing the elevated plateau between Mauna Kea and Mauna Loa, the Saddle Road represents the Big Island's last frontier. Some locals use this mountain "shortcut" to travel between Hilo and Kona, but rental car companies ban the use of the road (more because of its remoteness than its occasional rough edges). The narrow shoulders can be dangerous, however, and the road is often misted in. Besides desolate moonscapes, the main attraction of the Saddle is the Mauna Kea Summit Road halfway along.

If you just want to see Mauna Kea and return the same way, the more scenic approach is from the Kona/Kohala side. Start early, before the clouds roll in. Mamalahoa Highway (Route 190) runs inland between Kailua and Waimea. Six miles south of the latter, take the turnoff to the Saddle Road. The terrain resembles the Kohala Mountain Road as you climb through rolling green pastures and tree-covered knolls. Behind you, Maui's Haleakalā becomes the fifth volcano in a panorama of island castles floating in the sky.

The road eventually climbs above the foothills and enters the wide valley of the saddle. Cinder cones dot the open savannah as the road straightens out and the tree cover fades. Looking up at the twin towers on either side of the road, you can see how much larger the smooth, flattened dome of Mauna Loa is than the more vertical jagged-peaked Mauna Kea. Most of the cinder cones come from the older Mauna Kea, while ribbons of fresh lava run down the slopes of Mauna Loa. The highway begins to cross these flows, changing the landscape to a more barren plain. The live ammo tested at Pahakuloa Military Camp here makes this one place to avoid going off the beaten path. About 20 miles in, near the 35-mile marker, a turnoff leads to the ***Mauna Kea State Recreation Area*** (808-587-0300; dlnr.hawaii.gov/recreation/hunting/gma/maunakea).

Seven miles farther, next to the 28-mile marker, the ***Mauna Kea Summit Road*** begins its ascent through open cattle range. Switchbacks become steep as you climb 6 miles to Hale Pōhaku at the 9,200-foot level. Astronomers working at the summit observatories inhabit the base camp on this flat plateau, nestled behind a wall of cinder cones. The ***Onizuka Visitor Information Station*** (808-934-4550; ifa.hawaii.edu) provides an overview of the summit observatories and some general information about Mauna Kea's unique environment. If you're continuing to the summit, you should spend at least 1 hour here to acclimatize to the altitude. The visitor center is open daily from 9 a.m. to 5 p.m. (You must provide your own four-wheel-drive transport. Children younger than age 13 and pregnant women are not allowed.) Free. Note the rare silversword plants growing outside. Found only on the top of Hawai'i's three tallest volcanos, the plants here on Mauna Kea have to be hand-pollinated by biologists with a paintbrush because the insect that used to serve that function is now extinct.

The remaining 8 miles to the summit require four-wheel drive. ***Harper's*** (808-969-1478 or 800-488-6624; harpershawaii.com) rents these in both Hilo and Kona. If you'd rather someone else do the driving, several companies offer summit tours; most include evening stargazing. See the hiking companies in the chapter introduction for a partial list. The first part of the road traverses unpaved cinders, and the grade is very steep. Be prepared for summit weather conditions that can change rapidly, with summer blizzards not unheard of. Call (808) 935-6268 for an updated forecast. You can also expect your car's engine to labor somewhat in the thin air. (Be sure to loosen your gas cap to prevent vapor lock.) WARNING: Children, pregnant women, and those with respiratory ailments may suffer harm from the lack of oxygen on the summit. On the way up, you pass from the space age to the Stone Age in less than a mile. An important adze quarry used by the ancient Hawaiians lies above "Moon Valley," where the *Apollo* astronauts test-drove their lunar lander. One of the cinder cones near the quarry conceals Lake Waiau, an alpine pool fed by melted runoff from the layer of permafrost that lies hidden beneath cinder topsoil. A half-mile trail to get to the lake begins at the last switchback before the summit.

The summit area consists of a cluster of red cinder hills topped with the white-and-silver domes of the world's most powerful "eyes to the sky." Mauna Kea's elevation and isolation combine to create unbeatable viewing conditions at night. While scientists on neighboring Kīlauea and Mauna Loa probe the inner secrets of the earth, these lonely outposts peer across time and space, scanning the heavens for clues to the mysteries of the universe. Mauna Kea's most powerful telescopes, the Keck I and II, stand on nearby hills. Their unique honeycomb pattern of 36 hexagonal mirrors (weighing 15.9 tons in glass alone) function as a single unit, providing unprecedented light-gathering power. Mauna Kea's summit has been the subject of news headlines in recent years, as Native Hawaiian groups and protesters have stood against the construction of a proposed Thirty Meter Telescope on Mauna Kea. The dormant volcano happens to be the ideal location for the segmented mirror reflecting telescope, according to scientists, while also being the most sacred mountain in Native Hawaiian culture, religion, and mythology. After months-long standoffs and confrontations, the telescope construction was granted new permits to build on the site, but the situation is still developing.

In winter months you can count on snow here. Poliahu, the resident snow goddess of Hawaiian legend, had a hot-blooded sister, Pele. As with all of Pele's sisters, the two got caught up in epic battles over men. Pele's eruptions on Mauna Kea would be cooled by Poliahu's frosts, only to be melted by new flows of lava, and so on. These Hawaiian legends fit geologic evidence of eruptions during the eras when Mauna Kea had a dense glacial ice cap. Nowadays, the two goddesses maintain a truce. Poliahu's snows stick mostly to Mauna Kea, and Mauna Loa remains Pele's domain of fire. Pu'u Poliahu, the cinder cone on the summit most closely associated with the snow goddess, has been declared off-limits to observatory development.

After a snowfall, which can happen any time of year, families leave the beaches and flock to the mountain summit to toboggan, build snowmen, and generally frolic in the fresh white stuff. When enough snow falls, skiing takes place. ***Ski Guides of Hawai'i*** (808-885-4188; skihawaii.com) will provide clothing, equipment, and jeep-lift service for adventurous souls who want to earn their "Ski Hawai'i" T-shirts the hard way.

Mauna Kea's sunsets, bedded across a sea of clouds, number among the world's most beautiful. All vehicles must be off the upper summit road by nightfall, however, as headlights can impair observing conditions. On your way down the mountain, scan the heavens for the circling *'io,* the Hawaiian hawk. Found only on the Big Island, this high-flying hunter was a symbol of royalty. Just past the turnoff to the Mauna Kea Summit Road comes its Mauna Loa counterpart (heading in the opposite direction, naturally). This one doesn't quite make it to the summit. Scientists use it to access a meteorological observatory at the 11,000-foot level. At this elevation, the remaining 2,679-foot climb to the summit is far tougher than it seems. There is a wilderness cabin on the east rim of Moku'aweoweo Caldera, maintained by Volcanoes National Park.

hawai'itrivia

If viewed from its base on the ocean floor, 13,796-foot Mauna Kea mountain is the earth's tallest mountain.

Continuing along the saddle road leads you on a roller-coaster ride across undulating lava fields. As you approach Hilo, 'ōhi'a trees crop up as dry scrub cover and grow denser and taller as you move east. The final 12 miles of curving road descend through lush 'ōhi'a rain forest, which continues to the outskirts of the city itself.

Places to Stay on Hawai'i Island

CAPTAIN COOK

Manago Hotel
82-6155 Mamalahoa Hwy.
(808) 323-2642
managohotel.com
An institution in Kona, run by the third generation of Managos. A great place to soak up local hospitality and culture. Rates start at $91.

HILO

Dolphin Bay Hotel
333 Iliahi St.
(808) 935-1466
dolphinbayhotel.com
Has 18 rooms in a quiet section of Hilo town. Rates start at $139.

Hale Kai Hawai'i B&B
111 Honoli'i Pali
(808) 935-6330
halekaihawaii.com
Oceanfront rooms in a modern home from around $190.

HOLUALOA

Holualoa Inn
76-5932 Mamalahoa Hwy.
(808) 324-1121
holualoainn.com
Luxury bed-and-breakfast rooms in a hillside retreat, starting at $595.

HONOKA'A

Waipi'o Wayside Bed and Breakfast Inn
46-4226 Waipi'o Rd.
(808) 775-0275
waipiowayside.com
Gracious hospitality in a former plantation manager's home. Rates from $140 to $225.

KAMUELA

Jacaranda Inn
65-1444 Kawaihae Rd.
(808) 557-5068
jacarandainn.com
Luxury suites in a Waimea estate. Rates from $169.

VOLCANO VILLAGE

Chalet Kīlauea
19-4178 Wright Rd.
(808) 967-7786
volcano-hawaii.com
Offers a wide selection of bed-and-breakfasts and rentals from budget to luxury. Starting at $159.

WAIMEA

Waimea Gardens
65-1632 Kawaihae Rd.
(808) 885-8550
waimeagardens.com
Rustic country charm in an upcountry setting. Rates from $195 to $230.

Places to Eat on Hawai'i Island

HAWI

Bamboo Restaurant & Gallery
55-3415 Akoni Pule Hwy.
(808) 889-5555
bamboorestauranthawaii.com
Fresh island cuisine served in a vintage building with colorful Hawaiian ambience. Expensive to investment-caliber.

HILO

The Seaside Restaurant
1790 Kalaniana'ole Ave.
(808) 935-8825
A family-owned fish house serving fresh catch from the aquaculture fishpond right outside. Moderate.

KAILUA-KONA

Hualalai Grille
72-100 Ka'upulehu Dr.
(808) 325-8525
fourseasons.com/hualalai
Asian fusion and Pacific Rim cuisine lead the trendy menu listings. Investment-caliber.

La Bourgogne
77-6400 Nalani St., #101
(808) 329-6711
Classic French and Italian cuisine in an intimate venue. Investment-caliber.

FOR MORE INFORMATION ABOUT HAWAI'I ISLAND

gohawaii.com/islands/hawaii-big-island

stayhawaii.com

KAMUELA

CanoeHouse
68-1400 Mauna Lani Dr.
(808) 885-6622 or 800-367-2323
maunalani.com
Romantic beachfront venue for Pacific Rim cuisine. Investment-caliber.

Merriman's Restaurant
65-1227 Opelo Rd.
(808) 885-6822
merrimanshawaii.com
Inventive island cooking that pairs Pacific Rim flavors with classical technique. Investment-caliber.

KEALAKEKUA

Ke'ei Café
79-7511 Mamalahoa Hwy.
(808) 322-9992
Delivers impressive renditions of its eclectic menu offerings at moderate prices.

Teshima's
79-7251 Mamalahoa Hwy.
(808) 322-9140
teshimarestaurant.com
Family-owned local favorite for Japanese food. Inexpensive to moderate.

VOLCANO VILLAGE

Kīlauea Lodge and Restaurant
19-3948 Old Volcano Rd.
(808) 967-7366
Old World cuisine served in a former YWCA lodge. Expensive.

Index

I

J

K

L